Masterpieces of Latin literature: Terence, Lucretius, Catullus, Virgil, Horace, Tibullus, Propertius, Ovid, Petronius, Martial, Juvenal, Cicero, Caesar, Livy, Tacitus, Pliny the younger, Apuleius; with biographical sketches and notes

Gordon Jennings Laing

VIRGIL

Enlarged from a Gem

MASTERPIECES OF
LATIN LITERATURE

TERENCE: LUCRETIUS: CATULLUS: VIRGIL:
HORACE: TIBULLUS: PROPERTIUS: OVID:
PETRONIUS: MARTIAL: JUVENAL:
CICERO: CAESAR: LIVY: TACITUS:
PLINY THE YOUNGER:
APULEIUS

WITH BIOGRAPHICAL SKETCHES AND NOTES

EDITED BY

GORDON JENNINGS LAING, Ph. D.

ASSISTANT PROFESSOR OF LATIN IN
THE UNIVERSITY OF CHICAGO

HOUGHTON, MIFFLIN AND COMPANY
Boston: 4 Park Street ; New York: 85 Fifth Avenue
Chicago : 378-388 Wabash Avenue
The Riverside Press, Cambridge

The Riverside Press, Cambridge, Mass , U S A
Electrotyped and Printed by H O Houghton & Co

CONTENTS

[The names of translators are given in *italics*]

	PAGE
INTRODUCTION	vii
TERENCE	
BIOGRAPHICAL SKETCH	1
PHORMIO	4
LUCRETIUS	
BIOGRAPHICAL SKETCH	63
INVOCATION TO VENUS *H. A. J. Munro*	66
THE SACRIFICE OF IPHIGENIA. *Goldwin Smith*	67
ATOMS AND VOID *H. A. J. Munro*	69
THE GOSPEL ACCORDING TO EPICURUS *W. H. Mallock*	71
THE LIGHT OF THE WORLD. *H A J Munro*	74
THE FEAR OF DEATH. *R. Y. Tyrrell*	76
THE HONEY OF THE MUSES. *H. A. J Munro*	77
LOVE'S EXTRAVAGANCE *H. A J Munro*	78
THE DEVELOPMENT OF MAN. *H A. J. Munro*	81
CATULLUS.	
BIOGRAPHICAL SKETCH	100
ON THE DEATH OF LESBIA'S SPARROW *Sir Theodore Martin*	102
DEDICATION OF HIS PINNACE. *George Lamb*	103
TO LESBIA. *Robinson Ellis*	105
TO THE SAME. *Sir Theodore Martin*	105
TO HIMSELF, ON LESBIA'S INCONSTANCY *R. Y. Tyrrell*	106
VARUS' MISTRESS *J Hookham Frere*	108
TO FABULLUS *Sir Theodore Martin*	109
TO SIRMIO. *Leigh Hunt*	110
TO DIANA. *R. C. Jebb*	111
TO CORNIFICIUS. *Robinson Ellis*	112
ACME AND SEPTIMIUS. *Sir Theodore Martin*	112
TO LESBIA. *W. E Gladstone*	114
THE EPITHALAMIUM OF JULIA AND MANLIUS. *J. Hookham Frere*	115
REMORSE *Sir Theodore Martin, R Y. Tyrrell*	124
LOVE AND HATE *W S. Landor*	125

AT HIS BROTHER'S GRAVE. *Sir Theodore Martin*   . 126
CICERO
    BIOGRAPHICAL SKETCH   127
    THE SPEECH FOR CLUENTIUS. *W. Peterson* .   .   . 130
    FRIENDSHIP. (From *De Amicitia*) *Andrew P Peabody* . 151
    LETTERS. *E. S. Shuckburgh.*
        To Cn Pompeius Magnus, in Asia   .   .   . 158
        To his Wife and Family, in Rome   *G E. Jeans* . . 160
        To Atticus in Italy, on his Journey to Rome   . 162
        To Caesar, in Gaul   163
        To his Brother Quintus, in Gaul   .   .   . 165
        To C Trebatius Testa, in Gaul   .   .   . 166
        To Atticus, in Rome   167
        Cicero and his Son to Terentia and Tullia, in Rome . 169
        To Atticus, in Rome   171
        Servius Sulpicius to Cicero, at Astura   .   . 172
        To Atticus, in Rome   176
        Cicero, the Younger, to Tiro   .   .   . 176
        To Gaius Trebonius, in Asia 180
CAESAR
    BIOGRAPHICAL SKETCH   182
    THE SIEGE OF ALESIA. *T. Rice Holmes*   .   .   . 184
VIRGIL.
    BIOGRAPHICAL SKETCH   198
    DAMON AND ALPHESIBOEUS. *Sir Charles Bowen* .   . 201
    RULES OF HUSBANDRY *James Rhoades*   .   .   . 208
    SIGNS OF BAD WEATHER *James Rhoades* .   .   . 210
    AFTER CAESAR'S DEATH. *James Rhoades* .   .   212
    ITALY. *James Rhoades*   213
    THE BATTLE OF THE BEES *James Rhoades*   .   . 215
    AENEAS' DESCENT INTO HADES. *Sir Charles Bowen* . 216
HORACE.
    BIOGRAPHICAL SKETCH   273
    TO LYDIA *Sir Theodore Martin*   276
    WINTER. *Sir Theodore Martin*   .   .   .   277
    TO LEUCONOË. *John Conington*   .   .   .   278
    TO THE SHIP OF STATE. *R. M. Field*   .   .   . 278
    INNOCENCE. *Sir Theodore Martin* 280
    TO CHLOE. *Lord Ravensworth*   281
    ON THE DEATH OF A FRIEND. *Sir Theodore Martin* . 281
    TO LYDIA. *Sir Theodore Martin* 283
    SIMPLICITY. *W. E. Gladstone* 284
    A WOMAN'S WORD. *Lord Ravensworth*   .   .   . 284
    THE GOLDEN MEAN. *Lord Lytton* 285

CONTENTS

A RECONCILIATION. *Norma Rose Waterbury* . 286
TO THE SPRING OF BANDUSIA. *John Conington* . . 287
TO MAECENAS *Sir Stephen de Vere* 288
COUNTRY LIFE. *John Dryden* . . . 291
A CHALLENGE. *Lord Lytton* 294
A BORE. *John Conington* 295
A LETTER OF INTRODUCTION. *Sir Theodore Martin* . 299
TO HIS BOOK. *Sir Theodore Martin* . . 300
TIBULLUS
BIOGRAPHICAL SKETCH 302
THE POET'S IDEAL. *James Grainger* . . . 303
A RURAL FESTIVAL. *James Grainger* . . . 308
PROPERTIUS.
BIOGRAPHICAL SKETCH 312
BEAUTY UNADORNED. *Goldwin Smith* . . . 313
TO MAECENAS. *Thomas Gray* 314
A CHANGE OF VIEW *Thomas Gray* 318
A ROMAN MATRON TO HER HUSBAND. *Goldwin Smith* . 320
OVID
BIOGRAPHICAL SKETCH 325
DIDO TO AENEAS *Alexander Pope* . . 327
PHAETHON. *Henry King* 334
LIVY. *George Baker*
BIOGRAPHICAL SKETCH 348
THE HISTORIAN'S PREFACE 350
THE RAPE OF THE SABINE WOMEN 353
HORATIUS 356
BEFORE THE WAR 359
HANNIBAL 360
THE MARCH ACROSS THE ALPS . . 362
THE BATTLE OF CANNAE . . 372
THE CARTHAGINIANS IN CAPUA . . . 380
THE END OF THE WAR 381
THE DEATH OF HANNIBAL 385
PETRONIUS.
BIOGRAPHICAL SKETCH 387
AT TRIMALCHIO'S DINNER. *R. Y. Tyrrell* . . . 389
MARTIAL.
BIOGRAPHICAL SKETCH 393
A FRIEND. *Goldwin Smith* 394
THE DINER-OUT *Goldwin Smith* . . . 395
A LITERARY HOST. *James Elphinston* . . . 395
A ROMAN DAY *Goldwin Smith* . . . 396
THE TRUE BUSINESS OF LIFE. *Goldwin Smith* . . . 396

A Juggler. *James Elphinston* 397

Death of a Charioteer. *Goldwin Smith* 398

, TACITUS. *Arthur Murphy.*

Biographical Sketch 399

Customs of the Germans 401

The Mutiny of the Pannonian Legions . . . 410

The Great Fire at Rome 424

JUVENAL.

Biographical Sketch 432

Rome. *William Gifford* 433

PLINY THE YOUNGER. *John B. Firth.*

Biographical Sketch 450

To Cornelius Tacitus 451

To Sosius Senecio 452

To Septicius Clarus 453

To Calpurnia 454

To Tacitus 455

To Sura 460

To Geminus 464

To Maximus 465

To Fuscus 466

To Trajan 468

Trajan to Pliny 471

APULEIUS

Biographical Sketch 472

Cupid and Psyche. *Walter Pater* 473

Note — The several translations by Goldwin Smith from Lucretius, Propertius, and Martial are taken from his *Bay Leaves*, by his permission and that of The Macmillan Company, publishers of the volume. The following extracts also are used by permission of The Macmillan Company: Cicero's "Letters," from the translation by E S. Shuckburgh, "The Last Stand of Vereingetorix," from *Caesar's Conquest of Gaul*, by T Rice Holmes, Ode 29, Book III., from Sir Stephen de Vere's *Odes and Epodes of Horace*; and "Cupid and Psyche," from *Marius the Epicurean*, by Walter Pater.

The extract from Andrew Preston Peabody's translation of Cicero's *De Amicitia* is printed by arrangement with Messrs. Little, Brown & Co., the publishers, and the version of Horace's Ode 14, Book I., by permission of Messrs. Charles Scribner's Sons, publishers of *Echoes from the Sabine Farm*, by Eugene and Roswell Martin Field.

Acknowledgment is due also to Miss Norma R Waterbury for permission to use her prize translation of Horace's Ode 9, Book III.

INTRODUCTION

In this brief introduction an attempt will be made
to give an outline of the general tendencies of Latin
literature. The subject merits some attention, insomuch as the emphasis constantly laid upon the Greek
origin of Roman literary forms has tended to obscure
the fact that the strongest forces in Latin literature
were not due to Greek or any other influence, but were
its own, its peculiar birthright. They were qualities
derived from certain inherent characteristics of the
Roman people, which showed themselves in the very
earliest monuments of their literature, and which persisted throughout its history in spite of much running after foreign models and, in more than one
period, of an unfavorable social or political *milieu*. I
mean a certain seriousness of purpose, which found
its most splendid manifestation in the expression of
patriotism, in the glorification of the duties of citizenship, and in the construction of an enduring system
of law; and together with this, a shrewdness which
enabled them to see quickly the different aspects of
a question, to be swift to detect hypocrisy and fraud,
— the quality, in short, which, tempering their gravity,
saved it from being merely heaviness, and which made
them natural satirists. It is the former characteristic that we find exemplified in those religious observ-
ances of which the surviving chants formed a con-

stituent part, in the early collections of laws, and in
the historical records which the priests kept; it was
the latter that animated the Fescennine verses, and
formed the dominating element in the old *satura*. In
the literature that followed, in the great majority of
the works that were produced from the middle of the
third century before Christ, we can trace one or other
of these distinctly Roman tendencies.

Of the first we have innumerable examples in the
department of oratory. This lay close to the practice
of law, and ability in speaking was essential to every
one who aimed at a public career. So important a
rôle did oratory play in Roman life that its require-
ments practically controlled the whole system of education from the end of the primary school course, and
the question whether any particular subject should
find a place in the curriculum of the *ludus gram-
matici* or of the *schola rhetorici* was determined by
its advantages or disadvantages as a preliminary to
an orator's equipment. It is true that Roman orators
were trained in Greek rhetorical methods, made a
careful study of the great Greek orators, and were
familiar with all the details of the battle between the
Atticists and the Asiatics; but this, far from being
slavish imitation, was only part and parcel of their
desire for efficiency, their earnestness in everything
they undertook. Whatever complex of influences
may have been brought to bear on Cicero's oratorical
style, to whatsoever extent the form may be contribu-
tory to the final effect, it is as ever the spirit that
moves, the spirit of the Roman filled with a sense
of the high responsibility of office, of the greatness of
the Roman people. " The Senate and the People of
Rome," " the Senate and the People of Rome," — this

is the refrain that recurs again and again in all the great orations, as it does in the pages of Livy, for Livy's history is patriotism writ long, from the stately preface through the accounts of foreign wars and internal dissensions; and the chapters that more than others stir the blood are those that tell of the heroes who fought and died for their country, well content even at the cost of their lives to have deserved well of it.

Virgil's works breathe the same spirit of patriotism, his *Georgics* glorifying Italy with her mighty rivers, her cities crowning the hilltops, her teeming soil; his *Aeneid* exalting the race, descendants of gods and of heroes, men of prayer, yet withal strenuous in action, ready to suffer all things to attain their goal, gathering new strength from disaster, believing in the greatness of their destiny, fighting, waiting, enduring. And in Horace's lyrics we find from time to time the same note struck, as for example in the patriotic series at the beginning of the third book. These are not, perhaps, the odes that we turn to most frequently, yet they all show a consistent elevation. Tibullus too, with his love of fatherland, may be mentioned, and Propertius, pedantic and self-concentrated, but patriotic still.

Even in a branch so directly influenced by Greek work as philosophy there is a strong infusion of Roman spirit. In this department the Romans made absolutely no original contributions, founded no new schools, yet there is a sufficiently imposing list of men who in one way or another performed signal service. They emphasized the practical side of philosophic doctrine, made plain the drift of the teaching of this or that school, and brought philosophy down from the clouds to dwell among men.   In Lucretius' *De Rerum Natura* we have, so far as the subject matter goes, nothing more than an exposition of the theory of Epicurus, but in the intense seriousness with which the poet points out the practical bearing of the creed and its great importance for the conduct of life, the tone of the work is essentially Roman; and it is to this very Roman element that it owes its tremendous vigor of presentation, its glowing portrayal of the blessings of Epicureanism.   Widely different from the method of Lucretius is that which Cicero adopted in his philosophical works, in which we find urbanity instead of vehemence, and a tolerant eclecticism instead of the dogmatic teaching of a single creed.   Yet there are some points of similarity between the two in that Cicero also aimed at making Greek philosophy accessible to the Romans, and he too laid stress upon the value of literary form as an element of success. He did succeed, not only in his own day but in later centuries as well, when his writings were the principal medium through which Greek philosophy became known to western Europe.

Other writers, other fields, other periods might be drawn upon for further illustration of the serious practical trend of the Roman mind, as for example that great mass of legal lore which, accumulating year after year for centuries, found a final codification under Justinian, a κτῆμα ἐς ἀεί, the foundation of all modern law; or those writings in which agriculture had a long series of exponents, ranging from the dry didacticism of Cato to the poetic elevation of Virgil's *Georgics*.   Nor can I refrain from mentioning that sacred band, among whose ranks even so great a personage as Julius Caesar has a place, the Roman grammarians, who, zealous and acute, albeit sometimes misguided, exorcised the spirits of many a problem of tense and mood, of long and short, — ghosts that have even to this day wandered restlessly over the world, refusing to be laid, although more than the traditional three handfuls of dust have been thrown upon their remains.

The satirical vein was steadily productive, appearing either deliberately, of set purpose and intent, in writings aimed at various abuses, or incidentally in works of heavier calibre. It is represented, as we have seen, in such remnants as we have of the early literature. It found exuberant vent in the comedies of Plautus, and in a modified form enlivened the plays of Terence. In Lucilius it attained to full and free expression, and his fearlessness and vigor of attack, his keenness of vision and rapidity of execution became proverbial. Unfortunately he is not known to us except in fragments of his works and through the references of other writers, but we have enough to see that he was singularly virile of mind and facile of pen. As trenchant as he was merciless, he showed in his attacks on vice in high places a range of conception that does not remind us of a literature in the making. His technique was rude, as Augustan critics noted, but its rudeness or crudeness served in many cases to point the asperity of his invective.

Nor is satire wanting in the best of the later republican literature. It gave a Lucilian edge to more than one poem of Catullus, made the dicta of Caesar famous, was the salt of Cicero's orations, in urbane guise one of the charms of his letters.

Emergent still under the Empire it manifested within Horace's own work a striking development.

Conventional at first and having more than a modi-
cum of the old personal element, it presently adopted
broader methods, and by its substitution of types for
individuals, by its potentialities of suggestion, its creation of atmosphere, it gained in subtlety what it lost
in directness, and succeeded by its very lightness, its
elusiveness, its lack of insistence. In Persius we have
a tortured imitation of the same form, with frequent
echoes of Horace, but broken echoes only. The style
is recondite and obscure. Much studied and over
elaborated, it smells of the lamp. The poet's whole
manner, with its many phrases of but doubtful meaning, its hazy situations and invisible transitions, shows
that he wrote for an age which could be impressed
only by the unusual.

Of a different ilk is the satire of Petronius, coming
not out of the schools, but seeming to spring from the
ground soil of Italy. Spontaneous and exuberant, it
teems with broad characterizations and realistic pictures of low life. Elaborate descriptions of petty incidents are set off by the introduction of the quaint idiom
of popular speech with its proverbs, its slang, its many
expressions of mingled simplicity and shrewdness.

Later times furnish us with still further examples
of this race tendency to satire. We see it highly
developed in the writings of the historian Tacitus,
who was in some respects most Roman of them all,
— of more than Roman gravity, of more than Roman
keenness of satire, a man of republican ideals living
in an age which had seen tyranny. We find it in
Juvenal, whose style, strongly influenced by the standards of the public readings, is one of boundless vehemence, showing many vivid word-pictures and brilliant
sententiae. His rhetoric is sometimes pompous, on

occasion even blatant, and his expression not infrequently transcends his feeling, yet on the whole there seems to be a reasonably solid substratum of conviction. In Martial the satire is less pretentious, but there is no lack of effectiveness in his sharp attacks on contemporary conditions of life, his innumerable snapshots at the social farrago.

It is then in the great orations, the histories, the national epic, the patriotic lyrics, the practical expositions of philosophic systems, the codes of law on the one hand, and in the satirical writings on the other, that we get the purest traditions of the trend of Roman intellectual activity. In the former we have varying manifestations of that seriousness of purpose which the Romans themselves called *gravitas*, in the latter the output of that *satira* which was wholly theirs, — qualities which after all are not so much distinct as different aspects of the same character, for seriousness of purpose may reasonably enough be said to imply some degree of sensitiveness, and satire in its best form is the protest of wounded ideals.

The whole muster, it might seem, shows a woeful lack of productiveness along the higher lines of imaginative writing, but if we turn from the arid list of departments to the contents of the most representative works, the first impression is materially modified. It was only an imagination of rare power that could make a poem on the atomic theory of Epicurus so great a masterpiece as the *De Rerum Natura* of Lucretius. In it are descriptions that range from the exquisiteness of imagery to be found in the picture of the abodes of the gods, " where never creeps a cloud or moves a wind," to the Dantesque horrors of the Inferno that he did not believe in. Here we

have lines that sound with the clash of struggling battalions, there the perfect quiet of a lonely hillside;
now the peace and plenty of vineyards and olive-
yards, now battle-fields that show, like a picture by
Verestchagin, the grisly realities of war. His is not
the restraint of later art, but the storm of undisci-
plined power, seeing every detail in the white light
of his own imagination, and painting it as he saw it.
Virgil has less power, but his art is subtler, his work-
manship finer, and although the themes of many of
his pictures are drawn from Homer, the composition,
the details, the atmosphere are of his own creating.
His poems abound in golden words and phrases, in
lines of an exaltation that could be found only in one
who stood on the higher plane of poesy, who had
been touched by the divine afflatus. He was the inter-
preter of the muses, the *vates*, the inspired seer.

There were ventures in divers other fields; and even
if these constitute only a minor part of the message
which Roman literature has brought to the world,
they are none the less of abiding interest, not simply
as so many indications of the different influences that
bore on the evolution of literature and of society, but
by reason of their intrinsic worth. In lyric poetry,
for example, besides the patriotic odes of Horace we
have by the same hand many other pieces, of lighter
tone and not always showing the elevation of the
true lyric, yet of enduring charm, winning us by their
very restraint, by their perfect artistic form, their
many successes of phrase and line, their good humor,
their kindly philosophy; and Catullus, his predecessor, of more spontaneous utterance, more passionate,
of greater intensity, of rare depth of feeling and sincerity of expression. In elegy, too, the Romans were

conspicuously successful. This was a favorite medium of emotional expression, and shows a wide range of tone in the different works of Tibullus, Propertius, and Ovid. In pastoral poetry there are the *Eclogues* of Virgil, which, with all their inconsistencies of scenery and not infrequent political drift, rank with the best of his work. In epistolography the *Letters* of Cicero are an exemplar of the best Latin style with its toga off; while the correspondence of Pliny, an imitation of them, furnishes us with many glimpses of a personality that, even if not constructed on a large plan, is not without its interesting sides. Nor is fiction altogether wanting, as the *Satirae* of Petronius bear witness, and a hundred years later the *Golden Ass* of Apuleius, which gives us both by content and by style signs manifest that the old order of things was at an end.

Of strictly original dramatic composition there was but little. In consideration of their satirical tendencies it might have been expected that native Roman comedy would have flourished. The work done, moreover, by Plautus and Terence in the adaptation of Greek plays shows clearly that *vis comica* was not lacking. Yet at a comparatively early period we find legitimate comedy hardly able to hold its own against the mime and other doubtful forms of comic entertainment. Neither can the Romans be said to have succeeded in tragedy. It is true that the adaptations of Greek tragedies which the first wave of Hellenism brought with it seem to have had, to a very considerable extent, dignity of characterization and dramatic effectiveness. This is the judgment of Quintilian, and the fragments that remain confirm it. Yet the later examples, the plays of Seneca written in the

age of Nero, show that even at that date tragedy
had not escaped from its Greek leading-strings. Here
again we have the same old themes of Greek mythology,
and such changes of manner as we find in the introduction of lurid details and melodramatic situations,
in the constant striving for epigrammatic and senten-
tious effects, do not make for an increase in strength.
The fundamental cause of this failure in the higher
forms of dramatic expression is probably to be found
in the Roman lack of creative power in art. This
resulted in the production of plays which, adhering
closely to Greek models, failed by the very remote-
ness of their subjects to hold audiences which were,
for the most part, of a low grade of culture, and whose
interest in gladiatorial and similar exhibitions, part
of their heritage as a fighting people, was encouraged
more and more by the ruling class.

In the selections that follow an attempt has been
made to give a representation of Latin literature
in English translations. That some authors, some
works that might reasonably be looked for are not
represented is due either to lack of space or to the
fact that there are no good translations of them.
Plautus, for example, does not appear, for the reason
that, only a certain amount of space being available
for comedy, it seems probable that one play printed
in its entirety will give a better idea of the class to
which it belongs than shorter selections from different authors. The *Phormio* of Terence has accordingly the double function of representing both its author and the type known as the *Fabula Palliata*. This
plan of giving selections of considerable length and
of as much integrity as possible has been followed

throughout. In Lucretius, the last part of the fifth book is the *pièce de résistance ;* in Virgil the sixth book of the *Aeneid ;* in Cicero, for the orations the second division of the *Pro Cluentio,* for the philosophical works a portion of the *De Amicitia ;* in Livy, a series of chapters dealing with the career of Hannibal from his operations in Spain to his death in Bithynia. Where an author worked in several departments, these are represented, so far as their representation has been found to be compatible with the general plan of giving long selections. In the case of Cicero's orations one of the political speeches would have been preferred, but the *Pro Cluentio* has been substituted on account of the merit of the translation. In a few instances, where the translator's rendering seems somewhat more literal than the purpose of the book requires, changes have been made, for which the editor is solely responsible. Where the original is in verse, metrical translations have been regularly used, the only exceptions being the *Phormio,* where the version of the Roman Society of London has been drawn upon, and parts of Lucretius, where Munro's translation has been given. Throughout the book the aim has been to give the best translation, irrespective of the name or fame of the translator, and the fact that the renderings of the famous classicists of the eighteenth century have been very sparingly used is due to their seeming to be inferior to the more modern work.

GORDON JENNINGS LAING.

August 1, 1903.

TERENCE

BIOGRAPHICAL SKETCH

A NATIVE of Carthage, born about 190 B. C., Terence came at an early age to Rome, where from the lowly position of a slave in one of the patrician households he rose to distinction as one of the great representatives of Roman comedy. He belonged to the literary clique known as the Scipionic circle, of which the younger Scipio Africanus was the most conspicuous figure, and which included among others Laelius, whom Cicero afterwards made the principal interlocutor in his dialogue *On Friendship*, Polybius the historian, Panaetius the Stoic philosopher, Philus, and Metellus, — all of them men of broad culture and deeply imbued with a love of Greek literature.

His literary activity was confined to the production of *palliatae*, comedies the scenes of which were laid in Greece, and which obtained their name from the fact that the personages represented wore the Greek *pallium*. They were not original compositions, but were based on plays of Menander (342–292 B. C.), and other dramatists of the so-called New Attic Comedy, who, differing essentially in their aims from the playwrights of the Old Attic Comedy, avoided politics, and devoted themselves to the portrayal of social life. Their comedies were comedies of manners. In a majority of the plays the central interest is a love intrigue of more or less doubtful morality. The same types of character recur again and again : the tearful lover, the damsel in distress, the unscrupulous parasite,[1] the intriguing slave,

[1] The hanger-on, who in return for his support, assisted his patron in questionable transactions

the choleric old man, the guileful courtesan, the jealous wife, the shameless slave-trader, the thieving and insolent cook.

The *Phormio* is representative of the class. It bears the name of the parasite, through whose intrigues the action is carried on. Two brothers, Chremes and Demipho, had gone abroad, leaving their sons, Phaedria and Antipho respectively, in the care of Geta, a slave. He, however, instead of obeying the fathers' instructions, proceeded to abet the sons in their evil courses, and presently both of them were entangled in love affairs of distressing complexity. Phaedria fell desperately in love with a music girl, Pamphila, who was owned by Dorio, a slave-trader, and for whose release thirty minae [1] were requisite; while Antipho married an orphan, Phanium by name, quieting her guardian's objections by collusion with Phormio, who summoned him into court and charged him with being her next of kin, and so, by Athenian law, under obligation to marry her. It is at this point that the play opens. Phormio is confronted by two problems: to reconcile Antipho's father to the marriage, and to get the thirty minae for Phaedria. In the latter case he is successful through his own efforts; in the former, chance favors him. Demipho, on returning to Athens, is very angry at what his son has done, and declares that he will never recognize the marriage. After much wrangling, Phormio agrees to take her off his hands, and marry her himself, provided he be given thirty minae. The money is forthcoming, and Phormio promptly uses it to purchase the music girl for Phaedria. It then transpires that Phanium, instead of being poor and unknown, is the daughter of Chremes by a secret marriage, and there is no further objection to her as a wife for Antipho. Chremes, whose double life has been exposed, is not in a position to treat Phaedria harshly, and so all ends happily.

Besides the *Phormio*, five other plays of Terence have

---

[1] About $540

come down to us: *The Maid of Andros, The Self-Tor-mentor, The Eunuch, The Brothers,* and *The Mother-in-Law.* All of them were produced between 166 and 160 B. C. The poet died in the following year.

His work shows little or no originality. He followed his Greek masters closely, confining himself indeed to two, Menander and Apollodorus, the most careful workers of the school. Far from feeling this lack of creative power as a defect, he prided himself on the faithfulness and accuracy with which he reproduced his originals. The titles of all his plays are Greek, the names of all his characters are Greek, and there are few, if any, allusions to Roman customs or institutions. Only in one respect did he treat his sources more freely than Plautus, his predecessor in the same field, and that was in the use of the device known as *contamination,* the welding of the plots or parts of the plots of two or more plays into one. Comparing him with Plautus along other lines, while we miss the rollicking, boisterous merriment of the earlier playwright, there is a decided advance in the direction of more polished dialogue, more careful characterization, a more artistic construction of plot. In the matter of diction the contrast is still more striking. In Plautus we find the language of the street, but Terence used that of the salon, and its exquisite purity has been the admiration of both ancient and modern critics.

PHORMIO

CHARACTERS.

Davus, *a slave.*
Geta, *a slave of Demipho*
Antipho, *a young man, son of Demipho*
Phaedria, *a young man, son of Chremes*
Demipho, *an old man*
Phormio, *a parasite*
Hegio,
Cratinus, } *advisers of Demipho.*
Crito,
Dorio, *a slave-trader.*
Chremes, *an old man, brother of Demipho*
Sophrona, *a nurse.*
Nausistrata, *a matron, wife of Chremes.*
A Cantor.

Scene: *A street in Athens. In the background the houses of* Chremes, Demipho, *and* Dorio *The scene remains the same throughout the play.*

ACT I

Scene 1.

Enter Davus, *carrying a bag of money.*

Davus. My great friend and countryman, Geta, came to see me yesterday. I had owed him a trifling sum for a long time, the balance of a small account, and he asked me to get it for him I have done so, and am bringing it with me. I hear that his master's son has married a wife, and it is for her, I suppose, that this money is being scraped together. How unfair it is that the poor should always have to be adding to the treasures of the rich! This girl will carry off at one swoop everything that he, poor fellow, has saved with such difficulty and self-denial, out of his allowance, nor will she give a thought to the trouble he had in procuring it. They'll beat him out of another contribution when she has a baby, and another when the baby has a birthday, and another when it is initiated. The mother will take it all: the child will simply be the pretext for the presents. But I think I see Geta.

SCENE 2.

Enter GETA, *from* DEMIPHO'S *house*

Geta (speaking to some one within). If a red-headed fellow should ask for me —

Davus. Here he is, you need n't go on.

Geta. Oh, I was looking for you, Davus.

Davus (giving him the bag). There! Take it, it's good money. You'll find that it's just the amount of the debt.

Geta. Thank you. I'm very much obliged to you for not having forgotten me.

Davus. You well may be, especially when you consider how people act now-a-days. One has to take it as a great favor if anybody pays what he owes. But why do you look so sad?

Geta. Why, don't you know what terrible trouble we're in?

Davus. No. What is it?

Geta. I'll tell you, provided you can hold your tongue.

Davus. What a simpleton you are! After proving a man's reliability in money matters, are you afraid to trust him with words? What is there in it for me to deceive you?

Geta. Well, listen, then.

Davus. I'm all attention.

Geta. Do you know Chremes, my old master's elder brother?

Davus. Of course I do.

Geta. Well, do you know his son, Phaedria?

Davus. As well as I know you.

Geta. It happened that both the old gentlemen had to go abroad at the same time : Chremes to Lemnos, and my master to an old friend in Cilicia, who had written to him, holding out tempting prospects of all but mountains of gold.

Davus. What! to him who had so much!

Geta. Never mind, that's his way.

Davus. Oh, it's I who ought to have been a rich man.

Geta. Both these old gentlemen, when they went away, left me as a sort of guardian to their sons.

Davus. A hard office, Geta!

Geta. So I have found by experience. My protecting deity must have been angry with me when I was left in charge. At first I began to check them; but why make a long story of it? So long as I was faithful to the old gentlemen, my shoulders ached for it. I remembered the proverb about the folly of kicking against the pricks. I began to humor them and to do whatever they wanted.

Davus. You know how to suit your market.

Geta. My young master did not get into any mischief at first, but Phaedria straightway got hold of a little music girl, and fell head over heels in love with her. She belonged to a brutal slave-trader. Phaedria hadn't a penny to give for her — his father had seen to that — so all he could do was to feast his eyes on her, dangle after her, and escort her to her music lesson and home again. The rest of us had plenty

of time on our hands, and used to accompany him.
Now there was a barber shop opposite the school
where she took her lessons, and we generally waited
there till she was ready to go home. One day a young
fellow came in crying. Surprised, we asked him what
was the matter. "Never before," said he, "has poverty seemed to me so cruel and hard. I've just seen
a maiden in this neighborhood weeping for her dead
mother, who was buried right opposite. The girl had
no friend, acquaintance, or kinsman — nobody but one
old woman, to help her bury her mother. I felt for
her; she was such a stunning-looking girl!" Why
make a long story? He moved us all to compassion.
"Had n't we better go and see her?" said Antipho.
"I think so," said some one else; "show us the
way, please." We set out, reached the place, saw her.
She was beautiful, and there was all the more certainty about it because she had nothing to set off
her beauty: hair dishevelled — feet bare — untidy —
weeping — shabbily dressed. Her beauty had to be
brilliant indeed, not to be eclipsed by all that. Phaedria merely said, "She's not bad looking," but my
young master —

Davus. I know. He fell in love with her.

Geta. Yes, but do you know how deeply? Listen
to what happened. Next day he went straight to
the old woman, and implored her to let him have the
girl. She refused, and said that what he asked was
not right; that the girl was a citizen of Athens, a
good girl of a good family. If he wanted her for his
wife, she would agree to his marrying her legally; if
not, she would have nothing to do with him. My
young master did n't know what to do; he wanted to
marry her, but he feared his father.

Davus. Would n't his father, on his return, have forgiven him?

Geta. What! He forgive him for marrying a low-born, dowerless girl? Never.

Davus. What was the outcome of it?

Geta. The outcome of it? There 's a parasite named Phormio, an impudent fellow, the gods confound him!

Davus. What did he do?

Geta. He gave Antipho this advice: "It 's the law that orphan girls must marry their next of kin, and this same law commands their next of kin to marry them. Now, I 'll declare you to be next of kin, and will bring an action against you. I 'll pretend to be a friend of the girl's father. The matter will come before a jury; I 'll invent the whole story about who her father and mother were, and how she is related to you; and well shall I serve my own interest by so doing. You 'll make no defence to any of these charges, and I 'll win the case. Your father will come home. I 'll have a law-suit on my hands. But what difference will that make to me? The girl will be ours."

Davus. What consummate impudence!

Geta. He got the young fellow's consent, and it was done; we went into court — lost our case — he married her.

Davus. You don't say so!

Geta. Yes, I do.

Davus. Oh, Geta! what will become of you?

Geta. I'm sure I don't know; all I know is that I 'll bear patiently whatever may befall.

Davus. I like that; that 's the way a man should act.

Geta. My only hope is in myself.

Davus. That 's right.

Geta. However, I suppose that I must go to an intercessor, who will plead for me in this way : "Let him off just this once, I pray you ; if he offends again, I 'll not intercede for him." Lucky if he does not add, " As soon as my back is turned, kill him, for all I care."

Davus. How about the young fellow who was so attentive to the music girl ?   How is he getting on ?

Geta. But so so, poorly.

Davus. Has n't much to give her, perhaps ?

Geta. Nothing but unalloyed hope.

Davus. Has his father returned?

Geta. Not yet.

Davus. When do you expect your old master back?

Geta. I don't know for certain, but I heard just now that a letter had come from him, and had been taken to the custom-house officers;[1] I 'll go and ask for it.

Davus. Can I be of any further service, Geta ?

Geta. No, good-by. [*Exit* DAVUS. GETA *calls to slave within.*]   Hi, boy !   Is no one ever coming ? [*Enter a slave.* GETA *gives him the bag.*]   Here, give this to Dorcium.[2]   [*Exit.*

ACT II.

SCENE 1.

Enter ANTIPHO *and* PHAEDRIA *from* CHREMES' *house.*

Antipho. To think, Phaedria, that it should have come to this ; that I should be afraid of him who has

---

[1] They collected the port duties, and had the right to open letters.

[2] Geta's wife.

my interest most at heart, my own father, whenever
I think of his return ! Had I not been thoughtless, I
should have been looking forward to his arrival in the
proper spirit.

Phaedria. What's the matter?

Antipho. Do you ask, you who are my accomplice
in so bold a deed? Oh, that it had never come into
Phormio's head to advise me as he did, and that he
had not urged me (though I didn't need much urging) to that act which was the beginning of all my
troubles ! Suppose I had not won her, I should have
suffered for the next few days, but I shouldn't have
been racked by this daily anxiety —

Phaedria. Oh, doubtless!

Antipho. Expecting my father to come any day,
and put an end to my married life.

Phaedria. Other people fret because they see too
little of those they love; you complain because you
see too much of her. You have a surfeit of love,
Antipho. But, as a matter of fact, this life of yours
is one to be desired and longed for. So help me,
Heaven, I should be ready to lay down my life, if I
might enjoy my love as long as you have yours Just
think how I am suffering from want, while you are
revelling in plenty; to say nothing of the fact that
you have, without any expense, won a well-born, well-
bred wife; that you have, just as you wished, been
married publicly, and without any scandal. You would
be a happy man if there were not one thing wanting
— the temperament to bear your good fortune con-
tentedly. If you had to deal with the slave-trader
that I have, you would understand. But nearly all
men's dispositions are the same; we are always discontented with our lot.

Antipho. But, Phaedria, to me it is you who seem to be the lucky man, for you still have the power of doing what you choose · you can keep your sweetheart or let her go, whereas I, poor wretch, have got into such a fix that I can neither get rid of my wife nor keep her. But what is this? Is n't this Geta that I see running this way? So it is. Dear me! I wonder what news he brings.

SCENE 2.

Enter GETA, *running.*

Geta (to himself, not noticing ANTIPHO *and* PHAEDRIA). You 're a lost man, Geta, unless you quickly devise some plan of protection; so many disasters suddenly threaten, and you are so unprepared. I don't know how to avoid them, or how to get myself out of this scrape. Our bold stroke can't be kept secret any longer.

Antipho (aside to PHAEDRIA). What is it that he 's in such a flurry about?

Geta. Besides, I 've only a moment for this business. The master is here.

Antipho (aside). What disaster is this?

Geta. When he hears of it, what means shall I find to turn aside his anger? Suppose I speak? I should enrage him. Hold my tongue? I should aggravate him. Try to excuse myself? I might as well wash a brick. Oh, poor me! I 'm in for it. And then, too, I 'm on tenter-hooks about Antipho; I pity him; I fear him. It 's he who 's keeping me here now. But for him I should have taken good care of myself, and paid the old gentleman out for his ill temper; I should have got a few things together and bolted straightway.

Antipho (aside). What flight or theft is this that he's scheming?

Geta. But where shall I find Antipho? Which way shall I start to seek him?

Phaedria (aside). He's talking about you.

Antipho (aside). I expect to hear of some great disaster or other from this messenger.

Phaedria (aside). Oh, dear!

Geta. I'll go home; that's where he generally is.

Phaedria (aside). Let's call the fellow back.

Antipho. Stop, there!

Geta (without looking back). Umph! You speak haughtily enough, whoever you are.

Antipho. Geta!

Geta (looking back). It's the very man that I want to see.

Antipho. Pray, let me have the news that you bring, and tell it to me, if you can, in a word.

Geta. I will.

Antipho. Out with it.

Geta. At the harbor just now —

Antipho. Not my —?

Geta. You've guessed it.

Antipho. I'm undone.

Phaedria. Whew!

Antipho. What am I to do?

Phaedria. What is it you say?

Geta. I've seen his father, your uncle.

Antipho. Poor wretch that I am! How shall I ward off this sudden disaster? If my fortunes have fallen so low that I must be parted from you, Phanium, I don't care to live.

Geta. Well, then, if that's so, Antipho, you ought to be all the more on the alert; Fortune favors the brave.

Antipho. I 'm beside myself.

Geta. But, Antipho, this is just the time when you should n't be beside yourself, for if your father sees that you 're afraid he 'll think that you 're to blame.

Phaedria. That 's true.

Antipho. I can't change my character.

Geta. How would you manage if you had something harder to do?

Antipho. Why, since I can't do this, I should be still less able to do that.

Geta. There 's nothing in this, Phaedria; let 's be off. Why are we wasting time here? I 'm going.

Phaedria. And I too.

Antipho. Oh, pray! Suppose I pretend to be brave? (*feigning an expression of boldness*). Will this do?

Geta (*not turning round*). You 're talking nonsense.

Antipho. Look at my face, both of you. Now, will this do?

Geta. No.

Antipho. Well, then, this?

Geta. Almost.

Antipho. This, then.

Geta. That will do. Now stick to that, and see that you answer him word for word, tit for tat, and don't let him, however angry he may be, get the better of you by his savage abuse.

Antipho. I understand.

Geta. You were forced into it against your will by the law, the sentence passed upon you, do you understand? But who 's the old gentleman I see at the end of the street?

Antipho. 'T is he himself. I can't stay.

Geta. Oh, what are you doing, where are you going, Antipho? Stop, stop!

Antipho. I know myself and my offence; I leave Phanium and my life in your hands.   [*Exit hastily.*

Phaedria. What will happen now, Geta?

Geta. You'll get a lecture; and I, unless I'm very much mistaken, shall be tied up and flogged. But, Phaedria, we ourselves must now carry out the advice which we just gave to Antipho.

Phaedria. Away with your " musts," — give me your orders.

Geta. Do you remember what you used to say at the very beginning of this business, by way of shielding us from blame, — that the case against us was lawful and clear, sure to win, as good as it could be?

Phaedria. I remember.

Geta. Well, there's need of the selfsame defence now, or, if possible, of one better and more plausible.

Phaedria. I'll do my best.

Geta. Now do you attack first. I'll be here in reserve, ready to relieve you, if you fail.

Phaedria. Agreed. (*They retire to back of stage.*)

SCENE 3.

Enter DEMIPHO

Demipho (*to himself, not seeing* PHAEDRIA *and* GETA). To think of it, to think of it! Antipho married without my consent! Had he no regard for my authority? No, I'll say nothing about my authority, but for my displeasure? No shame? Oh, what an outrage! Oh, that Geta, his prompter!

Geta (*aside*). My turn at last!

Demipho. What will they say to me? What excuse will they find?

Phaedria (aside). Oh, I 'll find one ; don't let that trouble you.

Demipho. Will it be, " I did it against my will, the law compelled me " ? Well, I concede that.

Geta (aside). Good.

Demipho. But wittingly and without a word, to let your opponents win — did the law compel you to do that ?

Phaedria (aside). That 's a hard one.

Geta (aside). I 'll fix it ; leave it to me.

Demipho. I don't know what I 'm to do, seeing that this has happened. It 's such a surprise that I can hardly believe it even now. I 'm so upset that I can't bring myself to think it over. It shows that every one, even at the height of prosperity, should consider ways and means of bearing adversity — danger, loss, exile. A man returning from a journey should always keep in mind the possibility of his son being in a scrape, his wife being dead, or his daughter ill : he should remember that these are the common incidents of life, and so prevent their surprising him. Whatever turns out well contrary to his expectation, should be reckoned as so much gain.

Geta (aside). Oh, Phaedria, it 's hard to believe, but I 'm away ahead of my master in philosophy, for I 've considered all the disagreeable things which may befall me on his return : to grind corn in the mill, be flogged, wear chains, work as a field hand. None of these things will surprise me. Whatever turns out well contrary to my expectation, I shall reckon as so much gain. But why don't you go up to him and begin to coax him ?

Demipho. Why, here 's my nephew Phaedria.

Phaedria (going up to him). How do you do, uncle ?

Demipho. How do you do? but where 's Antipho?

Phaedria. Your safe return —

Demipho. Yes, I know what you would say, but answer my question.

Phaedria. He 's well, he 's here; have you found everything to your liking?

Demipho. I wish I had.

Phaedria. What is it that 's wrong?

Demipho. Need you ask me, Phaedria? A nice marriage you 've brought about here in my absence!

Phaedria. What, are you angry with him on that account?

Geta (*aside*). What an artist he is!

Demipho. How could I fail to be angry with him? Just let me set eyes on him. He 'll soon learn that his once lenient father has become harshness itself.

Phaedria. But, uncle, he has n't done anything for you to be angry at.

Demipho. Why, look you now! it 's all of a piece! they 're in it together! Know one and you know all.

Phaedria. It is n't so.

Demipho. When Number One has done something wrong, Number Two stands forth as his advocate; when Number Two is in trouble, Number One comes forward. It 's a mutual protection society.

Geta (*aside*). He does n't know it, but the old man has painted them in their true colors.

Demipho. If it were n't so, you would n't be siding with him, Phaedria.

Phaedria. If Antipho's fault, uncle, had been one that affected his fortune or good name, I should n't have said a word against his suffering the punishment which he deserved; but when some one, resorting to sharp practice and taking advantage of our youth, laid a trap for us, and won the case, is it our fault, or the fault of the jury, who often, as you know, cast the rich from envy, and find for the poor from compassion.

Geta (aside). If I did n't know the details of the trial, I should really believe that he was telling the truth.

Demipho. Can any juryman get at the right and wrong of a case, when the defendant acts as he did and says never a word?

Phaedria. Any other well-bred young fellow might have done the same: when he appeared in court he could n't deliver the speech he had prepared; his modesty was too much for him.

Geta (aside). Phaedria 's fine! But why don't I accost the old fellow? *(going up to him.)* How do you do, master? I 'm delighted to see you safe home again.

Demipho. O worthy guardian! true prop of the family! to whose care I commended my son when I went abroad!

Geta. I 've heard you for some time maligning us, and me most unjustly of all. Why, what did you expect me to do in this trial? The law does n't allow a slave to plead, nor can he be called as a witness.

Demipho. I pass over all that; I admit the defence that he was young, unsophisticated, afraid to speak; I allow your plea of being a slave; but however nearly related the girl might be, he need n't have married her. You should have given her a dowry, as the law directs, and she should have hunted up another husband. On what reckoning did he choose to marry a pauper?

Geta. It was n't a reckoning, but cash that we wanted

Demipho. He could have raised it somehow.

Geta. Where? It's easy to talk.

Demipho. Well, if he could n't get it in any other way, he might have borrowed it on interest.

Geta. A pretty idea that! As if any one would trust him while you 're alive!

Demipho. No, no, it shall not, it cannot be. I 'll not let her live with him one single day as his wife. This is not a case for leniency. I wish some one would point out that fellow to me, or show me the place where he lives.

Geta. You mean Phormio?

Demipho. The man who took up this woman's case.

Geta I 'll have him here presently.

Demipho. Where 's Antipho now?

Geta. Out.

Demipho. Go, find him, Phaedria, and bring him here.

Phaedria. I 'll go right away.

                [Exit into Dorio's house

Geta (aside). Yes, to Pamphila.

Demipho. I 'll go home, and greet my household gods; thence to the market place and ask some of my friends to stand by me in this matter, so that I may be ready for Phormio if he should come.

                [Exit into his house

ACT III

SCENE 1.

Enter PHORMIO *and* GETA.

Phormio. You say that he was so frightened at his father's return that he ran away.

Geta. Quite so.

Phormio. And Phanium is left alone?

Geta. Yes.

Phormio. And the old gentleman is angry?

Geta. Furious.

Phormio (to himself). Upon you alone, Phormio, devolves the conduct of this affair; you're the one who has made this dish, and you're the one who must eat it. Set about it then!

Geta. Pray, help us.

Phormio (to himself). Suppose he asks —

Geta. We're depending wholly on you.

Phormio (to himself). But see! What if he replies —

Geta. It was you who drove him to it.

Phormio (to himself). I have it, I think.

Geta. Do help us.

Phormio. Bring the old fellow out. I've all my plans arranged.

Geta. What are you going to do?

Phormio. Just what you want me to do, — have Phanium stay where she is, free Antipho from blame, turn aside the current of the old man's wrath upon myself.

Geta. You're a plucky fellow, and a friend indeed. But, Phormio, I'm often afraid that your dare-devil ways will land you in the stocks some day.

Phormio. Not a bit of it. I've had experience, and can see my way clearly now. Just think of all the people I've beaten out of their very lives — foreigners and citizens; the better I know the way, the oftener I try it. Come, tell me now, have you ever heard of any action for assault being brought against me?

Geta. How do you account for that?

Phormio. It 's this way : the net is not spread for the hawk or the kite, that do us harm ; it 's laid for those that do us none at all.   In the one case there 's profit, in the other mere labor lost   Men who have something to lose are exposed to divers perils, but I have nothing, and everybody knows it.   What 's that you say ?   Have me convicted, and take me to jail ? No, no ! they don't care to support a big eater, and to my mind they 're wise not to wish to requite an injury by the greatest of favors.

Geta. Antipho will never be able to reward you as you deserve.

Phormio. That 's true, but then no one is ever as grateful to his patron as he ought to be.   Just think ! You go to his house scot-free, you 've had your bath, been anointed, there 's not a care on your mind, while he has all the worry and expense.   You have a good time, he frets and fumes.   You may laugh, drink first, take your place first.   Then a puzzling dinner is set before you.

Geta. What do you mean by that?

Phormio. One where you are puzzled which dish you had better taste first.   Reckoning up how pleasant, how delicious these things are, should n't you regard the man who furnishes them as a god incarnate?

Geta. Here 's the old man !   Mind what you 're doing; it 's the first onset that 's always the fiercest. If you hold your own in that, all the rest will be mere play.   [*They retire to back of stage.*

Scene 2.

Enter DEMIPHO *and his three advisers.*

Demipho. Did you ever hear of anybody being wronged in a more insulting way than I have been in this matter? Stand by me, I pray you.

Geta (aside). He's furious.

Phormio (aside). Just keep your eye on me; I'll stir him up presently. (*Aloud.*) Good heavens! Phanium not related to him? Is that what Demipho says? Does Demipho say that she's not related to him?

Geta. That's what he says.

Demipho. I believe that this is the very man I was speaking of. Follow me.

Phormio. And says he does n't know who her father was?

Geta. That's what he says.

Phormio. And denies all knowledge of Stilpo?

Geta. Just so.

Phormio. Because the poor girl was left in want, people don't know her father, and she herself is neglected. Just see what avarice does.

Geta. If you cast any slurs on my master, you'll hear from me to your sorrow.

Demipho. The insolence of the fellow! He has actually come here to accuse me!

Phormio. As for the young man, I've no quarrel with him for not knowing much about my friend, who was well on in years, and in poor circumstances. He earned his living by the work of his hands, and so he generally stayed in the country, where he held some land under my father. I've often heard him tell how this kinsman of his neglected him. But what a man he was! the best I've ever known.

Geta. Something of a contrast between him and you!

Phormio. Oh, go and be hanged! If I had n't thought so highly of him, I never should have got into all this trouble with your family for the daughter's sake, whom your master is now treating so shabbily.

Geta. You scoundrel, are you going to continue abusing my master behind his back?

Phormio. But he deserves it.

Geta. You say so, you jail-bird?

Demipho. Geta!

Geta. You thief! You swindler!

Demipho. Geta!

Phormio (aside). Answer him.

Geta. Who is it? Oh!

Demipho. Silence!

Geta This fellow has never ceased to heap abuse on you behind your back, saying things which don't apply to you at all, but to himself.

Demipho. Hold your tongue. (*To* PHORMIO.) Young man, pray answer me, if you please. Just explain to me who that friend of yours was, and how he claimed kinship with me.

Phormio. Fishing, just as if you did n't know him!

Demipho. I know him?

Phormio. Yes.

Demipho. I tell you that I don't know him; recall him to my memory, since you say I do.

Phormio. What, not know your own cousin?

Demipho. You 'll be the death of me. Tell me his name.

Phormio. His name? Certainly.

Demipho. Why don't you tell it to me?

Phormio (aside). By Heaven, it's all over with me! I've forgotten his name.

Demipho. Eh! What's that you're saying?

Phormio (aside). Geta, if you remember what we said just now, prompt me. (*Aloud.*) Well, I won't tell you his name; you come to pump me, as if you did n't know.

Demipho. I pump you?

Geta (aside to PHORMIO). Stilpo.

Phormio. But after all, what do I care? His name was Stilpo.

Demipho. Whom did you say?

Phormio. Stilpo, I say; you knew him.

Demipho. I never knew him, and I never had a kinsman of that name

Phormio. So? Are you not ashamed? Now if he had left behind him a property worth ten talents —

Demipho. The gods confound you!

Phormio. You'd have been the very first to trace your ancestry from memory, going back to grandfather and great-grandfather.

Demipho. I take you at your word. In that case I should on my return home have told everybody how she was related to me. Now do you do likewise. Pray, how is she related to me?

Geta. Well done, our side! (*Aside to* PHORMIO) Look out, you there!

Phormio. I've already explained the whole matter clearly to those to whom it was my duty to explain it, the gentlemen of the jury. If what I said was untrue, why did n't your son disprove it?

Demipho. My son, indeed! I can't speak of his folly in the terms it deserves.

Phormio. But now do you, who are so wise, go to the magistrates, and ask them for a new trial, since it seems that you are sole monarch here, and can get judgment given twice in the same case.

Demipho. Though I 've been wronged, yet rather than be involved in a lawsuit, or listen to your talk, I 'll give her the dowry which the law orders, just as if she really were related to me. Away with her, and take five minae.

Phormio. Ha, ha! you 're delightful!

Demipho. What 's the matter? Isn't my request reasonable? Am I to be refused even this, the common right of citizens?

Phormio. And pray does the law order you to pay her off and get rid of her, after you 've done what you liked with her, just as if she were a courtesan? Does it not, on the contrary, order that she be given in marriage to her next of kin, to live with him all her days, lest poverty should drive her to evil courses? And this is what you forbid

Demipho. Yes, to her next of kin; but how do we come in? or why?

Phormio. Oh, my good sir, "don't plead a lost cause," as the saying is.

Demipho. What! not plead my cause? I 'll not stop till I 've gained my point.

Phormio. Nonsense!

Demipho. You 'll see.

Phormio. Besides, we have nothing to do with you, Demipho; judgment has been given against your son, not against you; your time for marrying has passed.

Demipho. You 're to think that he says everything that I say; or I 'll turn him out of doors, wife and all.

Geta (aside). He 's furious.

Phormio. Better turn yourself out.

Demipho. You scoundrel! Do you mean to thwart me in everything?

Phormio (*aside*). He's trying to hide it, but he's afraid of us all the same.

Geta (*aside*). You've made a good beginning.

Phormio (*aloud*). Now, why not bear what must be borne? Behave as you should, and let's be friends.

Demipho. I want your friendship, or wish to see or hear you!

Phormio. If you're on good terms with her, you'll have some one to comfort you in your old age; remember that you're getting on in years.

Demipho. Let her comfort you; take her for yourself.

Phormio. Don't let your anger run away with you.

Demipho. Now look here! Unless you're quick about taking that woman away, I'll throw her out of the house; that's all I have to say, Phormio.

Phormio. If you treat her in any way unbecoming a lady I'll bring a heavy action against you; that's all I have to say, Demipho. (*Aside.*) If I'm wanted, send to my house for me.

Geta (*aside*). I understand. [*Exit* PHORMIO.

SCENE 3

Demipho. What trouble and anxiety my son has caused me by entangling us in this marriage! And he won't let me see him, so that I might at least know what he has to say about the matter, or what his opinion is. (*To* GETA.) Go, find out whether he has come home yet.

Geta. Yes   [*Exit into* DEMIPHO'S *house.*

Demipho. You see how the matter stands. What am I to do? Speak, Hegio.

Hegio. What, I? With your permission, I think that Cratinus had better speak.

Demipho. Speak, Cratinus.

Cratinus. What, do you want me to speak?

Demipho. Yes, you.

Cratinus. I should like to see you do what is to your advantage. This is how I look at it: it's right and just that what your son has done in your absence should be undone; and you'll be able to manage it. That's what I say.

Demipho. Now do you speak, Hegio.

Hegio. I think that Cratinus has spoken to the best of his ability; but the fact is, "Many men, many minds!" Every one has his own way. It seems to me that what has been done by the law can't be undone, and that it's wrong to try.

Demipho. Now, Crito.

Crito. I reserve my decision; the matter is an important one.

Hegio. Can we be of any further service?

Demipho. You have done well. (*Exeunt advisers.*) I'm much more uncertain now than I was before.

Geta (*entering from* DEMIPHO'S *house*). They say that he hasn't come back.

Demipho. I must wait till my brother comes; I'll do whatever he advises me. I'll go down to the harbor and inquire when he is to return.   [*Exit.*

Geta. But I'll look for Antipho, and let him know what's been done here. Ah, there I see him coming back in the very nick of time!

Scene 4

Enter Antipho

Antipho. There's no doubt about it, Antipho, you're a great deal to blame for your cowardice. Just think of going off as you did and leaving your very life to be protected by others! Did you think that others would look after your interests better than yourself? However other matters stood, you certainly ought to have done your best for her whom you now have at home, and seen to it that she should not be deceived and harmed through you. All her hopes and resources, poor thing, rest in you alone.

Geta (coming forward). Well, as a matter of fact, master, we've been blaming you this long time for going away.

Antipho. You're the very man I was looking for.

Geta. But we haven't on that account been any the less zealous in your cause.

Antipho. Tell me, pray, how stand my affairs and my fortune? Does my father suspect anything?

Geta. Nothing as yet.

Antipho. Is there any hope for the future?

Geta. I don't know.

Antipho. Oh, dear!

Geta. Except that Phaedria has never ceased to fight for you.

Antipho. Nothing new in him.

Geta. And Phormio has shown himself as strenuous in this as in other matters.

Antipho. What has he done?

Geta. He silenced the old gentleman, who was in a great rage.

Antipho. Well done, Phormio!

Geta. And I, too, did what I could.

Antipho. My Geta, I love you all.

Geta. The affair has begun as I've told you. So far everything's quiet, and your father's going to wait for your uncle's arrival.

Antipho. Why is he waiting for him?

Geta. He said that he wished to follow his advice in the matter.

Antipho. O Geta, how greatly I fear my uncle's return, for he, as it seems, is to decide whether I am to live or die.

Geta. Here's Phaedria.

Antipho. Where?

Geta. There, coming out of his training-school.[1]

SCENE 5.

Enter DORIO *and* PHAEDRIA *from* DORIO'S *house.*

Phaedria. Dorio, listen to me, I beseech you.

Dorio. No, I won't.

Phaedria. Just a moment.

Dorio. Let me alone.

Phaedria. Do listen to what I have to say.

Dorio. But I'm tired of listening to the same thing a thousand times over.

Phaedria. But this time I'll tell you something that you'll be pleased to listen to.

Dorio. Go on, I'm listening.

Phaedria. Can't I prevail on you to wait for the next three days? Where are you going now?

Dorio. I was wondering whether you'd tell me anything new.

---

[1] Humorously applied to Dorio's house.

Antipho (aside). Ah! I 'm afraid the slave-trader may —

Geta (aside). Get his head broken. I 'm afraid of that too.

Phaedria. Won't you trust me?

Dorio. Nonsense!

Phaedria. If I give you my word of honor?

Dorio. Stuff!

Phaedria. You 'll say that you were well repaid for your kindness.

Dorio. Words!

Phaedria. Believe me, you 'll be glad that you did it; indeed that 's true.

Dorio. Dreams!

Phaedria. Try me; it 's not for long.

Dorio. The same old song!

Phaedria. I 'll regard you as my kinsman, my parent, my friend, my —

Dorio. Chatter away.

Phaedria. To think of your being so hard and inexorable that neither pity nor entreaties have any effect on you!

Dorio. To think, Phaedria, of your being so thoughtless and shameless as to expect to bamboozle me with fine words, and get my girl for nothing!

Antipho (aside). I 'm so sorry for him!

Phaedria. Alas! What he says is too true.

Geta (aside). How like himself each is!

Phaedria. I wish that this piece of bad luck had not happened to me at a time when Antipho has troubles of his own!

Antipho. Eh? What 's that you 're saying, Phaedria?

Phaedria. Oh, you lucky fellow!

Antipho. I lucky ?

Phaedria. You 've got your sweetheart, and you 've never had to face a trouble like this.

Antipho. Got her! no, I 'm like the man in the proverb, I " hold a wolf by the ears." [1]

Dorio. That 's just my difficulty with this fellow.

Antipho. Oh, don't be a slave-trader by halves! (*To* PHAEDRIA.)   Has he done anything final ?

Phaedria. He ? Yes, acted like a perfect brute, sold my Pamphila.

Geta. What! Sold her ?

Antipho. What 's that you say ?   Sold her ?

Phaedria. That 's what he 's done.

Dorio. What a crime, for a man to sell a girl that he bought with his own money !

Phaedria. I can't get him to wait for me and put off his other purchaser for just the next three days, while I get together the money that I 've been promised by my friends. If I don't give it you then, don't wait an hour longer.

Dorio. Still dinning that into my ears !

Antipho. It 's not a long time that he asks for. Agree to his proposition.   He 'll repay twice over the benefit you confer.

Dorio. That 's all talk.

Antipho. Will you let Pamphila be banished from the city ?   Have you the heart to sunder their love ?

Dorio. Neither you nor I need trouble about that.

Geta. May all the gods give you what you deserve !

Dorio. I 've borne with you against my will for several months, you 've been all promises and tears, but no cash; now, instead, I 've found a man with cash and no tears.   Make way for your betters.

---

[1] Difficult to hold, dangerous to let go

Antipho. But, if I remember rightly, a day was fixed long ago, by which you were to pay him.

Phaedria. So it was.

Dorio. Do I deny it?

Antipho. Has that day passed?

Dorio. No, but this one has come before it.

Antipho. Are n't you ashamed of your treachery?

Dorio. Not a bit, if I make anything out of it.

Geta. Dirt! '

Phaedria. Dorio, is this the way to act?

Dorio. It 's my way; take it or leave it.

Antipho. And you deceive him like this?

Dorio. But, Antipho, it 's he who 's deceiving me. He knew what I was; I thought he was something different. He 's taken me in; I 've been to him just what I always was. But however that may be, I 'll do this much for you. The soldier said that he 'd give me the money early to-morrow morning. If you bring it to me before he does, Phaedria, I 'll act on my old rule, "First come, first served." That 's all.

[*Exit*

SCENE 6

Phaedria. What am I to do? Miserable man that I am, how can I find the money for him on such short notice, I who have less than nothing? If we could have got him to wait, it was promised me in three days.

Antipho. Geta, can we let him be so unhappy, him who helped me so kindly a little while ago, as you told me? Now that he needs it, let 's try to repay our debt of gratitude to him.

Geta. That 's what we ought to do, I know.

ACT IV

Scene 1.

Enter Demipho *and* Chremes.

Demipho. Well, have you brought back your daughter with you, on whose account you went to Lemnos?

Chremes. No.

Demipho. And why not?

Chremes. When her mother saw that I was staying here rather a long time, and the girl's age did n't admit of neglect on my part, she set out, so they said, with all her household, to come to me.

Demipho. Pray, then, why did you stay there so long after you had heard this?

Chremes. Hang it![1] I was ill; that delayed me.

Demipho. What caused your illness? The circumstances?

Chremes. Do you ask me? Why, old age itself is an illness. However, I've heard, from the sailor who brought them over, that they got here safely.

Demipho. Have you heard, Chremes, what has happened to my son while I was away?

Chremes. Yes; and his action makes me uncertain what to do; for if I offer my daughter in marriage to an outsider, I'll have to explain in detail how and by whom she is mine. Now I know that I can trust you as myself; whereas, if an outsider wishes to form a connection with me, he'll say nothing so long as we're on good terms, but if we fall out, he'll know more than there's any need of his

[1] Chremes is restive under his brother's cross-questioning, and makes somewhat evasive answers

knowing. Moreover, I'm afraid of this coming somehow to my wife's ears, and if that happens there's
nothing left for me to do but to clear out and run
away from home. I've only myself, of all my be-
longings, that I can call my own.

Demipho. I know, and it makes me anxious. But
I'll never tire of trying to accomplish what I promised.

Scene 2.

Enter Geta.

Geta. Phormio is the cleverest man I've ever known.
I went to him to tell him that money was wanted, and
how it was to be got. Before I was half through, he
understood. He was delighted, praised me, inquired
where the old gentleman was, and thanked Heaven
that he had been given an opportunity of proving
himself no less a friend to Phaedria than he had been
to Antipho. I told him to wait for me at the market-
place, and I would bring Demipho there. But there's
the old gentleman himself now! And who is that
behind him? Whew! it's Phaedria's father come
home! But why should I be afraid, simpleton that I
am? Because I've got two men to cheat instead of
one? It's better, I take it, to have two strings to
one's bow. I'll ask Demipho for the money, as I
intended to do; if he gives it to me, all right. If I
can get nothing out of him, then I'll tackle the new-
comer.

Scene 3.

Enter Antipho, *unobserved, from* Demipho's *house.*

Antipho. I wonder how soon Geta will be back.
But I see my uncle standing with my father! Heavens! how I fear what his return may mean for me!

Geta (aside). I 'll approach them. (*Aloud.*) Our own Chremes! How do you do?

Chremes How do you do, Geta?

Geta. It 's a great pleasure to see you safe home again.

Chremes. Yes, yes.

Geta. How goes it?

Chremes. I 've found a good many changes here — the usual experience of one coming home.

Geta. True, indeed. Have you heard what Antipho has done?

Chremes. Yes, the whole story.

Geta (to DEMIPHO). Did you tell him? What a shame it was, Chremes, that he should be overreached in that way!

Demipho. That 's what I was just telling Chremes.

Geta. Well, I 've turned the matter over carefully in my mind, and I think I 've found a remedy.

Chremes. What is it, Geta?

Demipho. What 's your remedy?

Geta. After leaving you, I happened to meet Phormio.

Chremes. Who 's Phormio?

Geta. The man by whom that girl —

Chremes. I understand.

Geta. I thought I might as well sound him, so I took him aside. "Come, Phormio," I said, "why should n't we settle this business in a friendly way, instead of quarrelling over it? My master 's a gentleman, and does n't care to go to law, though, by Heaven, all his friends just now agreed in advising him to turn her out of doors."

Antipho (aside). What 's he up to? Where will all this end?

Geta. I went on, " Do you say that he would have
to pay the legal penalty, if he cast her forth? That
matter has been looked into already. Oh, but you'll
sweat if you go to law with that man. Such a speaker
as he is! And even suppose you win, after all, it's
only his money, not his life that's at stake." When
I saw that I had made some impression on him by
this sort of talk, I added, " We're all by ourselves
here now; tell me what you'll take, cash down, the
understanding being that my master desists from the
lawsuit, the girl takes herself off, and you trouble us
no more."

Antipho (aside). Has Heaven deprived him of his
wits?

Geta. " For I'm quite sure that if you say anything like what's fair and right, he's such a good
fellow that you'll not have to exchange three words
this day."

Demipho. Who ordered you to say this?

Chremes. But, Demipho, we can't get what we want
on better terms.

Antipho (aside). It's all over with me!

Demipho. Go on with your story.

Geta. At first he talked like a madman.

Chremes. Pray what did he ask?

Geta. Far too much.

Chremes. But how much? tell me.

Geta. If we would give him a great talent [1]—

Demipho. A great drubbing, he means! The impudence of him!

Geta. Just what I said to him. " Pray what more
could my master do, even if he were arranging the
marriage of an only daughter? He's not gained much

[1] About $1180.

by not having had one, seeing that a girl's been found
for him to provide with a dowry." His last words
were, "From the very beginning I've been willing, as
in duty bound, to marry my friend's daughter, for I
thought how much she would suffer if, poor as she was,
she were handed over to some rich man as his slave.
But to speak plainly with you, I wanted some one who
would bring me a trifle of money to pay my debts.
Even now, if Demipho is willing to pay me as much
as I shall get with the girl I'm engaged to, there's
no one I should sooner have for my wife than Phanium."

Antipho (aside). Is this stupidity or malice? Has
he something in view, or does n't he know what he's
doing? It's more than I can tell.

Demipho. But suppose he's head over heels in
debt?

Geta. "My land," he said, "is mortgaged for ten
minae."[1]

Demipho. All right, he shall marry her. I'll give
the money.

Geta. "And my house for ten more."

Demipho. Oh, no! that's too much.

Chremes (to Demipho). Be quiet. (*To Geta*)
Draw on me for those ten.

Geta. "I must buy a maid for my wife; I need a
little more furniture; then there are the expenses of
the wedding. Call that another ten."

Demipho. Let him straightway bring a thousand actions against me! I won't give him anything! Shall
this infamous scoundrel insult as well as cheat me?

Chremes. Do be quiet. I'll pay it; all you have
to do is to see that your son marries the girl we want
him to marry.

[1] About $197.

Antipho (aside). Woe's me! Geta, you 've undone me with your tricks.

Chremes. It 's for my sake that she 's being turned out; it 's only right that I should lose the money.

Geta. " Let me know as soon as possible," he said, " whether they will give her to me, so that I may break off my engagement, and not be left in suspense. The other parties, you understand, have promised me a dowry."

Chremes. Let him have the money directly; he shall break off his engagement, and marry Phanium.

Demipho. And much good may it do him !

Chremes. By good luck I have some money with me now, the rent of my wife's estate in Lemnos; I 'll take it, and tell my wife that you wanted it.

[*Exeunt* Chremes *and* Demipho *into the former's house.*

SCENE 4.

Antipho (coming forward). Geta!

Geta. Well !

Antipho. What have you done ?

Geta. Cleaned the old gentlemen out of their money.

Antipho. And is that enough ?

Geta. I don't know. 'T was all I was told to do.

Antipho. What, you scoundrel, won't you answer my question ?

Geta. Why, what are you talking about?

Antipho. Talking about ? Thanks to you, I may as well go and hang myself. May all the gods and goddesses in heaven above and hell beneath make an example of you ! Look you, if you want anything done, put it in this man's hands, and he 'll bring you out of smooth water unto a rock. What worse policy could there have been than to touch this sore, and mention my wife? You 've given my father hopes of being able to turn her out. Come now, if Phormio gets this dowry, he 'll have to marry her. What 's to be done then?

Geta. But he won't marry her.

Antipho. Oh, no! of course not! And when they demand their money back, on my account, forsooth, he 'll prefer the stocks!

Geta. There 's no story, Antipho, that can't be spoiled in the telling. You leave out all the strong points, and put in all the weak ones. Now hear the other side. If he receives the money, he 'll have to marry her, as you say, and I agree with you so far. But at least some little time will be given for getting ready the nuptials, for invitations, for sacrificing. Meanwhile, Phaedria's friends will give him the money that they have promised, and then Phormio will pay it back again.

Antipho. On what ground? What excuse will he make?

Geta. Do you ask? Why, he 'll say, " So many evil omens have befallen me since this business was begun: a strange black dog came into my house; a snake fell from the tiles through the skylight; a hen crowed; the soothsayer has forbidden it; the diviner has put a stop to it; to begin any new business before winter " — an excellent reason. That 's how things will go.

Antipho. I sincerely hope so.

Geta. They will; trust me. Here 's your father coming out of the house. Be off, and tell Phaedria that we 've got the money. [*Exit* ANTIPHO.

SCENE 5.

Enter DEMIPHO *and* CHREMES *from the latter's house*

Demipho. Never you mind, I say; I 'll take care that he does n't cheat us. I 'll never be fool enough to let this money out of my hands without having witnesses present; I 'll tell them to whom I give it, and for what.

Geta (aside). How careful he is when care is n't needed!

Chremes. That 's how you ought to do it; and make haste, while he 's of the same mind, for if that other girl becomes more urgent, he may throw us over.

Geta. You 've hit it exactly.

Demipho (to GETA). Then take me to him.

Geta. I 'm all ready.

Chremes. When you 've done this, come over and see my wife, and she 'll call on the girl before she goes away. She 'll tell her, by way of preventing her being angry, that we 're going to marry her to Phormio; that he 's much better suited to her, insomuch as he 's more closely connected with her; that we 've not failed in our duty, and have given him as much dowry as he wanted.

Demipho. What the deuce have you to do with that?

Chremes. A great deal, Demipho. It 's not sufficient to do your duty; you must win the world's approval as well. I want her to act of her own free will, so that she won't say that she was turned out.

Demipho. I can do all this myself.

Chremes. Yes, but it takes a woman to manage a woman.

Demipho. Well, I 'll ask your wife to do it.

[*Exeunt* DEMIPHO *and* GETA, R

Chremes. Now I wonder where I 'm to find those women.

Enter SOPHRONA *from* DEMIPHO'S *house.*

Sophrona. What am I to do? Wretched woman that I am, whom can I find to befriend me? Whom can I ask for advice? Where turn for help? I 'm afraid that, as a result of my counsel, my mistress may be shamefully treated, for I hear that the young man's father is furious at what he 's done.

Chremes (aside). Now, who in the world is this old woman coming out of my brother's house in such a fluster?

Sophrona. It was want that drove me to it. I knew that this marriage was invalid, but I wanted her to be safe in the meantime.

Chremes (aside). By Heaven, unless my mind deceives me or my eyesight 's failing, this is my daughter's nurse.

Sophrona. And the man who is her father —

Chremes (aside). What am I to do?

Sophrona. Can't as yet be discovered.

Chremes (aside). Shall I go up to her, or wait till I understand better what she 's saying?

Sophrona. But if I could find him now I should have nothing to fear.

Chremes (aside). It 's she herself; I 'll speak to her.

Sophrona. Who 's talking here?

Chremes. Sophrona!

Sophrona. And mentioning my name?

Chremes. Look at me.

Sophrona. For Heaven's sake, is it Stilpo?

Chremes. No.

Sophrona. You deny it?

Chremes. Pray, Sophrona, come a little away from the door of that house, and don't ever call me by that name again.

Sophrona. What? Are n't you the man you always said you were?

Chremes. Hush!

Sophrona. Why do you fear that door?

Chremes. I 've a savage wife caged up there. I used to call myself by that false name lest you might inadvertently talk too much, and so somehow it might come to her ears.

Sophrona. Then, by the powers, that 's why we poor women could never find you here in Athens.

Chremes. But tell me, what have you to do with that house you 've just left? Where are my wife and daughter?

Sophrona. Oh, dear me!

Chremes. What 's the matter? Are n't they alive?

Sophrona. Your daughter is, but all this trouble killed her mother.

Chremes. That 's too bad!

Sophrona. So I — being an old woman, all alone, poor, and friendless — did the best I could for the girl, and married her to the young master of this house.

Chremes. What, to Antipho?

Sophrona. Yes, that 's the man.

Chremes What, has he two wives?

Sophrona. No, only this one.

Chremes. Then what about the other who was said to be his kinswoman?

Sophrona. Why, this is she, of course.

Chremes. What's that?

Sophrona. We made up that story, so that her lover might get her without a dowry.

Chremes. Gracious Heavens! How often things one dares not hope for are brought about by mere chance! On my return home I've found my daughter married to the man I wanted and in the way I wanted. With great trouble to himself, but without troubling us in the least, he, all alone, has done what my brother and I were trying so hard to do.

Sophrona. Now see what's to be done. The young man's father has come home, and they say that he's very angry.

Chremes. Never fear; but in the name of gods and men don't let anybody know that she's my daughter.

Sophrona. Nobody shall know through me.

Chremes. Come with me; I'll tell you the rest inside. [*Exeunt* Chremes *and* Sophrona *into* Demipho's *house.*

ACT V.

Scene 1.

Enter Demipho *and* Geta, R.

Demipho. It's our own fault that we make it men's interest to be rogues. We're too eager to be called good and kind. "Run, but not past your own house," as the saying is[1] Wasn't it enough for me to have been

---

[1] Run away, if it is necessary, but not so precipitately as to pass your natural shelter; don't let your panic drive you to extremes

wronged by the fellow, without actually throwing away money, and giving him means of subsistence until he can bring off some new villainy?

Geta. Assuredly.

Chremes. The people who get rewarded nowadays are those who put wrong for right.

Geta. Very true.

Demipho. So we 've managed matters very badly in dealing with him.

Geta. It 'll be all right, provided you can end the affair as you planned, by getting him to marry her.

Demipho. What! Is there any doubt about that?

Geta. Indeed, I 'm rather inclined to fear (knowing the man's character) that he may change his mind.

Demipho. What! Change his mind?

Geta. I don't know, I only say " he might."

Demipho. I 'll do as my brother advised : I 'll bring his wife here to talk to her. Geta, go on ahead, and tell Phanium that Nausistrata is coming.

[*Exit* DEMIPHO *into* CHREMES' *house.*

Geta. We 've found the money for Phaedria ; there has n't been a word said about the lawsuit ; we 've arranged that the girl shan't leave just yet. What next? What 's to be done now? You 're still in the same fix, Geta; it 's a case of paying one with what you 've borrowed from another. The punishment that was close at hand has been staved off for a while, but your score of stripes will mount up unless you look out. Now I 'll go home and explain matters to Phanium, so that she won't be afraid of Phormio or of what Nausistrata may say.

[*Exit into* DEMIPHO'S *house.*

Enter DEMIPHO *and* NAUSISTRATA *from* CHREMES' *house.*

Demipho. Now, Nausistrata, with your wonted tact, get her into a good humor with us, so that she 'll do willingly what she has to do.

Nausistrata. I will.

Demipho. You 're helping me by your services now, just as you assisted me with your money a little while ago.

Nausistrata. You 're quite welcome, but indeed I 'm less able to help you, through my husband's fault, than I ought to be.

Demipho. Why?

Nausistrata. Because he 's careless of my father's honest earnings. My father used to get two talents a year regularly out of those estates. What a difference there is between one man and another!

Demipho. Two talents, you say?

Nausistrata. Yes, two talents, and that, too, when things were much cheaper than they are now.

Demipho. Heavens!

Nausistrata. What do you think of that?

Demipho. Oh, I quite agree with you.

Nausistrata. I wish I 'd been born a man, I should have shown them —

Demipho. I 'm sure you would.

Nausistrata. How to —

Demipho. Pray, spare yourself for your interview with the girl, lest, being so young, she tire you out.

Nausistrata. I 'll do as you wish, but I see my husband coming out of your house.

Scene 3.

Enter Chremes *from* Demipho's *house.*

Chremes (not seeing his wife). 'St, Demipho, have you paid him the money?

Demipho. I looked after that at once.

Chremes. I wish you had n't. Oh! I see my wife! I had almost said too much.

Demipho. Why do you wish I had n't paid it, Chremes?

Chremes. It does n't matter.

Demipho. What do you mean? Have you been talking to the girl on whose account we 're bringing Nausistrata?

Chremes. I 've settled it all.

Demipho. What does she say?

Chremes. She can't be taken away.

Demipho. Why can't she?

Chremes. Because they 're in love with one another.

Demipho. Well, what 's that to us?

Chremes. A great deal; and, besides, I find that she 's related to us.

Demipho. What? You 're raving.

Chremes. You 'll find it so. I know what I 'm saying ; I 've just recalled the matter.

Demipho. Are you in your right mind?

Nausistrata. Oh, I pray you, don't wrong a kinswoman.

Demipho. She is n't a kinswoman.

Chremes. Don't contradict me. Her father went under a different name; that 's how you made the mistake.

Demipho. Did n't she know her father?

Chremes. Yes.

Demipho. Then why did she call him by a wrong name?

Chremes. Won't you ever give in or understand?

Demipho. How can I understand when you tell me nothing?

Chremes. There you go again.

Nausistrata. I wonder what all this is about?

Demipho. I 'm sure I don't know.

Chremes. Do you want to know? Well, the girl has no nearer relatives than you and I, and that 's the truth.

Demipho. Good Heavens! let 's go to her. I want all of us to know the right and wrong of the case together.

Chremes. Oh, Demipho!

Demipho. What 's the matter?

Chremes. To think that you should have so little faith in me!

Demipho. Oh, you want me to believe you, do you? You want me to stop asking questions? Well, so be it. But what about our friend's daughter?

Chremes. That 's all right.

Demipho. Then are we to send Nausistrata away?

Chremes. Of course.

Demipho. And Phanium is to stay?

Chremes. Yes.

Demipho. Then you may go home, Nausistrata.

Nausistrata. And indeed I think that her staying is a much better arrangement for all of us than what you intended at first. I thought her a very well-bred girl, when I saw her.   [*Exit into* CHREMES' *house.*

Demipho. Now, what 's all this about?

Chremes. Has she shut the door yet?

Demipho. Yes.

Chremes. Heavens, what luck! I've found my daughter married to your son.

Demipho. Eh! how could that be?

Chremes. I can't explain here. It's not safe.

Demipho. Well, come inside, then.

Chremes. I tell you I don't want even our sons to know this.   [*Exeunt into* DEMIPHO'S *house.*

SCENE 4.

Enter ANTIPHO

Antipho. However my own affairs may turn out, I'm glad my cousin has got what he wanted. How shrewd to have a love affair of the kind that when things go wrong, a remedy is possible! As soon as Phaedria found the money, all his troubles were at an end; but I can't by any device free myself from my difficulties. To keep my secret means to live in dread; to reveal it, disgrace. I shouldn't go home now, if some hope of keeping her hadn't been held out to me. But where can I find Geta?

SCENE 5.

Enter PHORMIO

Phormio (not seeing ANTIPHO). I've received the money, paid it over to the slave-trader, and taken the girl away. I've seen that Phaedria has her for his very own; she's been set free. Now, I've still one thing left to do, and that's to get away from the old gentlemen for a spree. That's how I'll spend the next few days.

Antipho. Why, there's Phormio. Say!

Phormio. What?

Antipho. Tell me Phaedria's plans. What does he intend to do?

Phormio. He's going to play your rôle.

Antipho. My rôle?

Phormio. Yes, keep out of his father's sight. He's asked that you play his, and plead his cause, for he's coming to my house to take a few drinks. I'll tell the old gentlemen that I'm going to the fair at Sunium to buy that slave girl whom Geta was talking about just now, so that when they miss me they won't think that I'm squandering their money. But listen, there's some one at your door.

Antipho. See who's coming out.

Phormio. It's Geta.

SCENE 6.

Enter GETA *from* DEMIPHO'S *house.*

GETA (*not seeing the others*). O Fortune! O lucky Fortune! What blessings you have showered on my master Antipho this day!

Antipho. What does the fellow mean?

Geta. And freed us, his friends, from fear! But I'm wasting time in not throwing my cloak over my shoulder,[1] and hurrying to tell him what has befallen him.

Antipho (*to* PHORMIO). Do you understand what he's talking about?

Phormio. No, do you?

Antipho. No, not a word.

Phormio. No more do I.

---

[1] The cloak was thrown back over the shoulder to make running easier.

Geta. I 'll go to the slave-trader's; that's where they are now.

Antipho. Hi, Geta!

Geta. There you are! Is it a new or clever thing to call me back just when I 've started running?[1]

Antipho. Geta!

Geta. By the powers, he 's urgent. Well, you shan't get the better of me by pestering me.

Antipho. Won't you stop?

Geta. To the whipping-post with you!

Antipho. That 's where you 'll be presently, unless you halt, you scoundrel.

Geta. This must be some one who knows me pretty well: he threatens me with punishment. Is it the man I 'm looking for? Why, so it is. I 'll accost him.

Antipho. What 's the matter?

Geta. Oh, you luckiest of all men in the whole wide world! there can be no doubt, Antipho, but that you 're the special favorite of the gods.

Antipho. I would that I were; but I should like to be told why I 'm to believe this.

Geta. To be steeped in joy — will that be enough for you?

Antipho. How you do keep me on the rack!

Phormio. Enough of your promises! Tell us your news.

Geta. Oh, are you here too, Phormio?

Phormio. Yes, but won't you tell us?

Geta. Listen, then. As soon as we had paid you the money at the bank, we started straight home; then my master sent me to your wife.

Antipho. What for?

[1] To hail a slave who seemed to be in a hurry was a common joke.

Geta. I 'll not speak of that, Antipho, for it has nothing to do with this story. When I was about to enter the women's apartments, the page Midas ran up to me, caught me by the cloak behind, and pulled me back. I looked around, and asked him why he was detaining me , he answered that his mistress could n't be seen — those were his orders. "Sophrona," he said, "has just brought in Chremes, the old man's brother, and he 's inside with them now." When I heard this, I proceeded to go quietly up to the door on tiptoe — reached it — stood there — held my breath — put my ear close to: so I began to listen, trying in this way to catch what they were saying.

Antipho. Brave, Geta!

Geta. There I heard this glorious thing, so that I all but shouted aloud for joy.

Antipho. What was it?

Geta. What do you think?

Antipho. I don't know.

Geta. Well, it 's a truly wonderful story. Your uncle turns out to be your wife's father.

Antipho. Eh, what do you say?

Geta. He had a clandestine affair with her mother at Lemnos.

Phormio. It 's a dream. Can we suppose that she did n't know her own father?

Geta. There was some reason for that, Phormio, you may be sure; but do you think that outside the door I could understand everything that was going on inside?

Antipho. As a matter of fact, I 've had an inkling of that tale too.

Geta. Well, I 'll give you a proof to make you believe it. While this was going on your uncle crossed over from that house to this; presently he went back again with your father. They both say that they consent to your keeping her. And, to clinch the matter, I 've been sent to find you and to take you to them.

Antipho. Then away with me instantly! Why don't you go?

Geta. I will.

Antipho. Good-by, my dear Phormio.

Phormio. Good-by, Antipho. It 's turned out well, so help me Heaven!

[*Exeunt* ANTIPHO *and* GETA *to* DEMIPHO'S *house.*

SCENE 7.

Phormio. I 'm glad that these two have had such an unexpected piece of luck. Now I have an excellent chance of outwitting the old gentlemen and relieving Phaedria of his financial worries, so that he won't have to ask favors of any of his friends; for this money shall be given to him just as it was given to me, whether they like it or not. I 've found in the facts of the case the means to make them give it. Now I must assume a new bearing and expression. I 'll go into this alley hard by, and come out upon them when they leave the house. I 'm not going to the fair, as I pretended. [*Withdraws into alley.*

SCENE 8

Enter DEMIPHO *and* CHREMES *from the former's house.*

Demipho. Brother, I am indeed truly thankful to Heaven for this satisfactory settlement.

Chremes. Is n't she a lady, as I said?

Demipho. She certainly is. Now we must get

hold of Phormio as soon as possible, and get our thirty minae away from him before he squanders them.

Phormio (coming forward). I should like to see Demipho, if he's at home, to —

Demipho. Why, we were just going to you, Phormio.

Phormio. For the same reason, perhaps?

Demipho. Yes.

Phormio. That's what I thought. And why were you coming to me?

Demipho. Such a question!

Phormio. Did you think that I would n't do what I had once undertaken? Now, mark you, I may be poor, but I 've always made a point of preserving my honor. So I 've come to you, Demipho, to say that I 'm ready. Give me my wife as soon as you please, for on seeing how you had set your hearts on this I deferred all other business, as it was right I should.

Demipho. But my brother here has counselled me not to give her to you. "Think," he says, "what a scandal it will make, if you do; she was n't given before, when it might have been done honorably, and it 's a shame to drive her out of doors now as a divorced woman." He used pretty nearly the same arguments as you did to me a little while ago.

Phormio. You 're treating me pretty cavalierly.

Demipho. How so?

Phormio. Do you ask? Because I shan't be able to marry the other girl either, for how could I have the face to go back to her whom I jilted?

Chremes (aside to DEMIPHO). Say, "Besides, I see that Antipho does n't want to part with her."

Demipho. Besides, I see that my son does n't want to part with his wife. But, Phormio, pray come to the bank, and have that money paid back to me.

Phormio. What! the money I paid out at once to my creditors?

Demipho. What's to be done, then?

Phormio. If you like to give me the girl whom you've promised me, I'll marry her; but if you choose that she should stay with you, her dowry must stay with me; for it's not right that I should be disappointed to suit your convenience, seeing that, on your account, I jilted the other girl, who was bringing me a dowry of the same amount.

Demipho. To perdition with you, you swaggering scoundrel! Do you think that we know so little of you and your doings as that?

Phormio. I'm getting angry.

Demipho. As if you would marry her if she were offered to you!

Phormio. Try me!

Demipho. Your plan was that my son should keep his wife in your house.

Phormio. Pray, what are you talking about?

Demipho. Just you give me my money.

Phormio. No, you give me my wife.

Demipho. Then to court with you.

Phormio. Indeed, if you trouble me any more —

Demipho. What will you do?

Phormio. I? Perhaps you think that I act as champion for dowerless women only? I do the same for women with dowries.

Chremes. What has that to do with us?

Phormio. Oh, nothing. I knew a married woman here in Athens whose husband —

Chremes. Eh?

Demipho. What's that?

Phormio. Had another wife in Lemnos.

Chremes. I'm a lost man.

Phormio. And he had a daughter by her, whom he brought up secretly.

Chremes. I'm dead and buried.

Phormio. So I'm going now to tell her this story. (*Starts towards* CHREMES' *house.*)

Chremes I entreat you, don't.

Phormio. Oho! were you the man?

Demipho. How he mocks us!

Chremes. We grant you a quittance.

Phormio. Oh, nonsense!

Chremes. What more do you want? We make you a present of the money that you have.

Phormio. Yes, yes! You silly old men, what the mischief do you mean by playing with me in this way, like children that don't know their own minds? " I will " and " I won't " — " I will," and then again " I won't " — " take her," " give her up," — " what has been said is all unsaid; the bargain which has just been struck is void."

Chremes (*to* DEMIPHO). How or from whom did he learn this?

Demipho (*to* CHREMES) I don't know, but I'm quite sure that I did n't tell anybody.

Chremes (*to* DEMIPHO). So help me Heaven, it's like a miracle.

Phormio (*aside*). I've put a spoke in their wheel.

Demipho (*to* CHREMES). Come, is this fellow to carry off so large a sum of money from us, and laugh at us so openly? Better to die, by Heaven! Prepare to act boldly, and with presence of mind. You see that your transgression has got abroad, and you can't keep it from your wife any longer. Now, Chremes, the best way to win forgiveness is to tell her ourselves what she's certain to learn some day from others; then we shall be able to take vengeance on this scoundrel in our own way.

Phormio (aside). Hello! unless I keep a sharp lookout I'll be in a fix; they're coming at me with the spirit of gladiators.

Chremes (to DEMIPHO). But I'm afraid she'll never forgive me.

Demipho (to CHREMES). Cheer up, I'll restore you to favor with her, Chremes. There's the fact that the girl's mother has passed away to fall back upon.

Phormio. So this is how you treat me? A clever enough plan of attack! But, Demipho, you've done your brother no good in goading me on. (*To* CHREMES.) What! after amusing yourself as you pleased in foreign parts, and showing so little respect to your wife here, a lady of birth too, as to insult her in this outrageous way. you mean to go whining to her for forgiveness, do you? By telling her the whole story, I'll so kindle her wrath that you'll never quench the flames, even though you dissolved in tears.

Demipho. To think of any man being so impudent! The scoundrel ought to be transported at the public expense to some desert land.

Chremes. He's got me in so tight a place that I really don't know what to do with him.

Demipho. I know; let's go to law.

Phormio. To law, certainly. In this court, if you please. (*Goes towards* CHREMES' *house.*)

Chremes. After him! Hold him back, while I call the slaves out! (DEMIPHO *takes hold of* PHORMIO.)

Demipho. But I can't hold him alone; come and help me. (CHREMES *takes hold of* PHORMIO.)

Phormio (to DEMIPHO). One action for assault against you.

Demipho. Go to law, then.

Phormio. Another against you, Chremes.

Chremes. Drag him away.

Phormio. Is that your game? then I must use my voice.   Nausistrata, come forth.

Chremes. Stop his vile mouth; see how strong he is!

Phormio. Nausistrata, I say!

Demipho. Won't you be quiet?

Phormio. I be quiet?

Demipho. If he won't come along, punch him in the belly.

Phormio. Or knock his eye out; the time is coming when I shall have a fine revenge on you.

SCENE 9.

Enter NAUSISTRATA *from* CHREMES' *house.*

Nausistrata. Who's calling me?   Why, husband, what in the world is all this disturbance about?

Phormio (to CHREMES). Well, why do you stand like a mute?

Nausistrata. Who's this man?   Why don't you answer me?

Phormio. He answer you!   Why, he does n't know where he is.

Chremes. Mind you, don't believe a word he says.

Phormio. Go up to him, touch him; if he is n't in a cold sweat all over, you may kill me.

Chremes. It's all a lie.

Nausistrata. What's a lie?   What story is he telling?

Phormio. You shall know presently. Listen.

Chremes. What, will you believe him?

Nausistrata. And pray how can I believe him before he has told me anything?

Phormio. The wretch is scared out of his wits.

Nausistrata. Indeed, it can't be for nothing that you're so afraid.

Chremes. I afraid?

Phormio. Oh, no, not at all! Since you're not afraid, and the story I tell is all a lie, do you tell it yourself.

Demipho. Scoundrel! Is he to tell it to please you?

Phormio. You've done your brother a good turn, you have!

Nausistrata. Husband, won't you tell me?

Chremes. But —

Nausistrata. But what?

Chremes. It isn't worth telling.

Phormio. It isn't worth your while to tell, but it is worth her while to hear. In Lemnos —

Chremes. Here, what are you saying?

Demipho. Hold your tongue, will you?

Phormio. Without your knowledge —

Chremes. I'm in for it!

Phormio. He married a wife.

Nausistrata. Oh, husband, the gods forbid!

Phormio. That's the truth.

Nausistrata. Unhappy woman that I am, it's all over with me!

Phormio. And by her he's had one daughter already, while you're in a state of blissful ignorance.

Chremes (aside to DEMIPHO). What are we to do?

Nausistrata. A wicked and terrible thing, by the immortal gods'

Phormio (overhearing CHREMES). Do? There's nothing left to do.

Phormio. Was there ever anything more disgraceful?

Nausistrata. I address you, Demipho, for it makes me sick to talk to that creature. Was this the reason of his travelling so often to Lemnos and staying there so long? Was this the cause of the fall in prices which brought down our income?

Demipho. Nausistrata, I admit that he deserves blame in this matter, but it is n't an unpardonable offence.

Phormio (aside). He's pleading for the dead.

Demipho. It was n't, you must understand, because he was tired of you, or because he disliked you, that he did this. It all happened about fifteen years ago. He had been drinking when he met the woman. This girl was born, but he never had anything to do with the mother afterwards. She's dead and gone now; the only difficulty is removed. So, I beg you, be patient in this, as you have been in all other matters.

Nausistrata. I patient? I am indeed sorely anxious that this should be his last offence, but how can I hope for that? Am I to suppose that he will grow steadier as he grows older? Why, he was old when he did it; so much for years bringing steadiness! Are my looks and age likely to be more attractive to him now than they were then, Demipho? What grounds do you give me for expecting or hoping that he won't do it again?

Phormio. Now's the time for all who would attend the funeral of Chremes! That 's the way I'll give it to him. Such is the fate of those who attack Phormio, so let any one who likes come on, and I'll lay him as low as this man here. But I'm willing that he should be pardoned; he's had punishment enough to satisfy me. His wife has something to din into his ears as long as he lives.

Nausistrata. Well, I've deserved this, I suppose. What's the good of my telling you now in detail, Demipho, what a good wife I've been to him?

Demipho. I know it all as well as you do.

Nausistrata. Then do you think that I deserved such treatment?

Demipho. Not in the least. But seeing that what's done can't be undone by reproaches, forgive him. He begs your pardon, acknowledges his sin, and makes a clean breast of it. What more do you want?

Phormio (aside). Before she forgives him, I must look out for myself and for Phaedria. Look here, Nausistrata, before you give any rash answer, listen to me.

Nausistrata. What have you to say?

Phormio. I got thirty minae out of him by a trick; I've given them to your son, who has bought his mistress with them from a slave-trader.

Chremes. Eh, what's that you say?

Nausistrata. Pray, do you think it such a heinous crime that your son, who is a young man, should have a mistress, while you have two wives? Have you no shame? Will you have the face to blame him? Answer me.

Demipho. He'll do as you wish.

Nausistrata. No, to tell you my feeling in the matter, I don't mean to pardon him or to make any promise, or even to give an answer, until I've seen my son; I leave it all to him to decide; I'll do what he bids me.

Phormio. You're a sensible woman, Nausistrata.

Nausistrata (to CHREMES). Are you satisfied with that?

Chremes. Yes. (*Aside.*) I'm coming off finely, — much better than I expected.

Nausistrata. Tell me your name.

Phormio. Phormio, a friend of your family, and especially of your son Phaedria.

Nausistrata. Well, Phormio, I assure you, after this I'll do whatever I can for you, both in word and deed.

Phormio. You're very kind.

Nausistrata. Not at all, you deserve it.

Phormio. Would you like, Nausistrata, to do something to-day that would please me, and at the same time vex your husband's sight?

Nausistrata. I certainly should.

Phormio. Then invite me to dinner.

Nausistrata. Indeed I do.

Demipho. Let's go inside, then.

Nausistrata. Yes, but where's Phaedria, our judge?

Phormio. I'll have him here presently.

> [*Exeunt* PHORMIO *towards the forum, the others into* CHREMES' *house.*

Cantor [1] (*to the audience*). Farewell, and give us your applause.

---

[1] The *cantor*, whose principal function was to sing the lyrical parts of the play, always spoke the last words.

LUCRETIUS

BIOGRAPHICAL SKETCH

St. Jerome in his *Chronicle* places the birth of Lucretius in the year 94, adding that after having become insane
by drinking a love philtre he wrote some books in the lucid
intervals of his madness; that he committed suicide in his
forty-fourth year, and that Cicero revised his work. From
other sources it seems probable that 97 and not 94 was the
year of the poet's birth. The remaining statements of St.
Jerome's notice are likewise open to grave question. The
story of the love philtre may be dismissed without discussion; and there is no confirmation of the assertions concerning his madness and suicide. The Cicero mentioned is
probably the famous orator, but even this is uncertain.

His poem *On the Nature of Things* consists of six books,
and is an exposition of the doctrines of the Epicurean philosophy. The first two books are devoted to the atomic
theory in its more general aspects. Starting from the two
fundamental principles that nothing is produced from nothing and that nothing returns to nothing, he explains
the existence of the universe, of all forms of life, of all
natural phenomena, as due to the chance combination of an
infinite number of atoms moving in an infinite void. The
atoms have existed from all eternity, and are indestructi-
ble. They are of extreme minuteness, indivisible, and im-
perceptible by any of the senses. Having an inherent
power of deflection they swerve from the straight line as
they fall, and, colliding, combine in forms of manifold variety. The third book deals with the constitution of the

soul, which is, like everything else, material, consisting of small round atoms of unusual fineness. It cannot exist apart from the body. In the fourth book we have a treatment of sense perceptions, in the fifth, of the formation of the world, the origin of life, and the development of man ; in the sixth, of such natural phenomena as thunder, lightning, and earthquakes. The poem concludes with an account of the plague at Athens

It was not, however, so much the theory of Epicurus that attracted Lucretius as its practical application. In his view of life there were two principal causes of unhappiness : belief in the interference of the gods in the affairs of the world, and fear of death. He welcomed the Epicurean philosophy, because, as he believed, it proved that both were groundless. Epicurus did, it is true, believe in the existence of gods, but the atomic theory excluded them from all part in the creation and management of the world. They lived in perfect tranquillity somewhere in the vast spaces between the worlds, and paid no attention to terrestrial things. There was accordingly no reason why men should dread them. In the same way, the soul having been proved to be subject to immediate disintegration on separating from the body, death should have no more terrors

The most conspicuous feature of the book is the poet's splendid enthusiasm. His theme does not at first sight seem to be an inspiring one, but the atomic theory came to him as a revelation, and the realization of what it meant for him and for all who would believe filled him with a sort of frenzy. He had what the Greeks called μανία, *possession,* something stronger than inspiration as ordinarily used, and this, carrying him without a sign of weariness through long and intricate disquisitions on details of the theory, manifests itself every now and then with increased intensity in some arraignment of religion so-called, or some fine piece of descriptive writing, or a glorification of Epicurus. All his references to the master show a rare earnestness   Epicurus is to him something more than mortal, — something of a god.   He it was who first pointed out the way of truth, who showed a light in the darkness, who made happiness possible for men.   The ultra sombre, almost morbid view of life that we find in many passages of the poem is in part due to the same impassioned zeal for the doctrines he was preaching ; for while his keen sense of the misery and suffering in the world had much to do with his embracing Epicureanism in the first place, the enthusiasm with which he embraced it tended to make him exaggerate the evils which he was combatting.   The note sounded in the second book (v. 578 *seq.*), " nor did night ever follow day, or morning night, that heard not, mingling with the cries of sickly infants, wailings the attendants on death and black funeral " recurs again and again.   In depicting the different phases of nature he stands in the first rank among Roman poets.   His descriptions, introduced from time to time to relieve the tension of philosophic argument, are marked by an accuracy, a truthfulness, a startling vividness, that could come only from highly trained powers of observation ; but they have besides the charm which springs from a genuine feeling for the beauty of the external world. Nor does the compression which so many of them show detract at all from their effectiveness.   The " shells that paint the lap of earth, where the sea with gentle waves beats on the thirsty sand of the winding shore," the " grey-green strip of olives running between vineyards," — such descriptions as these linger in the memory, when more elaborate pictures might fail.

On the side of language Lucretius was hampered by the fact that Latin had not in his time developed a philosophical vocabulary.   So we find him complaining of the " poverty of the Latin language."   The Latin hexameter, too, was a medium which, although it had been used before by Ennius, had not as yet attained to any very great degree of flexibility.

INVOCATION TO VENUS[1]

(I, 1-43)

MOTHER of the Aeneadae,[2] darling of men and gods, increase-giving Venus, who beneath the gliding signs of heaven fillest with thy presence the ship-carrying sea, the corn-bearing lands, since through thee every kind of living things is conceived, rises up and beholds the light of the sun. Before thee, goddess, flee the winds, the clouds of heaven; before thee and thy advent; for thee earth manifold in works puts forth sweet-smelling flowers; for thee the levels of the sea do laugh and heaven propitiated shines with outspread light. For soon as the vernal aspect of day is disclosed, and the birth favoring breath of favonius[3] unbarred is blowing fresh, first the fowls of the air, O lady, shew signs of thee and thy entering in, throughly smitten in heart by thy power. Next the wild herds bound over the glad pastures and swim the rapid rivers: in such wise each made prisoner by thy charm follows thee with desire, whither thou goest to lead it on. Yes, throughout seas and mountains and sweeping rivers and leafy homes of birds and grassy plains, striking fond love into the breasts of all thou constrainest them each after its kind to continue their races with desire. Since thou then art sole mistress of the nature of things, and without thee nothing rises up into the divine borders of light, nothing grows to be glad or lovely, I would have thee for a helpmate in writing the verses which I essay to pen on the nature

[1] Venus is invoked as the procreative power in nature
[2] The Romans   According to legend Aeneas, son of Venus, was the founder of the Roman race
[3] The west wind

of things for our own son of the Memmii,[1] whom thou, goddess, hast willed to have no peer, rich as he ever is in every grace. Wherefore all the more, O lady, lend my lays an ever living charm. Cause meanwhile the savage works of war to be lulled to rest throughout all seas and lands; for thou alone canst bless mankind with calm peace, seeing that Mavors[2] lord of battle controls the savage works of war, Mavors who often flings himself into thy lap quite vanquished by the never-healing wound of love; and then with upturned face and shapely neck thrown back feeds with love his greedy sight gazing, goddess, open-mouthed on thee; and as backward he reclines, his breath stays hanging on thy lips. While then, lady, he is reposing on thy holy body, shed thyself about him and above, and pour from thy lips sweet discourse, asking, glorious dame, gentle peace for the Romans. For neither can we in our country's day of trouble with untroubled mind think only of our work, nor can the illustrious offset of Memmius in times like these be wanting to the general weal.

H A J. MUNRO.

THE SACRIFICE OF IPHIGENIA.[3]

(I , 62–101)

PROSTRATE lay human life beneath the spell
Of dark Religion lowering from the skies;

---

[1] The poem was dedicated to Gaius Memmius.   [2] Mars

[3] Iphigenia was the daughter of Agamemnon, the leader of the Greeks in their expedition against Troy. Her sacrifice was intended to appease Diana, to whose anger the contrary winds, which delayed the fleet at Aulis, were attributed. The preparations were made ostensibly for her marriage with Achilles, and it was only at the last moment that she realized the situation

Nor was one found to break that thraldom fell
　　Until a man of Greece dared lift his eyes,　　65
One whom no vengeful thunderbolts could quell
　　Nor wrath of gods   But on his high emprise,
Chafed to sublimer daring and intent,
To burst through Nature's portals forth he went.

Thus his undaunted spirit for mankind　　70
　　O'er Superstition's power the victory won;
Past the world's flaming walls his venturous mind
　　Through the unmeasured universe pressed on;
Thence brought us word how Being is defined
　　By bounds fast set which nothing may o'er-run.　　75
So trampled under foot Religion lies
While Science soars victorious to the skies.

Nor deem it sin by Reason to be freed,
　　Or think I lead thee an unholy way;
Rather to many a dark and bloody deed　　80
　　Religion hurries those who own her sway.
Was not Iphigenia doomed to bleed
　　By the Greek chiefs, though first of men were
　　　　they,
Staining the altar of the Trivian Maid
　　At Aulis where the fleet by winds was stayed?　　85

Lo! on her tresses fair for bridal tire
　　The sacrificial fillet they have bound;
Beside the altar weeping stands her sire:
　　In all the crowd no tearless eye is found.
The priests make ready for their office dire,　　90
　　Yet pitying hide the knife.   When gazing round
The Maiden sees her doom, her spirit dies,
Her limbs sink down, speechless on earth she lies.

The firstborn of his children she in vain
   Had brought the name of father to the king.   95
In arms upborne she goes, not by a train
   Of youths that the loud hymeneal sing
Around a happy bride in joyous strain
   Bearing her home, but a sad offering,
There to be slain by him who gave her birth.   100
Such evil hath Religion wrought on earth.

GOLDWIN SMITH

ATOMS AND VOID

(I, 503–550)

FIRST of all then, since there has been found to exist a two-fold and widely dissimilar nature of two things, that is to say of body and of place in which things severally go on, each of the two must exist for and by itself and quite unmixed. For wherever there is empty space which we call void, there body is not; wherever again body maintains itself, there empty void nowise exists. First bodies[1] therefore are solid and without void. Again since there is void in things begotten, solid matter must exist about this void, and no thing can be proved by true reason to conceal in its body and have within it void, unless you choose to allow that that which holds it in is solid. Again that can be nothing but a union of matter which can keep in the void of things. Matter therefore, which consists of a solid body, may be everlasting, though all things else are dissolved. Moreover if there were no empty void, the universe would be solid; unless on the other hand there were certain bodies to fill up whatever places they occupied, the existing universe would be

---

[1] The atoms.

empty and void space. Therefore sure enough body and void are marked off in alternate layers, since the universe is neither of a perfect fulness nor a perfect void. There are, therefore certain bodies which can vary void space with full. These can neither be broken in pieces by the stroke of blows from without, nor have their texture undone by aught piercing to their core nor give way before any other kind of assault; as we have proved to you a little before. For without void nothing seems to admit of being crushed in or broken up or split in two by cutting, or of taking in wet or permeating cold or penetrating fire, by which all things are destroyed. And the more anything contains within it of void, the more thoroughly it gives way to the assault of these things. Therefore if first bodies are as I have shown solid and without void, they must be everlasting. Again unless matter had been eternal, all things before this would have utterly returned to nothing and whatever things we see would have been born anew from nothing. But since I have proved above that nothing can be produced from nothing, and that what is begotten cannot be recalled to nothing, first beginnings must be of an imperishable body, into which all things can be dissolved at their last hour, that there may be a supply of matter for the reproduction of things. Therefore first-beginnings are of solid singleness, and in no other way can they have been preserved through ages during infinite time past in order to reproduce things.

H. A. J. MUNRO.

THE GOSPEL ACCORDING TO EPICURUS[1]

(II, 1 *seq*)

I.

WHEN storms blow loud, 't is sweet to watch at ease
From shore, the sailor laboring with the seas:
    Because the sense, not that such pains are his,
But that they are not ours, must always please.

II.

Sweet for the cragsman, from some high retreat
Watching the plains below where legions meet,
    To wait the moment when the walls of war
Thunder and clash together. But more sweet,

III.

Sweeter by far on Wisdom's rampired height
To pace serene the porches of the light,
    And thence look down — down on the purblind herd
Seeking and never finding in the night

IV.

The road to peace — the peace that all might hold,
But yet is missed by young men and by old,
    Lost in the strife for palaces and powers,
The axes, and the lictors, and the gold.

V.

Oh sightless eyes! Oh hands that toil in vain!
Not such your needs. Your nature's needs are twain,

---

[1] This selection bears on the principal aim of Epicurean ethics, —
to teach men how best to live in peace and tranquillity. The version
is taken from Mr Mallock's *Lucretius on Life and Death*, in the metre
of Omar Khayyám

And only twain : and these are to be free —
Your minds from terror, and your bones from pain.

VI.

Unailing limbs, a calm unanxious breast —
Grant Nature these, and she will do the rest.
   Nature will bring you, be you rich or poor,
Perhaps not much — at all events her best.

VII.

What though no statued youths from wall and wall
Strew light along your midnight festival,
   With golden hands, nor beams from Lebanon
Keep the lyre's languor lingering through the hall,

VIII.

Yours is the table 'neath the high-whispering trees ;
Yours is the lyre of leaf and stream and breeze,
   The golden flagon, and the echoing dome —
Lapped in the Spring, what care you then for these ?

IX.

Sleep is no sweeter on the ivory bed
Than yours on moss ; and fever's shafts are sped
   As clean through silks damasked for dreaming
      kings,
As through the hood that wraps the poor man's head.

X.

What then, if all the prince's glittering store
Yields to his body not one sense the more,
   Nor any ache or fever of them all
Is barred out by bronze gates or janitor —

XI.

What shall the palace, what the proud domain
Do for the mind — vain splendors of the vain ?
　　How shall these minister to a mind diseased,
Or raze one written trouble from the brain ?

XII.

Unless you think that conscience, with its stings
And misery, fears the outward pomp of things —
　　Fears to push swords and sentinels aside,
And sit the assessor of the king of kings.

XIII.

The mind ! Ay — there 's the rub. The root is there
Of that one malady which all men share.
　　It gleams between the haggard lids of joy ;
It burns a canker in the heart of care.

XIV.

Within the gold bowl, when the feast is set,
It lurks. 'T is bitter in the laborer's sweat.
　　Feed thou the starving, and thou bring'st it back —
Back to the Starving, who alone forget.

XV.

Oh you who under silken curtains lie,
And you whose only roof-tree is the sky,
　　What is the curse that blights your lives alike ?
Not that you hate to live, but fear to die.

XVI.

Fear is the poison. Wheresoc'er you go,
Out of the skies above, the clouds below,

The sense thrills through you of some pitiless Power
Who scowls at once your father and your foe;

XVII.

Who lets his children wander at their whim,
Choosing their road, as though not bound by him:
    But all their life is rounded with a shade,
And every road goes down behind the rim!

XVIII.

And there behind the rim, the swift, the lame,
At different paces, but their end the same,
    Into the dark shall one by one go down,
Where the great furnace shakes its hair of flame.

XIX.

Oh ye who cringe and cower before the throne
Of him whose heart is fire, whose hands are stone,
    Who shall deliver you from this death in life —
Strike off your chains, and make your souls your
        own ?

W H MALLOCK.

THE LIGHT OF THE WORLD

(III., 1–30)

THEE,[1] who first wast able amid such thick darkness to raise on high so bright a beacon and shed
a light on the true interests of life, thee I follow,
glory of the Greek race, and plant now my footsteps
firmly fixed in thy imprinted marks, not so much from
a desire to rival thee as that from the love I bear thee
I yearn to imitate thee; for why need the swallow

---

[1] Epicurus.

contend with swans, or what likeness is there between the feats of racing performed by kids with tottering limbs and by the powerful strength of the horse? Thou, father, art discoverer of things, thou furnishest us with fatherly precepts, and like as bees sip of all things in the flowery lawns, we, O glorious being, in like manner feed from out thy pages upon all the golden maxims, golden I say, most worthy ever of endless life. For soon as thy philosophy issuing from a godlike intellect has begun with loud voice to proclaim the nature of things, the terrors of the mind are dispelled, the walls of the world part asunder, I see things in operation throughout the whole void; the divinity of the gods[1] is revealed and their tranquil abodes which neither winds do shake nor clouds drench with rains, nor snow congealed by sharp frosts harms with hoary fall: an ever cloudless ether o'er-canopies them, and they laugh with light shed largely round. Nature too supplies all their wants and nothing ever impairs their peace of mind. But on the other hand the Acherusian quarters[2] are nowhere to be seen.

H. A. J. Munro.

[1] The well-known description of the gods of the Epicureans in Tennyson's *Lucretius* is a reminiscence of this passage, which in its turn goes back to some lines in the *Odyssey* of Homer

[2] No abiding place of the dead is discerned by the poet in the plan of the universe revealed to him. As an argument in favor of the mortality of the soul, this is hardly cogent.

THE FEAR OF DEATH [1]

(III., 894 *seq.*)

" No more shall look upon thy face
Sweet spouse, no more with emulous race
Sweet children court their sire's embrace.[2]

" To their soft touch right soon no more
Thy pulse shall thrill ; e'en now is o'er   5
Thy stewardship, Death is at the door.

" One dark day wresteth every prize
From hapless man in hapless wise,
Yea, e'en the pleasure of his eyes. "

Thus men bewail their piteous lot ;   10
Yet should they add, " 'T is all forgot,
These things the dead man recketh not."

Yea, could they knit for them this chain
Of words and reasons, men might gain
Some dull narcotic for their pain,   15

Saying, " The dead are dead indeed ;
The dead, from all heart-sickness freed,
Sleep and shall sleep and take no heed."

Lo, if dumb Nature found a voice,
Would she bemoan, and not make choice   20
To bid poor mortals to rejoice,

---

[1] The use of the metre of Tennyson's *Two Voices* was suggested to
Mr. Tyrrell by the similarity of theme. See his *Latin Poetry*, p 72.
The first three stanzas are put into the mouth of some friend of the
deceased, while the rest of the selection gives the Epicurean view.
[2] Comparison with Gray's *Elegy* is inevitable

Saying, " Why weep thy wane, O man?
Wert joyous e'en when life began,
When thy youth's sprightly freshets ran?

" Nay, all the joys thy life e'er knew   25
As poured into a sieve fell through,
And left thee but to rail and rue."

Go, fool, as doth a well-filled guest
Sated of life : with tranquil breast
Take thine inheritance of rest.   30

Why seekest joys that soon must pale
Their feeble fires, and swell the tale
Of things of nought and no avail?

Die, sleep!   For all things are the same;
Tho' spring now stir thy crescent frame,   35
'T will wither : all things are the same.

R. Y. TYRRELL.

THE HONEY OF THE MUSES

(IV., 1-25)

I TRAVERSE the pathless haunts of the Pierides [1]
never yet trodden by sole of man. I love to approach
the untasted springs and to quaff, I love to cull fresh
flowers and gather for my head a distinguished crown
from spots whence the muses have yet veiled the brows
of none; first because I teach of great things and essay
to release the mind from the fast bonds of religious
scruples, and next because on a dark subject I pen
such lucid verses o'erlaying all with the muses' charm.

[1] The muses.

For that too would seem to be not without good grounds : even as physicians when they propose to give nauseous wormwood to children, first smear the rim round the bowl with the sweet yellow juice of honey, that the unthinking age of children may be fooled as far as the lips, and meanwhile drink up the bitter draught of wormwood and though beguiled yet not betrayed, but rather by such means recover health and strength : so I now, since this doctrine seems generally somewhat bitter to those by whom it has not been handled, and the multitude shrinks back from it in dismay, have resolved to set forth to you our doctrine in sweet-toned Pierian verse and o'erlay it as it were with the pleasant honey of the muses, if happily by such means I might engage your mind on my verses, till such time as you apprehend all the nature of things and thoroughly feel what use it has.

H. A. J. Munro

LOVE'S EXTRAVAGANCE [1]

(IV., 1121–1191)

Then too they[2] waste their strength and ruin themselves by the labor, then too their life is passed at the beck of another. Meanwhile their estate runs away and is turned into Babylonian coverlets; duties are neglected and their good name staggers and sickens. On her feet laugh elastic and beautiful Sicyonian[3] shoes, yes, and large emeralds with green light are set in gold and the sea-colored dress is worn constantly and much

---

[1] Love finds a place in Lucretius's poem as one of the phenomena connected with the senses, which constitute the theme of the fourth book   [2] He has been speaking of lovers.

[3] From Sicyon, a town in the northeast of the Peloponnesus.

used drinks in the sweat. The noble earnings of their
fathers are turned into hairbands, head-dresses; sometimes are changed into a sweeping robe and Aliden-
sian and Cean dresses.[1] Feasts set out with rich coverlets and viands, games, numerous cups, perfumes,
crowns and garlands are prepared; all in vain, since
out of the very well-spring of delights rises up something bitter, to pain amid the very flowers; either
when the conscience-stricken mind haply gnaws itself
with remorse to think that it is passing a life of sloth
and ruining itself in brothels, or because she has
launched forth some word and left its meaning in doubt
and it cleaves to the love-sick heart and burns like
living fire, or because it fancies she casts her eyes too
freely about or looks on another, and it sees in her face
traces of a smile.

And these evils are found in love that is lasting and
highly prosperous; but in crossed and hopeless love
are ills such as you may seize with closed eyes, past
numbering; so that it is better to watch beforehand
in the manner I have prescribed, and be on your
guard not to be drawn in. For to avoid falling into
the toils of love is not so hard as, after you are caught,
to get out of the nets you are in and to break through
the strong meshes of Venus. And yet even when you
are entangled and held fast you may escape the mischief, unless you stand in your own way and begin by
overlooking all the defects of her mind or those of
her body, whoever it is whom you court and woo. For
this men usually do, blinded by passion, and attribute
to the beloved those advantages which are not really
theirs. We therefore see women in ways manifold

[1] From Alıda, in the southwest of Asia Minor, and Ceos, an island
in the Aegean Sea

deformed and ugly to be objects of endearment and
held in the highest admiration. And one lover jeers
at others and advises them to propitiate Venus, since
they are troubled by a disgraceful passion, and often,
poor wretch, gives no thought to his own ills, greatest
of all. The black is a brune, the filthy and rank has
not the love of order; the cat-eyed is a miniature
Pallas, the stringy and wizened a gazelle: the dumpy
and dwarfish is one of the graces, from top to toe all
grace; the big and overgrown is awe-inspiring and
full of dignity. She is tongue-tied, cannot speak, then
she has a lisp; the dumb is bashful; then the fire-spit,
the teasing, the gossiping, turns to a shining lamp.
One becomes a slim darling then when she cannot live
from want of flesh; and she is only spare, who is half
dead with cough. Then the fat and big-breasted is a
Ceres' self big-breasted from Iacchus;[1] the pug-nosed
is a she Silenus and a satyress: the thick-lipped a very
kiss. It were tedious to attempt to report other things
of the kind. Let her however be of ever so great
dignity of appearance; such that the power of Venus
goes forth from all her limbs; yet there are others
too; yet have we lived without her before; yet does
she do, and we know that she does, in all things the
same as the ugly woman; and fumigates herself, poor
wretch, with nauseous perfumes, her very maids running from her and giggling behind her back. But the
lover, when shut out, often in tears covers the threshold with flowers and wreaths, and anoints the haughty
doorposts with oil of marjoram and imprints kisses,
poor wretch, on the doors. When, however, he has
been admitted, if on his approach but one single
breath should come in his way, he would seek specious

[1] Bacchus, who was, according to one account, the son of Ceres

reasons for departing, and the long-conned deep-drawn complaint would fall to the ground ; and then he would blame his folly, on seeing that he had attributed to her more than it is right to concede to a mortal. Nor is this unknown to our Venuses ; wherefore all the more they themselves hide with the utmost pains all that goes on behind the scenes of life from those whom they wish to retain in the chains of love ; but in vain, since you may yet draw forth from her mind into the light all these things and search into all her smiles ; and if she is of a fair mind and not troublesome, overlook them in your turn and make allowance for human failings.

H A J MUNRO.

THE DEVELOPMENT OF MAN [1]

(V , 925-1457)

BUT the race of man then in the fields was much hardier, as beseemed it to be, since the hard earth had produced it ; and built on a groundwork of larger and more solid bones within, knit with powerful sinews throughout the frame of flesh ; not lightly to be disabled by heat or cold or strange kinds of food or any malady of body. And during the revolution of many lustres of the sun through heaven they led a life after the roving fashion of wild beasts. No one then was a sturdy guider of the bent plough or knew how to labor the fields with iron or plant in the ground young saplings or lop with pruning-hooks old boughs

---

[1] The importance of man's place in the nature of things is recognized by this long section at the end of the fifth book, in which the development of the race is traced through all the stages from primitive savagery to civilization and culture.

from the high trees. What the sun and rains had given, what the earth had produced spontaneously, was guerdon sufficient to content their hearts. Among acorn-bearing oaks they would refresh their bodies for the most part; and the arbute-berries which you now see in the winter-time ripen with a bright scarlet hue, the earth would then bear in greatest plenty and of a larger size; and many coarse kinds of food besides the teeming freshness of the world then bare, more than enough for poor wretched men. But rivers and springs invited to slake thirst, even as now a rush of water down from the great hills summons with clear plash far and wide the thirsty races of wild beasts. Then too as they ranged about they would occupy the well-known woodland haunts of the nymphs, out of which they knew that smooth-gliding streams of water with a copious gush bathed the dripping rocks, trickling down over the green moss; and in parts welled and bubbled out over the level plain. And as yet they knew not how to apply fire to their purposes or to make use of skins and clothe their body in the spoils of wild beasts, but they would dwell in woods and mountain-caves and forests and shelter in the brushwood their squalid limbs when driven to shun the buffeting of the winds and the rains. And they were unable to look to the general weal and knew not how to make a common use of any customs or laws. Whatever prize fortune threw in his way, each man would bear off, trained at his own discretion to think of himself and live for himself alone. And Venus would join the bodies of lovers in the woods; for each woman was gained over either by mutual desire, or the headstrong violence and vehement lust of the man, or a bribe of some acorns and arbute-berries or choice pears. And trusting to the marvellous powers of their hands and feet they would pursue the forest-haunting races of wild beasts with showers of stones and club of ponderous weight; and many they would conquer, a few they would avoid in hiding-places; and like to bristly swine just as they were they would throw their savage limbs all naked on the ground, when overtaken by night, covering themselves up with leaves and boughs. Yet never with loud wailings would they call for the daylight and the sun, wandering terror-stricken over the fields in the shadows of night, but silent and buried in sleep they would wait, till the sun with rosy torch carried light into heaven; for accustomed as they had been from childhood always to see darkness and light begotten time about, never could any wonder come over them, nor any misgiving that never-ending night would cover the earth and the light of the sun be withdrawn for evermore. But what gave them trouble was rather the races of wild beasts which would often render repose fatal to the poor wretches. And driven from their home they would fly from their rocky shelters on the approach of a foaming boar or a strong lion, and in the dead of night they would surrender in terror to their savage guests their sleeping-places strawn with leaves.

Nor then much more than now would the races of mortal men leave the sweet light of ebbing life. For then this one or that other one of them would be more likely to be seized, and torn open by their teeth would furnish to the wild beasts a living food, and would fill with his moaning woods and mountains and forests as he looked on his living flesh buried in a living grave. But those whom flight had saved with body eaten into, holding ever after their quivering palms over the noisome sores would summon death with appalling cries, until cruel gripings had rid them of life, forlorn of help, unwitting what wounds wanted. But then a single day gave not over to death many thousands of men marching with banners spread, nor did the stormy waters of the sea dash on the rocks men and ships. At this time the sea would often rise up and rage without aim, without purpose, without result, and just as lightly put off its empty threats; nor could the winning wiles of the calm sea treacherously entice any one to his ruin with laughing waters, when the reckless craft of the skipper had not yet risen into the light. Then too want of food would consign to death their fainting frames, now on the contrary 't is plenty sinks into ruin. They unwittingly would often pour out poison for themselves; now with nicer skill men give it to their son's wife instead.

Next after they had got themselves huts and skins and fire, and the woman united with the man passed with him into one domicile and the duties of wedlock were learnt by the two, and they saw an offspring born from them, then first mankind began to soften. For fire made their chilled bodies less able now to bear the frost beneath the canopy of heaven, and Venus impaired their strength and children with their caresses soon broke down the haughty temper of parents. Then too neighbors began to join in a league of friendship, mutually desiring neither to do nor suffer harm; and asked for indulgence to children and womankind, when with cries and gestures they declared in stammering speech that meet it is for all to have mercy on the weak. And though harmony could not be established without exception, yet a very large portion observed their agreements with good faith, or else the race of man would then have been wholly cut off, nor could breeding have continued their generations to this day.

But nature impelled them to utter the various sounds of the tongue and use struck out the names of things, much in the same way as the inability to speak is seen in its turn to drive children to the use of gestures, when it forces them to point with the finger at the things which are before them. For every one feels how far he can make use of his peculiar powers. Ere the horns of a calf are formed and project from his forehead, he butts with it when angry and pushes out in his rage. Then whelps of panthers and cubs of lions fight with claws and feet and teeth at a time when teeth and claws are hardly yet formed. Again we see every kind of fowl trust to wings and seek from pinions a fluttering succor. Therefore to suppose that some one man at that time apportioned names to things, and that men from him learnt their first words, is sheer folly. For why should this particular man be able to denote all things by words and to utter the various sounds of the tongue, and yet at the same time others be supposed not to have been able to do so? Again if others as well as he had not made use of words among themselves, whence was implanted in this man the previous conception of its use, and whence was given to him the original faculty, to know and perceive in mind what he wanted to do? Again one man could not constrain and subdue and force many to choose to learn the names of things. It is no easy thing in any way to teach and convince the deaf of what is needful to be done; for they never would suffer nor in any way endure sounds of voice hitherto unheard to continue to be dinned fruitlessly into their ears.

Lastly what is there so passing strange in this circumstance, that the race of men whose voice and tongue were in full force, should denote things by different words as different feelings prompted? since dumb brutes, yes, and the races of wild beasts are accustomed to give forth distinct and varied sounds, when they have fear or pain and when joys are rife. This you may learn from facts plain to sense: when the large spongy open lips of Molossian [1] dogs begin to growl enraged and bare their hard teeth, thus drawn back in rage they threaten in a tone far different from that in which they bark outright and fill with sounds all the places around. Again when they essay fondly to lick their whelps with their tongue or when they toss them with their feet and snapping at them make a feint with lightly closing teeth of swallowing though with gentle forbearance, they caress them with a yelping sound of a sort greatly differing from that which they utter when left alone in a house they bay, or when they slink away howling from blows with a crouching body. Again is not the neigh, too, seen to differ, when a young stallion in the flower of age rages among the mares smitten by the goads of winged love, and when with wide-stretched nostrils he snorts out the signal to arms, and when as it chances on any other occasion he neighs with limbs all shaking? Lastly the race of fowls and various birds, hawks and ospreys and gulls seeking their living in the salt water mid the waves of the sea, utter at a different time noises widely different from those they make when they are fighting for food and struggling with their prey. And some of them change together with the

[1] The Molossi were a people of Epirus, in the northwest of Greece. Molossian hounds were famous in antiquity.

weather their harsh croakings, as the long-lived races of crows and flocks of rooks when they are said to be calling for water and rain and sometimes to be summoning winds and gales. Therefore if different sensations compel creatures, dumb though they be, to utter different sounds, how much more natural it is that mortal men in those times should have been able to denote dissimilar things by many different words!

And lest haply on this head you ask in silent thought this question, it was lightning that brought fire down on earth for mortals in the beginning; thence the whole heat of flames is spread abroad. Thus we see many things shine dyed in heavenly flames, when the stroke from heaven has stored them with its heat. Ay and without this when a branching tree sways to and fro and tosses about under the buffeting of the winds, pressing against the boughs of another tree, fire is forced out by the power of the violent friction, and sometimes the burning heat of flame flashes out, the boughs and stems rubbing against each other. Now either of these accidents may have given fire to men. Next the sun taught them to cook food and soften it with the heat of flame, since they would see many things grow mellow, when subdued by the strokes of the rays and by heat throughout the land.

And more and more every day men who excelled in intellect and were of vigorous understanding, would kindly shew them how to exchange their former way of living for new methods. Kings began to build towns and lay out a citadel as a place of strength and of refuge for themselves, and divided cattle and lands and gave to each man in proportion to his personal beauty and strength and intellect; for beauty and vig-

orous strength were much esteemed. Afterwards
wealth was discovered and gold found out, which soon
robbed of their honors strong and beautiful alike ; for
men however valiant and beautiful of person generally follow in the train of the richer man. But were
a man to order his life by the rules of true reason, a
frugal subsistence joined to a contented mind is for
him great riches; for never is there any lack of a little. But men desired to be famous and powerful, in
order that their fortunes might rest on a firm foundation and they might be able by their wealth to lead a
tranquil life ; but in vain, since in their struggle to
mount up to the highest dignities they rendered their
path one full of danger ; and even if they reach it, yet
envy like a thunderbolt sometimes strikes and dashes
men down from the highest point with ignominy into
noisome Tartarus ; since the highest summits and
those elevated above the level of other things are
mostly blasted by envy as by a thunderbolt; so that
far better it is to obey in peace and quiet than to
wish to rule with power supreme and be the master of
kingdoms. Therefore let men wear themselves out to
no purpose and sweat drops of blood, as they struggle
on along the straight road of ambition, since they
gather their knowledge from the mouths of others
and follow after things from hearsay rather than the
dictates of their own feelings ; and this prevails not
now nor will prevail by and by any more than it has
prevailed before.

Kings therefore being slain the old majesty of
thrones and proud sceptres were overthrown and laid
in the dust, and the glorious badge of the sovereign
head bloodstained beneath the feet of the rabble
mourned for its high prerogative ; for that is greedily

trampled on which before was too much dreaded. It would come then in the end to the lees of uttermost disorder, each man seeking for himself empire and sovereignty. Next a portion of them taught men to elect legal officers, and drew up codes, to induce men to obey the laws. For mankind, tired out with a life of brute force, lay exhausted from its feuds; and therefore the more readily it submitted of its own free will to laws and stringent codes. For as each one moved by anger took measures to avenge himself with more severity than is now permitted by equitable laws, for this reason men grew sick of a life of brute force. Thence fear of punishment mars the prizes of life; for violence and wrong enclose all who commit them in their meshes and do mostly recoil on him whom they began; and it is not easy for him who by his deeds transgresses the terms of the public peace to pass a tranquil and a peaceful existence. For though he eludes God and man, yet he cannot but feel a misgiving that his secret can be kept for ever; seeing that many by speaking in their dreams or in the wanderings of disease have often we are told betrayed themselves and have disclosed their hidden deeds of evil and their sins.

And now what cause has spread over great nations the worship of the divinities of the gods and filled towns with altars and led to the performance of stated sacred rites, rites now in fashion on solemn occasions and in solemn places, from which even now is implanted in mortals a shuddering awe which raises new temples of the gods over the whole earth and prompts men to crowd them on festive days, all this it is not so difficult to explain in words. Even then in sooth the races of mortal men would see in waking mind glorious forms, would see them in sleep of yet more marvellous size of body. To these then they would attribute sense, because they seemed to move their limbs and to utter lofty words suitable to their glorious aspect and surpassing powers. And they would give them life everlasting, because their face would appear before them and their form abide ; yes, and yet without all this because they would not believe that beings possessed of such powers could lightly be overcome by any force. And they would believe them to be preëminent in bliss, because none of them was ever troubled with the fear of death, and because at the same time in sleep they would see them perform many miracles, yet feel on their part no fatigue from the effort. Again they would see the system of heaven and the different seasons of the years come round in regular succession, and could not find out by what cause this was done ; therefore they would seek a refuge in handing over all things to the gods and supposing all things to be guided by their nod And they placed in heaven the abodes and realms of the gods, because night and moon are seen to roll through heaven, moon, day and night, and night's austere constellations and night-wandering meteors of the sky and flying bodies of flame, clouds, sun, rains, snow, winds, lightnings, hail, and rapid rumblings and loud threatful thunderclaps.

O hapless race of men, when that they charged the gods with such acts and coupled with them bitter wrath! what groanings did they then beget for themselves, what wounds for us, what tears for our children's children ! No act is it of piety to be often seen with veiled head to turn to a stone and approach every altar and fall prostrate on the ground and spread out

the palms before the statues of the gods and sprinkle
the altars with much blood of beasts and link vow on
to vow, but rather to be able to look on all things with
a mind at peace. For when we turn our gaze on the
heavenly quarters of the great upper world and ether
fast above the glittering stars, and direct our thoughts
to the courses of the sun and moon, then into our
breasts burdened with other ills that fear as well begins to exalt its reawakened head, the fear that we
may haply find the power of the gods to be unlimited,
able to wheel the bright stars in their varied motion;
for lack of power to solve the question troubles the
mind with doubts, whether there was ever a birth-time
of the world, and whether likewise there is to be any
end; how far the walls of the world can endure this
strain of restless motion; or whether gifted by the
grace of the gods with an everlasting existence they
may glide on through a never-ending tract of time and
defy the strong powers of immeasurable ages. Again
who is there whose mind does not shrink into itself
with fear of the gods, whose limbs do not cower in
terror, when the parched earth rocks with the appalling thunderstroke and rattlings run through the great
heaven? Do not peoples and nations quake, and
proud monarchs shrink into themselves smitten with
fear of the gods, lest for any foul transgression or
overweening word the heavy time of reckoning has
arrived at its fulness? When too the utmost fury of
the headstrong wind passes over the sea and sweeps
over its waters the commander of a fleet together with
his mighty legions and elephants, does he not draw
near with vows to seek the mercy of the gods and ask
in prayer with fear and trembling a lull in the winds
and propitious gales; but all in vain, since often caught

up in the furious hurricane he is borne none the less
to the shoals of death? so constantly does some hidden power trample on human grandeur and is seen to
tread under its heel and make sport for itself of the
renowned rods and cruel axes.[1] Again when the whole
earth rocks under their feet and towns tumble with
the shock or doubtfully threaten to fall, what wonder
that mortal men abase themselves and make over to
the gods in things here on earth high prerogatives and
marvellous powers, sufficient to govern all things?

To proceed, copper and gold and iron were discovered and at the same time weighty silver and the substance of lead, when fire with its heat had burnt up
vast forests on the great hills, either by a discharge
of heaven's lightning, or else because men waging
with one another a forest-war had carried fire among
the enemy in order to strike terror, or because drawn
on by the goodness of the soil they would wish to
clear rich fields, and bring the country into pasture,
or else to destroy wild beasts and enrich themselves
with the booty; for hunting with the pitfall and with
fire came into use before the practice of enclosing the
lawn with toils and stirring it with dogs. Whatever
the fact is, from whatever cause the heat of flame had
swallowed up the forests with a frightful crackling
from their very roots and had thoroughly baked the
earth with fire, there would run from the boiling veins
and collect into the hollows of the ground a stream of
silver and gold, as well as of copper and lead. And
when they saw these afterwards cool into lumps and
glitter on the earth with a brilliant gleam, they would
lift them up attracted by the bright and polished lus-

---

[1] A bundle of rods enclosing an axe was the emblem of magisterial
authority at Rome

tre, and they would see them to be moulded in a shape the same as the outline of the cavities in which each lay. Then it would strike them that these might be melted by heat and cast in any form or shape soever, and might by hammering out be brought to tapering points of any degree of sharpness and fineness, so as to furnish them with tools and enable them to cut the forests and hew timber and plane smooth the planks, and also to drill and pierce and bore, and they would set about these works just as much with silver and gold at first as with the overpowering strength of stout copper, but in vain, since their force would fail and give way and not be able like copper to stand the severe strain. At that time copper was in higher esteem and gold would be neglected on account of its uselessness, with its dull blunted edge; now copper lies neglected, gold has mounted up to the highest place of honor. Thus time as it goes round changes the seasons of things. That which was in esteem, falls at length into utter disrepute; and then another thing mounts up and issues out of its degraded state and every day is more and more coveted and blossoms forth high in honor when discovered and is in marvellous repute with men.

And now, Memmius, it is easy for you to find out ' " yourself in what way the nature of iron was discovered. Arms of old were hands nails and teeth and stones and boughs broken off from the forests, and flame and fire, as soon as they had become known. Afterwards the force of iron and copper was discovered, and the use of copper was known before that of iron, as its nature is easier to work and it is found in greater quantity. With copper they would labor the soil of the earth, with copper stir up the billows of

war and deal about wide gaping wounds and seize cattle and lands; for everything defenceless and unarmed
would readily yield to them with arms in hand. Then
by slow steps the sword of iron gained ground and the
make of the copper sickle became a by-word; and
with iron they began to plough through the earth's
soil, and the struggles of wavering war were rendered
equal, and the custom of mounting in arms on the
back of a horse and guiding him with reins and shew-
ing prowess with the right hand is older than that of
tempting the risks of war in a two-horsed chariot;
and yoking a pair of horses is older than yoking four
or mounting in arms scythed chariots. Next the
Poeni [1] taught the lucan kine [2] with towered body,
hideous of aspect, with snake-like hand, to endure the
wounds of war and to disorder the mighty ranks of
Mars. Thus sad discord begat one thing after another, to affright nations of men under arms, and
every day made some addition to the terrors of war.

They made trial of bulls too in the service of war
and essayed to send savage boars against the enemy,
and some sent before them valorous lions with armed
trainers and courageous keepers to guide them and to
hold them in chains; but in vain since heated with
promiscuous slaughter they would disorder in their
rage the troops without distinction, shaking all about
the frightful crests upon their heads: and the horsemen were not able to calm the breasts of the horses
scared by the roaring and turn them with the bridle
upon the enemy. The lionesses with a spring would
throw their enraged bodies on all sides and would

[1] The Carthaginians

[2] Elephants were so called because the Romans first saw them in
Lucania, in southern Italy, in the army of Pyrrhus

attack in the face those who met them, and others off
their guard they would tear down from above, and
twining round them would bring them to the ground
overpowered by the wound, fastening on them with
firm bite and with hooked claws The bulls would
toss their own friends and trample them under foot
and gore with their horns the flanks and bellies of the
horses underneath and turn up the earth with threatening front. The boars too would rend their friends
with powerful tusks, in their rage dyeing with their
blood the weapons broken in them, ay dyeing with
their blood the weapons broken in their own bodies ;
and would put to promiscuous rout horse and foot ;
for the tame beasts would try to avoid by shying to
the side the cruel push of the tusk, or would rear up
and paw the winds, all in vain, since you might see
them tumble down with their tendons severed and straw
the ground in their heavy fall. Those whom they
believed before to have been sufficiently broken in at
home, they would see lash themselves into fury in the
heat of action from wounds and shouting, flight panic
and uproar ; and they could not rally any portion of
them ; for all the different kinds of wild beasts would
fly all abroad ; just as now the lucan kine when cruelly mangled by the steel fly often all abroad, after
inflicting on their friends many cruel sufferings. But
men chose thus to act not so much in any hope of victory, as from a wish to give the enemy something to
rue at the cost of their own lives, when they mistrusted
their numbers and were in want of arms.

A garment tied on the body was in use before a
dress of woven stuff. Woven stuff comes after iron,
because iron is needed for weaving a web : and in no
other way can such finely polished things be made, as

heddles and spindles, shuttles and ringing yarn-beams. And nature impelled men to work up the wool before womankind ; for the male sex in general far excels the other in skill and is much more ingenious ; until the rugged countrymen so upbraided them with it, that they were glad to give it over into the hands of the women and take their share in supporting hard toil, and in such hard work hardened body and hands.

But nature parent of things was herself the first model of sowing and first gave rise to grafting, since berries and acorns dropping from the trees would put forth in due season swarms of young shoots underneath ; and hence also came the fashion of inserting grafts in their stocks and planting in the ground young saplings over the fields.   Next they would try another and yet another kind of tillage for their loved piece of land and would see the earth better the wild fruits through genial fostering and kindly cultivation, and they would force the forests to recede every day higher and higher up the hillside and yield the ground below to tilth, in order to have on the uplands and plains meadows tanks runnels cornfields and glad vineyards, and allow a gray-green strip of olives to run between and mark the divisions, spreading itself over hillocks and valleys and plains ; just as you now see richly dight with varied beauty all the ground which they lay out and plant with rows of sweet fruit-trees, and enclose all round with plantations of other goodly trees.

But imitating with the mouth the clear notes of birds was in use long before men were able to sing in tune smooth-running verses and give pleasure to the ear.   And the whistlings of the zephyr through

the hollows of reeds first taught peasants to blow into
hollow stalks. Then step by step they learned sweet
plaintive ditties, which the pipe pours forth pressed by
the fingers of the players, heard through pathless woods
and forests and lawns, through the unfrequented haunts
of shepherds and abodes of unearthly calm. These
things would soothe and gratify their minds when sated
with food ; for then all things of this kind are welcome. Often therefore stretched in groups on the soft
grass beside a stream of water under the boughs of
a high tree at no great cost they would pleasantly refresh their bodies, above all when the weather smiled
and the seasons of the year painted the green grass
with flowers. Then went round the jest, the tale, the
peals of merry laughter; for the peasant muse was
then in its glory; then frolick mirth would prompt to
entwine head and shoulders with garlands plaited with
flowers and leaves, and to advance in the dance out of
step and move the limbs clumsily and with clumsy feet
beat mother earth ; which would occasion smiles and
peals of merry laughter, because all these things then
from their greater novelty and strangeness were in
high repute, and the wakeful found a solace for want
of sleep in this, in drawing out a variety of notes and
going through tunes and running over the reeds with
curving lip; whence even at the present day watch-
men observe these traditions and have lately learned to
keep the proper tune ; and yet for all this receive not
a jot more of enjoyment than erst the rugged race of
sons of earth received. For that which we have in our
hands, if we have known before nothing pleasanter,
pleases above all and is thought to be the best ; and as
a rule the later discovery of something better spoils
the taste for the former things and changes the feel-

ings in regard to all that has gone before. Thus
began distaste for the acorn, thus were abandoned
those sleeping places strawn with grass and enriched
with leaves. The dress too of wild beasts' skin fell
into neglect; though I can fancy that in those days it
was found to arouse such jealousy that he who first
wore it met his death by an ambuscade, and after all it
was torn in pieces among them and drenched in blood
was utterly destroyed and could not be turned to any
use. In those times therefore skins, now gold and purple plague men's lives with cares and wear them out
with war. And in this methinks the greater blame
rests with us; for cold would torture the naked sons
of earth without their skins; but us it harms not in
the least to do without a robe of purple, spangled
with gold and large figures, if only we have a dress
of the people to protect us. Mankind therefore ever
toils vainly and to no purpose and wastes life in
groundless cares, because sure enough they have not
learnt what is the true end of getting and up to what
point genuine pleasure goes on increasing: this by
slow degrees has carried life out into the deep sea and
stirred up from their lowest depths the mighty billows
of war.

But those watchful guardians sun and moon travers-
ing with their light all round the great revolving
sphere of heaven taught men that the seasons of the
year came round and that the system was carried on
after a fixed plan and fixed order.

Already they would pass their life fenced about with
strong towers, and the land, portioned out and marked
off by boundaries, be tilled: the sea would be filled
with ships scudding under sail; towns have auxiliaries
and allies as stipulated by treaty, when poets began to

consign the deeds of men to verse; and letters had not been invented long before. For this reason our age cannot look back to what has gone before, save where reason points out any traces.

Ships and tillage, walls, laws, roads, dress, and all such like things, all the prizes, all the elegancies too of life without exception, poems, pictures, and the chiselling of fine-wrought statues, all these things practice together with the acquired knowledge of the untiring mind taught men by slow degrees as they advanced on the way step by step. Thus time by degrees brings each several thing forth before men's eyes and reason raises it up into the borders of light; for things must be brought to light one after the other and in due order in the different arts, until these have reached their highest point of development.

H A J. Munro

CATULLUS

BIOGRAPHICAL SKETCH

SWEETEST of Roman singers, Catullus has won the hearts of his readers both in ancient and in modern times by his perfect sincerity, his exquisite tenderness, his absolute ingenuousness. Strange anomaly, a love poet with a really great love, he has told his story with simple directness, expressed its varying phases with compelling candor, traced its course, which ran any way but smoothly, with a range of feeling that places his lyrics among the truest and most spontaneous utterances in literature. At once buoyant and moody, with equal capacity for great happiness and for great suffering, his poems show him now striking the stars, now plunged in depths of woe. Yet all told, after reading his "little book," with its alternate sunshine and shadow, it is the more sombre tone that prevails, and the lighter pieces. while of lasting charm in themselves from their exuberance of spirits, their air of good fellowship, their humorous and satirical touches, have another and perhaps, from the point of view of the book as a whole, a still more striking effect in that they act as foils to those poems of the Lesbia group in which the poet's feelings find their most passionate expression. These are of singular intensity, some of them written in the heyday of his hopes and happiness, some in times of doubt and disillusion, some telling of his struggle between his love for Lesbia and his knowledge of her faithlessness, more than one a renunciation, — all examples of genuine self-revelation, the record of a rare spirit who happened upon misfortune.

He was born at Verona in 84 B. C. Almost the whole period of his literary activity, however, was spent in Rome, and it was there that he met Lesbia, as she is called in his poems, who seems to have given the first stimulus to his lyrical gift. While her identity has not been finally determined, it is probable that she was none other than Clodia, the sister of Clodius, the notorious enemy of Cicero. His affair with her lasted about four years, from 61–58. In 57 he joined the suite of the propraetor Memmius, who was going out to Bithynia. On returning to Rome in the following year, he showed an increased interest in politics, bitterly opposing Caesar and his party. There is no reference in his writings to any event later than 54, and it is assumed that he died soon after that year.

Besides the Lesbia lyrics, the verses to different friends, and other occasional pieces, we have a number of epigrams and some longer poems, among which may be mentioned the *Marriage of Peleus and Thetis*, an epyllion or miniature epic, into which is woven the story of Theseus and Ariadne ; the *Attis*, describing the self-mutilation of a young devotee of Cybele ; the *Epithalamium of Julia and Manlius*, one of the finest products of the poet's genius ; and *Berenice's Hair*, in which the hair itself gives the true history of its elevation from the head of Berenice, the sister, wife, and queen of Ptolemy Energetes, to a place in the heavens. While these, in contrast to the best of the shorter poems, show in many respects the influence of the tenets of the group of " new poets," among whom Catullus' closest literary friends were, and who, in violent reaction from the standards of the older national school, looked to Alexandrian poetry as the only means of literary salvation, yet there are in almost all of them striking manifestations of those qualities of imagination and true poetic insight which make Catullus one of Rome's greatest poets.

ON THE DEATH OF LESBIA'S SPARROW

(III.) [1]

Loves and Graces mourn with me,
Mourn, fair youths, where'er ye be !
Dead my Lesbia's sparrow is,
Sparrow, that was all her bliss,
Than her very eyes more dear;   5
For he made her dainty cheer,
Knew her well, as any maid
Knows her mother, never strayed
From her bosom, but would go
Hopping round her, to and fro,   10
And to her, and her alone,
Chirrup'd with such pretty tone.
Now he treads that gloomy track,
Whence none ever may come back.
Out upon you, and your power,   15
Which all fairest things devour,
Orcus' gloomy shades, that e'er
Ye took my bird that was so fair !
Ah, the pity of it !   Thou
Poor bird, thy doing 't is, that now   20
My loved one's eyes are swollen and red,
With weeping for her darling dead.

Sir Theodore Martin.

[1] The number of the poem in the complete collection.

DEDICATION OF HIS PINNACE [1]

(IV.)

THAT pinnace, friends, can boast that erst
　'T was swiftest of its kind ;
Nor swam the bark whose fleetest burst
　It could not leave behind ;
Whether the toiling rower's force　　　　　5
Or swelling sail impell'd its course.

This boast, it dares the shores that bound
　The Adrian's [2] stormy space,
The Cyclad [3] islands sea-girt round,
　Bright Rhodes or rugged Thrace,　　　　10
The wide Propontis [4] to gainsay,
Or still tempestuous Pontic bay.

There, ere it swam 'mid fleetest prows,
　A grove of spreading trees
On high Cytorus' [5] hill, its boughs　　　　15
　Oft whisper'd in the breeze.
Amastris,[6] pride of Pontic floods,
Cytorus, green with boxen woods,

---

[1] Pointing out to some friends an old pinnace beached somewhere near his villa on the shore of the Lago di Garda, Catullus tells how it had once borne him home from Asia Minor. After mentioning the most important places touched at or passed on the voyage, he dedicates the hulk to Castor and Pollux, twin gods of navigation

[2] The Adriatic Sea. The voyage is traced backward from Italy to Asia.

[3] In the Aegean Sea.

[4] Sea of Marmora

[5] A hill near the south coast of the Black Sea.

[6] A city on the Black Sea.

Ye knew it then, and all its race,
  And know the pinnace too,   20
Which from its earliest rise, to grace
  Thy lofty summit grew;
And in the waves that wash thy shores
Which moisten'd first its sturdy oars.

Thence many vainly raging seas   25
  It bore its master through;
Whether from right or left the breeze
  Upon the canvas blew;
Or prosperous to its course the gale
Spread full and square the straining sail.   30

No vows to Ocean's gods it gave,
  For then no storm could shake;
When erst from that remotest wave
  It sought this limpid lake:[1]
But, ah! those days are fled at length,   35
And fled with them are speed and strength.

Now old, worn out, and lost to fame,
  In rest that 's justly due,
It dedicates this shatter'd frame,
  Ye glorious Twins,[2] to you —   40
To you, whose often cheering ray
Beam'd light and safety on its way.
                                GEORGE LAMB

[1] Lake Benacus, now the Lago di Garda. The last part of the voyage was up the rivers Po and Mincio.
[2] The constellation Gemini was supposed to be Castor and Pollux.

TO LESBIA

(V)

LIVING, Lesbia, we should e'en be loving.
Sour severity, tongue of eld maligning,
All be to us a penny's estimation.

Suns set only to rise again to-morrow.
We, when sets in a little hour the brief light,   5
Sleep one infinite age, a night for ever.

Thousand kisses, anon to these an hundred,
Thousand kisses again, another hundred,
Thousand give me again, another hundred.

Then once heedfully counted all the thousands,   10
We'll uncount them as idly ; so we shall not
Know, nor traitorous eye shall envy,[1] knowing
All those myriad happy many kisses.

ROBINSON ELLIS.

TO THE SAME

(VII.)

DOST thou, Lesbia, ask that I
    Say how many of thy kisses
Would my craving satisfy,
    Yes, would surfeit me with blisses ?

---

[1] Information as to the exact number of blessings of any kind was supposed to enable an enemy to exert an evil influence.

Count the grains of sand besprent   5
   O'er Cyrene's [1] spicy plain,
'Twixt old Battus' [2] monument
   And the sweltering Hammon's [3] fane.

Count the silent stars of night,
   That be ever watching, when   10
Lovers tasting stol'n delight
   Dream not of their silent ken.

When these numbers thou hast told,
   And hast kisses given as many,
Then I may, perchance, cry hold!   15
   And no longer wish for any.

But, my love, there's no amount
   For a rage like mine too vast,
Which a curious fool may count,
   Or with tongue malignant blast.   20
SIR THEODORE MARTIN

TO HIMSELF

ON LESBIA'S INCONSTANCY

(VIII)

Ah, poor Catullus, learn to put away
   Thy childish things.
The lost is lost, be sure ; the task essay
   That manhood brings.

[1] A city in Libya
[2] The founder of Cyrene
[3] A name under which Jupiter was worshipped in Africa

Fair shone the skies on thee when thou to fare   5
    Wast ever fain
Where the girl beckon'd, lov'd as girl shall ne'er
    Be lov'd again.

Yes, fain thou wast for merry mirth; and she —
    She ne'er said nay.   10
Ah, gayly then the morning smil'd on thee
    Each happy day.

Now, she saith nay; but thou be strong to bear,
    Harden thy heart;
Nor nurse thy grief, nor cling to her so fair,   15
    So fixt to part.

Farewell! I've learn'd my lesson: I'll endure,
    Nor try to find
Words that might wake thy ruth, or even cure
    Thy poison'd mind.   20

Yet will the time come when thy heart shall bleed,
    Accursèd one,
When thou shalt come to eld with none to heed,
    Unwooed, unwon.

Who then will seek thee? Who will call thee fair?
    Call thee his own?   26
Whose kisses and whose dalliance wilt thou share?
    Be stone, my heart, be stone.

                          R. Y. TYRRELL.

VARUS' MISTRESS

(X)

Varus, whom I chanced to meet
The other evening in the street,
Engaged me there, upon the spot,
To see a mistress he had got.
She seem'd, as far as I can gather, 5
Lively and smart, and handsome rather.
There, as we rested from our walk,
We enter'd into different talk —
As, how much might Bithynia bring?
And had I found it a good thing? 10
I answer'd, as it was the fact,
The province had been stript and sack'd;
That there was nothing for the praetors,
And still less for us wretched creatures,
His poor companions and toad-eaters. 15
"At least," says she, "you bought some fellows
To bear your litter; for they tell us,
Our only good ones come from there."
I chose to give myself an air;
"Why, truly, with my poor estate, 20
The difference was n't quite so great
Betwixt a province, good or bad,
That where a purchase could be had,
Eight lusty fellows, straight and tall,
I should n't find the wherewithal 25
To buy them." But it was a lie;
For not a single wretch had I —
No single cripple fit to bear
A broken bedstead or a chair.
She, like a strumpet, pert and knowing, 30

Said — " Dear Catullus, I am going
To worship at Serapis' [1] shrine —
Do lend me, pray, those slaves of thine ! "
I answer'd — " It was idly said, —
They were a purchase Cinna made   35
(Caius Cinna, my good friend) —
It was the same thing in the end,
Whether a purchase or a loan —
I always used them as my own ;
Only the phrase was inexact —   40
He bought them for himself, in fact.
But you have caught the general vice
Of being too correct and nice,
Over curious and precise ;
And seizing with precipitation   45
The slight neglects of conversation."

J. HOOKHAM FRERE.

TO FABULLUS

(XIII)

You dine with me, Fabullus mine,
  On Friday next, at half-past two :
And I can promise that you 'll dine
  As well as man need wish to do ;

If you bring with you, when you come,   5
  A dinner of the very best,
And lots of wine and mirth, and some
  Fair girl to give the whole a zest.

But bring all these you must, I vow,
  If you 're to find yourself in clover,   10

[1] An Egyptian divinity, whose cult was fashionable in Catullus' time.

For your Catullus' purse just now
    With spiders' webs is running over.

But anyhow, a welcome warm
    And loving shall be yours, I ween;
And, for a rarer, daintier charm,   15
    A perfume which the Paphian queen[1]

Gave to my girl, — so rare, so sweet,
    That, when you smell it, in the throes
Of ecstasy you 'll straight entreat
    The gods to make you wholly nose.   20
                    Sir Theodore Martin.

TO SIRMIO [2]

(XXXI)

O best of all the scattered spots that lie
In sea or lake — apple of landscape's eye —
How gladly do I drop within thy nest,
With what a sigh of full contented rest,
Scarce able to believe my journey o'er,   5
And that these eyes behold thee safe once more.
Oh, where 's the luxury like the smile at heart,
When the mind, breathing, lays its load apart —
When we come home again, tired out, and spread
The loosened limbs o'er all the wished-for bed;   10
This, this alone is worth an age of toil!
Hail lovely Sirmio! Hail paternal soil!
Joy, my bright waters, joy, your master 's come!
Laugh, every dimple on the cheek of home!
                    Leigh Hunt.

[1] Venus
[2] A peninsula in the Lago di Garda, where Catullus had a villa

TO DIANA

(XXXIV.)

DIANA guardeth our estate,
Girls and boys immaculate:
Boys and maidens pure of stain,
Be Diana our refrain.

O Latonia,[1] pledge of love
Glorious to most glorious Jove,
Near the Delian[2] olive-tree
Latona gave thy life to thee,

That thou shouldst be forever queen
Of mountains and of forests green;
Of every deep glen's mystery;
Of all streams and their melody:

Women in travail ask their peace
From thee, our Lady of Release:
Thou art the Watcher of the Ways:
Thou art the moon with borrow'd rays;

And as thy full or waning tide
Marks how the monthly seasons glide,
Thou, Goddess, sendest wealth of store
To bless the farmer's thrifty floor.

Whatever name delights thine ear,
By that name be thou hallow'd here

[1] Diana, daughter of Latona
[2] The island of Delos, one of the Cyclades, was supposed to be the birthplace of Apollo and Diana

And as of old be good to us,
The lineage of Romulus.

R. C. Jebb.

TO CORNIFICIUS

(XXXVIII.)

Cornificius, ill is your Catullus,
Ill, ah heaven, a weary weight of anguish,
More, more weary with every day, with each hour.

You deny me the least, the very lightest
Help, one whisper of happy thought to cheer me.　5

Nay, I 'm sorrowful.　You to slight my passion?
Ah! one word, but a tiny word to cheer me,
Sad as ever a tear Simonidean.[1]

Robinson Ellis

ACME AND SEPTIMIUS

(XLV.)

Septimius cried, as on his breast
His darling Acme he caressed,
"My Acme, if I love not thee
To madness, ay, distractedly,
And with a love that well I know　　　　　5
With time shall fonder, wilder grow
In Libya may I then, my sweet,
Or India's burning deserts meet

---

[1] The allusion is to the pathetic quality of the work of Simonides,
the Greek lyric poet (556–467 B c)

The green-eyed lion's hungry glare,
And none be by to help me there!"   10

As thus he whispered, Love was pleased,
And on the right propitious sneezed.

Then bending gently back her head,
And with that mouth, so rosy-red,
Impressing on his eyes a kiss,   15
His eyes, that drunken were with bliss,
"Oh, Septimillus, life!" cried she,
"So love our only master be,
As burns in me, thine Acme true,
A fire that thrills my marrow through,   20
Intenser, mightier, more divine,
Than any thou canst feel in thine!"

As thus she whispered, Love was pleased,
And on the right propitious sneezed.

Now hallowed by such omens fair,   25
Each dotes on each, that happy pair.
He, sick with love, rates Acme's smiles
Above the East or Britain's isles;
Whilst Acme, to Septimius true,
For him, him only, doth renew   30
Love's first delights, and to her boy
Unfolds fresh treasuries of joy.

Were ever souls so lapped in bliss!
Was ever love so blest as this!

SIR THEODORE MARTIN.

TO LESBIA

(LI)

Him rival to the gods I place,
  Him loftier yet, if loftier be,
Who, Lesbia, sits before thy face,
  Who listens and who looks on thee ;

Thee, smiling soft.   Yet this delight   5
  Doth all my sense consign to death ;
For when thou dawnest on my sight,
  Ah, wretched ! flits my laboring breath.

My tongue is palsied.   Subtly hid
  Fire creeps me through from limb to limb :   10
My loud ears tingle all unbid :
  Twin clouds of night mine eyes bedim.

Ease is my plague : ease makes thee void,
  Catullus, with these vacant hours,
And wanton : ease that hath destroyed   15
  Great kings, and states with all their powers.

W. E. GLADSTONE.

THE EPITHALAMIUM OF JULIA AND MAN-LIUS [1]

(LXI.)

I. [2]

You that from the mother's side
Lead the lingering, blushing bride,
    Fair Urania's son —
Leave awhile the lonely mount,
The haunted grove and holy fount   5
    Of chilling Helicon.

II.

With myrtle wreaths enweave thy hair —
Wave the torch aloft in air —
    Make no long delay :
With flowing robe and footsteps light,   10
And gilded buskins glancing bright,
    Hither bend thy way.

III.

Join at once, with airy vigor,
In the dance's varied figure,
    To the Cymbal's chime :   15
Frolic unrestrain'd and free —
Let voice, and air, and verse agree,
    And the torch beat time.

[1] The poem was written for the marriage of Manlius Torquatus, one of Catullus' friends

[2] Stanzas i.-viii contain an invocation to Hymen, God of marriage.

IV.

Hymen, come, for Julia
Weds with Manlius to-day,   20
    And deigns to be a bride.
Such a form as Venus wore
In the contest famed of yore,
    On Mount Ida's side ; [1]

V.

Like the myrtle or the bay,   25
Florid, elegant, and gay,
    With foliage fresh and new ;
Which the nymphs and forest maids
Have foster'd in sequester'd shades,
    With drops of holy dew.   30

VI.

Leave, then, all the rocks and cells
Of the deep Aonian [2] dells,
    And the caverns hoar ;
And the dreary streams that weep
From the stony Thespian steep,[3]   35
    Dripping evermore.

VII.

Haste away to new delights,
To domestic happy rites,
    Human haunts and ways ;
With a kindly charm applied,   40
Soften and appease the bride,
    And shorten our delays.

[1] When Paris awarded to her the golden apple.
[2] Aonia was the name of that part of Boeotia in which Mount Helicon was situated.
[3] Mount Helicon, at the foot of which was the city of Thespiae

VIII.

Bring her hither, bound to move,
Drawn and led with bands of love,
    Like the tender twine   45
Which the searching ivy plies,
Clinging in a thousand ties
    O'er the clasping vine.

IX.

Gentle virgins, [1] you besides,
Whom the like event betides,   50
    With the coming year;
Call on Hymen! call him now!
Call aloud!   A virgin now
    Best befits his ear.

X.

" Is there any deity   55
More beloved and kind than he —
    More disposed to bless;
Worthy to be worshipp'd more;
Master of a richer store
    Of wealth and happiness?   60

XI.

" Youth and age alike agree,
Serving and adoring thee,
    The source of hope and care:
Care and hope alike engage
The wary parent sunk in age   65
    And the restless heir.

[1] A choir of girls had been chosen to sing the hymeneal, which is given in stanzas x.-xvi.

XII.

" She the maiden, half afraid,
  Hears the new proposal made,
        That proceeds from thee ;
  You resign and hand her over   70
  To the rash and hardy lover
        With a fix'd decree.

XIII.

" Hymen, Hymen, you preside,
  Maintaining honor and the pride
        Of women free from blame,   75
  With a solemn warrant given,
  Is there any power in heaven
        That can do the same ?

XIV.

" Love, accompanied by thee,
  Passes unreproved and free,   80
        But without thee, not :
  Where on earth, or in the sky,
  Can you find a deity
        With a fairer lot ?

XV.

" Heirship in an honor'd line   85
  Is sacred as a gift of thine,
        But without thee, not :
  Where on earth, or in the sky,
  Can you find a deity
        With a fairer lot ?   90

XVI.

" Rule and empire — royalty,
  Are rightful as derived from thee,

But without thee, not :
Where on earth, or in the sky,
Can you find a deity   95
With a fairer lot ? "

XVII. [1]

Open locks ! unbar the gate !
Behold the ready troop that wait
  The coming of the bride ;
Behold the torches, how they flare ! 100
Spreading aloft their sparkling hair,
  Flashing far and wide.

XVIII.

Lovely maiden ! here we waste
The timely moments; come in haste !
  Come then . . . . Out, alack ! 105
Startled at the glare and din,
She retires to weep within,
  Lingering, hanging back.

XIX.

Bashful honor and regret
For a while detain her yet, 110
  Lingering, taking leave :
Taking leave and lingering still,
With a slow, reluctant will,
  With grief that does not grieve.

XX.

Aurunculeia, [2] cease your tears, 115
And when to-morrow's morn appears,

---

[1] In this and the following stanzas we have a picture of the scene
in front of the bride's house, where a throng is waiting impatiently to
escort her in torch-light procession to her husband's house.

[2] The bride's full name was Julia Aurunculeia.

Fear not that the sun
Will dawn upon a fairer face, —
Nor in his airy, lofty race
    Behold a lovelier one.   120

XXI.

Mark and hear us, gentle bride;
Behold the torches nimbly plied,
    Waving here and there;
Along the street and in the porch,
See the fiery-tressed torch   125
    Spreads its sparkling hair.

XXII.

Like a lily, fair and chaste,
Lovely bride, you shall be placed
    In a garden gay,
A wealthy lord's delight and pride;   130
Come away then, happy bride,
    Hasten, hence away!

XXIII.

Mark and hear us — he, your lord,
Will be true at bed and board,
    Nor ever walk astray,   135
Withdrawing from your lovely side;
Mark and hear us, gentle bride,
    Hasten, hence away!

XXIV.

Like unto the tender vine,
He shall ever clasp and twine,   140
    Clinging night and day,

Fairly bound and firmly tied;
Come away then, happy bride,
Hasten, hence away!

XXVI.

Make ready.   There I see within
The bride is veil'd; the guests begin
    To muster close and slow:
Trooping onward close about,
Boys, be ready with a shout —   155
    "Hymen! Hymen! Ho!"

XXVII.

Now begins the free career,[1] —
For many a jest and many a jeer,
    And many a merry saw;
Customary taunts and gibes,   160
Such as ancient use prescribes,
    And immemorial law.

XXVIII. [2]

"Some at home, it must be fear'd,
Will be slighted, and cashier'd,
    Pride will have a fall;   165
Now the favorites' reign is o'er,
Proud enough they were before, —
    Proud and nice withal.

XXIX.

"Full of pride and full of scorn;
Now you see them clipt and shorn,   170

---

[1] The procession was conducted with the greatest hilarity.

[2] Stanzas xxviii.-xxxii. seem to have been sung by a choir of boys, who forecast the changes in the bridegroom's household after his marriage.

Humbler in array;
Sent away, for fear of harm,
To the village or the farm, —
Pack'd in haste away.

XXX.

"Other doings must be done,   175
Another empire is begun,
        Behold your own domain!
Gentle bride!   Behold it there!
The lordly palace proud and fair: —
        You shall live and reign   180

XXXI.

"In that rich and noble house,
Till age shall silver o'er the brows,
        And nod the trembling head,
Not regarding what is meant,
Incessant uniform assent   185
        To all that 's done or said.

XXXII.

"Let the faithful threshold greet,
With omens fair, those lovely feet,
        Lightly lifted o'er;[1]
Let the garlands wave and bow   190
From the lofty lintel's brow
        That bedeck the door."

XXXIII.

See the couch[2] with crimson dress —
Where, seated in the deep recess,

---

[1] The lifting of the bride over the threshold of her new home was probably a survival of the marriage by capture.

[2] The bridegroom is represented as reclining at a wedding supper, which had been prepared in anticipation of the coming of the bride

With expectation warm,   195
The bridegroom views her coming near, —
The slender youth [1] that led her here
      May now release her arm.

XXXIV.

With a fix'd intense regard
He beholds her close and hard   200
      In awful interview :
Shortly now she must be sped
To the chamber and the bed,
      With attendance due.

XXXV.

Let the ancient worthy wives,   205
That have pass'd their constant lives
      With a single mate,[2]
As befits advised age,
With council and precaution sage
      Assist and regulate.   210

XXXVI.

She the mistress of the band
Comes again with high command,
      " Bridegroom, go your way ;
There your bride is in the bower,
Like a lovely lily flower,   215
      Or a rose in May.

---

[1] Probably one of the boys who had conducted her during the procession.

[2] Only matrons who had been but once married were allowed to assist.

XXXIX.

" Ay, and you yourself in truth
Are a goodly, comely youth,   .   230
        Proper, tall, and fair;
Venus and the graces too
Have befriended each of you
        For a lovely pair."

XLII.

Fear not! with the coming year,
The new Torquatus will be here,
        Him we soon shall see
With infant gesture fondly seek   250
To reach his father's manly cheek,
        From the mother's knee.

XLIII.

With laughing eyes and dewy lip,
Pouting like the purple tip
        That points the rose's bud;   255
While mingled with the mother's grace,
Strangers shall recognize the trace
        That marks the Manlian blood.

                              J. Hookham Frere.

REMORSE

(LXXVI, *vv.* 10 *seq.*)

Why longer keep thy heart upon the rack?
    Give to thy soul a higher, nobler aim.
And tho' thou tear thy heart out, look not back
    In tears upon a love that was thy shame.

'T is hard at once to fling a love away   5
    That has been cherish'd with the faith of years.
'T is hard : but shrink not, flinch not. Come what
      may,
    Crush every record of its joys and fears.

O ye great gods, if ye can pity feel,
    If e'er to dying wretch your aid was given,   10
See me in agony before you kneel,
    To beg this plague from out my core be driven,

Which creeps in drowsy horror thro' each vein,
    Leaves me no thought from bitter anguish free ;
I do nót ask that she be kind again,   15
    Nor pure : for that can never, never be.

I only crave the health that once was mine,
    Some little respite from this sore disease.
If e'er I earned your mercy, powers divine,
    Grant me — O grant to a sick heart some ease !   20

SIR THEODORE MARTIN.
R. Y. TYRRELL.

LOVE AND HATE

(LXXXV)

I LOVE and hate. Ah! never ask why so!
I hate and love — and that is all I know.
I see 't is folly, but I feel 't is woe.

W. S. LANDOR

AT HIS BROTHER'S GRAVE [1]

(CI.)

O'ER many a sea, o'er many a stranger land,
  I bring this tribute [2] to thy lonely tomb,
  My brother ! and beside the narrow room
That holds thy silent ashes weeping stand.
Vainly I call to thee.   Who can command   5
  An answer forth from Orcus' dreary gloom?
  Oh, brother, brother, life lost all its bloom,
When thou wert snatched from me with pitiless
    hand !

Woe, woe is me, that we shall meet no more !
  Meanwhile, these gifts accept, which to the grave 10
Of those they loved in life our sires of yore
  With pious hand and reverential gave —
Gifts that are streaming with a brother's tears !
And now, farewell, and rest thee from all fears !
SIR THEODORE MARTIN

[1] Catullus' brother died in the Troad, and was buried there.
[2] Offerings of wine, milk, and flowers

CICERO

BIOGRAPHICAL SKETCH

THE most casual survey of the life and works of Cicero leaves us with a strong impression of his wonderful versatility. Turning easily from politics to literature, he found time, amid the manifold activities of a crowded public career, to elaborate and cast in permanent literary form his numerous orations, to make a close study of the various systems of rhetoric, to familiarize himself with the tenets of the different schools of philosophy, to make ventures even in the fields of historiography and of poetry, and to carry on a voluminous correspondence, which has survived as one of our most precious heritages from Roman antiquity.

He was born in 106 B. C. at Arpinum, an ancient city of the Volscians, already famous as the birthplace of Marius. His father was of equestrian rank, and the family seems to have been one of some local importance. He was educated at Rome, and his formative years were spent in close contact with such men as the famous orators Marcus Antonius and Lucius Crassus, the poet Archias, whose citizenship he afterwards defended, Scaevola the augur, Phaedrus the Epicurean philosopher, Philo the academic, and Diodotus the Stoic. He had already established his reputation as an orator when he went to Greece in 79 to continue his rhetorical and philosophical studies. Returning to Rome two years later, he resumed activity as an advocate. His official career began in 75, when he was sent to Sicily as quaestor; in 69 he was elected curule aedile, in 66 *prae-*

tor urbanus, in 63 consul. The year of his consulship was marked by the conspiracy of Catiline. Successful in bringing about the execution of some of the most notorious of the conspirators, he was himself subsequently driven into exile through the machinations of enemies, who revived a law according to which any one who ordered the execution of a Roman citizen before he had been condemned by the people, was guilty of treason. He had been in banishment some ten months when in August, 57, he was recalled by a vote of the *comitia centuriata.* From 51 to 50 he was proconsul of Cilicia. Meanwhile the struggle between Caesar and Pompey had come to a crisis. After long hesitation Cicero declared for Pompey and followed him to Dyrrachium. When the supremacy of the Caesarians was established, he retired from political life and devoted himself to literature. After Caesar's assassination he emerged once more as an opponent of Mark Antony. This was the immediate cause of his fall. He was proscribed by the second triumvirate, and killed by their emissaries on the 7th of December, 43.

"Most eloquent of all the descendants of Romulus, as many as are, or have been, or ever shall be," — such is the characterization of Cicero by Catullus, and subsequent ages have indorsed his opinion Some of his speeches are, it is true, open to criticism, if judged by the standard of a modern law court. He does not always confine himself strictly to the points of law involved, or to the facts of the case in hand. For example, in the *Pro Archia,* the panegyric of literature has a much more conspicuous place than the legality of the defendant's citizenship. There is, too, another criticism that is often and perhaps justly made, namely, that even the most impassioned of his utterances on state questions show a lack of that moral earnestness which is so prominent a feature of the orations of Demosthenes. Yet even with these shortcomings, Cicero's orations are masterpieces of eloquence; and his vivid imagination, that finds play in descriptions of persons, places, and actions, in similes and metaphors of almost infinite number and variety, his extraordinary keenness, which enabled him to single out swiftly and effectively the weak points in an adversary's position, his wide range of information, his marvellous command of language, and his powers of invective make a combination of qualities difficult to parallel in the whole history of oratory.

His rhetorical writings have special value as the productions of one who, besides being conspicuously successful in the practice of oratory, had made a long and careful study of the methods and standards of the different schools.

It was during years of enforced retirement that most of his philosophical works were written. They are, in the main, a working over of Greek material, especially the treatises of the post-Aristotelian philosophers, and offer very little that is new or original. Apart from their literary merit, their most important function, both in his own and in subsequent ages, was in serving as a medium for the popularization of Greek philosophy. They are, for the most part, cast in the form of dialogues, and deal with such questions as Government, Law, the Theory of Knowledge, the Greatest Good and the Greatest Evil, the Nature of the Gods, and more practical problems of ethics, as in the treatise on Moral Duties addressed to his son Marcus. Among the most charming are the two short pieces on Old Age, in which we have a masterly characterization of Cato Major, and on Friendship, in which Laelius is the principal interlocutor.

Of greater interest are the letters, of which we have sixteen books addressed to his intimate friend Atticus, sixteen to other friends and members of his household, three to his brother Quintus, and one to Brutus. These furnish us with a large mass of material for the study of colloquial Latin, and are, in addition, of inestimable value for the light they throw upon the political history of the time, and upon Cicero's character and private life.

THE SPEECH FOR CLUENTIUS [1]

(The second division of the case, from section 164 to the end.)

THERE you have, gentlemen,[2] all that his accusers have succeeded in raking together for the whole case, after eight years' preparation, concerning the character of A. Cluentius, against whom, on his trial, they would fain stir up ill-feeling. How trivial are the allegations in themselves, how groundless in fact, how short to answer! Listen now to what concerns the oath you have sworn, to what belongs to your court, to what the statute of poisoning,[3] in obedience to whose summons you are here assembled, has imposed on you as an obligation. I should like to know how brief the statement of this case could have been made, and how much that I have said was spoken in deference to my client's wishes, but did not in any way concern your court.

It was alleged by the prosecution that A Cluentius made away with Vibius Capax [1] by poison. There is

[1] The trial took place in 66 B C The defendant. Aulus Cluentius Habitus, was accused of having poisoned or caused to be poisoned (1) Vibius Capax, (2) Balbutius, (3) Oppianicus, his step-father. The last was the principal count of the accusation The prosecution was instituted by Oppianicus' son, but the real instigator of the action was Sassia, the wife of the alleged victim, and the mother of the defendant Eight years before, Oppianicus, brought to trial by Cluentius on a charge of attempting to poison him had been convicted, and banished from the city He died in exile, apparently in consequence of a fall from his horse, but according to Sassia, from poison administered by an agent of Cluentius In the first part of the speech Cicero tries to remove the prejudice that existed against his client as a result of the feeling that he had had some part in the wholesale bribery of the jurors at the trial of Oppianicus in 74 In the second part he deals with the specific charges of poisoning.

[2] Of the jury

[3] The fifth chapter of the *Lex Cornelia de Sicariis et Veneficis*

[1] Not otherwise known.

opportunely present in court a most reputable and in every way worthy person, the Senator L. Praetorius, whose hospitality and intimate friendship this Vibius enjoyed, with whom he lived at Rome when he was taken ill, and at whose house he expired. I assert that he died intestate,·and that the succession to his estate was by edict of the praetor assigned to Numerius Cluentius, his sister's son, whom you see here in court, a most honorable and eminently estimable young man, and a Roman knight to boot.

The second charge of poisoning states that poison was, at the instigation of Habitus,[1] prepared for young Oppianicus [2] here, when a large company was breakfasting together, as is the custom at Larinum,[3] on the occasion of his marriage; and that when it was being offered him in honey wine, Balbutius,[4] one of his friends, intercepted it on its passage, drank it, and instantly expired. If I were to treat this matter as if I had an accusation to dispose of, I should state at greater length what I am now cursorily mentioning in my speech.

What has Habitus ever done that this monstrous deed should not be thought quite foreign to his character? And had he any reason for being in such fear of Oppianicus,[5] seeing he could not have said one single word in this case, while, as you will presently be made aware, so long as his mother lives my client can never be free from prosecution? Was it that he wanted his case to lose no element of danger, but rather

---

[1] The defendant   Habitus was his cognomen

[2] Son of Oppianicus

[3] A town near the borders of Apulia, where the most important personages of the trial lived

[4] Mentioned only in this speech.

[5] The son.

to have a fresh charge added on to it? What kind
of a time was that to choose for administering poison,
on such a day and before such a number of people?
By whom, moreover, was it offered? Where was it
procured? What about the stoppage of the cup?
And why was it not offered afresh? There is much
that might be said; but I shall not lay myself open to
the charge of wishing to say something while saying
nothing. The facts are their own defence. I assert
that the youth spoken of, who, according to you, expired immediately after draining the cup, did not die
on that day at all. It is a monstrous accusation and
a shameless falsehood. I say that when he came to
the breakfast he was suffering from indigestion; he
indulged his appetites too freely at the time, as young
men like him will do; and he died in consequence after
a few days' illness. Who will vouch for this? The
same man who will vouch for his own sorrow — his
father — the young man's father, I repeat. He who
for his grief of heart could have been induced by a
very faint suspicion to come forward on the other side
as a witness against A. Cluentius, gives him the support of his testimony instead. Read it. And do you,
sir,[1] if you please, stand up for a little, and endure the
pang of this indispensable allusion; on which I shall
not linger any longer, since by acting like the excellent
man you are, you have not permitted your sorrow to
involve the guiltless in the calamity of a baseless accusation.

I have still one similar charge remaining, gentlemen,
which will enable you thoroughly to appreciate the
truth of what I said in the beginning of my speech —
that whatever misfortune A Cluentius has seen during

[1] Balbutius' father

these past years, whatever anxiety and trouble he has had at this time, has been entirely due to the machinations of his mother. You allege that Oppianicus [1] lost his life by poison given him in a piece of bread by one M. Asellius, an intimate friend of his, who acted, you say, at the instigation of Habitus. Now I have first to ask what motive Habitus had for wishing to take the life of Oppianicus? I admit, indeed, that they had been at enmity. But it is either from feelings of fear or of hatred that men desire the death of their enemies; and what fear, I ask, could have prompted Habitus to seek to perpetrate such a monstrous crime? Was there any reason why any one should be afraid of Oppianicus now that he had been punished for his crimes and banished the country? What had he to fear? The attack of a ruined man? Impeachment by a felon? Harm from the evidence of an outlaw? If again it was because he hated his enemy that Habitus desired his death, was he such a fool as to think that the life which Oppianicus was then living — condemned, an outlaw, forsaken by all — was worthy of the name, when, owing to the monstrosity of his character, no one would receive him into his house, no one would go near him, no one would speak to him, no one would look at him? And was it to this man that Habitus grudged his life? If he hated him bitterly and with all his heart, ought he not to have wished him to live as long as possible? Was his enemy to hasten his death — death that in his troubles was for him the only refuge from misfortune? Why, had he possessed a spark of spirit or courage, he would have died by his own hand, as many brave men in like afflictions

[1] Cicero now comes to the principal charge against his client, the alleged poisoning of his stepfather, Oppianicus

have done before him , and wherefore should his enemy
have wished to put in his way what he ought to have
desired for himself? As it is, I wonder what evil
death has brought him ! Unless indeed, carried away
by idle tales, we imagine that he is suffering in the
nether world the punishment of the wicked, and that
he has fallen in with more enemies there than he left
behind him here ; that by the avenging furies of his
mother-in-law,[1] of his wives, of his brother, and of his
children, he has been driven headlong into the place
where the ungodly have their home. If, however,
these representations are untrue, as all must know they
are, what, I ask, has death taken away from him save
the sensation of misery ?

But again, by whom was the poison administered ?
By M. Asellius. What connection had he with Habitus ? None ; in fact, as he was very intimate with
Oppianicus, he was more probably even on bad terms
with him. Did he then choose the person who, as he
knew, was anything but friendly to himself, and who
was an intimate acquaintance of his intended victim,
to be the instrument of his own crime and of the jeop-
ardy of his foe ? Then why do you,[2] whom filial piety
has prompted to undertake this prosecution, suffer this
Asellius to go so long unpunished ? Why have you
not followed the example of Habitus, and so secured,
by the conviction of the man who proffered the poison,
a previous verdict prejudicing my client ? Again how
incredible it is, gentlemen, that poison should have
been administered in a piece of bread ! how unusual !
how strange ! Could it diffuse its effects more readily

[1] Oppianicus was said to have poisoned her as well as many others
of his relatives

[2] Oppianicus' son

thus than in a draught, or more widely when concealed
in a portion of bread than if it had been entirely dissolved in a liquid? Could it make its way into the
veins and into every part of the body more quickly
when taken in food than when taken in drink?
Would it be more likely, in the event of discovery, to
escape detection in the bread than in the draught,
where it would have been so mixed as to be altogether
incapable of separation? " But he died a sudden
death." Even had that been the case, it would nevertheless, owing to the frequency of such occurrences,
furnish no adequate ground at all for suspecting poison;
and even if there were room for such a suspicion it
would nevertheless fall on others before my client.
But it is just here that men lie in the most shameless
way, as you will see if you listen to the story of his
death, and of how after his death a charge against
Habitus was raked up by his mother.

Wandering an outlaw from place to place, and finding no entertainment anywhere, Oppianicus betook
himself to C. Quinctius,[1] in the Falernian territory;
there his illness began, and he remained for a long time
seriously indisposed. Sassia, who was with him, under
the idea that the purity and legitimacy of the marriage
tie had been set aside by her husband's conviction, was
holding closer intercourse with Sex. Albius, a lusty
yeoman who used to keep company with her, than her
husband, with all his looseness, could have endured in
the days of his prosperity; and much of this Nicostratus, a faithful slave of Oppianicus, very inquisi-
tive and very truthful, is said to have reported to
his master. Meanwhile Oppianicus began to recover.
Unable to put up any longer with the unconscionable

---

[1] He had been Oppianicus' counsel.

conduct of the Falernian yeoman, he set out for Rome, where he used to have some hired lodgings outside the city gates; but falling from his horse, he is said to have struck his side violently, in bad health as he was, and to have died a few days after reaching the city in a fever. Such, gentlemen, are the circumstances of his death. Either they involve no suspicion at all, or, if they do, it hangs upon some domestic tragedy comprised within the four walls of his house.

On his decease that abominable woman began at once to plot against her son. She resolved to hold an inquest on her husband's death. Having bought from A. Rupilius, who had been the medical attendant of Oppianicus, one Strato, — as if forsooth she entertained the same design as Habitus when he bought Diogenes,[1] — she gave out that she intended to examine Strato by torture, as well as Ascla, one of her own slaves; and she further called on young Oppianicus to give up for like examination the slave Nicostratus, whom she suspected of having been too communicative in his excessive fidelity to his master. At that time Oppianicus was but a boy; and being told that it was about his father's death that the inquest was to be held, he did not dare refuse, though he believed the slave had been well disposed to his father and was so also to himself. The friends and guest-friends of Oppianicus and of the woman herself are called together in large numbers, men of reputation and of every kind of distinction; and in the rigid inquiry which ensues all sorts of instruments of torture are brought into requisition. The slaves were wrought on both by hope and by fear to make them say something on the rack; but

[1] The slave of Cluentius' physician, whose coöperation Oppianicus' agent had tried to procure in attempting Cluentius' life

I suppose it was the high character of the spectators, and the intensity of the torture that led them to hold by the truth and to protest that they had nothing to tell. So by the advice of the friends the inquiry was adjourned for that day. After a considerable interval they are summoned a second time; the examination is begun over again, and all the most powerful and agonizing tortures are applied. Unable to stand it any longer, the witnesses expostulate. The bloodthirsty and unnatural woman is beside herself with rage at the utter disappointment of her designs; and though now the torturer and his very instruments were wearied out, she refused to desist. Then one of the spectators, a man whom his country had honored with high office, and who was personally of the most exalted worth, remarked that he saw her object was not to find out the truth, but to force them to make some false deposition. With this the rest agreed, and so it was unanimously resolved that, in their opinion, the inquiry had gone on long enough. Nicostratus is given back to Oppianicus, and Sassia herself departs with her people for Larinum, grieved at the thought that her son would now surely be beyond the reach of danger. Not even the fictions of suspicion, she reflected, far less a regular accusation, could touch him; and not even his mother's secret plottings, to say nothing of the open attack of his enemies, had been able to do him harm. On her arrival at Larinum, she who had pretended that she was fully convinced that Strato had in time past administered poison to her husband, forthwith made him a present of a shop in the town, equipped and fitted up for the practice of medicine.

For one, two, three years Sassia kept quiet; it seemed as if she were praying and desiring that some disaster might come upon her son, rather than planning and contriving it. In the interval, during the consulship of Q. Hortensius and Q. Metellus, designing to draw him on to this prosecution, though his attention was otherwise occupied and nothing was further from his thoughts, she betrothed to Oppianicus here, against his will, the daughter whom she had borne to her son-in-law,[1] in the hope that these matrimonial bonds, as well as the fetters of an expectant heir, would put him in her power. About this very time Doctor Strato committed a domestic theft, aggravated by murder, under the following circumstances There was in the house a cabinet which he knew contained a considerable sum in gold and silver. So by night he killed two of his fellow-slaves in their sleep, and flung them into the fishpond: and then, cutting out the bottom of the box with his own hands, he removed 150,000 sesterces[2] and five pounds' weight of the gold, one of the slaves, a mere boy, being privy to the deed. Next day the theft was discovered, and suspicion was directed exclusively against the slaves who were missing. But on noticing that the bottom of the box had been cut out, men began to ask by what means it could have been done; and one of Sassia's friends recollected that he had lately seen for sale at an auction, among other small effects, a bent crooked little saw, with teeth all over it, by which he thought the part removed could have been cut out. To be brief, on inquiry being made of the collectors,[3] it is discovered that the saw in question had found its way into the hands of Strato. This

---

[1] Sassia had induced A Aurius Melinus, her daughter's husband, to put away his wife, and marry her

[2] About $6000

[3] Those who collected the money from purchasers at public auctions

aroused suspicion; and when Strato was openly charged
with the crime, the boy who had been his accomplice
became greatly terrified and made a clean breast of the
matter to his mistress. The bodies were found in the
fishpond. Strato was thrown into prison, and fur-
thermore the money, though by no means all of it, is
discovered in his shop.

A criminal investigation is instituted into the theft.
What else can one suppose? Do you tell me that
after the pillaging of the box, the abstraction of the
money (which was not all recovered), and the murder
of the slaves, it was concerning the death of Oppianicus that the inquiry was appointed? Can you satisfy
any one of this? Is there anything more improbable
that you could have brought forward? To pass over
other points, was inquiry held into the death of Oppianicus three years after his decease? Aye, and even
on this occasion, inflamed by her former hatred, she
again demanded Nicostratus for a groundless examination. At first Oppianicus refused; but afterwards,
when she threatened to take away her daughter and
alter her will, a most faithful slave, to humor a most
bloodthirsty woman, was by him not given up for examination but simply handed over to the executioner.

Well, then, after an interval of three years, the
inquiry into her husband's death was reopened. Who
were the slaves examined? A fresh charge was alleged,
I suppose, and suspicion was directed against fresh
persons — Strato and Nicostratus? What! had not
these men been examined at Rome? Can it be that
you, Sassia, with guilt now to aggravate the distemper
that had before infuriated your woman's heart, after
having held an inquiry at Rome at which it had been
determined, on the representation of T. Annius, L.

Rutilius, P. Saturius, and the other honorable men, that the thing had evidently gone on long enough — can it be, I ask, that three years afterward, without inviting the presence, I shall not say of any man, or you might perhaps retort that the yeoman was in attendance, but of any respectable man, you attempted, about the same matter and on the same persons, to hold an inquiry that involved capital consequences to your son? Or do you say (for a possible argument occurs to me though you must remember that it has not yet been put forward) that it was when investigation was being made into the theft that Strato made a confession about the poison? In this very way, gentlemen, does it happen that truth raises her head out of the depths to which depravity ofttimes weighs her down, and the defence of innocence that has been stifled breathes again. Either cunning rogues have no daring in proportion to their invention, or they whose audacity is conspicuous and prominent have no knavish arts by which to back it. But if craft were daring or audacity cunning, resistance would be hardly possible. Was the theft not committed? Why, nothing was more notorious at Larinum. Then did suspicion not attach to Strato? Why, the saw was his accuser, and the boy who had been his accomplice informed on him. Was this not the object of the inquiry? What other ground, then, was there for holding it? Will you not have to say what Sassia said more than once at the time — that when investigation was being made about the theft Strato while on the rack made a statement about the poison? Here we have an instance of what I said above: the woman has audacity enough and to spare, but is wanting in prudence and tact. Several minutes of the depositions made at the inquiry are brought forward; they have been read aloud and communicated to you, and they are the very minutes which she said were attested by the signature of the witnesses at the inquiry. But in them not a syllable about the theft is to be found. It never occurred to her first to write out Strato's deposition about the theft, and afterwards to tack on some statement about the poison which might seem not to have been elicited by direct questioning, but to have been wrung from him in his agony. The subject of the inquiry is the theft. The suspicion of poisoning had been done away with by the previous inquiry, as, indeed, the woman herself had admitted; for after deciding at Rome, on the representation of her friends, that it had gone far enough, she had during the three years that followed shown a fondness for this Strato above all her slaves, holding him in high esteem, and conferring on him every mark of favor. Well, then, the inquiry was being made about the theft — the theft, namely, which beyond all dispute he had committed — did he without saying a word upon the subject of that inquiry make a statement at once about the poison? If he did not speak of the theft when one might have expected him to do so, did he never, even at the end, or in the middle, or at least in some part or other of the inquiry, say a single word about it?

You see now, gentlemen, that with the same hand with which, if opportunity were given her, she would gladly slay her son, this abominable woman has forged her account of the inquiry. And even with regard to it, can you mention the name of any single individual who witnessed it with his hand and seal? You will find no one, except perhaps a person [1] whose charac-

---

[1] The Falernian yeoman, Sassia's paramour.

ter is such that I should prefer his being brought
forward to no name being mentioned at all. What
say you, T. Accius?[1] Are you actually bringing
before a court a capital charge, a criminal information, a written instrument involving the fortunes of
another, without giving the name of any voucher for
that instrument, of any one who sealed it, of any
one who witnessed its signature? And will this honorable court admit the weapon which you have drawn
forth from a mother's bosom for the ruin of a most
guiltless son? But enough; the document has no
weight. As to the inquiry itself, however, why was
it not reserved for the court? why not for the friends
and guest-friends of Oppianicus, whom she had invited to be present on the former occasion? why not
at least for the existing conjuncture? What was done
with these men? I ask you, Oppianicus, to say
what happened to your slave, Nicostratus. You were
shortly about to impeach my client, and you ought
therefore to have brought him to Rome, allowed him
to give information, aye, and preserved him in safety
for examination, for this court, and for this occasion.
As to Strato, gentlemen, I have to inform you that
he was crucified after having had his tongue cut out,
as is known to every one at Larinum. It was not her
own evil conscience that the distraught woman feared,
it was not the detestation of the townsmen, it was
not the public scandal. Just as if every one were not
to be a witness to her crime, what she dreaded was
lest the dying words of a slave should testify against
her.

Gracious Heaven! what a prodigy have we in this
woman! Where in the whole world can we point to

[1] He was conducting the prosecution

such a monster of iniquity, where to such a hateful
and horrible abomination as having ever had its birth?
Surely you see now, gentlemen, that it was only under
constraint of the weightiest reasons that I spoke as I
did of a mother at the beginning of my speech. Yes,
there is no form of evil or of crime that she has not
from the first desired, longed for, contrived, and put into
execution against her son. I say nothing of her first
outrageous lust, I say nothing of her accursed union
with her son-in-law, I say nothing of how a mother's
passion drove a daughter from her husband's arms; all
this, though it brought dishonor on the whole family, did
not go so far as to put my client in danger of his life.
I do not arraign her second marriage with Oppianicus,
by contracting which — but not till he had given her
his children's lives in pledge [1] — she plunged a family
in mourning for the death of those who should have
been her step-sons. I pass by the fact that, though she
knew that it was Oppianicus who had procured the
proscription and assassination of A. Aurius, whose
mother-in-law once and whose wife she herself but a
short time before had been, she chose for herself a
habitation and a home in which the tokens of her husband's death and his despoiled estate would day by
day be present to her eyes. My first charge relates to
the criminal attempt at poisoning by Fabricius,[2] which
has now at length been brought to light. What was
even at that early date matter of suspicion to men in
general, and of incredulity to my client, now appears
evident and obvious to all : the mother cannot of course
have been kept in ignorance of that attempt. Oppi-

---

[1] Oppianicus was charged with having removed his widower's en-
cumbrance on Sassia's request

[2] Oppianicus' agent in the attempt on Cluentius' life.

anicus contrived nothing apart from the woman's coöperation. Had he acted alone, she would surely have left him after the detection of his design, and left him not as one separating herself from a wicked husband, but as fleeing from a most ruthless foe ; she would surely have turned her back for all time upon a house that was a very sink of iniquity. But so far was she from doing this that from that time forth she lost no opportunity of hatching some plot or other, devoting all her powers of thought every day and every night to the destruction of the son of her bosom. And first, by way of nerving Oppianicus there for the prosecution of her son, she bound him to herself by gifts and presents, bestowing on him her daughter's hand in marriage, and holding out the hope of succession to her estate.

Thus whereas in most cases, when unaccustomed enmity has sprung up among kinsmen, we see divorces and the severing of relationships ensue, this woman thought that no one would be strong enough for the prosecution of her son except one who had previously taken his sister [1] to wife. New relationships often lead others to lay aside long-standing animosities ; she thought that in the bond of relationship she would have a pledge that would give a backbone to her feud. Nor did she bestow all her pains on securing a prosecutor for her son ; she also pondered with what weapons she could furnish him. To this end it was, that by means of threats and promises alike she worked upon the slaves ; to this end did she hold those everlasting and more barbarous inquests on the death of Oppianicus, which were at last brought to a close not by any moderation on her part, but by the influence

[1] Auria, Cluentius' half-sister.

of her friends. In the same inquiry originated the
inquiries held three years afterward at Larinum ; in
the same distraction of mind the forgery of the depositions there made ; in the same frenzy also the execrable amputation of Strato's tongue. She it was, in
short, who found and got ready all the materials of
this elaborate indictment. And after dispatching
thus equipped to Rome a prosecutor for her son, she
herself tarried awhile at Larinum in order to seek out
and hire witnesses ; but on being informed of the near
approach of the defendant's trial, she hastened hither
with all speed, for fear that the prosecution might
fail in diligence, or else that the witnesses might want
money, or that she might perchance miss seeing this
man's garb of mourning,[1] and his unkempt appearance, a spectacle so dear to her mother's heart.

But what, think you, were the circumstances which
attended her journey to the capital? I live in the
neighborhood of Aquinum and Fabrateria,[2] and from
many citizens I have heard and ascertained the facts.
What crowds ran together in these towns! What
loud groans were uttered alike by the men and by
the women! The idea of a lady of Larinum actually
setting out for Rome from the very shores of the Adriatic, with a crowd of attendants and a store of money,
in order to be able more readily to compass in a capital trial the ruin and destruction of her son! There
was, I might almost say, not a man among them but
thought that every spot on which she had set her
foot would require to be freed from pollution ; not a
man but thought that the footprints of that crime-
stained mother were a profanation to the earth, the

---

[1] Accused persons wore a dark-colored toga.
[2] Towns in Latium, not far from Arpinum, Cicero's birthplace.

mother of all. So in no town was she permitted to
make a halt.   Inns were there in abundance, but nowhere was there found a host who did not shun the
contagion of her presence. She preferred to intrust
herself to the solitude of night rather than to any
city or hostelry. And thinks she now that any one of
us are unaware of her schemes, her intrigues, her daily
stratagems? Full well we know those whom she has
approached, to whom she has promised money, whose
honesty she has attempted to shake by proffers of
reward ; aye, and we have heard of her nightly sacrifices, which she imagines are a secret, of her impious
prayers and her abominable vows, by which she makes
the very gods in heaven witnesses to her crime; not
knowing that it is piety, and holy fear, and the prayers
of the righteous that avail to turn their hearts, not
the defilements of superstition, nor the blood of victims sacrificed for the furtherance of crime. Her
unnatural frenzy I am confident the immortal gods
have spurned from their altars and their shrines

Do you, gentlemen, whom fortune has appointed to
play the part of another Providence to A Cluentius
here for all the rest of his life, ward off from the person of her son the monstrous inhumanity of this mother.
Men have often on the bench pardoned the offences of
children out of compassion for their parents ; do not
you, we pray you, sacrifice to his mother's unnatural
cruelty the life this man has most virtuously led, especially as you may see a whole township arrayed in
evidence against her. You must know, gentlemen,
that all the men of Larinum — incredible though it
is, I say it in all truth — all who were able made the
journey to Rome, to give my client, so far as in them
lay, the support of their sympathy and numbers in

this hour of danger. Their town has at this time been committed to the care of the women and children, and is at present under the protection, not of its ordinary defenders, but only of the general peace which prevails in Italy. And yet even they, no less than these whom you see here in court, are kept day and night in suspense and disquietude about the issue of this trial. For in their view it is not on the fortunes of a single townsman that you are about to give verdict, but on the standing of the whole municipality, on its credit, and the whole body of its interests. Gentlemen, the defendant is conspicuous for devotion to the public good of his town, for kindliness to the inhabitants individually, for righteousness and conscientiousness towards all men ; and he moreover maintains in his own circle the position of high rank bequeathed him by his forefathers in such a way as to emulate their gravity, their force of character, their popularity, their generosity. And therefore do they in the name of the community pronounce his eulogy in language which not only expresses their deliberate opinion of his character, but bears witness also to their solicitude and sorrow ; and while this eulogy is being read I must ask you who have brought it to stand up. From the tears of those present, gentlemen, you may infer that when they passed this decree every member of the town council was also in tears. Again as to the neighbors, what enthusiasm, what incredible goodwill, what anxiety do they display ! They have not sent in writing the panegyric they decreed, but have instructed men of the highest reputation, well known to all of us, to be present here in large numbers and to pronounce his eulogy in person. Illustrious citizens of Ferentum [1] are here in court, and men of the Mar-

---

[1] In Apulia

rucini[1] no less distinguished than they ; from Teanum
Apulum[2] and from Luceria[2] you see honorable Roman knights come to speak his praise ; from Bovia-
num and from the length and breadth of Samnium
most flattering panegyrics have been forwarded, and
men of the highest consideration and renown have
also come in person.   And as to those who have property, business avocations, or grazing stock in the territory of Larinum, honorable men of the highest distinction, it were hard to speak of their solicitude and
anxiety.   Few, I think, are loved by one as this man
is by them all.   How sorry I am that L. Volusienus, a
man of the greatest distinction and worth, is not present at this trial !   Would that P. Helvidius Rufus,
an eminently illustrious Roman knight, could be here
when I speak his name !   Sleepless day and night in
my client's interests, while he was instructing me in the
case he fell seriously and dangerously ill : and yet even
in his illness he is as anxious about the defendant's
safety as about his own recovery.   His evidence and
eulogy will make you aware of no less enthusiasm on
the part of that excellent and honorable senator Cn.
Tudicus.   Of you, P. Volumnius, I speak in the same
expectation but with greater reserve, inasmuch as you
are on the jury in this case.   To be brief, the whole
neighborhood, I tell you, cherishes the greatest good-
will towards the defendant.   Their unanimous enthusiasm, solicitude, and painstaking care ; my exertions
— and I have pleaded this case from beginning to end
single-handed, as I have long been wont to do ; and
also the justice and clemency of this court, are combated by one woman, the defendant's mother.   And

---

[1] Their territory extended along the right bank of the river Ater-
nus to the Adriatic Sea

[2] In Apulia.

what kind of mother? You see how she is carried
along in all the blindness of cruelty and crime. No
depths of dishonor have ever proved a hindrance to
her lust. In the depravity of her mind she has overturned in the foulest manner all the binding ordinances of society, too infatuated to be called a human
being, too outrageous for the name of woman, too unnatural for that of mother. Aye, and she has ever
confounded the designations of kinship as well as the
name and ordinances of nature. Her son-in-law's
wife, a step-mother to her son, the mistress of her
daughter's husband, she has, in a word, sunk so low
as to have nothing left her in the likeness of man
except her external form.

Now by your hate of crime, gentlemen, debar a
mother from access to the life-blood of her son. In-
flict on her who gave him birth the pang, incredible as
it is, of seeing the deliverance and triumph of her offspring; suffer the mother to depart vanquished by
your justice, and so deprive her of the joy of being bereft of her child. And again, by that love which, if
true to your nature, you have for honor, truth, and
virtue, raise at length from the ground the suppliant
now before you, after so many years of groundless
prejudice and peril. Now for the first time since the
avaricious conduct of others fanned that prejudice into
flame has he begun to take heart, and in reliance on
your impartiality in some degree to breathe again, for-
getting fear. His all is in your hands; many there
are who desire his deliverance, but you alone are able
to secure it. Habitus entreats you, gentlemen, and
beseeches you with tears not to sacrifice him to the
prejudice which in courts of law ought to be of no
avail; not to the mother whose vows and prayers you

must put far from your minds; not to the execrable Oppianicus, a convicted criminal now in his grave. But if at this trial the stroke of some disaster lay my guiltless client low, then will he verily in his wretchedness — if indeed he continue to live, which it will be hard for him to do — often bitterly lament that the poison of Fabricius was ever detected. For had it not been exposed at the time it would have been to this most miserable man, not poison, but the antidote of his many sorrows; aye, and his mother might perchance have followed in his funeral procession, counterfeiting grief for the death of her son. But as it is what good will have been done, save that it will seem as if his life were preserved only for affliction out of the midst of deathful snares — only that in death he might be robbed of the sepulchre of his fathers? Long enough has he been in trouble, gentlemen; years enough has he suffered from prejudice. None save her who gave him birth was ever so bitter against him but that we may believe his vengeance is now fully satisfied. Do you who are just towards all men, who tenderly sustain all those that are cruelly assailed, preserve A. Cluentius. Restore him to his townsmen unharmed; give him back to the friends, the neighbors, the guest-friends of whose zeal for him you are witnesses; lay him under an eternal obligation to yourselves and your children. To you, gentlemen, this appertains, to your dignity, your clemency; with justice do we require you to deliver at last from his distresses a most worthy and altogether guiltless man, and one who to very many people is most beloved and dear. Thus will you give all men to know that, while prejudice may find a place in public meetings, truth reigns supreme in courts of law.

W PETERSON

FRIENDSHIP [1]

(De Amicitia, VI -IX)

Laelius. Friendship is nothing else than entire fellow-feeling as to all things, human and divine, with mutual good-will and affection , and I doubt whether anything better than this, wisdom alone excepted, has been given to man by the immortal gods. Some prefer riches to it ; some, sound health ; some, power ; some, posts of honor , many, even sensual gratification. This last properly belongs to beasts ; the others are precarious and uncertain, dependent not on our own choice so much as on the caprice of Fortune. Those, indeed, who regard virtue as the supreme good are entirely in the right ; but it is virtue itself that produces and sustains friendship, nor without virtue can friendship by any possibility exist. In saying this, however, I would interpret virtue in accordance with our habits of speech and of life ; not defining it, as some philosophers do, by high-sounding words, but numbering on the list of good men those who are commonly so regarded, — the Pauli, the Catos, the Galli, the Scipios, the Phili. Mankind in general are content with these. Let us then leave out of the account such good men as are nowhere to be found. Among such good men as there really are, friendship has more advantages than I can easily name. In the first place, as Ennius says : —

> " How can life be worth living, if devoid
> Of the calm trust reposed by friend in friend ?

[1] This dialogue is part of the output of the years 45 and 44, which Cicero devoted almost exclusively to literature. The interlocutors are Laelius, the intimate friend of Scipio the younger, and his two sons-in-law Fannius and Scaevola

What sweeter joy than in the kindred soul,
Whose converse differs not from self-communion ? "

How could you have full enjoyment of prosperity, unless with one whose pleasure in it was equal to your
own ?   Nor would it be easy to bear adversity, unless
with the sympathy of one on whom it rested more
heavily than on your own soul.   Then, too, other objects of desire are, in general, adapted, each to some
specific purpose, — wealth, that you may use it;
power, that you may receive the homage of those around
you ; posts of honor, that you may obtain reputation ;
sensual gratification, that you may live in pleasure ;
health, that you may be free from pain, and may have
full exercise of your bodily powers and faculties.   But
friendship combines the largest number of utilities.
Wherever you turn, it is at hand.   No place shuts it
out.   It is never unseasonable, never annoying.   Thus,
as the proverb says, " You cannot put water or fire to
more uses than friendship serves."   I am not now
speaking of the common and moderate type of friendship, which yet yields both pleasure and profit, but of
true and perfect friendship, like that which existed in
the few instances that are held in special remembrance.
Such friendship at once enhances the lustre of prosperity, and by dividing and sharing adversity lessens
its burden.

Moreover, while friendship comprises the greatest
number and variety of beneficent offices, it certainly
has this special prerogative, that it lights up a good
hope for the time to come, and thus preserves the
minds that it sustains from imbecility or prostration in
misfortune.   For he, indeed, who looks into the face
of a friend beholds, as it were, a copy of himself.   Thus
the absent are present, and the poor are rich, and the

weak are strong, and — what seems stranger still — the dead are alive, such is the honor, the enduring remembrance, the longing love, with which the dying are followed by the living ; so that the death of the dying seems happy, the life of the living full of praise. But if from the condition of human life you were to exclude all kindly union, no house, no city, could stand, nor, indeed, could the tillage of the field survive. If it is not perfectly understood what virtue there is in friendship and concord, it may be learned from dissension and discord. For what house is so stable, what state so firm, that it cannot be utterly overturned by hatred and strife ? Hence it may be ascertained how much good there is in friendship. It is said that a certain philosopher [1] of Agrigentum sang in Greek verse that it is friendship that draws together and discord that parts all things which subsist in harmony, and which have their various movements in nature and in the whole universe. The worth and power of friendship, too, all mortals understand, and attest by their approval in actual instances. Thus, if there comes into conspicuous notice an occasion on which a friend incurs or shares the perils of his friend, who can fail to extol the deed with the highest praise? What shouts filled the whole theatre at the performance of the new play of my guest and friend Marcus Pacuvius, when — the king not knowing which of the two was Orestes [2] — Pylades said that he was Orestes, while Orestes persisted in asserting that he was, as in fact he was, Orestes ! The whole assembly rose in applause at this

[1] Empedocles, born about 485 B. c

[2] The friendship of Orestes and Pylades was proverbial. On this occasion each insisted that he should be the one to suffer. The king referred to is Thoas, of the Tauric Chersonesus

mere fictitious representation. What may we suppose that they would have done, had the same thing occurred in real life? In that case Nature herself displayed her power, when men recognized that as rightly done by another, which they would not have had the courage to do themselves. Thus far, to the utmost of my ability, as it seems to me, I have given you my sentiments concerning friendship. If there is more to be said, as I think that there is, endeavor to obtain it, if you see fit, of those who are wont to discuss such subjects.

Fannius. But we would rather have it from you. Although I have often consulted those philosophers also, and have listened to them not unwillingly, yet the thread of your discourse differs somewhat from that of theirs.

Scaevola. You would say so all the more, Fannius, had you been present in Scipio's garden at that discussion about the republic, and heard what an advocate of justice he showed himself in answer to the elaborate speech of Philus.

Fannius. It was indeed easy for the man preëminently just to defend justice.

Scaevola. As to friendship, then, is not its defence easy for him who has won the highest celebrity [1] on the ground of friendship maintained with preëminent faithfulness, consistency, and probity?

Laelius. This is, indeed, the employing of force; for what matters the way in which you compel me? You at any rate do compel me; for it is both hard and unfair not to comply with the wishes of one's sons-in-law, especially in a case that merits favorable consideration.

---

[1] He refers to the great friendship of Laelius and Scipio

In reflecting, then, very frequently on friendship, the foremost question that is wont to present itself is, whether friendship is craved on account of conscious infirmity and need, so that in bestowing and receiving the kind offices that belong to it each may have that done for him by the other which he is least able to do for himself, reciprocating services in like manner; or whether, though this relation of mutual benefit is the property of friendship, it has yet another cause, more sacred and more noble, and derived more genuinely from the very nature of man. Love, which in our language gives name [1] to friendship, bears a chief part in unions of mutual benefit; for a revenue of service is levied even on those who are cherished in pretended friendship, and are treated with regard from interested motives. But in friendship there is nothing feigned, nothing pretended, and whatever there is in it is both genuine and spontaneous. Friendship, therefore, springs from nature rather than from need, — from an inclination of the mind with a certain consciousness of love rather than from calculation of the benefit to be derived from it. Its real quality may be discerned even in some classes of animals, which up to a certain time so love their offspring, and are so loved by them, that the mutual feeling is plainly seen, — a feeling which is much more clearly manifest in man, first, in the affection which exists between children and parents, and which can be dissolved only by atrocious guilt; and in the next place, in the springing up of a like feeling of love, when we find some one of manners and character congenial with our own, who becomes dear to us because we seem to see in him an illustrious example of probity and virtue. For there

[1] *Amor, amicitia*

is nothing more lovable than virtue, — nothing which more surely wins affectionate regard, insomuch that on the score of virtue and probity we love even those whom we have never seen. Who is there that does not recall the memory of Caius Fabricius, of Manius Curius, of Tiberius Coruncanius, whom he never saw, with some good measure of kindly feeling? On the other hand, who is there that can fail to hate Tarquinius Superbus, Spurius Cassius, Spurius Maelius? Our dominion in Italy was at stake in wars under two commanders, Pyrrhus and Hannibal. On account of the good faith of the one,[1] we hold him in no unfriendly remembrance; the other because of his cruelty our people must always hate.

But if good faith has such attractive power that we love it in those whom we have never seen, or — what means still more — in an enemy, what wonder is it if the minds of men are moved to affection when they behold the virtue and goodness of those with whom they can become intimately united?

Love is, indeed, strengthened by favors received, by witnessing assiduity in one's service, and by habitual intercourse; and when these are added to the first impulse of the mind toward love, there flames forth a marvellously rich glow of affectionate feeling. If there are any who think that this proceeds from conscious weakness and the desire to have some person through whom one can obtain what he lacks, they assign, indeed, to friendship a mean and utterly ignoble origin, born, as they would have it, of poverty and neediness. If this were true, then the less of resource one was conscious of having in himself, the better fitted would he be for friendship. The contrary is the

---

[1] Pyrrhus, King of Epirus, who invaded Italy in 280 B C.

case ; for the more confidence a man has in himself,
and the more thoroughly he is fortified by virtue and
wisdom, so that he is in need of no one, and regards
all that concerns him as in his own keeping, the more
noteworthy is he for the friendships which he seeks
and cherishes. What? Did Africanus[1] need me?
Not in the least, by Hercules. As little did I need
him. But I was drawn to him by admiration of his
virtue, while he, in turn, loved me, perhaps, from some
favorable estimate of my character ; and intimacy
increased our mutual affection. But though utilities
many and great resulted from our friendship, the cause
of our mutual love did not proceed from the hope of
what it might bring. For as we are beneficent and
generous, not in order to exact kindnesses in return
(for we do not put our kind offices to interest), but are
by nature inclined to be generous, so, in my opinion,
friendship is not to be sought for its wages, but because its revenue consists entirely in the love which
it implies. Those, however, who, after the manner of
beasts, refer everything to pleasure, think very differ-
ently. Nor is it wonderful that they do ; for men
who have degraded all their thoughts to so mean and
contemptible an end can rise to the contemplation of
nothing lofty, nothing magnificent and divine. We
may, therefore, leave them out of this discussion.
But let us have it well understood that the feeling of
love and the endearments of mutual affection spring
from nature, in case there is a well-established assurance of moral worth in the person thus loved. Those
who desire to become friends approach each other,
and enter into relation with each other, that each
may enjoy the society and the character of him whom

[1] Scipio

he has begun to love; and they are equal in love, and on either side are more inclined to bestow obligations than to claim a return, so that in this matter there is an honorable rivalry between them. Thus will the greatest benefits be derived from friendship, and it will have a more solid and genuine foundation as tracing its origin to nature than if it proceeded from human weakness. For if it were utility that cemented friendships, an altered aspect of utility would dissolve them. But because nature cannot be changed, therefore true friendships are eternal. This may suffice for the origin of friendship, unless you have, perchance, some objection to what I have said.

ANDREW P. PEABODY.

LETTERS [1]

TO CN. POMPEIUS MAGNUS, IN ASIA

(Fam. V , 7.) [2]

ROME, B. C. 62

M. TULLIUS CICERO, son of Marcus, greets Cn. Pompeius, son of Cneius, Imperator.

If you and the army are well I shall be glad. From your official dispatch I have, in common with every one else, received the liveliest satisfaction; for you

---

[1] In the Letters Mr. E. S Shuckburgh's translation has been used, except in the case of Fam XIV , 2, where Mr. G E. Jeans's version has been given   The chronological order has been followed.

[2] This letter, one of the collection *Ad Familiares*, was written shortly after Pompey's dispatches, containing the news of his victory over Mithridates, had been received at Rome

have given us that strong hope of peace, of which, in sole reliance on you, I was assuring every one. But I must inform you that your old enemies [1] — now posing as your friends — have received a stunning blow by this dispatch, and, being disappointed in the high hopes they were entertaining, are thoroughly depressed. Though your private letter to me contained a somewhat slight expression of your affection, yet I can assure you it gave me pleasure : for there is nothing in which I habitually find greater satisfaction than in the consciousness of serving my friends ; and if on any occasion I do not meet with an adequate return, I am not at all sorry to have the balance of kindness in my favor. Of this I feel no doubt — even if my extraordinary zeal in your behalf has failed to unite you to me — that the interests of the state will certainly effect a mutual attachment and coalition between us. To let you know, however, what I missed in your letter I will write with the candor which my own disposition and our common friendship demand. I did expect *some* congratulation in your letter on my achievements,[2] for the sake at once of the ties between us and of the Republic. This I presume to have been omitted by you from a fear of hurting any one's feelings. But let me tell you that what I did for the salvation of the country is approved by the judgment and testimony of the whole world. You are a much greater man than Africanus,[3] but I am not much inferior to Laelius either ; and when you come home you will recognize that I have acted with such prudence

[1] Caesar and his party

[2] Cicero had written him an account of his suppression of the Catilinarian conspiracy.

[3] Scipio, whose name, together with that of Laelius, has been already mentioned in connection with the dialogue *On Friendship*.

and spirit, that you will not be ashamed of being coupled with me in politics as well as in private friend ship.

TO HIS WIFE AND FAMILY IN ROME [1]

(Fam. XIV., 2)

THESSALONICA, B. C. 58.

I SEND this, my dear Terentia, with much love to you, and my little Tullia, and my Marcus.

I hope you will never think that I write longer letters to other people, unless it so happens that any one has written to me about a number of matters that seem to require an answer. In fact, I have nothing to say, nor is there anything just now that I find more difficult. But to you and my dear little girl I cannot write without shedding many tears, when I picture to myself, as plunged in the deepest affliction, you whom my dearest wish has been to see perfectly happy ; and this I ought to have secured for you ; yes, and I would have secured, but for our being all so faint-hearted.

I am most grateful to our friend Piso [2] for his kind services. I did my best to urge that he would not forget you when I was writing to him : and have now thanked him as in duty bound. I gather that you think there is hope of the new tribunes ; that will be a safe thing to depend on, if we may on the profession of Pompeius, but I have my fears of Crassus. It is true I see that everything on your part is done both bravely and lovingly, nor does that surprise me, but what pains me is that it should be my fate to expose you to such severe suffering to relieve my own. For Publius Vale-

---

[1] Written during his exile.   [2] Tullia's husband

rius, who has been most attentive, wrote me word, and it cost me many tears in the reading, how you had been forced to go from the temple of Vesta to the Valerian office.[1] Alas, my light, my love, whom all used once to look up to for relief!—that you, my Terentia, should be treated thus; that you should be thus plunged in tears and misery, and all through my fault! I have indeed preserved others, only for me and mine to perish.

As to what you say about our house [2]—or rather its site—I for my part shall consider my restoration to be complete only when I find that it has been restored to me. But these things are not in our hands: what troubles me is, that in the outlay which must be incurred you, unhappy and impoverished as you are, must necessarily share. However, if we succeed in our object, I shall recover everything; but then, if ill-fortune continues to persecute us, are you, my poor dear, to be allowed to throw away what you may have saved from the wreck? As to my expenses, I entreat you, my dearest life, to let other people, who can do so perfectly if they will, relieve you; and be sure as you love me not to let your anxiety injure your health, which you know is so delicate.[3] Night and day you are always before my eyes! I can see you making every exertion on my behalf, and I fear you may not be able to bear it. But I know well that all our hopes are in you; so be very careful of your

[1] Terentia's half-sister Fabia was a Vestal, and it is possible that she had taken refuge with her. The "Valerian office" was probably a bank, where she was required to make a declaration about her husband's property.

[2] His house on the Palatine had been destroyed and a temple of Liberty built on its site

[3] Terentia is said to have lived to the age of 103.

health, that we may be successful in what you hope
and are working for.

As far as I know there is nobody I ought to write
to except those who write to me, or these whom you
mention in your letters. Since you prefer it I will
not move any further from here, but I hope you will
write to me as often as possible, especially if we have
any surer grounds for hoping. Good bye, my dar-
lings, good bye.

TO ATTICUS IN ITALY, ON HIS JOURNEY TO ROME

(Att. IV., 4 b.)

ANTIUM,[1] B. C. 56.

IT will be delightful if you come to see us here.
You will find that Tyrannio[2] has made a wonderfully
good arrangement of my books, the remains of which
are better than I had expected. Still, I wish you would
send me a couple of your library slaves for Tyrannio
to employ as gluers,[3] and in other subordinate work,
and tell them to get some fine parchment[4] to make
title-pieces, which you Greeks, I think, call "sillybi."
But all this is only if not inconvenient to you.
In any case, be sure you come yourself, if you can
halt for a while in such a place, and can persuade
Pilia[5] to accompany you. For that is only fair, and

---

[1] A town in Latium, on the Mediterranean, where one of Cicero's
villas was situated.

[2] His librarian.

[3] Their duty would be to glue together the separate leaves of papy-
rus used in making up a roll.

[4] A strip of parchment, on which the title of the book was written,
was attached to the roll.

[5] Atticus' wife.

Tullia is anxious that she should come. My word! You have purchased a fine troop![1] Your gladiators, I am told, fight superbly. If you had chosen to let them out you would have cleared your expenses by the last two spectacles. But we will talk about this later on. Be sure to come, and, as you love me, see about the library slaves.

TO CAESAR, IN GAUL

(Fam. VII., 5.)[2]

ROME, B. C. 54.

CICERO greets Caesar, *imperator*. Observe how far I have convinced myself that you are my second self, not only in matters which concern me personally, but even in those which concern my friends. It had been my intention to take Gaius Trebatius with me for whatever destination I should be leaving town, in order to bring him home again honored as much as my zeal and favor could make him. But when Pompey remained home longer than I expected, and a certain hesitation on my part (with which you are not unacquainted) appeared to hinder, or at any rate to retard, my departure, I presumed upon what I will now explain to you. I begin to wish that Trebatius should look to you for what he had hoped from me, and in fact. I have been no more sparing of my promises of good-will on your part than I had been wont to be of my

---

[1] Atticus speculated in gladiators

[2] A letter of recommendation in behalf of C. Trebatius Testa, the jurist We have seventeen letters of Cicero addressed to him, most of them written in a semi-humorous strain, and all indicating a close friendship between the two men

own.   Moreover, an extraordinary coincidence has
occurred which seems to support my opinion and to
guarantee your kindness.   For just as I was speaking
to our friend Balbus about this very Trebatius at my
house, with more than usual earnestness, a letter from
you was handed to me, at the end of which you say:
" Miscinius Rufus, whom you recommend to me, I
will make king of Gaul, or, if you choose, put him
under the care of Lepta.[1]   Send me some one else to
promote."   I and Balbus both lifted our hands in
surprise: it came so exactly in the nick of time, that
it appeared to be less the result of mere chance than
something providential.   I therefore send you Trebatius, and on two grounds, first that it was my spontaneous idea to send him, and secondly, because you
have invited me to do so.   I would beg you, dear
Caesar, to receive him with such a display of kindness as to concentrate on his single person all that
you can be possibly induced to bestow for my sake
upon my friends.   As for him I guarantee — not in the
sense of that hackneyed expression of mine, at which,
when I used it in writing to you about Milo, you very
properly jested, but in good Roman language such as
sober men use — that no honester, better, or more
modest man exists.   Added to this, he is at the top
of his profession as a jurisconsult, possesses an un-
equalled memory, and the most profound learning.
For such a man I ask neither a tribuneship, prefec-
ture, nor any definite office, I ask only your good-will
and liberality: and yet I do not wish to prevent your
complimenting him, if it so please you, with even
these marks of distinction.   In fact, I transfer him
entirely from my hand, so to speak, to yours, which is

[1] A friend of Cicero's, who was with Caesar in Gaul

as sure a pledge of good faith as of victory. Excuse my being somewhat importunate, though with a man like you there can hardly be any pretext for it — however, I feel that it will be allowed to pass. Be careful of your health and continue to love me as ever.

TO HIS BROTHER QUINTUS, IN GAUL

(Q Fr III., 7)

Tusculum,[1] b. c 54.

AT Rome, and especially on the Appian road as far as the temple of Mars, there is a remarkable flood. The promenade of Crassipes has been washed away, pleasure grounds, a great number of shops. There is a great sheet of water right up to the public fishpond. That doctrine of Homer's is in full play: —

> " The days in autumn when in violent flood
> Zeus pours his waters, wroth at sinful men " —

for it falls in with the acquittal of Gabinius —

> " Who wrench the law to suit their crooked ends
> And drive out justice, recking naught of Gods."

But I have made up my mind not to care about such things. When I get back to Rome I will write and tell you my observations, and especially about the dictatorship, and I will also send a letter to Labienus and one to Ligurius. I write this before daybreak by the carved wood lampstand, in which I take great delight, because they tell me that you had it made when you were at Samos. Good-bye, dearest and best of brothers.

[1] About ten miles southeast of Rome. Cicero had a villa there.

TO C. TREBATIUS TESTA, IN GAUL

(Fam VII, 16)

ROME, B. C. 54.

IN the " Trojan Horse," [1] just at the end, you remember the words, " Too late they learn wisdom."
You, however, old man, were wise in time.   Those first
snappy [2] letters of yours were foolish enough, and
then . . . !   I don't at all blame you for not being
over-curious in regard to Britain. [3]   For the present,
however, you seem to be in winter quarters somewhat
short of warm clothing, and therefore not caring to
stir out: —

> " Not here and there, but everywhere,
>   Be wise and ware.
> No sharper steel can warrior bear "

If I had been by way of dining out, I would not have
failed your friend Cn. Octavius ; to whom, however, I
did remark upon his repeated invitations, " Pray, who
are you ? "   But, by Hercules, joking apart, he is a
pretty fellow : I could have wished you had taken him
with you !   Let me know for certain what you are doing and whether you intend coming to Italy at all this
winter.   Balbus has assured me that you will be rich.
Whether he speaks after the simple Roman fashion,
meaning that you will be well supplied with money, or
according to the Stoic dictum, that " all are rich who
can enjoy the sky and the earth," I shall know here-

---

[1] A play by one of the earlier Roman dramatists, either Livius or
Naevius

[2] The first letters written by Trebatius after going to Gaul seem to
have been full of complaints

[3] Trebatius did not cross the Channel.

after. Those who come from your part accuse you of pride, because they say you won't answer men who put questions to you. However, there is one thing that will please you : they all agree in saying that there is no better lawyer than you at Samarobriva !

TO ATTICUS IN ROME

(Att. V., 1)

MINTURNAE,[1] B. C. 51.

YES, I saw well enough what your feelings were as I parted from you; what mine were I am my own witness. This makes it all the more incumbent on you to prevent an additional decree being passed, so that this mutual regret of ours may not last more than a year. As to Annius Saturninus, your measures are excellent. As to the guarantee,[2] pray, during your stay at Rome, give it yourself. You will find several guarantees on purchase, such as those of the estates of Mennius, or rather of Attilius. As to Oppius,[3] that is exactly what I wished, and especially your having engaged to pay him the 800 sestertia,[4] which I am determined shall be paid in any case, even if I have to borrow to do so, rather than wait for the last day of getting in my own debts. I now come to that last line of your letter written crossways, in which you give me a word of caution about your sister.[5] The facts of the matter are these. On arriving at my place at Ar-

[1] In Latium, on the Via Appia. The letter was written by Cicero on his way to Cilicia, whither he was going as proconsul.
[2] Of the title to some property that Cicero was selling
[3] The agent of Caesar
[4] About $34,000
[5] Atticus' sister Pomponia was the wife of Cicero's brother Quintus.

pinum, my brother came to see me, and our first subject of conversation was yourself, and we discussed it
at great length.   After this I brought the conversation
round to what you and I had discussed at Tusculum,
on the subject of your sister.   I never saw anything so
gentle and placable as my brother was on that occasion
in regard to your sister : so much so, indeed, that if
there had been any cause of quarrel on the score of expense, it was not apparent.   So much for that day.
Next day we started from Arpinum.   A country festival caused Quintus to stop at Arcanum ; I stopped
at Aquinum ; but we lunched at Arcanum.   You know
his property there.   When we got there Quintus said,
in the kindest manner, " Pomponia, do you ask the
ladies in ; I will invite the men."   Nothing, as I
thought, could be more courteous, and that, too, not
only in the actual words, but also in his intention and
the expression of face.   But she, in the hearing of us
all, exclaimed, " I am only a stranger here ! "   The
origin of that was, as I think, the fact that Statius had
preceded us to look after the luncheon.   Thereupon
Quintus said to me, " There, that's what I have to put
up with every day ! "   You will say, " Well, what does
that amount to ? "   A great deal ; and, indeed, she
had irritated even me : her answer had been given
with such unnecessary acrimony, both of word and look.
I concealed my annoyance.   We all took our places at
table except her.   However, Quintus sent her dishes
from the table, which she declined.   In short, I thought
I never saw anything better-tempered than my brother,
or crosser than your sister : and there were many par-
ticulars which I omit that raised my bile more than
they did that of Quintus himself.   I then went on to
Aquinum ; Quintus stopped at Arcanum, and joined

me early the next day at Aquinum. He told me that
she had refused to sleep with him, and when on the
point of leaving, she behaved just as I had seen her.
Need I say more? You may tell her herself that in
my judgment she showed a marked want of kindness
on that day. I have told you this story at greater
length, perhaps, than was necessary, to convince you
that you, too, have something to do in the way of giving her instruction and advice.

There only remains for me to beg you to complete
all my commissions before leaving town; to give
Pomptinus [1] a push, and make him start; to let me
know as soon as you have left town, and to believe
that, by heaven, there is nothing I love and find more
pleasure in than yourself.

I said a most affectionate good-bye to that best of
men, A. Torquatus, at Minturnae, to whom I wish you
would remark, in the course of conversation, that I
have mentioned him in my letter.

CICERO AND HIS SON TO TERENTIA AND TULLIA, IN ROME [2]

(Fam XIV., 14.)

MINTURNAE, B C. 49.

TULLIUS to Terentia, her father to Tullia, his two
sweethearts, and Cicero to his excellent mother and
darling sister, send warm greetings. If you are well,
we are so too. It is now for you to consider, and not

---

[1] An old friend of Cicero's, who was to be one of his lieutenants in
Cilicia

[2] Cicero had taken part in the general flight from Rome that followed the news of Caesar's having crossed the Rubicon.

for me only, what you must do.   If Caesar means to
come to Rome in a peaceable manner, you can stay at
home with safety for the present : but if in his madness he is going to give up the city to plunder, I fear
Dolabella [1] himself may not be able to protect us sufficiently.   Besides, I am alarmed lest we should be cut
off from you, so that when you do wish to leave town
you may be prevented.   There is one other thing,
which you are in the best position to observe yourselves
— are other ladies of your rank remaining in Rome ?
If not, it deserves consideration whether you can do so
with propriety.   As things stand at present, indeed,
always provided that I am allowed to hold this district,
you will be able to stay with me or on one of our estates with the greatest comfort.   There is another
thing I am afraid of — a want of provisions in the city
before long.   On these points pray consult with Pom-
ponius,[2] with Camillus, with anybody you think right :
above all don't be frightened.   Labienus has made
things better for us.   Piso, too, is helpful in quitting
the city and declaring his own son-in-law guilty of
treason.   Do you, dear hearts, write to me as often as
possible, and tell me how you are and what is going
on around you.   Quintus and his son and Rufus send
their love.   Good-bye !

[1] Tullia's second husband, who belonged to Caesar's party.
[2] Atticus.

TO ATTICUS IN ROME [1]

(Att VII, 20.)

CAPUA, B. C 49.

I HAVE no choice but to be brief. I have given up all hope of peace, and as to war, our men are not stirring a finger. Don't, pray, suppose that our consuls care for anything less than that: though it was in hopes of hearing something and learning what preparations we were making that I came to meet them in a pelting rain on the 4th, according to orders. They, however, had not arrived, and were expected on the 5th — empty-handed and unprepared. Pompey, again, is said to be at Luceria, and on his way to join some cohorts of the Appian legions, which are far from being in a very satisfactory state. But he,[2] they say, is hurrying along and is expected at Rome every hour, not to fight a battle — for who is there to fight with? — but to prevent the flight from town. For myself, if it is to be in Italy — " if die I must," etc.! I don't ask your advice about that: but if it is to be outside Italy — what can I do? On the side of remaining there are the winter season, my lictors, the improvidence and carelessness of our leaders: on the side of flight, my friendship for Pompey, the claims of the loyalist cause, the disgrace of having anything to do with a tyrant; as to whom it is uncertain whether he will copy Phalaris or Pisistratus.[3] Pray unravel these

[1] One of the many letters in which Cicero asks Atticus for advice and guidance He complains of the apathy of the consuls, comparing it with Caesar's energetic movements

[2] Caesar

[3] Tyrants of Agrigentum and Athens respectively.

perplexities for me, and help me with your advice, though I expect by this time you are in a warm corner yourself at Rome. However, do the best you can. If I learn anything fresh to-day, I will let you know. For the consuls will be here directly on the 5th, the date they fixed themselves. I shall look for a letter from you every day. But do answer this as soon as you can. I left the ladies and the two boys at For-miae.

SERVIUS SULPICIUS[1] TO CICERO, AT ASTURA [2]

(Fam. IV., 5)

ATHENS, B. C. 45.

WHEN I received the news of your daughter Tullia's death, I was indeed as much grieved and distressed as I was bound to be, and looked upon it as a calamity in which I shared. For if I had been at home, I should not have failed to be at your side, and should have made my sorrow plain to you face to face. That kind of consolation involves much distress and pain, because the relations and friends, whose part it is to offer it, are themselves overcome by an equal sorrow. They cannot attempt it without many tears, so that they seem to require consolation themselves rather than to be able to afford it to others. Still I have decided to set down briefly for your benefit such

[1] The collection of letters *Ad Familiares* includes many letters to Cicero by various correspondents. Among the best known is this letter of consolation written by the distinguished jurist and orator Servius Sulpicius Rufus, on the death of Cicero's daughter, Tullia.

[2] Cicero had a villa upon an island at the mouth of the Astura, a river in Latium flowing into the Mediterranean

thoughts as have occurred to my mind, not because I
suppose them to be unknown to you, but because your
sorrow may perhaps hinder you from being so keenly
alive to them.

Why is it that a private grief should agitate you
so deeply? Think how fortune has hitherto dealt
with us. Reflect that we have had snatched [1] from us
what ought to be no less dear to human beings than
their children — country, honor, rank, every political
distinction. What additional wound to your feelings
could be inflicted by this particular loss? Or where is
the heart that should not by this time have lost all
sensibility and learn to regard everything else as of
minor importance? Is it on her account, pray, that
you sorrow? How many times have you recurred to
the thought — and I have often been struck with the
same idea — that in times like these theirs is far from
being the worst fate to whom it has been granted
to exchange life for a painless death? Now what was
there at such an epoch that could greatly tempt her to
live? What scope, what hope, what heart's solace?
That she might spend her life with some young and
distinguished husband? How impossible for a man
of your rank to select from the present generation of
young men a son-in-law, to whose honor you might
think yourself safe in trusting your child! Was it
that she might bear children to cheer her with the
sight of their vigorous youth? who might by their
own character maintain the position handed down to
them by their parent, might be expected to stand for
the offices in their order, might exercise their freedom
in supporting their friends? What single one of these
prospects has not been taken away before it was given?

---

[1] By the triumph of the Caesarian party

But, it will be said, after all it is an evil to lose one's children.   Yes, it is: only it is a worse one to endure and submit to the present state of things.

I wish to mention to you a circumstance which gave me no common consolation, on the chance of its also proving capable of diminishing your sorrow.   On my voyage from Asia, as I was sailing from Aegina towards Megara, I began to survey the localities that were on every side of me.   Behind me was Aegina, in front Megara, on my right Piraeus, on my left Corinth: towns which at one time were most flourishing, but now lay before my eyes in ruin and decay.   I began to reflect to myself thus: " Ah! do we manikins feel rebellious if one of us perishes or is killed — we whose life ought to be still shorter — when the corpses of so many towns lie in helpless ruin?   Will you please, Servius, restrain yourself and recollect that you are born a mortal man?"   Believe me, I was no little strengthened by that reflection.   Now take the trouble, if you agree with me, to put this thought before your eyes.   Not long ago all those most illustrious men perished at one blow:[1] the empire of the Roman people suffered that huge loss: all the provinces were shaken to their foundations.   If you have become the poorer by the frail spirit of one poor girl, are you agitated thus violently? If she had not died now, she would yet have had to die a few years hence, for she was mortal born   You, too, withdraw soul and thought from such things, and rather remember those which become the part you have played in life: that she lived as long as life had anything to give her; that her life outlasted that of the Republic; that she lived to see you — her own father — praetor, consul, and augur; that she

---

[1] The defeat of the Pompeians by Caesar at Pharsalus

married young men of the highest rank; that she had
enjoyed nearly every possible blessing; that, when the
Republic fell, she departed from life. What fault
have you or she to find with fortune on this score? In
fine, do not forget that you are Cicero, and a man
accustomed to instruct and advise others; and do not
imitate bad physicians, who in the diseases of others
profess to understand the art of healing, but are unable to prescribe for themselves. Rather suggest to
yourself and bring home to your own mind the very
maxims which you are accustomed to impress upon
others. There is no sorrow beyond the power of time
at length to diminish and soften: it is a reflection on
you that you should wait for this period, and not
rather anticipate that result by the aid of your wisdom. But if there is any consciousness still existing
in the world below, such was her love for you and her
dutiful affection for all her family, that she certainly
does not wish you to act as you are acting. Grant
this to her — your lost one! Grant it to your friends
and comrades who mourn with you in your sorrow!
Grant it to your country, that if the need arises she
may have the use of your services and advice.

Finally — since we are reduced by fortune to the
necessity of taking precautions on this point also — do
not allow any one to think that you are not mourning
so much for your daughter as for the state of public
affairs and the victory of others. I am ashamed to
say any more to you on this subject, lest I should appear to distrust your wisdom. Therefore I will only
make one suggestion before bringing my letter to an
end. We have seen you on many occasions bear good
fortune with a noble dignity which greatly enhanced
your fame: Now is the time for you to convince us that

you are able to bear bad fortune equally well, and that it does not appear to you to be a heavier burden than you ought to think it. I would not have this be the only one of all the virtues that you do not possess.

As far as I am concerned, when I learn that your mind is more composed, I will write you an account of what is going on here, and of the condition of the province. Good-bye.

TO ATTICUS, IN ROME

(Att. XV, 16 a)

Astura, b. c 44

AT length a letter-carrier from my son?[1] And, by Hercules, a letter elegantly expressed, showing in itself some progress. Others also give me excellent reports of him. Leonides,[2] however, still sticks to his favorite " at present." But Herodes[2] speaks in the highest terms of him. In short, I am glad even to be deceived in this matter, and am not sorry to be credulous. Pray let me know if Statius has written to you anything of importance to me.

CICERO, THE YOUNGER, TO TIRO[3]

(Fam. XVI, 21)

Athens, b. c. 44

AFTER I had been anxiously expecting letter-carriers day after day, at length they arrived forty-six

[1] Marcus, who was at the time a student in Athens
[2] Whose lectures Marcus was attending
[3] Cicero's freedman and confidential secretary. It was he who

days after they left you. Their arrival was most welcome to me : for while I took the greatest possible pleasure in the letter of the kindest and most beloved of fathers, still your most delightful letter put a finishing stroke to my joy. So I no longer repent of having suspended writing for a time, but am rather rejoiced at it ; for I have reaped a great reward in your kindness from my pen having been silent. I am therefore exceedingly glad that you have unhesitatingly accepted my excuse. I am sure, dearest Tiro, that the reports about me which reach you answer your best wishes and hopes. I will make them good, and will do my best that this belief in me, which day by day becomes more and more *en évidence*, shall be doubled. Wherefore you may with confidence and assurance fulfil your promise of being the trumpeter of my reputation. For the errors of my youth have caused me so much remorse and suffering, that not only does my heart shrink from what I did, my very ears abhor the mention of it. And of this anguish and sorrow I know and am assured that you have taken your share. And I don't wonder at it! for while you wished me all success for my sake, you did so also for your own ; for I have ever meant you to be my partner in all my good fortunes. Since, therefore, you have suffered sorrow through me, I will now take care that through me your joy shall be doubled. Let me assure you that my very close attachment to Cratippus[1] is that of a son rather than a pupil: for though I enjoy his lectures, I am also specially

---

edited the letters *Ad Familiares* The modern tone of this letter, written by a university student to his father's man of business, will be noticed.

[1] The distinguished Peripatetic philosopher.

charmed with his delightful manners. I spend whole
days with him, and often part of the night: for
I induce him to dine with me as often as possible.
This intimacy having been established, he often drops
in upon us unexpectedly while we are at dinner, and
laying aside the stiff airs of a philosopher joins in our
jests with the greatest possible freedom. He is such
a man — so delightful, so distinguished — that you
should take pains to make his acquaintance at the earliest possible opportunity. I need hardly mention Bruttius,[1] whom I never allow to leave my side. He is a
man of a strict and moral life, as well as being the most
delightful company. For in him fun is not divorced
from literature and the daily philosophical inquiries
which we make in common. I have hired a residence
next door to him, and as far as I can with my poor
pittance [2] I subsidize his narrow means. Further-
more, I have begun practising declamation in Greek
with Cassius ; in Latin I like having my practice
with Bruttius. My intimate friends and daily company are those whom Cratippus brought with him
from Mitylene — good scholars, of whom he has the
highest opinion. I also see a great deal of Epicrates,
the leading man at Athens, and Leonides,[3] and other
men of that sort. So now you know how I am going
on.

You remark in your letter on the character of Gor-
gias.[4] The fact is, I found him very useful in my
daily practice of declamation ; but I subordinated

---

[1] Known only from this passage.

[2] About $4000 a year.

[3] He had written to Cicero somewhat unfavorably about his son.

[4] A distinguished rhetorician but a man of dissolute habits. He
seems to have encouraged young Marcus in dissipation, and Cicero
had objected to his son's intimacy with him.

everything to obeying my father's injunctions, for
he had written ordering me to give him up at once.
I would n't shilly-shally about the business, for fear
my making a fuss should cause my father to harbor
some suspicion. Moreover, it occurred to me that it
would be offensive for me to express an opinion on a
decision of my father's. However, your interest and
advice are welcome and acceptable. Your apology for
lack of time I quite accept; for I know how busy you
always are. I am very glad that you have bought
an estate, and you have my best wishes for the success
of your purchase. Don't be surprised at my congratulations coming in at this point in my letter, for it was
at the corresponding point in yours that you told me
of your purchase. You are a man of property! You
must drop your city manners: you have become a
Roman country gentleman. How clearly I have your
dearest face before my eyes at this moment! For I
seem to see you buying things for the farm, talking
to your bailiff, saving the seeds at dessert in the
corner of your cloak. But as to the matter of money,
I am as sorry as you that I was not on the spot to
help you. But do not doubt, my dear Tiro, of my
assisting you in the future, if fortune does but stand
by me; especially as I know that this estate has been
purchased for our joint advantage. As to my commissions about which you are taking trouble — many
thanks! But I beg you to send me a secretary at
the earliest opportunity — if possible a Greek; for
he will save me a great deal of trouble in copying
out notes. Above all, take care of your health, that
we may have some literary talk together hereafter.
I commend Anteros [1] to you.

[1] The slave who brought the letter.

TO GAIUS TREBONIUS, IN ASIA[1]

(Fam X., 28)

ROME, B. C. 43.

How I could wish that you had invited me to that most glorious banquet on the Ides of March![2] We should have had no leavings![3] While, as it is, we are having such a trouble with them, that the magnificent service which you men then did the state leaves room for some grumbling In fact, for Antony's having been taken out of the way by you, — the best of men, — and that it was by your kindness that this pest still survives, I sometimes do feel, though perhaps I have no right to do so, a little angry with you. For you have left behind an amount of trouble which is greater for me than for every one else put together.

For as soon as a meeting of the senate could be freely held, after Antony's very undignified departure, I returned to that old courage of mine, which along with that gallant citizen, your father, you ever had upon your lips and in your heart. For the tribunes having summoned the senate for the 20th of December, and having brought a different piece of business before it, I reviewed the situation as a whole,[4] and spoke with the greatest fire, and tried all I could to recall the now languid and wearied senate to its ancient and traditional valor, more by an exhibition of high spirit than of eloquence.

[1] Trebonius had taken a prominent part in the conspiracy which resulted in the assassination of Caesar. He afterwards went as proconsul to the province of Asia.

[2] The date of the assassination

[3] Cicero would have had Antony killed too.

[4] The speech alluded to is the third Philippic.

This day and this earnest appeal from me were the first things that inspired the Roman people with the hope of recovering its liberty. And had not I supposed that a gazette of the city and of all acts of the senate was transmitted to you, I would have written you out a copy with my own hand, though I have been overpowered with a multiplicity of business. But you will learn all that from others. From me you shall have a brief narrative, and that a mere summary. Our senate is courageous, but the consulars are partly timid, partly disaffected. We have had a great loss in Servius.[1] Lucius Caesar entertains the most loyal sentiments, but, being Antony's uncle, he refrains from very strong language in the senate. The consuls are splendid. Decimus Brutus is covering himself with glory. The youthful Caesar [2] is behaving excellently, and I hope he will go on as he has begun. You may at any rate be sure of this — that, had he not speedily enrolled the veterans, and had not the two legions transferred themselves from Antony's army to his command, and had not Antony been confronted with that danger, there is no crime or cruelty which he [3] would have omitted to practise. Though I suppose these facts too have been told you, yet I wished you to know them still better. I will write more when I get more leisure.

[1] Servius Sulpicius Rufus, who had died while on an embassy to Antony.

[2] Afterwards Augustus.

[3] Antony

CAESAR

BIOGRAPHICAL SKETCH

INDISPUTABLY the greatest personality in Roman history, Caesar, in addition to his epoch-making achievements as a statesman and as a general, showed throughout his career a keen interest in various branches of literature and science. His writings included commentaries on the Gallic and on the Civil War, a grammatical treatise on Analogy which is said to have been composed during a journey from Italy to Transalpine Gaul, a work dealing with some problems of astronomy, a pamphlet against Cato Minor, written in the camp at Munda in answer to the panegyric which Cicero had published shortly after Cato's suicide at Utica, some poems, and many letters and speeches (Of these the commentaries alone have come down to us) the others being known only through the testimony of contemporary or later authors or from a few fragments which have survived.

He was born in 100 B. C. The Julian gens, to which he belonged, was of patrician rank, and more than one of its members had already attained to the consulship. Of his early life and education, little is known, but one of his tutors is said to have been the Gaul M Antonius Gnipho, a rhetorician of some repute. Through the marriage of his father's sister to Marius, he was during his boyhood and youth brought in close contact with the great popular leader, and this connection undoubtedly did much to develop in him the democratic spirit which helped to make him the idol of the Roman masses. His wife was Cornelia, the daughter of Cinna, the famous adherent of Marius. He began his military service under M. Minucius Thermus in Asia. On his return to Rome in 78, he came forward with an accusation of extortion against Cn. Dolabella, who had been proconsul of Macedonia. Although unsuccessful in this and in a similar attempt directed against Gaius Antonius, formerly proconsul in Greece, his speeches won high praise, and he was regarded as one of the best orators of the time. He subsequently pursued his rhetorical studies under Molon at Rhodes. After holding office as quaestor, aedile, and praetor, he went in 61 to Further Spain as propraetor. The year 60 saw the formation of the first triumvirate, which made him, together with Pompey and Crassus, supreme in the state. Consul in 59, he was in the following year appointed to the proconsulship of Gaul, where he spent the greater part of nine years, actively engaged in military and administrative work. In the mean time a rupture between him and Pompey had taken place. In the Civil War which followed, the victories at Pharsalus (48), Thapsus (46), and Munda (45) made him absolute master of the Roman world. His triumph, however, was short-lived; he was assassinated on the 15th of March, 44.

The commentaries on the Gallic War are a record of his career in Gaul during the years 58–52, and were in all probability written in 51. There are seven books, each giving an account of the events of a single year. The last two years of his command are treated by his lieutenant Hirtius in the eighth book. The gap between the Gallic War and the Civil War, that is, the years 51–49, is filled by the narratives of others of his lieutenants dealing with the Alexandrian, the African, and the Spanish wars. His commentaries on the Civil War consist of three books, the first two taking up the events of 49, the third those of 48. His aim in writing the account of the Gallic War seems to have been to impress the Roman people with the greatness of his services in extending the bounds of their empire. In his work on the Civil War he doubtless desired to show that he had done everything in his power to avert the War.

It is perhaps the element of restraint and reserve that contributes most to the effectiveness of Caesar's style. His narrative, moreover, is marked by a sustained objectivity: he writes as if he had been only a spectator of the events of which he was so great a part. Carefully avoiding all merely rhetorical devices, and using only the purest Latin, he tells his story with the utmost directness, simplicity, and clearness.

THE SIEGE OF ALESIA[1]

Taken from the narrative based on *De Bello Gallico*, VII., 69–89, in T. Rice Holmes' *Caesar's Conquest of Gaul*.

NEXT day the Romans arrived at Alesia, where Vercingetorix was preparing to make his final stand. The column descended a valley closed on the right and the left by the hills of Bussy and Pevenel. On their left front, connected with Pevenel by a broad neck of land, rose a hill, much lower than Gergovia,[2] but still too steep to be taken by assault. The Gauls were swarming on the eastern slope, beneath the scarped rocks of the plateau, on which stood the town; and Vercingetorix had made them build a wall and dig a ditch to protect their encampment. Just at their feet the legions saw a stream, the Oze, winding like a steely thread through the greenery that fringed the north of the hill; and beyond its southern side,

---

[1] Alesia, the capital of the Mandubii, now Alise Ste. Reine on Mont Auxois, west of Dijon, was the scene of the last concerted attempt on the part of the Gauls to free themselves from Roman rule. That this rebellion of 52 B.C., which had begun in the country of the Arverni, the modern Auvergne, became a national one was due very largely to the enthusiastic patriotism and personal magnetism of the young Arvernian chieftain Vercingetorix. It was only after many months of fighting that Caesar forced the rebels to retreat to Alesia.

[2] The capital of the Arverni, upon which Caesar had made an unsuccessful attack.

parallel to the Oze, but invisible, flowed the little river Ozerain. Moving down past the hill of Réa, the soldiers came to a miniature plain, which extended, three miles in length, beneath the western slope of Alesia, and was bounded on its further side by a range of heights; the river Brenne, which received the waters of the Oze and the Ozerain, meandered through it from south to north; and beyond the Ozerain the steep declivities of Flavigny completed the zone of hills.

Caesar harangued his troops and encouraged them to brace themselves for a toilsome effort. As it was evident that the place could not be taken except by a blockade, he drew a line of investment, fully ten miles in length, along which a ring of camps was constructed. Those intended for the cavalry were on low ground, — three in the plain and one in the valley of the Rabutin, which entered the Oze from the north. The rest were strongly placed upon the slopes of the outlying hills. Close to the camps redoubts or blockhouses, twenty-three in all, were thrown up; and strong pickets were placed in them, to guard against any sudden sortie.

Soon after the commencement of the works, Vercingetorix sent all his cavalry down the hill; and a desperate combat was fought in the western plain. Caesar's Gallic[1] and Spanish horse were soon in trouble; and he sent his Germans to reinforce them. The legions were drawn up in front of their camps, to deter the enemy's foot from attempting a sortie. The Gauls were beaten, and galloped back along the valleys of the Oze and the Ozerain, hotly pursued by the Germans: but the gates of the camp being too

[1] Some of the Gauls had adhered to Caesar

narrow, many of the thronging fugitives were cut down, while others threw themselves off their horses and tried to scramble over the wall. The legions, by Caesar's order, moved forward a little. The Gauls inside the wall were smitten with panic: "To arms!" they cried, "To arms!" Many of them fled helter-skelter up the hillside; and Vercingetorix was obliged to shut the gates of the town, for fear the camp should be left unprotected.

He saw with dismay that the toils were closing around him. He had never expected that Caesar, who had failed so ignominiously at Gergovia, would be strong enough to attempt a systematic blockade. But there were now ten legions instead of six; and wherever he looked, over the plain or down in the valleys, there were soldiers at work with axe or spade. There was nothing for it but to appeal to the whole Gallic people to extricate him from the trap in which he was caught. The ring of redoubts was not yet complete: the Romans were far too few to blockade the whole circuit of the mountains: and the cavalry might perhaps steal out in the dark without attracting notice. He charged them to go, each to his own country, and bring back with them every man who could wield a sword. He reminded them of all that he had done for the good cause, and adjured them not to abandon him to the vengeance of the Romans. Everything depended on their using all speed: if they left him to perish, the whole garrison would perish with him. By reducing the rations, he reckoned that he might make the provisions last a little over a month. Silently up each river valley sped the shadowy cavalcade, until it was lost to view.

Caesar learned the whole story from some deserters.

Its only effect was to stimulate his inventive genius. If he could keep the army of Vercingetorix from breaking out, he could also keep the relieving force from breaking in. The most vulnerable part of his position was the open meadow on the western side of the mountain. Across this expanse, from the Oze to the Ozerain, a trench was dug, twenty feet wide with perpendicular sides, to prevent the enemy from attacking the troops while they were constructing the proper works. About four hundred yards behind the ends of this trench, but bending outwards, was traced the line of contravallation, which was prolonged so as to surround Alesia, and ran along the lower slopes of the encircling hills and across the valley of the Rabutin. First of all, two parallel trenches were dug, each fifteen feet wide and eight feet deep, the outer of which extended only across the plain, while the inner, embracing the whole circuit of the hill, was filled, where the level permitted, with water drawn from the Ozerain and the Rabutin. Just behind the outer trench, and also behind that portion of the other which encompassed the rest of the position, a rampart was erected, surmounted by a palisade, with an embattled fence of wattle-work in front, from the bottom of which projected stout forked branches. The combined height of rampart and palisade was twelve feet. Wooden towers were erected upon the western section of the rampart at intervals of eighty feet, and also at certain points along the rest of the contravallation.

To repel the reinforcements for which Vercingetorix had sent, a line of works somewhat similar to these, forming the circumvallation, was traced along the heights of Flavigny, Pevenel and Bussy, and across the intervening valleys and the plain. The circuit of this line was fully ten miles.

But even these works were not deemed sufficient. The Gauls made frequent and furious sallies. Comparatively few of the Romans were available as combatants; for many had to go in quest of corn and timber, while others were laboring on the works. Caesar therefore invented various subsidiary defences. Ditches, five feet deep, were dug just inside the large moat that was filled with water; and five rows of strong boughs were fixed in each, with one end protruding above ground, sharpened and with the branches projecting so as to form a kind of abatis. In front of them and rising a few inches above the ground, but purposely concealed by brushwood, were sharp pointed logs embedded in small pits. In front of these again, concealed, but barely concealed, beneath the turf, were barbed spikes fixed in pieces of wood. Fringed by these formidable defences, Caesar expected that contravallation and circumvallation would be alike impregnable.

Nevertheless, the struggle was likely to be prolonged; and it would certainly tax to the utmost the endurance and the fighting power of the men. As soon as the relieving army should arrive, the Romans would be hemmed in between two desperate enemies. Every moment for preparation was precious. Flying parties scoured the country for corn and provender: but they could not collect a sufficient supply; and the rations had to be reduced. Every day, — even by night, when the moon was up, or in the glow of the watch-fires, — the besieged could see the indefatigable legionaries laboring to finish their works before the time for the great hazard should arrive.

Meanwhile Vercingetorix had abandoned his camp, and withdrawn the troops who occupied it into the town. He took every precaution to husband his scanty resources. He ordered the whole of the grain to be thrown into one common stock and brought to him for safe keeping; and he let it be known that disobedience would be punished with death. From time to time each man received his scanty ration. Meat was tolerably abundant; for the Mandubii had driven large numbers of cattle into the stronghold.

The appeal of Vercingetorix had meanwhile been answered. A council of chieftains met to consider the situation. Vercingetorix, in his great need, had asked for an universal levy: but the cooler judgment of the council rejected his demand. So vast a multitude would become unmanageable; and it would be impossible to find food for so many mouths. It was resolved, therefore, to call upon each tribe for a limited contingent. The summons was obeyed with alacrity; and from north and south and east and west, from the Seine, the Loire and the Garonne, from the marshes of the Scheldt and the Sambre and the mountains of the Vosges and the Cevennes, from the Channel and the Atlantic Ocean, horse and foot came swarming to save the hero of Gaul. But even in this supreme moment, in one instance, tribal jealousy prevailed over patriotism. The Bellovaci peremptorily refused to send a single man. They intended, they said, to attack Caesar on their own account, and had no intention of being dictated to by any one. They consented, however, as a personal favor to Commius, king of the Atrebates, who had great influence with them, to despatch a small contingent. Four generals were chosen; for, except Vercingetorix

himself, there was no one leader of sufficient eminence
to command universal confidence. And, as if this
weakening of authority were not enough, the generals
were fettered by civil commissioners, whose instructions they were to follow in the conduct of the campaign. One of the four was Commius, who had, in
former years, rendered good service to Caesar, but
was now swept away on the wave of patriotic enthusiasm. He had indeed good reason to abhor the Roman name. Just before the outbreak of the rebellion,
Labienus[1] had discovered that he was conspiring
against Caesar, and had sent the tribune Volusenus
to assassinate him. He escaped with a wound ; and
now he saw a prospect of taking his revenge. His
brother generals were Eporedorix and Viridomarus,
representing the Aedui, and Vercassivellaunus, a cousin of Vercingetorix. The vast host mustered in the
country of the Aedui, eight thousand horsemen and
nearly two hundred and fifty thousand foot, and
marched for Alesia in the certain confidence of victory.

By this time the garrison were in great straits.
Their grain was all consumed.[2] Day after day they
strained their eyes, trying to catch a glimpse of the
relieving army: but there was never a sign. At
length the chieftains called a council of war. Some
advised surrender : others were clamorous for a grand
sortie : but one proposal equalled in atrocity the
worst that has been told of Jerusalem or Samaria.
An Arvernian chieftain, called Critognatus, reminded
his hearers that their fathers, when driven into their

[1] At this time Caesar's most trusted officer. At the outbreak of the
Civil War he deserted to Pompey

[2] According to Napoleon I (*Précis des guerres de César*, 1836, p
110), more than 50 days must have elapsed between the departure
of Vercingetorix's cavalry and the arrival of the relieving army

fastnesses by the Cimbri and Teutoni, had sustained life by feeding upon the flesh of those who were useless for warfare; and he urged that, to give the garrison strength to hold out to the last against the tyrants who made war only to enslave, this glorious precedent should be followed. Finally it was decided that all who were too old, too young, or too feeble to fight should be expelled from the town; that those who remained should try every expedient before having recourse to the desperate remedy of Critognatus; but that, if the relieving army failed to arrive in time, they should even follow his counsel rather than surrender. Accordingly the Mandubii, to whom the town belonged, were compelled to depart, with their wives and children. They presented themselves before the Roman lines. Many of them were weeping. They piteously begged the soldiers to receive them as slaves, — only give them something to eat. To grant their prayer was impossible; and a line of guards, whom Caesar posted on the rampart, forbade any attempt to escape.

But suspense was nearly at an end. It was just after the expulsion of the Mandubii when the anxious watchers on the hill saw, moving over the plain, a multitude of cavalry. The infantry were on the heights of Mussy-la-Fosse behind. In a fever of exultation men ran to and fro, exchanging congratulations. The garrison descended the hill, prepared for a sortie. Vercingetorix had forgotten nothing. His men were provided with fascines [1] for filling up the trenches, and movable huts to protect their approach. Soon a fierce combat of horse was raging over the plain. The legionaries were posted, ready for emer-

---

[1] Bundles of sticks.

gencies, along the outer and the inner lines. Archers were scattered among the Gallic ranks; and the arrows fell so thick and fast that scores of wounded horsemen were seen riding off the field. Every man fought like a hero; for they knew that from the heights around friends and enemies alike were anxiously watching. The numbers of the Gauls began to tell; and their countrymen, behind and before, encouraged them by loud yells. All through the afternoon the battle raged uncertain. But towards sunset the ever-victorious Germans charged in a compact body, and threw the division opposed to them into disorder: the archers were exposed and killed: the rout was general; and the besieged who had sallied forth turned in despair, and reascended the hill.

But Commius and his brother generals were still hopeful. Next day their men were hard at work, making fascines and scaling ladders for a grand assault on the Roman lines. About midnight they quitted their camp, and moved in silence across the plain. As they approached the works, they raised a simultaneous shout, to put the besieged on the alert; and, as they flung their fascines into the ditch, the trumpet was heard, calling the garrison to arms. Stones flew from slings: arrows whizzed through the air; and, though the Romans too plied their slings, and supports hurried from the neighboring redoubts to the relief of any point that was too hardly pressed, the enemy were too many for them, and they suffered heavily: but when those ghost-like companies rushed in to storm the rampart, they trod upon the spikes, or, stumbling into the holes, impaled themselves on the pointed logs, while heavy pikes were hurled down from the towers into the seething multitude. The

Roman artillery made great havoc. The losses on either side were very heavy; for they were fighting in the dark, and shields were of little use. Towards dawn the Gauls retreated, fearing an attack in flank; and the besieged, who had lost much valuable time in attempting to cross the inner trench, went back before they could strike a blow.

One more chance remained. The leaders of the relieving army questioned the rustics about the lie of the ground on the north and the nature of the Roman defences. Mont Réa, which bounded the plain and rose above the further bank of the Oze, extended so far to the north that Caesar had not been able to enclose it in his line of circumvallation. On the southern slope, close to the stream, stood one of the Roman camps. It was held by two legions, — perhaps about eight thousand men, — under Reginus and Caninius. In order to avoid observation, it would be necessary to approach the camp by a wide détour. The Gauls sent scouts to reconnoitre. It appeared that Mont Réa was connected by a ridge with a further group of heights. Just after dark sixty thousand picked men, under the command of Vercassivellaunus, left the Gallic camp, and, passing right round the sweep of the northern hills, halted at daybreak for a rest in a hollow north-east of Mont Réa. About noon, just as they were moving down on the camp, the cavalry, by a preconcerted arrangement, streamed over the plain towards the Roman lines: the rest of the infantry showed themselves in front of their encampment; and Vercingetorix, observing these movements from the citadel, descended the hill and moved towards the plain.

This time there was no delay. The inner trench

was filled up, where necessary, with earth and fascines : stout sappers' huts, destined to protect the men when they should approach to storm the lines, long poles fitted with hooks for tearing down the rampart, and other implements which Vercingetorix had provided, were carried across ; and the besieged moved on to make their last effort.

A desperate struggle then began.   Wherever there was a weak spot in the defences, the Gauls threw themselves upon it ; and the Romans, comparatively few in numbers, and scattered owing to the vast extent of their lines, found great difficulty in massing themselves upon the exposed points.   Moreover, they were painfully distracted by the roar of battle in their rear ; for both on the inner and the outer line men felt, as they fought, that they must perish if their comrades behind suffered the enemy to break through.   Yet, agitated as they were, they combated with a nervous eager energy ; and the besieged struggled as desperately as they ; for both knew that that day's fight would decide all : — the Gauls were lost unless they could break the line ; the Romans, if they could but hold that line, saw their long toil at an end.   From the slope of Flavigny, south of the Ozerain, the view from which embraced the whole plain, Caesar directed the battle, and sent supports to every point where he saw his men hard pressed.   The attack on the circumvallation in the plain was comparatively feeble ; for the bulk of the relieving force was formidable only in numbers. Nor were those numbers wisely directed.   The Aedui may have been treacherous : the generals may have disagreed, or they may have been fettered by the civil commissioners ; anyhow the Gauls made no attempt upon the circumvallation, except on Mont Réa

and in the plain. The fighting was fiercest on Mont
Réa. The Gauls were so numerous that Vercassivellaunus could always send fresh men to relieve their
comrades. Coming down on the camp from a higher
level, the assailants hurled their missiles with fatal
momentum : they shot earth in heaps over the pointed
logs and the spikes, and, locking their shields over
their heads, passed unscathed to the rampart ; and,
then their numbers began to tell. Suddenly a gal-
loper rode up and told Caesar that the garrison were
worn out, and their stock of missiles failing. He immediately sent Labienus with six cohorts to the rescue, telling him to hold on as long as he could, and
when he could hold on no longer, to sally forth, and
fight it out in the open. Then, riding down between
the lines on to the plain, he harangued his weary soldiers and adjured them not to give in : just one short
hour, and the prize was won. At last the besieged
abandoned in despair the attempt to break through,
and, wheeling to the left, crossed the Ozerain, and
flung themselves against the works at the foot of Flavigny. They drove the artillerymen from the towers
with volleys of missiles : they shot earth and fascines
into the ditch, and made their way across : they tore
down the palisading of the rampart : six cohorts, then
seven more were sent down to help, and still they
pressed on, — till Caesar himself hurried to the spot
with fresh reinforcements, and drove them away.
Everywhere, except at Mont Réa, the victory was won.
Caesar called out four cohorts from the nearest re-
doubt, told his cavalry to follow him, and sent a horse-
man galloping to the northern cavalry camp to send
another detachment down upon the enemy's rear.
They were now swarming over the rampart : and, as

a last resource, Labienus summoned every available
man from the neighboring redoubts to his aid. By
good luck these reinforcements amounted to eleven
cohorts, — perhaps four thousand men. And now,
conspicuous in his crimson cloak, Caesar was descried,
hurrying across the plain. The enemy made a supreme effort. Labienus and his men took heart, and
rushed into the thick of the stormers. As Caesar approached, he heard the shouts of the combatants: he
saw the camp abandoned and the short swords flashing over the slopes beyond. Suddenly the cavalry
appeared on the heights above the enemy's rear:
Caesar's reserves came up to attack them in front;
and they fled in bewilderment, — into the midst of
the hostile squadrons. Vercassivellaunus himself was
captured, and seventy-four standards; and of the
sixty thousand chosen men who had marched out of
camp the night before only a remnant returned. The
whole scene was visible from the town; and in despair
the officers left in command sent to recall their comrades from below. The vast host without vanished in
the gathering darkness. The legions were too tired
to follow, or all might have been destroyed: but at
midnight the cavalry were sent in pursuit; and when
day broke, they were still hunting the fugitives and
capturing or slaying them in scores.

All was lost: so Vercingetorix clearly saw. In the
night he formed his resolve. Next morning he gathered the tribal chiefs around him. He told them that
he had fought, not for himself but for his countrymen; and, since they must needs all bow to fortune, he
was ready to place himself at their disposal, — to die,
if they wished to appease the Romans by his death,
or to yield himself up as a prisoner of war. They

accepted his offer, and consented to purchase life by sacrificing the leader of their own choice. Ambassadors were sent to learn the pleasure of the conqueror. He ordered the chiefs of the garrison to be brought out, and all the arms to be surrendered. The chiefs were led forth; and Caesar, seated on his tribunal, received their submission. Vercingetorix, mounted on a gaily caparisoned charger, rode round the tribunal, and then, leaping to the ground, took off his armor, laid down his sword, and bowed himself at Caesar's feet. He was sent to Rome, and imprisoned in a dungeon. Six years later he was brought out, to adorn Caesar's triumph; and then he was put to death.

T. RICE HOLMES.

VIRGIL

BIOGRAPHICAL SKETCH

WHILE in true poetic inspiration Virgil does not rank with Lucretius or Catullus, yet in his larger conception of the poet's function, in his more artistic handling of his themes, and in his mastery of technique he is far superior to them. He is a product of the Augustan age, with its more settled political and social atmosphere, its wider culture, and its higher ideals of literary art. We miss, it is true, the individual note that marks the work of some of the earlier poets, but in its place is something of fuller volume, an essentially national tone, emanating from one who was possessed with the idea of his country's greatness. In his *Georgics* he sings the praise of Italian agriculture; his *Aeneid* is a glorification of the Roman race.

He was born in Mantua in 70 B. C. His parents were plebeians, but sufficiently prosperous to give their son a good education. He received his first training at Cremona, went afterwards to Naples, and finally to Rome. How long he remained at the capital on this occasion is not certain, but we know from the *Eclogues* that he was in his native place during the troubles caused by the confiscation of lands in northern Italy for the benefit of the veterans of Octavian [1] after the battle of Philippi in 42 B. C. The soldiers, not satisfied with the lands which had been assigned to them around Cremona, proceeded to seize those near Mantua; and it was only through the protection afforded him by Asinius Pollio, the legate in the district, and afterwards

[1] Afterwards the Emperor Augustus.

by the intervention of Octavian himself, that the poet was secured in the possession of his farm. From this time on he enjoyed the patronage of Maecenas and Octavian, living for the most part either at Naples or at Rome. About 37 B. C., possibly at the suggestion of Maecenas, he began the composition of the *Georgics*, and the next seven years were spent upon this work. The writing of the *Aeneid* followed, and he had devoted eleven years to it when he died in 19 B. C. while returning from a journey to Athens.

Not to mention some minor poems attributed to him, Virgil's works consist of the *Eclogues*, ten in number, the *Georgics*, in four books, and the *Aeneid*, in twelve. The *Eclogues* are either genuine pastoral poems following more or less strictly the form used by his model Theocritus, or pastoral allegories in which, while the speakers are ostensibly shepherds and the pastoral background is preserved, prominent personages of the time are really represented and topics discussed which have no connection whatever with any phase of shepherd life. To the first class the second, third, fifth, seventh, and eighth belong, some of them (the third, seventh, and eighth) showing the amoebaean structure that is characteristic of bucolic poetry. In the second class are the first, the sixth, the ninth, and the tenth. The fourth is altogether outside the bucolic sphere.

The content of the *Georgics* is aptly summed up in the opening lines : —

> What makes the cornfield smile, beneath what star,
> Maecenas, it is meet to turn the sod
> Or marry elm with vine ; how tend the steer ;
> What pains for cattle keeping, or what proof
> Of patient trial serves for thrifty bees, —
> Such are my themes.

Among the many sources used by the poet in the composition of the work we find writers as far removed from one another as Homer and Hyginus. A large element, however, came from his own experience on his Mantuan estate. A striking feature of the poem is the artistic interweaving of episodes having in themselves little or nothing to do with the main theme. The first book, for example, has a fine description of the portents that appeared just after Caesar's assassination; the second, the famous passage in which the praises of Italy are sung; the fourth, the story of Aristaeus. But this is only one of the devices adopted to lighten a theme that in less skilful hands could hardly have failed to become tedious. We have besides many finely elaborated pictures of nature, picturesque descriptions of rural occupations and activities, little touches of realism, wise saws and homely maxims, — all wrought into a perfect whole by the sure hand of the artist.

In the *Aeneid* Virgil enters the epic field. It is the story of the coming of Aeneas of Troy and his followers to Italy, and the founding of the Roman state. In the first six books we are told of the sack of Troy by the Greeks, the flight of Aeneas with a remnant of the Trojans, their long wanderings, their visit to Sicily, their stay at Carthage, and Aeneas' descent into Hades. The second half of the poem describes the wars with the natives, ending with the death of Turnus, the young chieftain of the Rutulians, at the hands of Aeneas.

While we must admit the justice of some of the criticisms of the *Aeneid*, — that the poet has in many passages imitated and even plagiarized from Homer, that there is, especially in the last six books, a lack of that variety of incident which is so characteristic of the Homeric epics, — the poem shows, nevertheless, qualities which give it one of the first places in the list of the world's great epics: descriptive powers of a high order, a wealth of imagery that manifests itself sometimes in similes and metaphors, sometimes in a single word or phrase charged with poetic associations, a rare skill in handling dramatic situations, a perfect mastery of language, and lastly a marvellous command of the dactylic hexameter.

DAMON AND ALPHESIBOEUS [1]

(Eclogue VIII.)

SONGS of the shepherds Damon and Alphesiboeus,
    my theme :
Hearkening to whom with rapture as each in rivalry
    sung,
Heifers forgot their pasture, upon whose melodies
    hung
Lynxes smitten with wonder, and every listening
    stream
Loitered with altered current along its watery way ; 5
Damon and Alphesiboeus shall be our burden to-day.

Sailing already abreast of the great Timavus's hill,[2]
Whether I find thee,[3] or coasting around Illyria still,
Comes not the bright day ever when this poor tongue
    shall be free
Thy fair deeds to proclaim ?   Shall I ne'er at liberty
    be   10
Proudly to waft thy verse o'er earth and her every
    clime,
Only of Athens worthy, and buskin'd tragedy's prime ?
Thou my Muse's beginning, her song shall finish with
    thee.

[1] The Eclogue contains the songs of the two shepherds Damon and Alphesiboeus, the former telling of the faithlessness of his mistress, the latter giving the song of a Thessalian girl who is trying by magic to win back her lover.

[2] The rocks near the mouth of the river Timavus on the north shore of the Adriatic

[3] Pollio, to whom the poem is addressed, was on his way home from a successful campaign in Illyricum, on the east coast of the Adriatic.

Take these strains at thy bidding essayed, and grant
me to lay
Round thy brow these ivies to twine with the conqueror's bay.   15

Hardly as yet from the skies had the night's chill
shadow dispersed,
Dew lay sweet on the spring-tide grass for the cattle
athirst;
Propped on an olive staff thus sang young Damon,
the first:
(*Damon sings.*)
Rise, fair star of the morning, and herald the genial
day.
I, whom a passion for Nysa the false has served to
betray,   20
Here will lament; and to gods — whose presence
attested in vain
Naught has availed me — in death's last hour once
more will complain.
Begin, my flute of the mountains, with me my Maenalus [1] strain.

Maenalus ever has forests that sing to him; ever a
sigh
Speaks in his pines; to the loves of the shepherds he
listens for aye;   25
Hears Pan piping, who brooked not that reeds should
idle remain.
Begin, my flute of the mountains, with me my Maenalus strain.

[1] Mt. Maenalus in Arcadia was a haunt of Pan, the god of shepherds.

Nysa with Mopsus[1] weds ; what next is a lover to
see ?
Soon will the griffin be matched with the mare, and
in summers to be
Timid fawns with the hounds come down to the pools
on the plain. 30
Begin, my flute of the mountains, with me my Maenalus strain.

Hew fresh torches[2] the bridal to grace; thy bride is
in sight,
Mopsus — the bridegroom thou — go scatter the
nuts[3] to her train !
Hesper[4] from Oeta's summit for thee sails into the
night.
Begin, my flute of the mountains, with me my Maenalus strain. 35

Worthy the lord they give thee to wed, who scornest
the world,
Holdest the pipe of the shepherd and these poor goats
in disdain,
Thinkest light of a brow untrimmed and a beard un-
curled,
Deeming the gods untroubled by mortal passion and
pain !
Begin, my flute of the mountains, with me my Maenalus strain. 40

[1] His rival.
[2] The bride was escorted in torchlight procession from her old
home to the bridegroom's house.
[3] Nuts were scattered among those who took part in the procession
[4] The evening star rises over Mt. Oeta   The scene is laid in
Thessaly, which was famous for its witchcraft.

'T was in our crofts I saw thee, a girl thy mother beside,
Plucking the apples dewy, myself thy pilot and
 guide;
Years I had finished eleven, the twelfth was beginning to reign;
Scarce was I able to reach from the ground to the
 branches that snapped.
Ah, when I saw! how I perished! to fatal folly was
 rapt!   45
Begin, my flute of the mountains, with me my Maenalus strain.

Now have I learned what love is. Among rocks savage and wild
Tmaros [1] or Rhodope [1] bare him or far Garamantes [2]
 for child, —
Mortal his lineage is not, nor human blood in his veins.
Begin, my flute of the mountains, with me my Maenalus strains.   50

Fell love taught one mother [3] her sinful hands to
 imbrue
Once in her children's blood, and the mother was
 heartless too.
Heartless the mother most? Or was love more cruel
 and fell?
Cruel was love; thou also, the mother, heartless as
 well.
Begin, my flute of the mountains, with me my Maenalus strain.   55

---

[1] Names of mountains: Tmaros in Epirus, Rhodope in Thrace.
[2] A savage tribe in the interior of Africa.
[3] Medea.

Now let the wolf turn tail to the sheep; oaks stubborn
    have power
Apples golden to bear, on the alder the daffodil
    flower!
Droppings of amber rich from the bark of the tama-
    risk rain;
Screech-owls vie with the swan, and to Orpheus
    Tityrus [1] change;
Orpheus play for the woods, as Arion [2] with dolphins
    range.   60
Begin, my flute of the mountains, with me my Mae-
    nalus strain.

Nay, let the sea drown all. Farewell to the woods.
    I will leap
Here from this mountain crest that for ever watches
    the deep;
This death-song of the dying for last sad gift let her
    keep.
Cease, my flute, it is ended, the Maenalus mountain
    refrain.   65

Thus sang Damon. The answer of Alphesiboeus
    again,
Muses, recount! Frail mortals to all things cannot
    attain.

           (Alphesiboeus sings.)

Fetch me the water; with soft wreaths circle the
    altar divine;
Burn to the gods rich boughs, heap frankincense on
    the fire;

----
[1] Used here for any shepherd

[2] According to the fable he was saved from drowning by a dolphin which he had charmed by his music.

So to the passionless heart of this ice-cold lover of
    mine   70
I may reach with my magic; it is but a chant we
    require.
Homeward bring from the city, my chants, bring
    Daphnis again.

Chants from her heavenly station can draw down even
    the moon !
Circe once with a chant transformed Ulysses' train.
Cold snakes split in the meadows asunder with chant
    and with tune !   75
Homeward bring from the city, my chants, bring
    Daphnis again.

These three threads, each tinted a separate color, I
    twine
Round thee first in a circle; and thrice these altars
    around
Carry the image — a number uneven is dear to the
    shrine ; —
In three knots, Amaryllis,[1] let each of the colours be
    wound.   80
Wind them, prithee, and cry, " I am weaving Venus's
    chain "
Homeward bring from the city, my chants, bring
    Daphnis again.

As in a fire that is one and the same, grows harder
    the clay,
Softer the wax, may Daphnis be wrought by passion
    to-day.

[1] She addresses herself.

Crumble the cake, let the boughs of the bay-tree
    crackle and blaze.   85
Daphnis has fired me with passion, I light over
    Daphnis the bays.
Homeward bring from the city, my chants, bring
    Daphnis again.

May such love upon Daphnis be laid as the heifer's,
    who hies
Wearily after her mate through the forest and hills
    in the quest.   89
Down by the river bank upon greenest sedges she lies,
Lost in her grief, nor remembers at nightfall late to
    arise.
Such may his love be, nor I care ever to heal his
    unrest.
Homeward bring from the city, my chants, bring
    Daphnis again.

These worn garments he left me, my faithless love, as
    he went;
Pledges dear of himself; — by the door let them
    buried remain.   95
Hold them, O Earth! they are pledges, and owe me
    the Daphnis I lent.
Homeward bring from the city, my chants, bring
    Daphnis again.

These green herbs, these poisons from Pontus[1]
    gathered in bloom,
Moeris[2] gave me; in plenty they grow on the Pontus
    plain;

---

[1] On the shores of the Black Sea.
[2] A shepherd and sorcerer.

Often the form of a wolf with these I have seen him
    assume,   100
And in the forests plunge, or the ghosts call forth from
    the tomb,
Often remove to an alien field rich harvests of grain.
Homeward bring from the city, my chants, bring
    Daphnis again.

Carry the ashes without, Amaryllis, and into the brook
Over thy shoulders fling them, nor venture behind
    thee to look!   105
These are for Daphnis; he recks nor of gods nor
    magical strain.
Homeward bring from the city, my chants, bring
    Daphnis again.

Look! As I linger to take it, the cinder itself from
    the grate
Catches the altar with flickering flames. Good luck
    on us wait!
Ay, there is something surely, and Hylax barks at
    the gate!   110
Ought I to hope? Or do lovers their own dreams
    fashion in vain?
Cease, my chants. From the city he comes, my
    Daphnis, again.

Sir Charles Bowen.

RULES OF HUSBANDRY

(Georgics, I., 176–203)

Many the precepts of the men of old,
I can recount thee, so thou start not back,
And such slight cares to learn not weary thee.

And this among the first : Your threshing-floor
With ponderous roller must be levelled smooth,   5
And wrought by hand, and fixed with binding chalk,
Lest weeds arise, or dust a passage win
Splitting the surface, then a thousand plagues
Make sport of it : oft builds the tiny mouse
Her home, and plants her granary, underground,   10
Or burrow for their bed the purblind moles,
Or toad is found in hollows, and all the swarm
Of earth's unsightly creatures ; or a huge
Corn-heap the weevil plunders, and the ant,
Fearful of coming age and penury.   15
Mark too, what time the walnut in the woods
With ample bloom shall clothe her, and bow down
Her odorous branches : if the fruit prevail,
Like store of grain will follow, and there shall come
A mighty winnowing-time with mighty heat ;   20
But if the shade with wealth of leaves abound,
Vainly your threshing-floor will bruise the stalks
Swoln but with chaff.   Many myself have seen
Steep, as they sow, their pulse-seeds, drenching them
With lees of oil and natron, that the fruit   25
Might swell within the treacherous pods, and they
Make speed to boil at howso' small a fire.
Yet, culled with caution, proved with patient toil,
These have I seen degenerate, did not man
Put forth his hand with power, and year by year   30
Choose out the largest.   So, by fate impelled,
Speed all things to the worse, and backward borne
Glide from us ; even as who with struggling oars
Up stream scarce pulls a shallop, if his arms
Relax but for one moment, and the boat   35
Is headlong swept adown the hurrying tide.

JAMES RHOADES

SIGNS OF BAD WEATHER

(Georgics, I, 351–392.)

Ay, and that these things we might win to know
By certain tokens, heats and showers, and winds
That bring the frost, the Sire of all himself
Ordained what warnings in her monthly round
The moon should give, what bodes the south wind's
      fall;   5
What oft-repeated sights the herdsman seeing
Should keep his cattle closer to their stalls.
No sooner are the winds at point to rise,
Than either Ocean's firths begin to toss
And swell, and a dry crackling sound is heard   10
Upon the heights, or one loud ferment booms
The beach afar, and through the forest goes
A murmur multitudinous.   By this
Scarce can the billow spare the curved keels,
When swift the sea-gulls from the middle main   15
Come winging, and their shrieks are shoreward borne,
When ocean-loving cormorants on dry land
Besport them, and the hern, her marshy haunts
Forsaking, mounts above the soaring cloud.
Oft, too, when wind is toward, the stars thou 'lt see   20
From heaven shoot headlong, and through murky
      night
Long trails of fire white-glistening in their wake,
Or light chaff flit in air with fallen leaves,
Or feathers on the wave-top float and play.
But when from regions of the furious North   25
It lightens, and when thunder fills the halls
Of Eurus[1] and of Zephyr, all the fields

[1] The southeast wind.

With brimming dykes are flooded, and at sea
No mariner but furls his dripping sails.
Never at unawares did shower annoy: 30
Or, as it rises, the high-soaring cranes
Flee to the vales before it, or, with face
Upturned to heaven, the heifer snuffs the gale
Through gaping nostrils, or about the meres
Shrill-twittering flits the swallow, and the frogs   35
Crouch in the mud and chant their dirge of old.
Oft, too, the ant from out her inmost cells,
Fretting the narrow path, her eggs conveys;
Or the huge bow sucks moisture; or a host
Of rooks from food returning in long line   40
Clamor with jostling wings.   Now mayst thou see
The various ocean-fowl and those that pry
Round Asian meads[1] within thy freshet-pools,
Cayster, as in eager rivalry,
About their shoulders dash the plenteous spray,   45
Now duck their head beneath the wave, now run
Into the billows, for sheer idle joy
Of their mad bathing-revel.   Then the crow
With full voice, good-for-naught, inviting rain,
Stalks on the dry sand mateless and alone.   50
Nor e'en the maids, that card their nightly task,
Know not the storm-sign, when in blazing crock
They see the lamp-oil sputtering with a growth
Of mouldy snuff-clots.

JAMES RHOADES.

[1] The meadows beside the river Cayster in Ionia.

AFTER CAESAR'S DEATH

(Georgics, I., 466–514.)

HE [1] too it was, when Caesar's light was quenched,
For Rome had pity, when his bright head he veiled
In iron-hued darkness, till a godless age
Trembled for night eternal ; at that time
Howbeit earth also, and the ocean-plains,   5
And dogs obscene, and birds of evil bode
Gave tokens   Yea, how often have we seen
Etna, her furnace-walls asunder riven,
In billowy floods boil o'er the Cyclops' fields,[2]
And roll down globes of fire and molten rocks!   10
A clash of arms through all the heaven was heard
By Germany ; strange heavings shook the Alps.
Yea, and by many through the breathless groves
A voice was heard with power, and wondrous-pale
Phantoms were seen upon the dusk of night,   15
And cattle spake, portentous ! streams stand still,
And the earth yawns asunder, ivory weeps
For sorrow in the shrines, and bronzes sweat.
Up-twirling forests with his eddying tide,
Madly he bears them down, that lord of floods,   20
Eridanus,[3] till through all the plain are swept
Beasts and their stalls together.   At that time
In gloomy entrails ceased not to appear
Dark-threatening fibres, springs to trickle blood,
And high-built cities night-long to resound   25
With the wolves' howling.   Never more than then
From skies all cloudless fell the thunderbolts,

[1] The sun.   An eclipse took place in November of the year of the
assassination, and there were rumors of many portents.
[2] Sicily, the fabled home of the Cyclops.
[3] The river Po.

Nor blazed so oft the comet's fire of bale.
Therefore a second time [1] Philippi saw
The Roman hosts, with kindred weapons rush   30
To battle, nor did the high gods deem it hard
That twice Emathia [2] and the wide champaign
Of Haemus [3] should be fattening with our blood.
Ay, and the time will come when thereanigh,
Heaving the earth up with his curved plough,   35
Some swain will light on javelins by foul rust
Corroded, or with ponderous harrow strike
On empty helmets, while he gapes to see
Bones as of giants from the trench untombed.

JAMES RHOADES.

ITALY

(Georgics, II., 136–176.)

BUT no, not Mede-land with its wealth of woods,
Fair Ganges, Hermus [4] thick with golden silt,
Can match the praise of Italy; nor Ind,
Nor Bactria, [5] nor Panchaia, [6] one wide tract
Of incense-teeming sand.   Here never bulls   5
With nostrils snorting fire upturned the sod
Sown with the monstrous dragon's teeth, nor crop
Of warriors bristled thick with lance and helm;
But heavy harvests and the Massic [7] juice

---

[1] Virgil's geography is vague. The decisive battle between Caesar and Pompey had been fought at Pharsalia in Thessaly. Philippi, where Brutus and Cassius were defeated by Octavian and Antony, was in Macedonia.

[2] A part of Macedonia.

[3] The Balkan range.

[4] A river in Aeolis in Asia Minor

[5] Properly Bactra, the capital of the province of Bactriana in Asia.

[6] The fabulous spice-isle off the coast of Arabia.

[7] Mons Massicus in Campania was famous for its vineyards.

Of Bacchus fill its borders, overspread   10
With fruitful flocks and olives.   Hence arose
The war-horse stepping proudly o'er the plain;
Hence thy white flocks, Clitumnus,[1] and the bull,
Of victims mightiest, which full oft have led,
Bathed in thy sacred stream, the triumph-pomp   15
Of Romans to the temples of the gods.
Here blooms perpetual spring, and summer here
In months that are not summer's; twice teem the
          flocks;
Twice doth the tree yield service of her fruit.
But ravening tigers come not nigh, nor breed   20
Of savage lion, nor aconite betrays
Its hapless gatherers, nor with sweep so vast
Doth the scaled serpent trail his endless coils
Along the ground, or wreathe him into spires.
Mark too her cities, so many and so proud,   25
Of mighty toil the achievement, town on town
Up rugged precipices heaved and reared,
And rivers undergliding ancient walls.
Or should I celebrate the sea that laves   29
Her upper[2] shores and lower?[3] or those broad lakes?
Thee, Larius,[4] greatest and, Benacus,[5] thee
With billowy uproar surging like the main?
Or sing her harbors, and the barrier cast
Athwart the Lucrine,[6] and how ocean chafes
With mighty bellowings, where the Julian wave   35

---

[1] A river of Umbria, in the neighborhood of which a famous breed
of white cattle was reared.

[2] The Adriatic Sea.   [3] The Tyrrhenian Sea
[4] Lago di Como   [5] Lago di Garda.

[6] Lucrinus and Avernus were two small lakes on the Campanian
coast, connected with the sea and with one another by a channel, and
used as a harbor. A strong breakwater had been built by Octavian
on the strip of land that separated Lucrinus from the sea.

Echoes the thunder of his rout, and through
Avernian inlets pours the Tuscan tide?
A land no less that in her veins displays
Rivers of silver, mines of copper ore,
Ay, and with gold hath flowed abundantly.   40
A land that reared a valiant breed of men,
The Marsi [1] and Sabellian youth, and, schooled
To hardship, the Ligurian, and with these
The Volscian javelin-armed, the Decii [2] too,
The Marii and Camilli, names of might,   45
The Scipios, stubborn warriors, ay and thee,
Great Caesar, who in Asia's [3] utmost bounds
With conquering arm e'en now art driving back
The unwarlike Indian from the heights of Rome.
Hail, land of Saturn, [4] mighty mother thou   50
Of fruits and heroes; 't is for thee I dare
Unseal the sacred fountains, and essay
Themes of old art and glory, as I sing
The song of Ascra [5] through the towns of Rome.

JAMES RHOADES.

THE BATTLE OF THE BEES

(Georgics, IV., 67–85.)

BUT if to battle they have hied them forth —
For oft 'twixt king and king with uproar dire

---

[1] The Marsi, Sabelli, and Volscians belonged to the Umbrian stock. The Ligurians were of doubtful origin

[2] Here and in the names that follow the reference is to distinguished Roman families

[3] After the battle of Actium Octavian made a triumphal progress through Syria, Palestine, and Asia Minor.

[4] Saturn was said to have dwelt in Italy during the Golden Age.

[5] A town in Boeotia, the native place of Hesiod, whose *Works and Days* had a strong influence upon Virgil's *Georgics*.

Fierce feud arises, and at once from far
You may discern what passion sways the mob,
And how their hearts are throbbing for the strife;   5
Hark! the hoarse brazen note that warriors know
Chides on the loiterers, and the ear may catch
A sound that mocks the war-trump's broken blasts;
Then in hot haste they muster, then flash wings,
Sharpen their pointed beaks and knit their thews,   10
And round the king, even to his royal tent,
Throng rallying, and with shouts defy the foe.
So when a dry spring and clear space is given,
Forth from the gates they burst, they clash on high;
A din arises; they are heaped and rolled   15
Into one mighty mass, and headlong fall,
Not denselier hail through heaven, nor pelting so
Rains from the shaken oak its acorn-shower.
Conspicuous by their wings, the chiefs themselves
Press through the heart of battle, and display   20
A giant's spirit in each pigmy frame,
Steadfast no inch to yield till these or those
The victor's ponderous arm has turned to flight.

JAMES RHOADES.

AENEAS' DESCENT INTO HADES

(Aeneid, VI.)

WEEPING he spake, then gave to his flying vessels the
     rein,
Gliding at last on the wind to Euboean Cumae's[1]
     plain.

[1] On the coast of Campania. It was colonized from Chalcis in
Euboea

Seaward the bows are pointed, an anchor's hook to
    the land
Fastens the ships, and the sterns in a long line border
    the strand.
Troy's young warriors leap with exultant hearts from
    the bark   5
Forth upon Italy's soil. Some look for the fiery
    spark
Hid in the secret veins of the flint; some scour the
    profound
Forest, and wild beasts' cover, and show where waters
    abound.
While the devout Aeneas a temple seeks on the
    height,
Phoebus's mountain throne, and a cavern vast as the
    night,   10
Where in mysterious darkness the terrible Sibyl[1] lies,
Maiden upon whose spirit the Delian seer[2] of the
    skies
Breathes his immortal thought, and the knowledge of
    doom untold.
Soon they arrive at Diana's grove and her palace of
    gold.

Flying, as legends tell, from the thraldom of Minos[3]
    the king,   15
Daedalus,[4] trusting the heavens, set forth on adven-
    turous wing;
Sailed for the ice-bound north by a way unimagined
    and strange;
Airily poising at last upon this Chalcidian range,

---

[1] The Cumaean Sibyl.   [2] Apollo.
[3] King of Crete.
[4] The famous artisan of Attic and Cretan mythology.

Here first touching the land, to Apollo hallowed his
    light   19
Oarage of wings; and a temple colossal built on the site.
Graved on the doors is the death of Androgeos;[1]
    yonder in turn
Attica's land, condemned each year in atonement to
    yield
Seven of her children; the lots are drawn, still stand-
    ing the urn;
Rising from midmost ocean, to match them, Crete is
    revealed.
Here is the gloomy romance of the bull, Pasiphaë's[2]
    blind   25
Passion; and twiformed Minotaur,[3] two bodies com-
    bined,
Record of lawless love; there, marvellous labor, were
    shaped
Palace and winding mazes,[4] from whence no feet had
    escaped,
Had not Daedalus pitied the lorn princess[5] and her
    love,
And of himself unentangled the woven trick of the
    grove,   30
Guiding her savior's[6] steps with a thread. Thee, too,
    he had wrought,

[1] Son of Minos, killed by the bull of Marathon, with which Aegeus,
king of Attica, had forced him to fight. To avenge his death Minos
made war upon Attica, and compelled the Athenians to send once in
every nine years seven boys and seven girls to Crete, to be devoured
by the Minotaur

[2] Wife of Minos.

[3] A monster with the body of a man and the head of a bull

[4] The Minotaur was kept in the labyrinth built by Daedalus

[5] Ariadne, daughter of Minos, who fell in love with Theseus, son
of Aegeus, when he came from Athens to kill the Minotaur.

[6] Theseus.

Icarus,[1] into the picture, had grief not baffled the
    thought.

Twice he essayed upon gold to engrave thine agony,
    twice

Faltered the hands of the father, and fell. Each
    noble device

Long their eyes had perused, but Achates[2] now is in
    sight ;   35

With him the priestess comes, dread servant of
    Phoebus and Night,

Daughter of Glaucus the seer. To the Trojan mon-
    arch she cries :

" 'T is not an hour, Aeneas, for feasting yonder thine
    eyes.

Better to slaughter from herds unyoked seven oxen
    and seven

Ewes of the yester year, as a choice oblation to
    Heaven."   40

Then, as the ministers hasten the rites ordained to
    prepare,

Into the depth of the temple she bids Troy's children
    repair.

There is a cavern hewn in the mountain's enormous
    side,

Reached by a hundred gates, and a hundred passages
    wide.

Thence roll voices a hundred, the seer's revelations
    divine.   45

When by the doors they stood : " 'T is the hour to
    inquire of the shrine,"

---

[1] Son of Daedalus, who was drowned while attempting to accompany his father's flight from Crete.

[2] Aeneas' faithful companion.

Cried the illumined maiden: "The God! lo, here is
    the God!"
Even as she spake, while still on the threshold only
    she trod,
Sudden her countenance altered, her cheek grew pale
    as in death,
Loose and disordered her fair hair flew, heart panted
    for breath,   50
Bosom with madness heaved. More lofty than wo-
    man's her frame,
More than mortal her voice, as the presence of
    Deity came
Nearer upon her. "And art thou slow to petition
    the shrine,
Troy's Aeneas a laggard at prayer? — nought else
    will incline
This charmed temple," she cries, "its colossal doors
    to unclose."   55
Then stands silent. The veteran bones of the Teu-
    crians[1] froze,
Chilled with terror, and prayer from the heart of the
    monarch arose:
"Phoebus! compassionate ever to Troy in the hour
    of her woe,
Who against haughty Achilles of old didst prosper
    the bow   59
Bent by the Dardan Paris, beneath thine auspices led
Many a sea I have travelled around great continents
    spread,
Far as Massylian[2] tribes and the quicksands lining
    their plain.
Italy's vanishing regions, behold, thy people attain!

[1] The Trojans.
[2] On the north coast of Africa.

Here may the evil fate of the Trojans leave us at last!
Spare, for 't is mercy's hour, this remnant of Per-
 gama's [1] race,   65
Gods and goddesses all, whose jealous eyes in the past
Looked upon Ilion's [1] glories! From thee I implore
 one grace,
Prophet of Heaven, dark seer of the future. Grant
 us the debt,
Long by the destinies owed us — a kingdom promised
 of yore —
Foot upon Latium's borders at length may Teucrians
 set,   70
Bearing their household gods by the tempests tossed
 evermore!
I, their votary grateful, in Phoebus' and Trivia's [2]
 praise
Hewn from the solid marble a glorious fane will raise,
Call by Apollo's name his festival. Also for thee
Shall in our future kingdom a shrine imperial be. 75
There shall thine own dark sayings, the mystic fates
 of our line,
Gracious seer, be installed, and a priesthood chosen
 be thine.
Only entrust not to leaves thy prophecy, maiden
 divine,
Lest in disorder, the light winds' sport, they be
 driven on the air;
Chant thyself the prediction." His lips here ended
 from prayer.   80

Still untamed of Apollo, to stature terrible grown,
Raves the prophetic maid in her cavern, fain to de-
 throne

---

  [1] Troy.   [2] Diana

This great God who inspires her — the more with bit
    doth he school
Fiery mouth and rebellious bosom and mould her to
    rule.
Wide on a sudden the hundred enormous mouths of
    her lair   85
Fly, of themselves unclosing, and answer floats on the
    air:
" Thou who hast ended at last with the dangers dread
    of the sea,
Greater on land still wait thee. Lavinium's[1] kingdom
    afar
Teucria's children shall find — of that ancient terror
    be free —
Yet shall repent to have found it. I see grim visions
    of war,   90
Tiber foaming with blood. Once more shall a Simois[2]
    flow,
Xanthus be there once more, and the tents of a
    Dorian[3] foe.
Yonder in Latium rises a second Achilles,[4] and
    born,
Even as the first, of a goddess; and neither at night
    nor at morn
Ever shall Juno leave thee, the Trojans' enemy
    sworn,   95
While thou pleadest for succor, besieging in misery
    sore
Each far people and city around Ausonia's[5] shore!

[1] The city founded by Aeneas in Latium.
[2] The Simois and Xanthus were the two rivers which flowed
through the Trojan plain.
[3] Greek
[4] Turnus, chief of the Rutuli.
[5] Italy.

So shall a bride [1] from the stranger again thy nation
    destroy,
Once more foreign espousals a great woe bring upon
    Troy.
Yield not thou to disasters, confront them boldly, and
    more   100
Boldly — as fortune suffers — and first from a town
    of the Greek,[2]
Marvel to say, shall be shown thee the way salvation
    to seek."

So from her awful shrine the Cumaean Sibyl intones
Fate's revelation dread, till the cavern echoes her
    groans,
Robing her truths in gloom. So shakes, as she fumes
    in unrest,   105
Phoebus his bridle reins, while plunging the spur in
    her breast.
After her madness ceased and her lips of frenzy were
    still,
Thus Aeneas replied: " No vision, lady, of ill
Comes unimagined now to the exile here at thy door;
Each has he counted and traversed already in spirit
    before.   110
One sole grace I entreat — since these be the gates,
    it is said,
Sacred to Death and the twilight lake by the Acheron [3]
    fed —
Leave to revisit the face of the sire [4] I have loved so
    well ;
Teach me the way thyself, and unlock yon portals of hell.

---

[1] Aeneas married Lavinia, daughter of king Latinus, who had been
previously betrothed to Turnus.

[2] Pallanteum, the city of Evander.

[3] One of the rivers of Hades   [4] Anchises.

This was the sire I bore on my shoulders forth from
    the flame, 115
Brought through a thousand arrows, that vexed our
    flight as we came,
Safe from the ranks of the foeman. He shared my
    journey with me ;
Weak as he was, braved ocean, the threats of sky and
    of sea ;
More than the common strength or the common fate
    of the old.
'T is at his bidding, his earnest prayer long since, I
    am fain 120
Thus in petition to seek thy gate. With compassion
    behold
Father and son, blest maid, for untold thy power, nor
    in vain
Over the groves of Avernus[1] hath Hecate[2] set thee
    to reign.
Grace was to Orpheus granted, his bride from the
    shadows to bring,
Strong in the power of his lyre and its sounding
    Thracian string. 125
Still in his turn dies Pollux,[3] a brother's life to re-
    deem,
Travels and ever retravels the journey. Why of the
    great
Theseus[4] tell thee, or why of Alcides[5] mighty relate ?

[1] Lake Avernus near Cumae, where there was supposed to be an entrance to the lower world
[2] Diana's name in the lower world
[3] Pollux shared his immortality with his brother Castor, who had been born mortal They lived and died alternately
[4] Thesus descended into Hades with Pirithous to assist him in carrying off Proserpina.
[5] Hercules, whose twelfth labor was to bring up the three-headed dog Cerberus from Hades.

My race, even as theirs, is descended from Jove the
    supreme." 129
So evermore he repeated, and still to the altar he clung.
She in reply: " Great Hero, of heaven's high lineage
    sprung,
Son of Anchises of Troy, the descent to Avernus[1] is
    light ;
Death's dark gates stand open, alike through the day
    and the night.
But to retrace thy steps and emerge to the sunlight
    above,
This is the toil and the trouble. A few, whom Jupi-
    ter's love 135
Favors, or whose bright valor has raised them thence
    to the skies,
Born of the gods, have succeeded. On this side
    wilderness lies,
Black Cocytus[2] around it his twilight waters entwines.
Still, if such thy desire, and if thus thy spirit inclines
Twice to adventure the Stygian lake,[3] twice look on
    the dark 140
Tartarus,[4] and it delights thee on quest so wild to
    embark,
Learn what first to perform. On a tree no sun that
    receives
Hides one branch all golden — its yielding stem and
    its leaves —
Sacred esteemed to the queen of the shadows. For-
    ests of night
Cover it, sloping valleys enclose it around from the
    light. 145

[1] Here used to designate the lower world   [2] A river of Hades.
[3] Where the river Styx widened
[4] That part of Hades where the souls of the wicked abode.

Subterranean gloom and its mysteries only may be

Reached by the mortal who gathers the golden growth
of the tree.

This for her tribute chosen the lovely Proserpina[1]
needs

Aye to be brought her.   The one bough broken, another succeeds,

Also of gold, and the spray bears leaf of a metal as
bright.   150

Deep in the forest explore, and if once thou find it
aright,

Pluck it ; the branch will follow, of its own grace and
design,

Should thy destiny call thee ; or else no labor of
thine

Ever will move it, nor ever thy hatchet conquer its
might.

Yea, and the corpse of a friend, although thou know'st
not," she saith,   155

"Lies upon shore unburied, and taints thy vessels
with death,

While thou tarriest here at the gate thy future to
know.

Carry him home to his rest, in the grave his body
bestow ;

Death's black cattle provide for the altar ; give to
the shades

This first lustral oblation, and so on the Stygian
glades,   160

Even on realms where never the feet of the living
come,

Thou shalt finally look."   Then, closing her lips, she
was dumb.

[1] Queen of Hades.

Sadly, with downcast eyes, Aeneas turns to depart,

Leaving the cave ; on the issues dark foretold by her
    words 164

Pondering much in his bosom. Achates, trusty of heart,

Paces beside him, plunged in a musing deep as his
    lord's.

Many the troubled thoughts that in ranging talk they
    pursue —

Who is the dead companion the priestess spake of,
    and who

Yonder unburied lies ? And advancing thither, they
    find

High on the beach Misenus, to death untimely con-
    signed, 170

Aeolus-born [1] Misenus, than whom no trumpeter
    bright

Blew more bravely for battle, or fired with music the
    fight ;

Comrade of Hector great, who at Hector's side to the
    war

Marched, by his soldier's spear and his trumpet known
    from afar.

After triumphant Achilles his master slew with the
    sword, 175

Troy's Aeneas he followed, a no less glorious lord.

Now while over the deep he was sounding his clarion
    sweet,

In wild folly defying the Ocean Gods to compete,

Envious Triton,[2] lo ! — if the legend merit belief —

Drowned him, before he was ware, in the foaming
    waves of a reef. 180

All now, gathered around him, uplift their voices in
    grief,

[1] Son of Aeolus of Troy.   [2] Son of Neptune.

Foremost the faithful chieftain.   Anon to their tasks
    they hie ;
Speed, though weeping sorely, the Sibyl's mission,
    and vie,
Building the funeral altar with giant trees to the
    sky.

Into the forest primeval, the beasts' dark cover, they
    go ;   185
Pine-trees fall with a crash and the holm-oaks ring to
    the blow.
Ash-hewn timbers and fissile oaks with the wedges
    are rent ;
Massive ash-trees roll from the mountains down the
    descent.
Foremost strides Aeneas, as ever, guiding the way,
Cheering his men, and equipped with a forester's axe
    as they.   190
Long in his own sad thoughts he is plunged — then
    raising his eyes
Over the measureless forest, uplifts his prayer to the
    skies.
" O that in this great thicket the golden branch of
    the tree
Might be revealed !   For in all she related yonder of
    thee   194
Ever, alas ! Misenus, the prophetess spake too true."
Lo ! at the words twain doves came down through the
    heavenly blue,
And at his side on the green turf lighted.   The hero
    of Troy
Knows the celestial birds of his mother,[1] and cries
    with joy :

[1] Venus.

"Guide us, if ever a way be, and cleaving swiftly the
    skies,

Wing for the grove where in shadow a golden branch
    overlies   200

One all-favored spot. Nor do thou in an hour that
    is dark,

Mother, desert thy son!" So saying, he pauses to
    mark

What be the omens, and whither the birds go. They
    in their flight,

Soaring, and lighting to feed, keep still in the Teu-
    crians' sight.

When they have come to the valley of baleful Aver-
    nus, the pair,   205

Shooting aloft, float up through a bright and radiant
    air ;

Both on a tree they have chosen at length their pin-
    ions fold

Through whose branches of green is a wavering
    glimmer of gold.

As in the winter forest a mistletoe often ye see   209

Bearing a foliage young, no growth of its own oak-tree,

Circling the rounded boles with a leafage of yellow-
    ing bloom ;

Such was the branching gold, as it shone through the
    holm-oak's gloom,

So in the light wind rustled the foil. Aeneas with bold

Ardor assails it, breaks from the tree the reluctant
    gold ;   214

Then to the Sibyl's palace in triumph carries it home.

Weeping for dead Misenus the Trojan host on the
    shore

Now to his thankless ashes the funeral offerings bore.

Rich with the resinous pine and in oak-hewn timbers
    cased
Rises a giant pyre, in its sides dark foliage laced;
Planted in front stand branches of cypress, gifts to
    the grave ;   220
Over it hang for adornment the gleaming arms of the
    brave.
Some heat fountain water, the bubbling caldron pre-
    pare ;
Clay-cold limbs then wash and anoint.   Wail sounds
    on the air.
Dirge at an end, the departed is placed on the funeral
    bed ;
O'er him they fling bright raiment, the wonted attire
    of the dead.   225
Others shoulder the ponderous bier, sad service of
    death ;
Some in ancestral fashion the lighted torches beneath
Hold with averted eyes.   High blaze on the burning
    pyre
Incense, funeral viands, and oil outpoured on the
    fire.
After the ashes have fallen and flames are leaping no
    more,   230
Wine on the smouldering relics and cinders thirsty
    they pour.
Next in a vessel of brass Corynaeus[1] gathers the
    bones,
Thrice bears pure spring water around Troy's sorrow-
    ing sons,
Sprinkles it o'er them in dew, from the bough of an
    olive in bloom,   234
Gives lustration to all, then bids farewell to the tomb.

[1] One of Aeneas' companions.

But the devout Aeneas a vast grave builds on the
    shore,
Places upon it the warrior's arms, his trumpet and
    oar,
Close to the sky-capped hill that from hence Misenus [1]
    is hight,
Keeping through endless ages his glorious memory
    bright.

Finished the task, to accomplish the Sibyl's behest
    they sped.   240
There was a cavern deep, — with a yawning throat
    and a dread, —
Shingly and rough, by a sombre lake and a forest of
    night
Sheltered from all approach. No bird wings safely
    her flight
Over its face, — from the gorges exhales such poison-
    ous breath,   244
Rising aloft to the skies in a vapor laden with death.
Here four sable oxen the priestess ranges in line ;
Empties on every forehead a brimming beaker of
    wine ;
Casts on the altar-fire, as the first-fruits due to the
    dead,
Hair from between both horns of the victim, plucked
    from its head ;
Loudly on Hecate calls, o'er heaven and the shadows
    supreme.   250
Others handle the knife, and receive, as it trickles,
    the stream
Warm from the throat in a bowl. Aeneas with fal-
    chion bright

[1] Properly Misenum, the promontory southeast of Cumae.

Slays himself one lamb of a sable fleece to the fell
Mother and queen of the Furies, and great Earth,
    sister of Night,
Killing a barren heifer to thee, thou mistress of
    Hell.   255
Next for the Stygian monarch a twilight altar he
    lays;
Flings on the flames whole bodies of bulls unquartered
    to blaze,
Pours rich oil from above upon entrails burning and
    bright.
When, at the earliest beam of the sun, and the dawn
    of the light,
Under his feet earth mutters, the mountain forests
    around   260
Seem to be trembling, and hell dogs bay from the
    shadow profound,
Night's dark goddess approaching. " Avaunt, ye un-
    hallowed, avaunt !"
Thunders the priestess. " Away from a grove that
    is Hecate's haunt.
Make for the pathway, thou, and unsheathe thy sword;
    thou hast need,   264
Now, Aeneas, of all thy spirit and valor indeed !"
When she had spoken, she plunged in her madness
    into the cave;
Not less swiftly he follows, with feet unswerving and
    brave.

Gods ! whose realm is the spirit-world, mute shadows
    of might,
Chaos, and Phlegethon [1] thou, broad kingdoms of
    silence and night,

      [1] A river of Hades.

Leave vouchsafe me to tell the tradition, grace to
    exhume   270
Things in the deep earth hidden and drowned in the
    hollows of gloom.

So unseen through darkness, amid lone night, they
    strode
Down the unpeopled realm of Death, and his ghostly
    abode,
As men journey in woods when a doubtful moon has
    bestowed
Little of light, when Jove has concealed in shadow
    the heaven,   275
When from the world by sombre Night Day's colors
    are driven.

Facing the porch itself, in the jaws of the gate of the
    dead,
Grief, and Remorse the Avenger, have built their
    terrible bed.
There dwells pale-cheeked Sickness, and Old Age
    sorrowful-eyed,
Fear, and the temptress Famine, and hideous Want
    at her side,   230
Grim and tremendous shapes.   There Death with
    Labor is joined,
Sleep, half-brother of Death, and the Joys unclean of
    the mind.
Murderous Battle is camped on the threshold.   Front-
    ing the door
The Iron cells of the Furies, and frenzied Strife,
    evermore
Wreathing her serpent tresses with garlands dabbled
    in gore.   285

Thick with gloom, an enormous elm in the midst of
    the way
Spreads its time-worn branches and limbs: false
    Dreams, we are told,
Make their abode thereunder, and nestle to every
    spray.
Many and various monsters, withal, wild things to
    behold,
Lie in the gateway stabled — the awful Centaurs [1] of
    old ;   290
Scyllas [2] with forms half-human ; and there with his
    hundred hands
Dwells Briareus ; [3] and the shapeless Hydra [4] of
    Lerna's lands,
Horribly yelling ; in flaming mail the Chimaera [5] ar-
    rayed ;
Gorgons [6] and Harpies, [7] and one three-bodied and
    terrible Shade. [8]

Clasping his sword, Aeneas in sudden panic of fear 295
Points its blade at the legion ; and had not the Hea-
    ven-taught seer
Warned him the phantoms are thin apparitions,
    clothed in a vain

[1] Fabled to have been half man, half horse.

[2] The monster Scylla is usually said to have dwelt in the cave
of a rock between Italy and Sicily. Virgil here speaks as if there
were several of them, and places them in the lower world

[3] A monstrous giant, one of the sons of Uranus and Gaea.

[4] The huge water serpent that lived in the marsh of Lerna near
Argos

[5] A fabulous composite of dragon, lion, and goat.

[6] Three daughters of Phorcys, whose hair was of snakes and whose
looks turned all beholders to stone.

[7] Mythical monsters, half bird and half woman.

[8] The giant Geryon.

Semblance of form, but in substance a fluttering bodi-
    less train,
Idly his weapon had slashed the advancing shadows
    in twain.   299

Here is the path to the river of Acheron, ever by mud
Clouded, for ever seething with wild, insatiate flood
Downward, and into Cocytus disgorging its endless
    sands.
Sentinel over its waters an awful ferryman stands,
Charon, grisly and rugged; a growth of centuries
    lies
Hoary and rough on his chin; as a flaming furnace
    his eyes.   305
Hung in a loop from his shoulders a foul scarf round
    him he ties;
Now with his pole impelling the boat, now trimming
    the sail,
Urging his steel-gray bark with its burden of corpses
    pale,
Aged in years, but a god's old age is unwithered and
    hale.

Down to the bank of the river the streaming shadows
    repair,   310
Mothers, and men, and the lifeless bodies of those
    who were
Generous heroes, boys that are beardless, maids un-
    wed,
Sons borne forth in the sight of their sires to the pile
    of the dead,
Many as forest leaves that in autumn's earliest frost
Flutter and fall, or as birds that in bevies flock to
    the coast   315

Over the sea's deep hollows, when winter, chilly and
    frore,
Drives them across far waters to land on a sunnier
    shore.
Yonder they stood, each praying for earliest passage,
    and each
Eagerly straining his hands in desire of the opposite
    beach.
Such as he lists to the vessel the boatman gloomy re-
    ceives,   320
Far from the sands of the river the rest he chases and
    leaves.

Moved at the wild uproar, Aeneas, with riveted eyes:
"Why thus crowd to the water the shadows, priest-
    ess?" he cries;
"What do the spirits desire? And why go some
    from the shore
Sadly away, while others are ferried the dark stream
    o'er?"   325

Briefly the aged priestess again made answer and
    spake:
"Son of Anchises, sprung most surely from gods
    upon high,
Yon is the deep Cocytus marsh, and the Stygian lake.
Even the Immortals fear to attest its presence and
    lie!
These are a multitude helpless, of spirits lacking a
    grave;   330
Charon the ferryman; yonder the buried, crossing the
    wave.
Over the awful banks and the hoarse-voiced torrents
    of doom

None may be taken before their bones find rest in a
    tomb.
Hundreds of years they wander, and flit round river
    and shore,
Then to the lake they long for are free to return once
    more."   335

Silent the hero gazed and his footstep halted, his
    mind
Filled with his own sad thoughts and compassion of
    doom unkind.
Yonder he notes, in affliction, deprived of the dues of
    the dead,
Near Leucaspis,[1] Orontes [1] who Lycia's vessels had led.
Over the wind-tossed waters from Troy as together
    they drave,   340
One wild storm overtook them, engulfing vessels and
    brave.
Yonder, behold, Palinurus the pilot gloomily went,
Who, while standing from Libya's shores, on the
    planets intent,
Fell but of late from the stern, and was lost in a
    watery waste.
Hardly he knows him at first, as in shadow sadly he
    paced :   345
Then at the last breaks silence and cries : " What
    God can it be
Robbed us of thee, Palinurus, and drowned thee deep
    in the sea ?
Answer me thou !   For Apollo I ne'er found false till
    to-day ;
Only in this one thing hath his prophecy led us
    astray.

[1] Former companions of Aeneas.

Safe with life from the deep to Italian shores, we
    were told,   350
Thou should'st come at the last! Is it thus that his
    promises hold ? ''

"Son of Anchises," he answers, " Apollo's tripod and
    shrine
Have not lied; no god overwhelmed me thus in the
    brine.
True to my trust I was holding the helm, stood ruling
    the course,
When by sad misadventure I wrenched it loose, and
    perforce   355
Trailed it behind in my fall. By the cruel waters I
    swear
Fear of mine own life truly I knew not, felt but a
    care
Lest thy bark, of her rudder bereft, and her helms-
    man lost,
Might be unequal to combat the wild seas round her
    that tossed.
Three long nights of the winter, across great waters
    and wide,   360
Violent south winds swept me; at fourth day's dawn
    I descried
Italy's coast, as I rose on the crest of a wave of the
    sea.
Stroke by stroke I was swimming ashore, seemed
    nearly to be
Safe from the billows; and weighted by dripping
    garments I clave,
Clutching my hands, to the face of a cliff that towered
    on the wave,   365

When wild people assailed me, a treasure-trove to
    their mind.
Now are the waves my masters; I toss on the beach
    in the wind.
O! by the pleasant sun, by the joyous light of the
    skies,
By thy sire, and Iulus,[1] the rising hope of thine eyes,
Save me from these great sorrows, my hero! Over
    me pour   370
Earth, as in truth thou canst, and return to the
    Velian[2] shore.
Else, if a heavenly mother hath shown thee yonder a
    way, —
Since some god's own presence, methinks, doth guide
    thee, who here
Seekest to cross these streams and the Stygian
    marshes drear, —
Give thy hand to thy servant, and take him with thee
    to-day,   375
So that in quiet places his wearied head he may
    lay!"
Thus, sad phantom, he cried; thus answered the seer
    of the shrine:
"Whence, Palinurus, comes this ill-omened longing
    of thine?
Thou cast eyes, unburied, on Stygian waves, the
    severe
Stream of the Furies, approach unbidden the banks
    of the mere!   380
Cease thy dream that the Fates by prayer may be
    ever appeased,
Yet keep this in remembrance, that so thy lot may be
    eased :—

---

[1] Aeneas' son   [2] Velia was a town on the Lucanian coast.

Many a neighboring people from cities far and un-
    known,
Taught by prodigies dire of the skies, thy bones shall
    atone,
Building thy tomb, and remitting their gifts each year
    to thy ghost ;   385
So Palinurus' [1] name shall for ever cleave to the
    coast."
Thus his affliction she soothes. For a little season
    his sad
Spirit has comfort; he thinks on his namesake land
    and is glad.
Thence they advance on the journey and now draw
    near to the flood.
Soon as the boatman saw them, from where on the
    water he stood,   390
Move through the silent forest and bend their steps
    to the beach,
Ere they arrive he accosts them, and first breaks si-
    lence in speech.
" Stranger, approaching in arms our river, whoever
    thou art,
Speak on the spot thine errand, and hold thee further
    apart.
This is the kingdom of shadows, of sleep and the
    slumberous dark ;   395
Bodies of living men are forbidden the Stygian bark.
Not of mine own good will was Alcides over the wave
Yonder, or Theseus taken, nor yet Pirithous brave,
Though from gods they descended, and matchless
    warriors were ;
One [2] from the monarch's presence to chains sought
    boldly to bear   400

---

[1] There was a promontory so called   [2] Hercules.

Hell's unslumbering warder,[1] and trailed him trem-
    bling away.
Two[2] from her bridal chamber conspired Death's
    queen to convey."

Briefly again makes answer the great Amphrysian
    seer:[3]
"Here no cunning awaits thee as theirs was, far be
    the fear.
Violence none our weapons prepare; Hell's warder
    may still   405
Bay in his cavern for ever, affrighting the phantoms
    chill;
Hell's chaste mistress keep to her kinsman's halls if
    she will.
Troy's Aeneas, a son most loving, a warrior brave,
Goes in the quest of his sire to the deepest gloom of
    the grave.
If thou art all unmoved at the sight of a love so
    true " —   410
Here she displays him the bough in her garment
    hidden from view —
"Know this branch."   In his bosom the tempest of
    anger abates.
Further he saith not.   Feasting his eyes on the wand
    of the Fates,
Mighty oblation, unseen for unnumbered summers be-
    fore,
Charon advances his dark-blue bows, and approaches
    the shore;   415

[1] Cerberus
[2] Theseus and Pirithous.
[3] The Sibyl   The epithet "Amphrysian" is applied to her as the
priestess of Apollo, who, according to the story, fed the flocks of
Admetus near the river Amphrysus in Thessaly.

Summons the rest of the spirits in row on the benches
who sate
Place to resign for the comers, his gangway clears,
and on board
Takes Aeneas. The cobbled boat groans under his
weight
Water in streams from the marshes through every
fissure is poured.
Priestess and hero safely across Death's river are
passed,   420
Land upon mud unsightly, and pale marsh-sedges, at
last.

Here huge Cerberus bays with his triple jaws through
the land,
Crouched at enormous length in his cavern facing the
strand.
Soon as the Sibyl noted his hair now bristling with
snakes,
Morsels she flings him of meal, and of honeyed opiate
cakes.   425
Maddened with fury of famine his three great throats
unclose ;
Fiercely he snatches the viand, his monstrous limbs
in repose
Loosens, and, prostrate laid, sprawls measureless over
his den.
While the custodian sleeps, Aeneas the entrance takes,
Speeds from the bank of a stream no traveller crosses
again.   430

Voices they heard, and an infinite wailing, as onward
they bore,
Spirits of infants sobbing at Death's immediate door,

Whom, at a mother's bosom, and strangers to life's
    sweet breath,
Fate's dark day took from us, and drowned in un-
    timeliest death.
Near them are those who, falsely accused, died guilt-
    less, although   435
Not without trial, or verdict given, do they enter be-
    low;
Here, with his urn, sits Minos[1] the judge, convenes
    from within
Silent ghosts to the council, and learns each life and
    its sin.
Near them inhabit the sorrowing souls, whose innocent
    hands
Wrought on themselves their ruin, and strewed their
    lives on the sands,   440
Hating the glorious sunlight. Alas! how willingly
    they
Now would endure keen want, hard toil, in the re-
    gions of day!
Fate forbids it; the loveless lake with its waters of
    woe
Holds them, and nine times round them entwined,
    Styx bars them below.

Further faring, they see that beyond and about them
    are spread   445
Fields of the Mourners, for so they are called in
    worlds of the dead.
Here dwell those whom Love, with his cruel sickness,
    hath slain.
Lost in secluded walks, amid myrtle groves overhead,

[1] Minos, king of Crete, became after his death one of the judges
in Hades

Hiding they go, nor in death itself are they eased of
the pain.
Phaedra,[1] and Procris,[2] here, Eriphyle[3] here they behold,   450
Sadly displaying the wounds that her wild son
wrought her of old.

Yonder Pasiphaë[4] stood and Evadne;[5] close to them
clung
Laodamia,[6] and Caenis,[7] a man once, woman at last,
Now by the wheel of the Fates in her former figure
recast.
Fresh from her death-wound still, here Dido,[8] the
others among,   455
Roamed in a spacious wood.   Through shadow the
chieftain soon
Dimly discerned her face, as a man, when the month
is but young,
Sees, or believes he has seen, amid cloudlets shining,
the moon.
Tears in his eyes, he addressed her with tender love
as of old:

[1] Wife of Theseus, who killed herself when her stepson Hippoly-
tus rejected her love.
[2] Wife of Cephalus, who, moved by jealousy to spy upon her husband, was accidentally killed by him.
[3] Killed by her son Alcmaeon, because, bribed with a necklace,
she had induced her husband to join the expedition of the Seven
against Thebes, in which he was slain
[4] Wife of Minos
[5] Wife of Capaneus, who threw herself on her husband's funeral
pyre and perished.
[6] Wife of Protesilaus, the first Greek who fell at Troy.
[7] A girl whom her lover Neptune transformed into a man, but who,
on being slain by the Centaurs, was retransformed
[8] She had committed suicide after Aeneas' departure from Carthage.

" True, then, sorrowful Dido, the messenger fires that
   told   460
Thy sad death, and the doom thou soughtest of choice
   by thy hand!
Was it, alas! to a grave that I did thee?   Now by
   the bright
Stars, by the Gods, and the faith that abides in
   realms of the Night,
'T was unwillingly, lady, I bade farewell to thy
   land.
Yet, the behest of Immortals, — the same which bids
   me to go   465
Through these shadows, the wilderness mire and the
   darkness below, —
Drove me imperious thence, nor possessed I power to
   believe
I at departing had left thee in grief thus bitter to
   grieve.
Tarry, and turn not away from a face that on thine
   would dwell;
'T is thy lover thou fliest, and this is our last farewell!"   470

So, with a burning heart and with glowering eyes as
   she went,
Melting vainly in tears, he essayed her wrath to re-
   lent;
She with averted gaze upon earth her countenance
   cast,
Nothing touched in her look by her lover's words to
   the last,   474
Set as a marble rock of Marpessus,[1] cold as a stone.
After a little she fled, in the forest hurried to hide,

---

[1] A mountain in the island of Paros in the Aegaean Sea.

Ever his foe ; Sychaeus[1], her first lord, there at her
    side,
Answers sorrow with sorrow, and love not less than
    her own.

Thence on the path appointed they go, and the utter-
    most plain
Reach ere long, where rest in seclusion the glorious
    slain.   480
Tydeus[2] here he discerns, here Parthenopaeus[2] of old
Famous in arms, and the ghost of Adrastus,[2] pallid
    and cold.
Wailed in the world of the sunlight long, laid low in
    the fray,
Here dwell Ilion's chiefs.   As his eyes on the gallant
    array
Lighted, he groaned.   Three sons of Antenor yonder
    they see,   485
Glaucus[3] and Medon and young Thersilochus, breth-
    ren three ;
Here Polyphaetes, servant of Heaven from his earliest
    breath ;
There Idaeus, the shield and the reins still holding in
    death.
Thickly about him gather the spectral children of
    Troy :
'T is not enough to have seen him, to linger round
    him is joy,   490
Pace at his side, and inquire why thus he descends to
    the dead.

[1] Her husband, after whose murder by her brother Pygmalion she
had come from Tyre to Africa, and founded Carthage

[2] One of the Seven against Thebes.

[3] In this and in the next two lines we have the names of distinguished Trojans who had been killed in the war.

But the Achaean [1] chiefs, Agamemnon's [2] legions ar-
    rayed,
When on the hero they looked, and his armor gleam-
    ing in shade,
Shook with an infinite terror, and some turned from
    him and fled,
As to the Danaan [1] vessels in days gone by they had
    sped.   495
Some on the air raise thinnest of voices; the shout of
    the fray
Seems, upon lips wide-parted, begun, then passing
    away.

Noble Deïphobus here he beholds, all mangled and
    marred,
Son of the royal Priam; — his visage cruelly scarred,
Visage and hands; from his ravaged temples bloodily
    shorn   500
Each of his ears, and his nostrils with wounds in-
    glorious torn.
Hardly he knew him in sooth, for he trembled, seek-
    ing to hide
These great wrongs; but at last in a voice most lov-
    ing he cried:
"Gallant Deïphobus, born of the Teucrian lineage
    bright,
Who had the heart to revenge him in this dire fashion
    and dread?   505
Who dared thus to abuse thee? On Troy's last
    funeral night,
Weary of endless slaughter and Danaan blood, it was
    said

[1] Greek   [2] The leader of the Greeks.

Thou hadst laid thee to die on a heap of the nameless dead.

Yea! and a vacant mound upon far Rhoetaeum's [1] coast

I there built thee, and thrice bade loud farewell to thy ghost.   510

Hallowed the spot by thine armor and name. Ere crossing the wave

Never, friend, could I find thee, nor give thee an Ilian grave."

"Nothing was left undone, O friend!" he replies; "thou hast paid

All that Deïphobus claims, all debt that was due to his shade.

'T was my destiny sad, and the crime accursed of the Greek   515

Woman,[2] in woe that plunged me, and wrote this tale on my cheek.

Well thou knowest — for ah! too long will the memory last —

How Troy's funeral night amid treacherous pleasures we passed;

When Fate's terrible steed [3] overcame our walls at a leap,

Carrying mailclad men in its womb towards Pergama's steep;   520

How, a procession feigning, the Phrygian [4] mothers she led

Round our city in orgy, with lighted torch at their head,

Waving herself the Achaeans to Ilion's citadel keep.

---

[1] A promontory north of Troy

[2] Helen, who after Paris' death had been given to Deïphobus

[3] The wooden horse.   [4] Trojan

I, that night, overburdened with troubles, buried in
    sleep,   524
Lay in the fatal chamber, delicious slumber and deep
Folding mine eyelids, like the unbroken rest of the
    slain.
She, meanwhile, my glorious spouse, from the palace
    has ta'en
Every weapon, and drawn from the pillow the fal-
    chion I bore,
Then Menelaus [1] summons, and straightway loosens
    the door,
Hoping in sooth that her lover with this great boon
    might be won,   530
Deeming the fame of her guilt in the past might so
    be undone.
Why on the memory linger? The foe streamed in
    at the gate
Led by Ulysses, the plotter. May judgment, Immor-
    tals, wait
Yet on the Greeks, if of vengeance a reverent heart
    may be fain!
Tell me in turn what sorrow has brought thee alive
    and unslain   535
Hither?" he cries; " art come as a mariner lost on
    the main,
Or by the counsel of Heaven ? What fortune drives
    thee in quest,
Hither, of sunless places and sad, the abodes of un-
    rest?"
Morn already with roseate steeds, while talk they
    exchange,
Now in her journey has traversed the half of the
    heavenly range,   540

[1] Brother of Agamemnon and husband of Helen.

And peradventure thus the allotted time had been
    passed,
Had not the faithful Sibyl rebuked him briefly at last.
" Night draws nigh, Aeneas.   In tears we are spend-
    ing the hours.
Here is the place where the path is divided.   This to
    the right,
Under the walls of the terrible Dis [1] — to Elysium [2] —
    ours.   545
Yonder, the left, brings doom to the guilty, and
    drives them in flight
Down to the sinful region where awful Tartarus
    lowers."

" Terrible priestess, frown not," Deïphobus cries ; " I
    depart,
Join our shadowy legion, restore me to darkness
    anon.
Go, thou joy of the race ; may the Fates vouchsafe
    thee a part   550
Brighter than mine ! "   And behold, as he uttered
    the word, he was gone.

Turning his eyes, Aeneas sees broad battlements
    placed
Under the cliffs on his left, by a triple rampart en-
    cased ;
Round them in torrents of ambient fire runs Phlege-
    thon swift,
River of Hell, and the thundering rocks sends ever
    adrift.   555

---

[1] The ruler of the world below, corresponding to the Greek Pluto.

[2] The abode of the blessed, as Tartarus was the place of punishment for the wicked.

One huge portal in front upon pillars of adamant
    stands ;
Neither can mortal might, nor the heavens' own
    warrior bands,
Rend it asunder.   An iron tower rears over the door,
Where Tisiphone[1] seated in garments dripping with
    gore
Watches the porch, unsleeping, by day and by night
    evermore.   560
Hence come groans on the breezes, the sound of a
    pitiless flail,
Rattle of iron bands, and the clanking of fetters that
    trail.

Silent the hero stands, and in terror rivets his eyes.
" What dire shapes of impiety these ?   Speak, priest-
    ess ! " he cries.
" What dread torment racks them, and what shrieks
    yonder arise ? "   565
She in return : " Great chief of the Teucrian hosts,
    as is meet
Over the threshold of sinners may pass no innocent
    feet.
Hecate's self, who set me to rule the Avernian glade,
Taught me of Heaven's great torments, and all their
    terrors displayed.
Here reigns dread Rhadamanthus,[2] a king no mercy
    that knows,   570
Chastens and judges the guilty, compels each soul to
    disclose
Crimes of the upper air that he kept concealed from
    the eye,

[1] One of the Furies.
[2] He acted, together with Aeacus and Minos, as judge of the dead.

Proud of his idle cunning, till Death brought punish-
　　ment nigh.
Straightway then the Avenger Tisiphone over them
　　stands,
Scourges the trembling sinners, her fierce lash arming
　　her hands;   575
Holds in her left uplifted her serpents grim, and from
　　far
Summons the awful troop of her sisters gathered for
　　war!
Then at the last with a grating of hideous hinges un-
　　close
Hell's infernal doors. Dost see what warders are those
Crouched in the porch? What presence is yonder
　　keeping the gate?   580
Know that a Hydra[1] beyond it, a foe still fiercer in
　　hate,
Lurks with a thousand ravening throats. See! Tar-
　　tarus great
Yawning to utter abysses, and deepening into the
　　night,
Twice as profound as the space of the starry Olym-
　　pian height.

"Here the enormous Titans,[2] the Earth's old progeny,
　　hurled   585
Low by the lightning, are under the bottomless waters
　　whirled.
Here I beheld thy children, Aloeus, giants[3] of might,
Brethren bold who endeavored to pluck down heaven
　　from its height,

---

[1] A water-snake.
[2] Sons of Uranus and Gaea, who were conquered by Zeus and cast
into Tartarus.　　　　　　　　　　　[3] Otus and Ephialtes.

Fain to displace great Jove from his throne in the
    kingdom of light.
Saw Salmoneus[1] too, overtaken with agony dire   590
While the Olympian thunder he mimicked and Jove's
    own fire.
Borne on his four-horsed chariot, and waving torches
    that glowed,
Over the Danaan land, through the city of Elis, he
    rode,
Marching in triumph, and claiming the honors due
    to a god.
Madman, thinking with trumpets and tramp of the
    steeds that he drove   595
He might rival the storms, and the matchless thun-
    ders of Jove!
But the omnipotent Father a bolt from his cloudy
    abyss
Launched — no brand from the pine, no smoke of the
    torchlight this —
And with an awful whirlwind blast hurled Pride to
    its fall.
Tityos[2] also, the nursling of Earth, great mother of
    all,   600
Here was to see, whose body a long league covers of
    plain;
One huge vulture, standing with hooked beak at his
    side,
Shears his liver that dies not, his bowel fruitful of pain,
Searches his heart for a banquet, beneath his breast
    doth abide,
Grants no peace to the vitals that ever renew them
    again.   605

[1] Son of Aeolus, who usurped the name and sacrifices of Jupiter.
[2] Son of Gaea, a giant of Euboea, who was punished for insulting
Artemis.

" Why of Pirithous tell, and Ixion, Lapithae [1] tall,
O'er whose brows is suspended a dark crag, ready to
    fall,
Ever in act to descend ? Proud couches raised upon
    bright
Golden feet are shining, a festal table in sight
Laden with royal splendor. The Furies' Queen [2] on
    her throne   610
Sits at the banquet by — forbids them to taste it —
    has flown
Now to prevent them with torch uplifted, and thun-
    dering tone.

" All who have hated a brother in lifetime, all who
    have laid
Violent hands on a parent, the faith of a client be-
    trayed ;
Those who finding a treasure have o'er it brooded
    alone,   615
Setting aside no portion for kinsmen, a numerous
    band ;
Those in adultery slain, all those who have raised in
    the land
Treason's banner, or broken their oath to a master's
    hand,
Prisoned within are awaiting an awful doom of their
    own.

" Ask me not, what their doom, — what form of re-
    quital or ill   620
Whelms them below. Some roll huge stones to the
    crest of the hill,

---

[1] A mythical people of Thessaly, ruled by Pirithous, son of Ixion.
[2] Either Alecto or Megaera.

Some on the spokes of a whirling wheel hang spread
    to the wind.
Theseus sits, the unblest, and will ever seated re-
    main;
Phlegyas[1] here in his torments a warning voice to
    mankind
Raises, loudly proclaiming throughout Hell's gloomy
    abodes :   625
' Learn hereby to be just, and to think no scorn of
    the Gods ! '
This is the sinner his country who sold, forged tyr-
    anny's chain,
Made for a bribe her laws, for a bribe unmade them
    again.
Yon wretch dared on a daughter with eyes unholy to
    look.   629
All some infamy ventured, of infamy's gains partook.
Had I a thousand tongues, and a thousand lips, and a
    speech
Fashioned of steel, sin's varying types I hardly could
    teach,
Could not read thee the roll of the torments suffered
    of each ! "

Soon as the aged seer of Apollo her story had done,
" Forward," she cries, " on the path, and complete
    thy mission begun.   635
Hasten the march ! I behold in the distance battle-
    ments great,
Built by the Cyclops' forge, and the vaulted dome at
    the gate

---

[1] King of the Phlegyae in Boeotia, who, to avenge his daughter,
set fire to the temple of Apollo at Delphi, and was killed by the
arrows of the god

Where the divine revelation ordains our gifts to be
    laid."
Side by side at her bidding they traverse the region
    of shade,
Over the distance hasten, and now draw nigh to the
    doors.   640
Fronting the gates Aeneas stands, fresh water he
    pours
Over his limbs, and the branch on the portal hangs
    as she bade.

After the rite is completed, the gift to the goddess
    addressed,
Now at the last they come to the realms where Joy
    has her throne ;
Sweet green glades in the Fortunate Forests, abodes
    of the blest,   645
Fields in an ampler ether, a light more glorious
    dressed,
Lit evermore with their own bright stars and a sun
    of their own.
Some are training their limbs on the wrestling-green,
    and compete
Gaily in sport on the yellow arenas, some with their
    feet
Treading their choral measures, or singing the hymns
    of the god ;   650
While their Thracian priest,[1] in a sacred robe that
    trails,
Chants them the air with the seven sweet notes of his
    musical scales,
Now with his fingers striking, and now with his ivory
    rod.

          Orpheus

Here are the ancient children of Teucer,[1] fair to be-
    hold,

Generous heroes, born in the happier summers of
    old, —   655

Ilus, Assaracus by him, and Dardan, founder of Troy.

Far in the distance yonder are visible armor and
    car

Unsubstantial, in earth their lances are planted, and
    far

Over the meadows are ranging the chargers freed from
    employ.

All the delight they took when alive · in the chariot
    and sword,   660

All of the loving care that to shining coursers was
    paid,

Follows them now that in quiet below Earth's breast
    they are laid.

Banqueting here he beholds them to right and to left
    on the sward,

Chanting in chorus the Paean, beneath sweet forests
    of bay,

Whence, amid wild wood covers, the river Eridanus,
    poured,   665

Rolls his majestic torrents to upper earth and the
    day.

Chiefs for the land of their sires in the battle wounded
    of yore,

Priests whose purity lasted until sweet life was no
    more,

Faithful prophets who spake as beseemed their god
    and his shrine,   669

All who by arts invented to life have added a grace,

[1] Teucer, Ilus, Assaracus, and Dardan all belonged, in different generations, to the royal house of Troy.

All whose services earned the remembrance deep of
    the race,
Round their shadowy foreheads the snow-white gar-
    land entwine.

Then, as about them the phantoms stream, breaks
    silence the seer,
Turning first to Musaeus,[1] — for round him the
    shadows appear
Thickest to crowd, as he towers with his shoulders
    over the throng —   675
" Tell me, ye joyous spirits, and thou, bright master
    of song,
Where is the home and the haunt of the great An-
    chises, for whom
Hither we come, and have traversed the awful rivers
    of gloom ? "
Briefly in turn makes answer the hero : " None has a
    home
In fixed haunts.   We inhabit the dark thick glades,
    on the brink   680
Ever of moss-banked rivers, and water meadows that
    drink
Living streams.   But if onward your heart thus wills
    ye to go,
Climb this ridge.   I will set ye in pathways easy to
    know."
Forward he marches, leading the way ; from the
    heights at the end
Shows them a shining plain, and the mountain slopes
    they descend.   685
There withdrawn to a valley of green in a fold of the
    plain

---

[1] A mythical poet of pre-Homeric times

Stood Anchises the father, his eyes intent on a train —
Prisoned spirits, soon to ascend to the sunlight
    again ; —
Numbering over his children [1] dear, their myriad
    bands,
All their destinies bright, their ways, and the work
    of their hands.   690
When he beheld Aeneas across these flowery lands
Moving to meet him, fondly he strained both arms to
    his boy,
Tears on his cheek fell fast, and his voice found
    slowly employ.

" Here thou comest at last, and the love I counted
    upon
Over the rugged path has prevailed. Once more, O
    my son,   695
I may behold thee, and answer with mine thy voice as
    of yore.
Long I pondered the chances, believed this day was
    in store,
Reckoning the years and the seasons. Nor was my
    longing belied.
O'er how many a land, past what far waters and wide,
Hast thou come to mine arms ! What dangers have
    tossed thee, my child !   700
Ah ! how I feared lest harm should await thee in
    Libya wild ! "

" Thine own shade, my sire, thine own disconsolate
    shade,
Visiting oft my chamber, has made me seek thee," he
    said.

[1] The Romans

" Safe upon Tusean waters the fleet lies. Grant me
    to grasp
Thy right hand, sweet father, withdraw thee not from
    its clasp." 705

So he replied; and a river of tears flowed over his
    face.
Thrice with his arms he essayed the beloved one's
    neck to embrace;
Thrice clasped vainly, the phantom eluded his hands
    in flight,
Thin as the idle breezes, and like some dream of the
    night.

There Aeneas beholds in a valley withdrawn from the
    rest 710
Far-off glades, and a forest of boughs that sing in the
    breeze;
Near them the Lethe[1] river that glides by abodes of
    the blest.
Round it numberless races and peoples floating he
    sees.
So on the flowery meadows in calm, clear summer,
    the bees
Settle on bright-hued blossoms, or stream in com-
    panies round 715
Fair white lilies, till every plain seems ringing with
    sound.

Strange to the scene Aeneas, with terror suddenly
    pale,
Asks of its meaning, and what be the streams in the
    distant vale,

[1] The river of forgetfulness.

Who those warrior crowds that about yon river await.
Answer returns Anchises : " The spirits promised by
    Fate   720
Life in the body again. Upon Lethe's watery brink
These of the fountain of rest and of long oblivion
    drink.
Ever I yearn to relate thee the tale, display to thine
    eyes,
Count thee over the children that from my loins shall
    arise,
So that our joy may be deeper on finding Italy's
    skies."   725

"O my father ! and are there, and must we believe
    it," he said,
" Spirits that fly once more to the sunlight back from
    the dead ?
Souls that anew to the body return and the fetters
    of clay ?
Can there be any who long for the light thus blindly
    as they ? "

" Listen, and I will resolve thee the doubt," Anchises
    replies.   730
Then unfolds him in order the tale of the earth and
    the skies.

"In the beginning, the earth, and the sky, and the
    spaces of night,
Also the shining moon, and the sun Titanic and bright
Feed on an inward life, and with all things mingled,
    a mind
Moves universal matter, with Nature's frame is com-
    bined.   735

Thence man's race, and the beast, and the bird that
    on pinions flies,
All wild shapes that are hidden the gleaming waters
    beneath.
Each elemental seed has a fiery force from the skies,
Each, its heavenly being, that no dull clay can dis-
    guise,
Bodies of earth ne'er deaden, nor limbs long destined
    to death.   740
Hence, their fears and desires; their sorrows and
    joys; for their sight,
Blind with the gloom of a prison, discerns not the
    heavenly light.

" Nor when at last life leaves them, do all sad ills, that
    belong
Unto the sinful body, depart; still many survive
Lingering within them, alas! for it needs must be
    that the long   745
Growth should in wondrous fashion at full completion
    arrive.
So, due vengeance racks them, for deeds of an earlier
    day
Suffering penance. and some to the winds hang view-
    less and thin
Searched by the breezes; from others, the deep in-
    fection of sin
Swirling water washes, or bright fire purges, away. 750
Each in his own sad ghost we endure; then pass to
    the wide
Realms of Elysium. Few in the fields of the happy
    abide,
Till great Time, when the cycles have run their
    courses on high,

Takes the inbred pollution, and leaves to us only the
    bright
Sense of the heaven's own ether, and fire from the
    springs of the sky.   755
When for a thousand years they have rolled their
    wheels through the night,
God to the Lethe river recalls this myriad train,
That with remembrance lost once more they may visit
    the light,
And, at the last, have desire for a life in the body
    again."

When he had ended, his son and the Sibyl maiden
    he drew   760
Into the vast assembly — the crowd with its endless
    hum ;
There on a hillock plants them, that hence they better
    may view
All the procession advancing, and learn their looks as
    they come.

"What bright fame hereafter the Trojan line shall
    adorn,
What far children be theirs, from the blood of Ital-
    ians born,   765
Splendid souls, that inherit the name and the glory
    of Troy,
Now will I tell thee, and teach thee the fates thy race
    shall enjoy.
Yon fair hero who leans on a lance unpointed and
    bright,
Granted the earliest place in the world of the day and
    the light,
Half of Italian birth, from the shadows first shall
    ascend,   770

Silvius,[1] Alban of name, thy child though born at the
     end,
Son of thy later years by Lavinia, consort of thine,
Reared in the woods as a monarch and sire of a royal
     line.
Next to him Procas, the pride of the race; then
     Capys, and far
Numitor; after him one who again thy name shall
     revive,   775
Silvius, hight Aeneas, in pious service and war
Noble alike, if to Alba's throne he shall ever arrive.
Heroes fair! how grandly, behold! their manhood is
     shown,
While their brows are shaded by leaves of the citizen-
     crown![2]
These on the mountain ranges shall set Nomentum[3]
     the steep,   780
Gabii's towers, Fidenae's town, Collatia's keep;
Here plant Inuus' camp, there Cora and Bola en-
     throne,
Glorious names ere long, now a nameless land and
     unknown.
Romulus, scion of Mars, at the side of his grandsire[4]
     see —
Ilia fair his mother, the blood of Assaracus he! 785
See on his helmet the doubled crest, how his sire has
     begun
Marking the boy with his own bright plumes for the
     world of the sun.

[1] In this and the following lines we have the names of princes of
Alba.
[2] A crown of oak leaves was awarded for saving a citizen's life in
battle.
[3] A town in Old Latium. So, too, the other places mentioned.
[4] Numitor, the father of Rhea Silvia, or Ilia.

Under his auspices Rome, our glorious Rome, shall
    arise,

Earth with her empire ruling, her great soul touching
    the skies.

Lo! seven mountains enwalling, a single city, she
    lies,   790

Blest in her warrior brood! So crowned with towers
    ye have seen

Ride through Phrygia's cities the great Berecynthian
    queen,[1]

Proud of the gods her children, a hundred sons at her
    knee,

All of them mighty immortals, and lords of a heavenly
    fee!   794

Turn thy glance now hither, behold this glorious clan,

Romans of thine. See Caesar, and each generation
    of man

Yet to be born of Iulus beneath heaven's infinite
    dome.

Yonder behold thy hero, the promised prince, upon
    whom

Often thy hopes have dwelt, Augustus Caesar, by
    birth   799

Kin to the godlike dead, who a golden age upon earth

Comes to renew where once o'er Latium Saturn
    reigned,

Holding remote Garamantes and India's tribes en-
    chained.

Far beyond all our planets the land lies, far beyond
    high

Heaven, and the sun's own orbit, where Atlas, lifting
    the sky,

[1] Cybele, the mother of the Gods. Mt Berecyntus in Phrygia was
one of the seats of her worship.

Whirls on his shoulders the sphere, inwrought with
    its fiery suns! 805
Ere his arrival, lo! through shivering Caspia [1] runs
Fear, at her oracle's answers. The vast Maeotian
    plain, [2]
Sevenfold Nile and his mouths, are fluttered and
    tremble again;
Ranges of earth more wide than Alcides ever sur-
    veyed,
Though he pursued deer brazen of limb, tamed Ery-
    manth's [3] glade, 810
Lerna [4] with arrows scared, or the Vinegod, [5] when from
    the war
Homeward with ivied reins he conducts his conquer-
    ing car,
Driving his team of tigers from Nysa's [6] summits afar.
Art thou loth any longer with deeds our sway to ex-
    pand?
Can it be fear forbids thee to hold Ausonia's land? 815

  " Who comes yonder the while with the olive branch
    on his brow,
Bearing the sacred vessels? I know yon tresses, I know
Yon gray beard, Rome's monarch, [7] the first with law
    to sustain
Rome yet young; from the lordship of Cures' [8] little
    domain

---

[1] The country of the Parthians, southeast of the Caspian Sea.
[2] Maeotis Palus is the ancient name of the Sea of Azof
[3] A mountain chain in the northwest corner of Arcadia, the haunt
of the wild boar destroyed by Alcides (Hercules).
[4] The marsh near Argos where Hercules killed the Hydra.
[5] Bacchus   [6] In India, the scene of Bacchus' nurture.
[7] Numa Pompilius, the second king of Rome.
[8] The ancient Sabine town from which Numa came.

Sent to an empire's throne. At his side goes one
    who shall break   820

Slumberous peace, to the battle her easeful warriors
    wake,

Rouse once more her battalions disused to the triumph
    so long,

Tullus the king ! Next, Ancus the boastful marches
    along,

See, overjoyed already by praises breathed from a
    crowd !

Yonder the royal Tarquins are visible ; yonder the
    proud   825

Soul of avenging Brutus,[1] with Rome's great fasces
    again

Made Rome's own ; who first to her consul's throne
    shall attain,

Hold her terrible axes : his sons, the rebellious pair,

Doom to a rebel's death for the sake of Liberty
    fair.

Ill-starred sire ! let the ages relate as please them the
    tale,   830

Yet shall his patriot passion and thirst of glory pre-
    vail.

Look on the Decii[2] there, and the Drusi ; hatchet in
    hand

See Torquatus the stern, and Camillus home to his
    land

Marching with rescued banners. But yonder spirits[3]
    who stand   834

---

[1] The leader of the revolution which resulted in the expulsion of
the Tarquins from Rome, and the establishment of the Republic.

[2] Like the following, heroes of Republican history.

[3] Caesar and Pompey. The civil wars of the last days of the Republic are foretold.

Dressed in the shining armor alike, harmonious now
While in the world of shadows with dark night over
       their brow —
Ah! what battles the twain must wage, what legions
       array,
What fell carnage kindle, if e'er they reach to the
       day!
Father[1] descending from Alpine snows and Monoe-
       cus's[2] height,
Husband ranging against him an Eastern[3] host for
       the fight!   840
Teach not your hearts, my children, to learn these
       lessons of strife;
Turn not a country's valor against her veriest life.
Thou be the first to forgive, great child of a heavenly
       birth,
Fling down, son of my loins, thy weapons and sword
       to the earth!

"See, who[4] rides from a vanquished Corinth in con-
       queror's car   845
Home to the Capitol, decked with Achaean spoils from
       the war!
Argos and proud Mycenae a second[5] comes to de-
       throne,
Ay, and the Aeacus-born,[6] whose race of Achilles is
       sown,

[1] Caesar, whose daughter was Pompey's wife.
[2] The modern Monaco. It is not certain that Caesar entered Italy by this route.
[3] Pompey had a large number of Eastern allies.
[4] The poet reverts to earlier Republican celebrities with a reference to Mummius
[5] Aemilius Paulus.
[6] Perseus, king of Macedonia.

Venging his Trojan sires and Minerva's outraged
    fane!
Who would leave thee, Cato, untold? thee, Cossus,
    unknown?   850
Gracchus's clan, or the Scipio pair, war's thunder-
    bolts twain,
Libya's ruin ; — forget Fabricius, prince in his need ;
Pass unsung Serranus, his furrows sowing with seed ?
Give me but breath, ye Fabians, to follow!   Yonder
    the great
Fabius thou, whose timely delays gave strength to
    the state.   855
Others will mould their bronzes to breathe with a
    tenderer grace,
Draw, I doubt not, from marble a vivid life to the face,
Plead at the bar more deftly, with sapient wands of
    the wise
Trace heaven's courses and changes, predict us stars
    to arise,   859
Thine, O Roman, remember, to reign over every race!
These be thine arts, thy glories, the ways of peace to
    proclaim,
Mercy to show to the fallen, the proud with battle to
    tame!' "

Thus Anchises, and then — as they marvelled — fur-
    ther anon :
" Lo, where decked in a conqueror's spoils Marcellus,[1]
    my son,
Strides from the war!   How he towers o'er all of the
    warrior train !   865
When Rome reels with the shock of the wild in-
    vaders' alarm,

[1] One of the chief Roman generals in the Second Punic War.

He shall sustain her state.   From his war-steed's sad-
　　dle, his arm
Carthage and rebel Gaul shall destroy, and the arms
　　of the slain
Victor a third time hang in his father Quirinus'
　　fane."

Then Aeneas, — for near him a youth [1] seemed ever
　　to pace,   870
Fair, of an aspect princely, with armor of glittering
　　grace,
Yet was his forehead joyless, his eye cast down as in
　　grief : —
" Who can it be, my father, that walks at the side of
　　the chief?
Is it his son, or perchance some child of his glorious
　　race
Born from remote generations?   And hark, how ring-
　　ing a cheer   875
Breaks from his comrades round!   What a noble
　　presence is here!
Though dark night with her shadow of woe floats over
　　his face ! "
Answer again Anchises began with a gathering tear :
" Ask me not, O my son, of thy children's infinite
　　pain !
Fate one glimpse of the boy to the world will grant,
　　and again   830
Take him from life.   Too puissant methinks to im-
　　mortals on high
Rome's great children had seemed, if a gift like this
　　from the sky

---

[1] Young Marcellus, the nephew of Augustus, probably intended
by the Emperor to be his successor   He died at the age of twenty.

Longer had been vouchsafed! What wailing of
    warriors bold
Shall from the funeral plain to the War-god's city be
    rolled!
What sad pomp thine eyes will discern, what pageant
    of woe,   885
When by his new-made tomb thy waters, Tiber, shall
    flow!
Never again such hopes shall a youth of thy lineage,
    Troy,
Rouse in his great forefathers of Latium! Never a
    boy
Nobler pride shall inspire in the ancient Romulus
    land!
Ah, for his filial love! for his old world faith! for his
    hand   890
Matchless in battle! Unharmed what foeman had
    offered to stand
Forth in his path, when charging on foot for the en-
    emy's ranks,
Or when plunging the spur in his foam-flecked
    courser's flanks!
Child of a nation's sorrow! if thou canst baffle the
    Fates'
Bitter decrees, and break for a while their barrier
    gates,   895
Thine to become Marcellus! I pray thee, bring me
    anon
Handfuls of lilies, that I bright flowers may strew on
    my son,
Heap on the shade of the boy unborn these gifts at
    the least,
Doing the dead, though vainly, the last sad service."
                        He ceased.

So from region to region they roam with curious eyes,
Traverse the spacious plains where shadowy darkness
    lies.   901
One by one Anchises unfolds each scene to his son,
Kindling his soul with a passion for glories yet to be
    won.
Speaks of the wars that await him beneath the Ital-
    ian skies,
Rude Laurentian [1] clans and the haughty Latinus'
    walls,   905
How to avoid each peril, or bear its brunt, as befalls.

Sleep has his portals twain; one fashioned of horn, it
    is said,
Whence come true apparitions by exit smooth from
    the dead ;
One with the polished splendor of shining ivory
    bright,
False are the only visions that issue thence from the
    night.   910
Thither Anchises leads them, exchanging talk by the
    way,
There speeds Sibyl and son by the ivory gate to the
    day.
Straight to his vessels and mates Aeneas journeyed,
    and bore
Thence for Caieta's harbor along the Italian shore.

                    SIR CHARLES BOWEN.

[1] Laurentum was the chief seat of Latinus, king of Latium

HORACE

BIOGRAPHICAL SKETCH

WHAT Virgil did for epic poetry, Horace did for lyric. Disregarding everything that Roman precursors in the same field had attempted, he looked to Greek poetry for his models. He even went so far as to speak slightingly of Catullus, whose lyrical gift far surpassed his own. His position in literature is unique. Without any very special inspiration, intensity of feeling, or profundity of thought, he produced a body of verse that not only succeeded in winning the interest of his own generation, but has held the attention of all subsequent ages. The real basis of this success is probably the character of the man, with his wide human sympathy, his practical wisdom and knowledge of the world, and his fund of humor and good fellowship, — qualities which find their expression through a medium to which felicity of phrase, unusual skill in handling metrical forms, and the fine sense of appropriateness in figure, word, and theme, which is an attribute of the artist only, give a rare distinction.

He was a freedman's son, born at Venusia, a town on the confines of Apulia, in 65 B. C. Of his education at Rome, which he owed to his father's foresight and self-sacrifice, he himself tells us something in his *Satires*.

> If pure and innocent I live, and dear
> To those I love (self-praise is venial here),
> All this I owe my father, who, though poor,
> Lord of some few lean acres, and no more,
> Was loath to send me to the village school,
> Whereto the sons of men of mark and rule —

Centurions and the like — were wont to swarm,
With slate and satchel on sinister arm,
And the poor dole of scanty pence to pay
The starveling teacher monthly to the day ;
But boldly took me when a boy to Rome,
There to be taught all arts, that grace the home
Of knight and senator.

He afterwards went to Athens to continue his studies, and he was there at the time of the assassination of Caesar. His sympathies at this period of his life seem to have been strongly Republican, for he joined the forces of Brutus and Cassius, and fought as a military tribune at Philippi. The seventh ode of the second book has a humorous reference to his experience as a soldier. When the war was over he was pardoned, and returned to Rome, where he became one of that coterie of literary men which was known as the Maecenas circle, enjoying the patronage of Augustus' prime minister, and of Augustus himself. Here or at his villa in the Sabine country, which he owed to the generosity of Maecenas, he spent his life, perfectly content with a modest competence and the fame which his writings won him.

His works consist of four books of *Odes*, the *Carmen Saeculare*, composed for the celebration of the Secular Games under Augustus, a number of *Epodes*, two books of *Satires*, and two books of *Epistles*. The collection of *Odes* shows a great variety of subjects. Some of them are love poems written in the mock serious tone which is peculiarly Horatian : for example, the thirteenth of the first book, addressed to Lydia, the sixteenth, to Tyndaris, the nineteenth, to Glycera, the twenty-third, to Chloe, the eighth of the second book, to Barine, the tenth of the third, to Lyce. The length of the list will serve to show that our poet's affections had a wider range than is altogether consistent with even a moderate standard of constancy. A much more serious vein appears in the odes devoted to questions of politics and morals, as the fourteenth of the first book, *To the Ship of State*, and the noble series at the beginning

of the third book. Another class consists of those in which
we see the poet in relation to his friends. As examples
may be cited from the first book the third, in which he gives
Godspeed to the ship on which Virgil sailed for Greece, the
twentieth, an invitation to Maecenas to visit him at his Sabine farm, and the twenty-ninth, in which he rallies Iccius
on his military ambition. The *Odes* are arranged within
the different books with regard to variety of theme and
metre. In the *Epodes*, which stand first, in order of composition, of all the poet's works, and which are written in
the iambic metre, there is a strong element of invective,
several of them being directed against individuals who in
one way or another had aroused the poet's ire, *e. g.*, the
parvenu whose ambition was to attract attention on the Sacra
Via by his elaborate dress (IV.), the alleged sorceress Cani-
dia (V.), and the writer who made better men than himself
the objects of his libellous attacks (VI.). The tone of the
Satires is much more moderate. These are in hexameters,
and are delightful sketches of different phases of Roman literary and social conditions. Among the most famous is the
fifth of the first book, which describes the various incidents
of a journey from Rome to Brundisium which Horace took
with Maecenas, Virgil, and other well-known men. The
ninth of the same book is a delightfully humorous account
of Horace's encounter with a bore on the Sacra Via. The
tenth deals with literary subjects. In the second book the
sixth contrasts life in the country and life in the town, the
eighth gives a picture of a parvenu's dinner party. In the
first book of the *Epistles* we have perhaps the poet's best
work. Some of the themes are not unlike those treated in
the *Satires*, but the style, informal and easy as ever, has
a still subtler charm that comes from greater maturity.
The second book is confined to literary topics, the third
epistle being the famous *Art of Poetry*, Horace's most pretentious essay in the field of literary criticism.

TO LYDIA

(Odes, I., 8.)

Why, Lydia, why,
I pray, by all the gods above,
    Art so resolved that Sybaris should die,
And all for love?

    Why doth he shun   5
The Campus Martius'[1] sultry glare?
    He that once recked of neither dust nor sun,
Why rides he there,

    First of the brave,
Taming the Gallic steed no more?   10
    Why doth he shrink from Tiber's yellow wave?
Why thus abhor

    The wrestler's oil,
As 't were from viper's tongue distilled?
    Why do his arms no livid bruises soil,   15
He, once so skilled,

    The disc or dart
Far, far beyond the mark to hurl,
    And tell me, tell me, in what nook apart,
Like baby-girl,   20

    Lurks the poor boy,
Veiling his manhood, as did Thetis' son,[2]
    To 'scape war's bloody clang, while fated Troy
Was yet undone?

                            Sir Theodore Martin.

[1] The plain by the Tiber, where the Roman youth exercised.
[2] Achilles, who was disguised as a girl by his mother to prevent
his being taken to the Trojan war.

WINTER

(Odes, I , 9)

SEE, Thaliarch, see, across the plain
    Soracte [1] white with snow !
Scarce may the laboring woods sustain
Their load, and locked in icy chain
    The streams have ceased to flow.   5

Logs on the fire, your biggest, fling,
    To thaw the pinching cold,
And from the time to take its sting
A pipkin forth of Sabine bring,
    Four mellowing summers old.   10

All else unto the Gods leave we ;
    When they have stilled the roar
Of winds that with the yeasty sea
Conflict and brawl, the cypress-tree,
    The old ash shake no more.   15

What with to-morrow comes forbear
    To ask, and count as gain
Each day fate grants, ere time and care
Have chilled thy blood, and thinned thy hair,
    Love's sweets do not disdain ;   20

Nor, boy, disdain the dance !   For, mark,
    Now is thy time to take
Joy in the play, the crowded park,
And those low whispers in the dark,
    Which trysting lovers make.   25

[1] Mt. Soracte, about twenty-five miles north of Rome

In the sweet laugh, that marks the spot
    Where hid the fair one lies,
The token from the wrist besought,
    Or from the finger wrung, that not
        Too cruelly denies.   ₃₀
               Sir Theodore Martin.

TO LEUCONOE

(Odes, I., 11.)

Ask not ('t is forbidden knowledge) what our destined
    term of year,
Mine and yours; nor scan the tables of your Baby-
    lonish seers.
Better far to bear the future, my Leuconoë, like the
    past,
Whether Jove has many winters yet to give, or this
    our last;
This, that makes the Tyrrhene billows spend their
    strength against the shore;   5
Strain your wine, and prove your wisdom; life is
    short; should hope be more?
In the moment of our talking, envious time has ebb'd
    away.
Seize the present: trust to-morrow e'en as little as
    you may.
                          John Conington

TO THE SHIP OF STATE[1]

(Odes, I., 14)

    O ship of state,
Shall new winds bear you back upon the sea?

[1] This ode was written at a time when there seemed to be some
possibility of civil war breaking out again.

What are you doing? Seek the harbor's lee
    Ere 't is too late!

    Do you bemoan   5
Your side was stripped of oarage in the blast?
Swift Africus has weakened, too, your mast;
    The sailyards groan.

    Of cables [1] bare,
Your keel can scarce endure the lordly wave. 10
Your sails are rent; you have no gods [2] to save,
    Or answer pray'r.

    Though Pontic pine,
The noble daughter of a far-famed wood,
You boast your lineage and title good, — 15
    A useless line!

    The sailor there
In painted sterns no reassurance finds;
Unless you owe derision to the winds,'
    Beware — beware! 20

    My grief erewhile,
But now my care — my longing! shun the seas
That flow between the gleaming Cyclades,[3]
    Each shining isle.

ROSWELL MARTIN FIELD.

[1] The ancients girded their vessels with cables in rough weather to prevent the planks from springing asunder.

[2] Images of gods were carried in the sterns of Roman ships Here they are represented as having been washed overboard.

[3] The Aegean Sea in the neighborhood of the Cyclades was proverbially dangerous

INNOCENCE

(Odes, I , 22)

FUSCUS, the man of life upright and pure,
Needeth nor javelin, nor bow of Moor,
Nor arrows tipped with venom deadly-sure,
    Loading his quiver :

Whether o'er Afric's burning sands he rides,   5
Or frosty Caucasus' bleak mountain-sides,
Or wanders lonely, where Hydaspes [1] glides,
    That storied river.

For as I strayed along the Sabine wood,
Singing my Lalage in careless mood,   10
Lo, all at once a wolf before me stood,
    Then turned and fled :

Creature so huge did warlike Daunia [2] ne'er
Engender in her forests' wildest lair,
Not Juba's [3] land, parched nurse of lions, e'er   15
    Such monster bred.

Place me, where no life-laden summer breeze
Freshens the meads, or murmurs 'mongst the trees,
Where clouds oppress, and withering tempests freeze
    From shore to shore ;   20

Place me beneath the sunbeams' fiercest glare,
On arid sands, no dwelling anywhere ;

[1] In India.
[2] Apulia, Horace's native province.
[3] King of Mauritania in northern Africa

Still Lalage's sweet smile, sweet voice even there
    I will adore.

Sir Theodore Martin.

TO CHLOE

(Odes, I , 23.)

You fly me, Chloe! like a vagrant fawn,
    Tracing the footprints of its parent deer
Through each sequestered path and mazy lawn,
    While woods and winds excite a causeless fear.

For should the aspen quiver to the breeze,   5
    Or the green lizards rustle in the brake,
It bounds in vague alarm among the trees,
    Its heart-pulse flutters, and its fibres quake.

Yet not as tigers do I follow you,
    Or Libyan lion, to destroy your charms ;   10
Then cease to linger in a mother's view,
    And learn the rapture of a lover's arms.

Lord Ravensworth

ON THE DEATH OF A FRIEND [1]

(Odes, I , 24)

Why should we stem the tears that needs must flow,
    Why blush, that they should freely flow and long,
To think of that dear head in death laid low ?
    Do thou inspire my melancholy song,

---

[1] Quintilius Varus, an intimate friend of Horace and Virgil. The ode is addressed to the latter.

Melpomene,[1] in whom the Muses' sire   5
Joined with a liquid voice the mastery of the lyre!

And hath the sleep that knows no waking morn
    Closed o'er Quintilius, our Quintilius dear?
Where shall be found the man of woman born
    That in desert might be esteemed his peer, —   10
Sincere as he, and resolutely just,
So high of heart, and all so absolute of trust?

He sinks into his rest, bewept of many,
    And but the good and noble weep for him,
But dearer cause thou, Virgil, hast than any,   15
    With friendship's tears thy friendless eyes to dim!
Alas, alas! Not to such woeful end
Didst thou unto the gods thy prayers unceasing send!

What though thou modulate the tuneful shell
    With defter skill than Orpheus of old Thrace,   20
When deftliest he played, and with its spell
    Moved all the listening forest from its place?
Yet never, never can thy art avail
To bring life's glowing tide back to the phantom pale,

Whom with his black inexorable wand,   25
    Hermes,[2] austere and pitiless as fate,
Hath forced to join the dark and spectral band
    In their sad journey to the Stygian gate.
'T is hard, great heavens, how hard! But to endure
Alleviates the pang we may nor crush nor cure!   30

SIR THEODORE MARTIN.

[1] The muse of tragedy.

[2] It was one of the functions of Hermes to conduct the souls of the dead to the lower world.

TO LYDIA

(Odes, I., 25)

SWAINS in numbers
Break your slumbers,
Saucy Lydia, now but seldom,
  Ay, though at your casement nightly,
  Tapping loudly, tapping lightly,   5
By the dozen once ye held them.

  Ever turning,
  Night and morning,
Swung your door upon its hinges ;
  Now, from dawn till evening's closing,   10
  Lone and desolate reposing,
Not a soul its rest infringes.

  Serenaders,
  Sweet invaders,
Scanter grow, and daily scanter,   15
  Singing, " Lydia, art thou sleeping?
  Lonely watch thy love is keeping !
Wake, oh wake, thou dear enchanter ! "

  Lorn and faded,
  You, as they did,   20
Woo, and in your turn are slighted ;
  Worn and torn by passion's fret,
  You, the pitiless coquette,
Waste by fires yourself have lighted,

  Late relenting,   25
  Half lamenting —

" Withered leaves strew wintry brooks !
　　Ivy garlands greenly darkling,
　　Myrtles brown with dewdrops sparkling,
Best beseem youth's glowing looks ! "　　　　30
　　　　　　　　　　SIR THEODORE MARTIN.

SIMPLICITY

(Odes, I., 38.)

OFF with Persian gear, I hate it,
　　Hate the wreaths with limebark bound,
Care not where the latest roses
　　Linger on the ground.

Bring me myrtle, naught but myrtle !　　　　5
　　Myrtle, boy, will well combine
Thee attending, me carousing,
　　'Neath the trellised vine.
　　　　　　　　　　W. E. GLADSTONE.

A WOMAN'S WORD

(Odes, II., 8.)

BARINE ! if some vengeance dread
Fell on your trebly perjured head,
Did but a single tooth or nail
Turn black, I might believe your tale !

But still the oftener that you dare　　　　5
To outrage heaven with oaths, more fair
That face becomes, and, still the more,
Admirers thicken and adore.

It answers then to treat with scorn [1]
A parent's ashes, and suborn 10
The silent stars and heavenly powers,
To favor falsehood such as yours.

For Venus laughs at woman's wiles ;
The Graces laugh, and Cupid smiles,
All as he barbs his glowing darts 15
On whetstone red with bleeding hearts.

Besides, each day augments your train,
Each hour new charms your slaves enchain ;
Nay, even those who late forswore
Your roof still linger round the door. 20

The mothers for their striplings dread,
Old men, and virgins lately wed,
Lest thine alluring air delay
The bridegroom on his homeward way.
LORD RAVENSWORTH.

THE GOLDEN MEAN

(Odes, II., 10.)

LICINIUS, wouldst thou steer life's wiser voyage,
Neither launch always into deep mid-waters,
Nor hug the shores, and, shrinking from the tempest,
Hazard the quicksand.

He who elects the golden mean of fortune, 5
Nor where dull squalor rots the time-worn hovel,
Nor where fierce envy storms the new-built palace,
Makes his safe dwelling.

[1] To swear falsely by them.

The wildest winds rock most the loftiest pine-trees,
The heaviest crash is that of falling towers, 10
The spots on earth most stricken by the lightning
    Are its high places.

The mind well-trained to cope with either fortune,
Takes hope in adverse things and fear in prosperous;
Deforming winters are restored or banished 15
    By the same Father.

If to-day frown, not therefore frowns to-morrow;
His deadly bow not always bends Apollo,
His hand at times the silent muse awakens
    With the sweet harpstring. 20

In life's sore straits brace and display thy courage;
Boldness is wisdom then: as wisely timid
When thy sails swell with winds too strongly fav'ring,
    Heed, and contract them.
                Lord Lytton.

A RECONCILIATION

(Odes, III., 9)

HORACE

When thy fair neck had never felt
Caress more dear than mine,
I happier lived than Persia's King,
    For I was thine.

LYDIA

When thy hot heart had never burned 5
For Chloe, and was mine,
I lived more famed than Ilia,[1]
    For I was thine.

[1] The mother of Romulus and Remus.

HORACE

To me my Thracian Chloe's rule
A joy most sweet doth give.   10
With songs and lute she charms ; I 'd die
    That she might live.

LYDIA

To me my Thurian[1] Calais
A burning love doth give ;
A mutual love, for I 'd twice die   15
    That he might live.

HORACE

What if I ope the door to thee,
And auburn Chloe spurn ;
If with a lasting yoke we 're joined,
    And love return ?   20

LYDIA

Though fickle thou as cork, and rough
As Hadria,[2] while he
Is fairer than a star, — I 'd live,
    I 'd die with thee.

NORMA ROSE WATERBURY.

TO THE SPRING OF BANDUSIA

(Odes, III , 13.)

BANDUSIA's fount, in clearness crystalline,
    O worthy of the wine, the flowers we vow !
        To-morrow shall be thine
        A kid, whose crescent brow

---

[1] Of Thurii, a city in Lucania   [2] The Adriatic Sea.

Is sprouting all for love and victory   5
 In vain: his warm red blood, so easily stirred,
  Thy gelid stream shall dye,
   Child of the wanton herd.

Thee the fierce Sirian star,[1] to madness fired,   9
 Forbears to touch: sweet cool thy waters yield,
  To ox with ploughing tired,
   And lazy sheep a-field.

Thou, too, one day shalt win proud eminence
 'Mid honored founts, while I the ilex sing
  Crowning the cavern whence   15
   Thy babbling wavelets spring.
        JOHN CONINGTON.

TO MAECENAS

(Odes, III., 29.)

MAECENAS, thou whose lineage springs
From old Etruria's Kings,
Come to my humble dwelling.[2]   Haste;
 A cask unbroached of mellow wine
Awaits thee, roses interlaced,   5
 And perfumes pressed from nard divine.
Leave Tibur[3] sparkling with its hundred rills;
 Forget the sunny slopes of Aesulae,[4]
And rugged peaks of Telegonian hills[5]
 That frown defiance on the Tuscan sea.   10

---

[1] The dog-star.   [2] His Sabine villa.
[3] The modern Tivoli, about sixteen miles northeast of Rome.
[4] Properly Aesula, a Latin town between Tibur and Praeneste.
[5] It was on a ridge of these mountains that Tusculum, said to have
been founded by Telegonus, son of Ulysses, was situated, about ten
miles southeast of Rome

Forego vain pomps, nor gaze around
   From the tall turret of thy palace home
On crowded marts, and summits temple-crowned,
   The smoke, the tumult, and the wealth of Rome.
   Come, loved Maecenas, come !   15

How oft in lowly cot
   Uncurtained, nor with Tyrian purple spread,
   Has weary state pillowed its aching head,
And smoothed its wrinkled brow, all cares forgot ?
Come to my frugal feast, and share my humble lot.
For now returning Cepheus [1] shoots again   21
   His fires long hid ; now Procyon and the star
Of the untamed Lion blaze amain :
   Now the light vapors in the heated air
Hang quivering : now the shepherd leads   25
His panting flock to willow bordered meads
By river banks, or to those dells
Remote, profound, where rough Sylvanus [2] dwells,
Where by mute margins voiceless waters creep,
And the hushed Zephyrs sleep.   30
Too long by civil cares opprest
Snatch one short interval of rest,
Nor fear lest from the frozen north
Don's arrowed thousands issue forth,
Or hordes from realms by Cyrus won,   35
Or Scythians from the rising sun.

Around the future Jove has cast
   A veil like night : he gives us power

[1] The constellation of which Cepheus formed a part, rose on the 9th of July, Procyon on the 15th of July, and Regulus, the brightest star of the Lion, on the 30th of July

[2] The deity who presided over fields and forests

To see the present and the past,
  But kindly hides the future hour,   40
And smiles when man with daring eye
Would pierce that dread futurity.

Wisely and justly guide thy present state,
  Life's daily duty: the dark future flows
  Like some broad river, now in calm repose,   45
Gliding untroubled to the Tyrrhene Shore,
Now by fierce floods precipitate,
  And on its frantic bosom bearing
    Homes, herds, and flocks,
      Drowned men, and loosened rocks;   50
  Uprooted trees from groaning forests tearing;
Tossing from peak to peak the sullen waters' roar.

Blest is the man who dares to say,
" Lord of myself, I 've lived to-day:
To-morrow let the Thunderer roll   55
Storm and thick darkness round the pole,
Or purest sunshine: what is past
Unchanged for evermore shall last.
Nor man, nor Jove's resistless sway
Can blot the record of one vanished day."   60
Fortune, capricious, faithless, blind,
  With cruel joy her pastime plays,
  Exalts, enriches, and betrays,
One day to me, anon to others kind.
  I praise her while she stays; —   65
But when she shakes her wanton wing
And soars away, her gifts to earth I fling,
And wrapped in Virtue's mantle live and die
Content with dowerless poverty.
When the tall ship with bending mast

Reels to the fury of the blast,
The merchant trembles, and deplores
Not his own fate, but buried stores
From Cyprian or Phoenician shores ; —
He with sad vows and unavailing prayer   75
  Rich ransom proffers to the angry Gods :
I stand erect: no groans of mine shall e'er
  Affront the quiet of those blest abodes :
My light unburthened skiff shall sail
Safe to the shore before the gale,   80
While the twin sons [1] of Leda point the way,
And smooth the billows with benignant ray.

Sir Stephen de Vere.

COUNTRY LIFE

(Epodes, II.)

" How happy in his low degree,
  How rich in humble poverty, is he
  Who leads a quiet country life;
  Discharg'd of business, void of strife,
  And from the griping scrivener free!   5
Thus ere the seeds of vice were sown,
  Liv'd men in better ages born,
Who plough'd, with oxen of their own,
  Their small paternal field of corn.
Nor trumpets summon him to war,   10
  Nor drums disturb his morning sleep,
Nor knows he merchants' gainful care,
  Nor fears the dangers of the deep.
The clamors of contentious law,
  And court and state, he wisely shuns,   15

---

[1] Castor and Pollux, who watched over mariners.

Nor brib'd with hopes, nor dar'd with awe,
  To servile salutations runs ;
But either to the clasping vine
  Does the supporting poplar wed,
Or with his pruning-hook disjoin   20
  Unbearing branches from their head,
  And grafts more happy in their stead :
Or, climbing to a hilly steep,
  He views his herds in vales afar,
Or shears his overburden'd sheep,   25
Or mead for cooling drink prepares,
  Of virgin honey in the jars.
Or, in the now declining year,
  When bounteous Autumn rears his head,
He joys to pull the ripen'd pear,   30
  And clust'ring grapes with purple spread.
The fairest of his fruit he serves,
  Priapus,[1] thy rewards :
Sylvanus too his part deserves,
  Whose care the fences guards.   35
Sometimes beneath an ancient oak,
  Or on the matted grass, he lies :
No god of Sleep he need invoke ;
  The stream, that o'er the pebbles flies,
  With gentle slumber crowns his eyes.   40
The wind, that whistles through the sprays,
  Maintains the consort of the song ;
And hidden birds, with native lays,
  The golden sleep prolong.
But when the blast of winter blows,   45
  And hoary frost inverts the year,
Into the naked woods he goes,
  And seeks the tusky boar to rear,

---

[1] A god of the fruitfulness of fields and of cattle.

With well-mouth'd hounds and pointed spear!
Or spreads his subtle nets from sight,   50
 With twinkling glasses, to betray
The larks that in the meshes light,
 Or makes the fearful hare his prey.
Amidst his harmless easy joys
 No anxious care invades his health,   55
Nor love his peace of mind destroys,
 Nor wicked avarice of wealth.
But if a chaste and pleasing wife,
To ease the business of his life,
Divides with him his household care,   60
Such as the Sabine matrons were,
Such as the swift Apulian's bride,
 Sun-burnt and swarthy though she be,
Will fire for winter nights provide,
 And without noise will oversee   65
 His children and his family;
And order all things till he come,
Sweaty and overlabor'd home;
If she in pens his flocks will fold,
 And then produce her dairy store,   70
With wine to drive away the cold,
 And unbought dainties of the poor;
Not oysters of the Lucrine lake[1]
 My sober appetite would wish,
 Nor turbot, or the foreign fish   75
That rolling tempests overtake,
 And hither waft the costly dish.
Not heathpout, or the rarer bird,
 Which Phasis[2] or Ionia yields,

[1] Properly an inner recess of the Bay of Cumae on the coast of Campania, famous for its oyster beds.

[2] A river of Colchis, an Asiatic province east of the Black Sea.

More pleasing morsels would afford   80
  Than the fat olives of my fields ;
Than shards or mallows for the pot,
  That keep the loosen'd body sound,
Or than the lamb that falls by lot
  To the just guardian [1] of my ground.   85
Amidst these feasts of happy swains,
  The jolly shepherd smiles to see
His flock returning from the plains ;
  The farmer is as pleas'd as he,
To view his oxen, sweating smoke,   90
Bear on their necks the loosen'd yoke :
To look upon his menial crew,
  That sit around his cheerful hearth,
And bodies spent in toil renew
  With wholesome food and country mirth."   95
This Morecraft [2] said within himself ;
  Resolv'd to leave the wicked town,
  And live retir'd upon his own,
    He call'd his money in ;
But the prevailing love of pelf   100
Soon split him on the former shelf,
  He put it out again.

JOHN DRYDEN.

A CHALLENGE

(Epodes, VI.)

WHY snap at the guests who do nobody harm,
  Turning tail at the sight of a wolf ?

---

[1] Terminus, the god of boundaries.
[2] Here at the end of the poem comes the surprise that the enthusiastic description of rural life is but the idle dream of a city money-lender

O cur! thy vain threats why not venture on me,
   Who can give back a bite for a bite?
Like mastiff Molossian[1] or Sparta's dun hound,   5
   Kindly friend to the shepherd am I,
But I prick up my ears and away through the snows,
   If a wild beast of prey run before;
But thou, if thou fillest the woods with thy bark,
   Art struck dumb at the sniff of a bone.   10
Ah, beware! I am rough when I come upon knaves,
   Ah, beware of a toss from my horns!
I'm as sharp as the wit[2] whom Lycambes deceived,
   Or the bitter foe[3] Bupalus roused;
Dost thou think, when a cur shows the grin of his
   teeth,   15
   That I'll weep, unavenged, like a child?

LORD LYTTON

A BORE

(Satires, I., 9)

ALONG the Sacred Road[4] I strolled one day,
Deep in some bagatelle (you know my way),
When up comes one whose name I scarcely knew —
"The dearest of dear fellows! how d'ye do?"
He grasped my hand — "Well, thanks: the same to
   you."   5
Then, as he still kept walking by my side,
To cut things short, "You've no commands?" I
   cried.

---

[1] From the country of the Molossi in the north of Greece
[2] The poet Archilochus (about 640 B. c), whose satirical attacks drove Lycambes to suicide.
[3] Hipponax, a poet of Ephesus (about 540 B. c.), whose satire had a similar result in the case of the sculptor Bupalus.
[4] It ran through the Forum

" Nay, you should know me : I'm a man of lore."
" Sir, I'm your humble servant all the more."
All in a fret to make him let me go,   10
I now walk fast, now loiter and walk slow,
Now whisper to my servant, while the sweat
Ran down so fast, my very feet were wet.
" O had I but a temper worth the name,
Like yours, Bolanus ! " [1] inly I exclaim,   15
While he keeps running on at a hand-trot,
About the town, the streets, I know not what.
Finding I made no answer, " Ah ' I see,
You're at a strait to rid yourself of me ;
But 't is no use : I 'm a tenacious friend,   20
And mean to hold you till your journey's end."
" No need to take you such a round : I go
To visit an acquaintance you don't know :
Poor man ! he 's ailing at his lodging, far
Beyond the bridge where Caesar's gardens are."   25
" Oh, never mind : I 've nothing else to do,
And want a walk, so I 'll step on with you."
Down go my ears, in donkey-fashion, straight ;
You 've seen them do it, when their load 's too great.
" If I mistake not," he begins, " you 'll find   30
Viscus [2] not more, nor Varius, to your mind :
There 's not a man can turn a verse so soon,
Or dance so nimbly when he hears a tune :
While, as for singing — ah ! my forte is there :
Tigellius' [3] self might envy me, I 'll swear."   35
He paused for breath : I falteringly strike in :
" Have you a mother ? have you kith or kin

[1] Some hot-headed friend of the poet.

[2] Viscus and Varius were members of the Maecenas circle, into
which the speaker was so anxious to be introduced

[3] A well-known musician to whom Julius Caesar and afterwards
Augustus showed favor

To whom your life is precious ? " " Not a soul :
My line 's extinct : I have interred the whole."
O happy they ! (so into thought I fell)   40
After life's endless babble they sleep well :
My turn is next : dispatch me : for the weird
Has come to pass which I so long have feared,
The fatal weird a Sabine beldame sung,
All in my nursery days, when life was young :   45
" No sword nor poison e'er shall take him off,
Nor gout, nor pleurisy, nor racking cough :
A babbling tongue shall kill him : let him fly
All talkers, as he wishes not to die."

    We got to Vesta's temple, and the sun   50
Told us a quarter of the day was done.
It chanced he had a suit, and was bound fast
Either to make appearance or be cast.
" Step here a moment, if you love me." " Nay ;
I know no law : 't would hurt my health to stay,   55
And then, my call." " I 'm doubting what to do,
Whether to give my lawsuit up or you."
" Me, pray ! " " I will not." On he strides again :
I follow, unresisting, in his train.

    " How stand you with Maecenas ? " he began :   60
" He picks his friends with care , a shrewd wise man :
In fact, I take it, one could hardly name
A head so cool in life's exciting game.
'T would be a good deed done, if you could throw
Your servant in his way ; I mean, you know,   65
Just to play second : in a month, I 'll swear,
You 'd make an end of every rival there."
" Oh, you mistake : we don't live there in league :
I know no house more sacred from intrigue :
I 'm never distanced in my friend's good grace   70
By wealth or talent : each man finds his place."

" A miracle ! if 't were not told by you,
I scarce should credit it."   " And yet 't is true."
" Ah, well, you double my desire to rise
To special favor with a man so wise."   75
" You 've but to wish it : 't will be your own fault,
If, with your nerve, you win not by assault :
He can be won : that puts him on his guard,
And so the first approach is always hard."
" No fear of me, sir : a judicious bribe   80
Will work a wonder with a menial tribe :
Say, I 'm refused admittance for to-day ;
I 'll watch my time ; I 'll meet him in the way,
Escort him, dog him.   In this world of ours
The path to what we want ne'er runs on flowers."   85
   'Mid all this prate there met us, as it fell,
Aristius, my good friend, who knew him well.
We stop : inquiries and replies go round :
" Where do you hail from ? "   " Whither are you
          bound ? "
There as he stood, impassive as a clod,   90
I pull at his limp arms, frown, wink, and nod,
To urge him to release me.   With a smile
He feigns stupidity : I burn with bile.
" Something there was you said you wished to tell
To me in private."   " Ay, I mind it well ;   95
But not just now : 't is a Jews' fast to-day :
Affront a sect so touchy ! nay, friend, nay."
" Faith, I 've no scruples."   " Ah ! but I 've a few :
I 'm weak, you know, and do as others do :
Some other time : excuse me."   Wretched me !   100
That ever man so black a sun should see !
Off goes the rogue, and leaves me in despair,
Tied to the altar with the knife in air :
When, by rare chance, the plaintiff in the suit

Knocks up against us : " Whither now, you brute ? " 105
He roars like thunder : then to me : " You 'll stand
My witness, sir ? "   " My ear 's at your command." [1]
Off to the court he drags him : shouts succeed :
A mob collects : thank Phoebus, I am freed.

John Conington

A LETTER OF INTRODUCTION

(Epistles, I , 9.)

Septimius [2] only understands, 't would seem,
How high I stand in, Claudius,[3] your esteem ;
For when he begs and prays me, day by day,
Before you his good qualities to lay,
As not unfit to share the heart and hearth   5
Of Nero, who selects his staff for worth ;
When he supposes you to me extend
The rights and place of a familiar friend, —
Much better than myself he sees and knows,
How far with you my commendation goes.   10
Plea upon plea, believe me, I have used,
In hope he 'd hold me from the task excused,
Yet feared the while, it might be thought I feigned
Too low what influence I perchance have gained ;
Dissembling it as nothing with my friends,   15
To keep it for my own peculiar ends.
So to escape such dread reproach, I put

[1] It was customary, on calling a person to witness, to touch his ear, apparently as an intimation that he was not to forget what he then heard.

[2] It is to this Septimius that Horace addresses the sixth ode of the second book

[3] Afterwards the Emperor Tiberius. His full name was Tiberius Claudius Nero

My blushes by, and boldly urge my suit.
If, then, you hold it as a grace, though small,
To doff one's bashfulness at friendship's call,   20
Enroll him in your suite, assured you 'll find
A man of heart in him, as well as mind.

SIR THEODORE MARTIN.

TO HIS BOOK [1]

(Epistles, I , 20)

I READ the meaning of that wistful look
Towards Janus [2] and Vertumnus, O my book!
Upon the Sosii's [3] shelves you long to stand,
Rubbed smooth with pumice by their skilful hand.
You chafe at lock and modest seal; you groan,   5
That you should only to a few be shown,
And sigh by all the public to be read,
You in far other notions trained and bred.
Well, go your way, whereso you please and when,
But once sent forth, you come not back again.   10
"Fool that I was! why did I change my lot?"
You 'll cry, when wounded in some tender spot,
And, out of fashion and of favor grown,
You 're crumpled up, and into corners thrown.
  Unless my ill-divining spirit be   15
Warped by chagrin at your perversity,
Thus with sure presage I forecast your doom ;
You will be liked by Rome, while in your bloom,
But soon as e'er the thumbing and the soil

[1] An epilogue to the first book of the *Epistles*
[2] There were bookshops in the neighborhood of the temple of Janus
and of Vertumnus
[3] A prominent firm of booksellers and publishers

Of vulgar hands shall your first freshness spoil,   20
You will be left to nibbling worms a prey,
Or sent as wrappers to lands far away.
Then one, whose warnings on your ears fell dead,
With a grim smile will note how you have sped,
Like him who, driven past patience by his mule,   25
Pushed o'er a precipice the restive fool, —
" Oho! so you 're determined to destroy
Yourself?   Well, do it, and I wish you joy!"
     Yet one thing more awaits your failing age;
That in suburban schools your well-thumbed page   30
Will be employed by pedagogues to teach
Young boys with painful pangs the parts of speech.
     But if, perchance, some sunny afternoon
To hear your voice shall eager ears attune,
Say, that though born a freedman's son, possessed   35
Of slender means, beyond the parent nest
I soared on ampler wing; thus what in birth
I lack, let that be added to my worth.
Say, that in war, and also here at home,
I stood well with the foremost men of Rome;   40
That small in stature, prematurely grey,
Sunshine was life to me and gladness; say
Besides, though hasty in my temper, I
Was just as quick to put my anger by.
Then, should my age be asked you, add that four   45
And forty years I 'd flourished, and no more,
In the December of that year, which fame
Will join with Lepidus'[1] and Lollius' name.

SIR THEODORE MARTIN.

[1] Lepidus and Lollius were the consuls in B. C. 21.

TIBULLUS

BIOGRAPHICAL SKETCH

FOUR books of *Elegies* have come down to us under the name of Tibullus, but of these only the first two and a part of the fourth are the work of that poet. Delia, whose real name is said to have been Plania, and Nemesis, whose identity has not been determined, are the central figures of the first and second book respectively. Most of the poems in the fourth book written by him relate to a love affair other than his own, *i. e*, that of Sulpicia and Cerinthus.

He was born about 54 B. C., probably at Pedum, a town in Latium, where his family, which belonged to the equestrian order, had an estate, apparently of considerable extent. Some part of this, if not all, escaped the confiscations of 41 B. C., and it was throughout his life the poet's favorite retreat. In Rome he was on terms of the greatest intimacy with Valerius Messala, who like Maecenas had surrounded himself with a group of literary men. Yet, while Messala's name occurs frequently in the *Elegies*, Tibullus' position does not at any time seem to have been one of dependence. Of the friendly relations which existed between him and Horace we know from the latter's works, one of the *Odes* (I. 33) and one of the *Epistles* (I. 4) being addressed to him. His death, which took place in 19 B. C., is the subject of the ninth elegy of the third book of Ovid's *Amores*.

Although of somewhat limited range, and not in any way the work of a poet of the first rank, Tibullus' elegies have an undeniable grace and charm of their own. Free from the frigid mythological pedantries that disfigure so large a part of elegiac literature, they reflect, probably faithfully enough, the character of the man, a conservative of conservatives, attached to old rites and customs simply because they were old, shrinking from the strenuous life of war and politics, gentle, sensitive, and, where women were concerned, of even more than elegiac susceptibility, a dreamer of dreams, eternally weaving vague fantasies of love and of the peace and quiet of rural seclusion.

THE POET'S IDEAL

(I 1.)

THE glittering ore let others vainly heap,
 O'er fertile vales extend th' enclosing mound;
With dread of neighb'ring foes forsake their
  sleep,
 And start aghast at every trumpet's sound.

Me humbler scenes delight, and calmer days; 5
 A tranquil life fair poverty secure;
Then boast, my hearth, a small but cheerful
  blaze,
 And, riches grasp who will, let me be poor.

Nor yet be hope a stranger to my door,
 But o'er my roof, bright goddess, still preside! 10
With many a bounteous autumn heap my floor,
 And swell my vats with must, a purple tide.

My tender vines I'll plant with early care,
 And choicest apples with a skilful hand;
Nor blush, a rustic, oft to guide the share, 15
 Or goad the sturdy ox along the land.

Let me, a simple swain, with honest pride,
    If chance a lambkin from its dam should roam,
Or sportful kid, the little wanderer chide,
    And in my bosom bear exulting home.   20

Here Pales [1] I bedew with milky showers,
    Lustrations yearly for my shepherd pay,
Revere [2] each antique stone bedeck'd with flowers
    That bounds the field, or points the doubtful way.

My grateful fruits, the earliest of the year,   25
    Before the rural god [3] shall duly wait.
From Ceres' gifts I 'll cull each browner ear,
    And hang a wheaten wreath before her gate.

The ruddy god [4] shall save my fruit from stealth,
    And far away each little plunderer scare ;   30
And you, the guardians once of ampler wealth,
    My household gods, shall still my off'rings share.

My numerous herds that wanton'd o'er the mead
    The choicest fatling then could richly yield ;
Now scarce I spare a little lamb to bleed   35
    A mighty victim for my scanty field.

And yet a lamb shall bleed, while, ranged around,
    The village youths shall stand in order meet,
With rustic hymns, ye gods, your praise resound,
    And future crops and future wines entreat.   40

[1] The tutelary deity of shepherds and cattle.
[2] In honor of Terminus, the god of boundaries
[3] Silvanus, who presided over woods and fields
[4] Statues of Priapus, colored red, were frequently placed in gardens

Then come, ye powers, nor scorn my frugal board,
    Nor yet the gifts clean earthen bowls convey ;
With these the first of men the gods adored,
    And form'd their simple shape of ductile clay.

My little flock, ye wolves, ye robbers, spare,   45
    Too mean a plunder to deserve your toil ;
For wealthier herds the nightly theft prepare ;
    There seek a nobler prey, and richer spoil.

For treasured wealth, nor stores of golden wheat,
    The hoard of frugal sires, I vainly call ;   50
A little farm be mine, a cottage neat,
    And wonted couch where balmy sleep may fall.

What joy to hear the tempest howl in vain,
    And clasp a fearful mistress to my breast;
Or lull'd to slumber by the beating rain,   55
    Secure and happy sink at last to rest.

These joys be mine ! — O grant me only these,
    And give to others bags of shining gold,
Whose steely heart can brave the boist'rous seas,
    The storm wide-wasting, or the stiff'ning cold. 60

Content with little, I would rather stay
    Than spend long months amid the wat'ry waste;
In cooling shades elude the scorching ray,
    Beside some fountain's gliding waters placed.

Oh perish rather all that's rich and rare,   65
    The diamond quarry, and the golden vein,
Than that my absence cost one precious tear,
    Or give some gentle maid a moment's pain.

With glittering spoils, Messala,[1] gild thy dome,
　　Be thine the noble task to lead the brave ;　　70
A lovely foe me captive holds at home,
　　Chain'd to her scornful gate, a watchful slave.

Inglorious post ! — and yet I heed not fame :
　　Th' applause of crowds for Delia I 'd resign :
To live with thee I 'd bear the coward's name,　　75
　　Nor 'midst the scorn of nations once repine.

With thee to live I 'd mock the ploughman's toil,
　　Or on some lonely mountain tend my sheep ;
At night I 'd lay me on the flinty soil,
　　And happy 'midst thy dear embraces sleep.　　80

What drooping lover heeds the Tyrian [2] bed,
　　While the long night is pass'd with many a sigh ;
Nor softest down with richest carpets spread,
　　Nor whisp'ring rills can close the weeping eye.

Of threefold iron were his rugged frame,　　85
　　Who, when he might thy yielding heart obtain,
Could yet attend the calls of empty fame,
　　Or follow arms in quest of sordid gain.

Unenvied let him drive the vanquished host,
　　Through captive lands his conquering armies lead ;
Unenvied wear the robe with gold emboss'd,　　91
　　And guide with solemn state his foaming steed.

Oh may I view thee with life's parting ray,
　　And thy dear hand with dying ardor press :

---

[1] His patron, who was in Asia Tibullus had been induced to accompany him, but falling ill at Corcyra had returned to Rome.
[2] Luxurious as those of the people of Tyre

Sure thou wilt weep — and on thy lover's clay,   95
    With breaking heart, print many a tender kiss!

Sure thou wilt weep — and woes unutter'd feel,
    When on the pile thou seest thy lover laid!
For well I know, nor flint, nor ruthless steel
    Can arm the breast of such a gentle maid.   100

From the sad pomp, what youth, what pitying fair,
    Returning slow, can tender tears refrain?
O Delia, spare thy cheeks, thy tresses spare,
    Nor give my ling'ring shade a world of pain.

But now while smiling hours the Fates bestow,   105
    Let love, dear maid, our gentle hearts unite!
Soon death will come and strike the fatal blow;
    Unseen his head, and veil'd in shades of night.

Soon creeping age will bow the lover's frame,
    And tear the myrtle chaplet from his brow: 110
With hoary locks ill suits the youthful flame,
    The soft persuasion, or the ardent vow.

Now the fair queen of gay desire is ours,
    And lends our follies an indulgent smile:
'T is lavish youth's t' enjoy the frolic hours,   115
    The wanton revel and the midnight broil.

Your chief, my friends and fellow-soldiers, I
    To these light wars will lead you boldly on:
Far hence, ye trumpets, sound, and banners fly;
    To those who covet wounds and fame begone.   120

And bear them fame and wounds; and riches bear;
    There are that fame and wounds and riches prize.

For me, while I possess one plenteous year,
I 'll wealth and meagre want alike despise.
JAMES GRAINGER.

A RURAL FESTIVAL[1]

(II 1.)

ATTEND! and favor! as our sires ordain,
The fields we lustrate, and the rising grain :
Come, Bacchus, and thy horns with grapes surround ;
Come, Ceres, with thy wheaten garland crowned ;
This hallow'd day suspend each swain his toil,　　　　5
Rest let the plough, and rest th' uncultured soil :
Unyoke the steer, his racks heap high with hay,
And deck with wreaths his honest front to-day.
Be all your thoughts to this grand work applied !
And lay, ye thrifty fair, your wool aside !　　　　10
Hence I command you mortals from the rite,
Who spent in amorous blandishment the night,
The vernal powers in chastity delight.
But come, ye pure, in spotless garbs array'd !
For you the solemn festival is made ;　　　　15
Come! follow thrice the victim round the lands !
In running water purify your hands !
See to the flames the willing victim come !
Ye swains with olive crown'd, be dumb! be dumb!
" From ills, O sylvan gods, our limits shield,　　　　20
To-day we purge the farmer and the field ;
Oh let no weeds destroy the rising grain ;
By no fell prowler be the lambkin slain ;

---

[1] The central theme of this elegy is the celebration of the Ambar-
valia, which took place annually in April Its purpose was the
purification of the fields

So shall the hind dread penury no more,
But gayly smiling o'er his plenteous store, 25
With liberal hand shall larger billets bring,
Heap the broad hearth, and hail the genial spring.
His numerous bond-slaves all in goodly rows,
With wicker huts your altars shall enclose.
That done, they 'll cheerly laugh, and dance, and play,
And praise your goodness in their uncouth lay." 31

The gods assent! see! see! those entrails show
That heaven approves of what is done below!
Now quaff Falernian, let my Chian wine,
Poured from the cask in massy goblets shine! 35
Drink deep, my friends; all, all, be madly gay,
'T were irreligion not to reel to-day!
Health to Messala, every peasant toast,
And not a letter of his name be lost!

O come, my friend, whom Gallic triumphs[1] grace,
Thou noblest splendor of an ancient race; 41
Thou whom the arts all emulously crown,
Sword of the state, and honor of the gown;
My theme is gratitude, inspire my lays!
Oh be my genius! while I strive to praise 45
The rural deities, the rural plain.
The use of foodful corn they taught the swain.
They taught man first the social hut to raise,
And thatch it o'er with turf, or leafy sprays;
They first to tame the furious bull essay'd, 50
And on rude wheels the rolling carriage laid.
Man left his savage ways; the garden glow'd
Fruits not their own admiring trees bestow'd,

---

[1] Messala was given a triumph in 27 B. C. for his victory over the Aquitanians in the battle of Atax

While through the thirsty ground meandering run-
　　nels flowed.
There bees of sweets despoil the breathing spring,　55
And to their cells the dulcet plunder bring.
The ploughman first to soothe the toilsome day
Chanted in measur'd feet his sylvan lay:
And, seed-time o'er, he first in blithesome vein
Piped to his household gods the hymning strain.　60
Then first the press with purple wine o'erran,
And cooling water made it fit for man.
The village lad first made a wreath of flowers
To deck in spring the tutelary powers:
Blest be the country, yearly there the plain　65
Yields, when the dog-star burns, the golden grain:
Thence too thy chorus, Bacchus, first began,
The painted clown first laid the tragic plan.
A goat, the leader of the shaggy throng,
The village sent it, recompensed the song.　70
There too the sheep his woolly treasure wears;
There too the swain his woolly treasure shears;
This to the thrifty dame long work supplies;
The distaff hence, and basket took their rise.
Hence too the various labors of the loom,　75
Thy praise, Minerva,[1] and Arachne's[2] doom!
'Mid mountain herds, Love first drew vital air,
Unknown to man, and man had nought to fear;
'Gainst herds, his bow th' unskilful archer drew;
Ah, my pierced heart, an archer now too true!　80
Now herds may roam untouch'd, 't is Cupid's joy,
The brave to vanquish, and to fix the coy.

[1] Spinning, weaving, and similar feminine activities were under the patronage of Minerva
[2] The story is that Arachne was changed into a spider through the machinations of Athene, who was jealous of her skill in weaving

The youth whose heart the soft emotion feels,
Nor sighs for wealth, nor waits at grandeur's heels ;
Age fired by Love is touch'd by shame no more,   85
But blabs its follies at the fair one's door !
Led by soft Love, the tender, trembling fair
Steals to her swain, and cheats suspicion's care,
With outstretched arms she wins her darkling way,
And tiptoe listens that no noise betray !   90

Ah, wretched those on whom dread Cupid frowns !
How happy they whose mutual choice he crowns !
Will Love partake the banquet of the day ?
O come — but throw thy burning shafts away.

Ye swains, begin to mighty Love the song,   95
Your songs, ye swains, to mighty Love belong !
Breathe out aloud your wishes for my fold,
Your own soft vows in whispers may be told.
But hark ! loud mirth and music fire the crowd —
Ye now may venture to request aloud !   100

Pursue your sports ; night mounts her curtain'd
        wain ;
The dancing stars compose her filial train ;
Black muffled sleep steals on with silent pace,
And dreams flit last, imagination's race !

JAMES GRAINGER

PROPERTIUS

BIOGRAPHICAL SKETCH

OF the life of Propertius, unquestionably the greatest of Roman elegiac poets, very little is known in addition to the few facts that he himself relates. He was an Umbrian, and of the various places which have claimed him, Assisi probably has the strongest case. The year 50 B. C. may be given as an approximate date for his birth. He was a member of the Maecenas circle in Rome, but of all his literary contemporaries Ovid alone mentions him. In none of his poems do we find a reference to any event later than 16 B. C., and with some show of reason his death is generally placed about that time.

Five books of *Elegies* bear witness to his unusual powers. The first, commonly known as the *Cynthia*, from the name of the woman who constitutes its principal theme, was published when he was only twenty. It shows extraordinary precocity on the technical as well as on the emotional side. In the second and third books the erotic element is still prominent, but Cynthia is no longer the poet's only thought. In the fourth and fifth books there is greater variety. National themes are introduced, and some poems dealing with the origins of Roman customs and institutions mark the first attempts by a Roman poet in the field of the aetiological elegy.

It is a somewhat disagreeable personality that Propertius' poems reveal. He seems to have been strangely self-centred, gloomy, and morbid. No matter what his theme may be, it is his own relation to it that interests him most, and to himself he almost invariably return ⁄ If his sufferings were great, the contemplation of them afforded him a pleasure that was, in part at least, a recompense. His happiness would seem to have reached its highest point in brooding over his own death and burial.

Unlike that of his contemporary Tibullus his work shows strong Alexandrian influence. His models were Callimachus and Philetas, and it is to his imitation of them that the undue preponderance of mythological lore and the tendency to recondite and abstruse allusion are largely due. To the same source must be ascribed the excessive elaboration of detail and superabundance of ornament that characterize some of his elegies. Yet in spite of these faults we find everywhere traces of a genius of rare brilliancy · imagination of great range and vividness, deftness in word and phrase, and a fine ear for rhythmical effects.

BEAUTY UNADORNED

(I., 2)

DEAR girl,[1] what boots it thus to dress thy hair,
Or flaunt in silken garment rich and rare,
To reek of perfume from a foreign mart,
And pass thyself for other than thou art —
Thus Nature's gift of beauty to deface   5
And rob thy own fair form of half its grace?
Trust me, no skill can greater charms impart;
Love is a naked boy and scorns all art.
Bears not the sod unbidden blossoms rare?
The untrained ivy, is it not most fair?   10
Greenest the shrub on rocks untended grows,
Brightest the rill in unhewn channel flows.

[1] Cynthia.

The beach is with unpolished pebbles gay,
And birds untutored trill the sweetest lay.
Not thus the damsels of the golden age   15
Were wont the hearts of heroes to engage :
Their loveliness was to no jewels due,
But to such tints as once Apelles [1] drew.
From vain coquettish arts they all were free,
Content to charm with simple modesty.   20
By thee despite to me will ne'er be done ;
The woman pleases well who pleases one.

GOLDWIN SMITH.

TO MAECENAS [2]

(II., 1.)

YOU ask, why thus my loves I still rehearse,
Whence the soft strain and ever-melting verse ?
From Cynthia all that in my numbers shines ;
She is my genius, she inspires the lines ;
No Phoebus else, no other Muse I know,   5
She tunes my easy rhyme, and gives the lay to flow.
If the loose curls around her forehead play,
Or lawless, o'er their ivory margin stray :
If the thin Coan web [3] her shape reveal,
And half disclose those limbs it should conceal ;   10
Of those loose curls, that ivory front I write ;
Of the dear web whole volumes I indite :
Or if to music she the lyre awake,
That the soft subject of my song I make,
And sing with what a careless grace she flings   15
Her artful hand across the sounding strings

[1] A Greek painter of the Alexandrian period
[2] The publication of the first book of his *Elegies* had won for the poet the favor of Maecenas.   [3] Of silk from the island of Coos

If sinking into sleep she seem to close
Her languid lids, I favor her repose
With lulling notes, and thousand beauties see
That slumber brings to aid my poetry.   20
When, less averse, and yielding to desires,
She half accepts, and half rejects, my fires,
While to retain the envious lawn she tries,
And struggles to elude my longing eyes,
The fruitful Muse from that auspicious night   25
Dates the long Iliad of the amorous fight.
In brief, whate'er she do, or say, or look,
'T is ample matter for a lover's book ;
And many a copious narrative you 'll see
Big with the important nothing's history.   30
Yet would the tyrant love permit me raise
My feeble voice, to sound the victor's praise,
To paint the hero's toil, the ranks of war,
The laurell'd triumph and the sculptured car ;
No giant race, no tumult of the skies,   35
No mountain-structures [1] in my verse should rise,
Nor tale of Thebes, nor Ilium there should be,
Nor how the Persian trod th' indignant sea ; [2]
Not Marius' Cimbrian [3] wreaths would I relate,
Nor lofty Carthage struggling with her fate.   40
Here should Augustus great in arms appear,
And thou, Maecenas, be my second care ;
Here Mutina [4] from flames and famine free,

[1] In their attempt to storm heaven, the giants, according to the old story, piled mountain upon mountain.

[2] On the occasion of the Persian invasion of Greece in 480 B C , Xerxes' host crossed the Hellespont by means of two bridges of boats.

[3] Marius won a decisive victory over the invading forces of the Cimbri, near Verona, in 101 B. C.

[4] A town in Cisalpine Gaul, where the consuls Hirtius and Pansa were killed in battle in 43 B C

And there th' ensanguined wave of Sicily,[1]
And sceptred Alexandria's [2] captive shore,   45
And sad Philippi,[3] red with Roman gore:
Then, while the vaulted skies loud Ios [4] rend,
In golden chains should loaded monarchs bend,
And hoary Nile with pensive aspect seem
To mourn the glories of his sevenfold stream,   50
While prows,[5] that late in fierce encounter met,
Move through the Sacred Way and vainly threat,
Thee too the Muse should consecrate to fame,
And with her garlands weave thy ever-faithful name.

   But nor Callimachus' [6] enervate strain   55
May tell of Jove, and Phlegra's [7] blasted plain;
Nor I with unaccustom'd vigor trace
Back to its source divine the Julian race.
Sailors to tell of winds and seas delight,
The shepherd of his flocks, the soldier of the fight,   60
A milder warfare I in verse display;
Each in his proper art should waste the day:
Nor thou my gentle calling disapprove,
To die is glorious in the bonds of love.

   Happy the youth, and not unknown to fame,   65
Whose heart has never felt a second flame.
Oh, might that envied happiness be mine!

---

  [1] Sextus Pompeius had been defeated in a number of naval battles near Sicily.

  [2] Alexandria was taken in B c. 30

  [3] In Macedonia, the scene of the victory of Antony and Octavian over Brutus and Cassius in 42 B. C.

  [4] " Io ! " was a cry of triumph

  [5] When a naval victory was celebrated, the beaks of ships were sometimes borne in the triumphal procession.

  [6] The famous Alexandrian poet who flourished about 260 B c

  [7] Perhaps the volcanic plain along the coast of Campania in the neighborhood of Cumae It was said to have been the battleground of the gods and the giants.

To Cynthia all my wishes I confine ;
Or if, alas ! it be my fate to try
Another love, the quicker let me die :   70
But she, the mistress of my faithful breast,
Has oft the charms of constancy confessed,
Condemns her fickle sex's fond mistake,
And hates the tale of Troy for Helen's sake.
Me from myself the soft enchantress stole ;   75
Ah ! let her ever my desires control,
Or if I fall the victim of her scorn,
From her loved door may my pale corse be borne.
The power of herbs can other harms remove,
And find a cure for every ill but love.   80
The Malian's [1] hurt Machaon could repair,
Heal the slow chief, and send again to war ;
To Chiron [2] Phoenix [3] owed his long-lost sight,
And Phoebus' son [4] recall'd Androgeos to the light.
Here arts are vain, e'en magic here must fail,   85
The powerful mixture and the midnight spell ;
The hand that can my captive heart release,
And to this bosom give its wonted peace,
May the long thirst of Tantalus [5] allay,
Or drive th' infernal vulture from his prey.[6]   90

[1] Philoctetes of Malis, a district in the south of Thessaly. Bitten by a snake on the way to Troy, he had been abandoned at Lemnos, but in the tenth year of the war he was healed by Machaon, son of Aesculapius, and joined the Greeks once more at Troy. It was he who killed Paris.

[2] The centaur who was entrusted with the education of Achilles.

[3] The friend of Achilles

[4] Aesculapius, who brought back to life Androgeos, son of Minos of Crete

[5] Afflicted with perpetual thirst in the lower world for revealing the secrets of Jove.

[6] Prometheus, who for stealing fire from heaven was fastened to one of the cliffs of Mt. Caucasus, where a vulture preyed upon his liver

For ills unseen what remedy is found?
Or who can probe the undiscover'd wound?
The bed avails not, nor the leech's care,
Nor changing skies can hurt, nor sultry air.
'T is hard th' elusive symptoms to explore;   95
To-day the lover walks, to-morrow is no more;
A train of mourning friends attend his pall,
And wonder at the sudden funeral.
    When then my fates that breath they gave shall
        claim,
And the short marble but preserve a name,   100
A little verse my all that shall remain,
Thy passing courser's slacken'd speed restrain,
(Thou envied honor of thy poet's days,
Of all our youth th' ambition and the praise!)
Then to my quiet urn awhile draw near,   105
And say, while o'er the place you drop a tear,
"Love and the fair were of his life the pride;
He lived, while she was kind; and when she frown'd,
        he died."

                                THOMAS GRAY

A CHANGE OF VIEW

(III, 5, 19 *seq*)

LONG as of youth the joyous hours remain,
Me may Castalia's [1] sweet recess detain,
Fast by th' umbrageous vale lull'd to repose,
Where Aganippe [2] warbles as it flows;
Or roused by sprightly sounds from out the trance,   5
I 'd in the ring knit hands, and join the Muses' dance.

[1] A spring on Mt Parnassus sacred to Apollo and the Muses.
[2] A spring on Mt Helicon in Boeotia

Give me to send the laughing bowl around,
My soul in Bacchus' pleasing fetters bound;
Let on this head unfading flowers reside,
There bloom the vernal rose's earliest pride;   10
And when, our flames commission'd to destroy,
Age step 'twixt love and me, and intercept the joy;
When my changed head these locks no more shall
    know,
And all its jetty honors turn to snow;
Then let me rightly tell of nature's ways;   15
To Providence, to Him my thoughts I'd raise,
Who taught this vast machine its steadfast laws,
That first, eternal, universal cause;
Search to what region yonder star retires,
That monthly waning hides her paly fires,   20
And whence, anew revived, with silver light
Relumes her crescent orb to cheer the dreary night:
How rising winds the face of ocean sweep,
Where lie th' eternal fountains of the deep,
And whence the cloudy magazines maintain   25
Their wintry war, or pour th' autumnal rain;
How flames, perhaps, with dire confusion hurl'd,
Shall sink this beauteous fabric of the world;
What colors paint the vivid arch [1] of Jove;
What wondrous force the solid earth can move,   30
When Pindus' [2] self approaching ruin dreads,
Shakes all his pines, and bows his hundred heads;
Why does yon orb, so exquisitely bright,
Obscure his radiance in a short-lived night;
Whence the seven Sisters' [3] congregated fires,   35
And what Boötes' [4] lazy wagon tires;
How the rude surge its sandy bounds control;

[1] The rainbow. [2] A mountain in Thessaly.
[3] The Pleiades. [4] The Little Bear.

Who measured out the year and bade the seasons
    roll;
If realms beneath those fabled torments know,
Pangs without respite, fires that ever glow,   40
Earth's monster brood [1] stretch'd on their iron bed,
The hissing terrors round Alecto's [2] head,
Scarce to nine acres Tityus' bulk confined,
The triple dog that scares the shadowy kind,
All angry heaven inflicts, or hell can feel,   45
The pendent rock, Ixion's whirling wheel,
Famine at feasts, and thirst amid the stream;
Or are our fears th' enthusiast's empty dream,
And all the scenes, that hurt the grave's repose,
But pictured horror and poetic woes.   50

    These soft inglorious joys my hours engage;
Be love my youth's pursuit, and science crown my
    age.
You, whose young bosoms feel a nobler flame,
Redeem what Crassus [3] lost, and vindicate his name.
                    THOMAS GRAY.

A ROMAN MATRON TO HER HUSBAND [4]

(V, 11.)

WEEP no more, Paullus, where thy wife is laid:
    At the dark gate thy prayer will beat in vain;

---

[1] The giants, sons of Earth, who rebelled against Jove
[2] One of the Furies.
[3] Crassus had been defeated by the Parthians in a disastrous battle
in 55 B. C.
[4] One of the most famous of Propertius's elegies. Cornelia is represented as addressing her husband from the tomb. She was the daughter of Publius Cornelius Scipio by Scribonia who was afterwards the
wife of Augustus Her husband was Paullus Aemilius Lepidus, consul in B C 34.

Once let the nether realm receive the shade,
    The adamantine bar turns not again.

Prayer may move heaven, but, the sad river passed, 5
    The grave relentless gives not back its dead :
Such sentence spake the funeral trumpet's blast,
    As sank in funeral flames thy loved one's head.

No honors that on Paullus' consort wait,
    No pride of ancestry or storied bust, 10
Could save Cornelia from her cruel fate :
    Now one small hand may hold her grandeur's dust.

Shades of the Dead and sluggish fens that gloom
    Around Hell's murky shores my steps to bind,
Before my hour, but pure in soul, I come, 15
    Then let the Judge of all the Dead be kind.

Call the dread court : let silence reign in Hell ;
    Set for an hour the damned from torture free,
And still the Guardian Hound. If aught I tell
    But truth, fall Hell's worst penalty on me. 20

Is honor to a glorious lineage due ?
    What my sires were, Afric and Spain proclaim ;
Nor poor the blood I from my mother drew,
    For well may Libo's match with Scipio's name.

And when, my virgin vesture laid aside, 25
    They placed the matron's wreath upon my head,
Thine, Paullus, I became, till death thy bride :
    " Wedded to one " shall on my tomb be read.

By glory's shrine I swear, great Scipio's tomb,
    Where sculptured Afric sits a captive maid, 30

By him [1] that led the Macedonian home
   In chains and all his pride in ruin laid,

Never for me was bent the censor's law;
   Never by me wrong to your honor done;
Your scutcheon to Cornelia owes no flaw,   35
   To her your roll of worthy names owes one.

Nor failed my virtue; faithful still I stood,
   And stainless from the bridal to the bier.
No law I needed save my noble blood;
   The basely born are innocent through fear.   40

Judge strictly as ye will, within the bound
   Of Death's wide realm not one, matron or maid,
Howe'er renowned in story, will be found
   To shun communion with Cornelia's shade.

Not she, the wife of purity unstained,   45
   At touch of whose pure hand Cybele moved,[2]
When hands less pure in vain the cable strained,
   Not she,[3] the virgin of the gods beloved,

For whom, when Vesta's sacred fire was lost,
   It from her votary's robe rekindled sprang.   50
And thou, dear mother, did thy child e'er cost
   Thee, save by her untimely fate, a pang?

Short was my span, yet children three I bore,
   And in their arms I drew my latest breath;

[1] Aemilius Paullus, who conquered Perseus in 168 B C. His son became a Scipio by adoption

[2] The ship that was bearing the image of Cybele to Rome ran aground in the Tiber, and it was only when the vestal Claudia laid her hand upon the cable that it could be moved

[3] The vestal Aemilia.

In these I live although my life is o'er;   55
  Their dear embraces took the sting from death.

Twice did my brother fill the curule chair,[1]
  There sat he when I parted.   Daughter, thou
Wast born a censor's child; be it thy care
  Like me, by wedded troth, his rule to show.   60

Now I bequeath our children to thy heart,
  Husband, though I am dust, that care is mine;
Father and mother too henceforth thou art;
  Around one neck now all those arms must twine.

Kiss for thyself and then for her that's gone;   65
  Thy love alone the whole dear burden bears;
If e'er for me thou weepest, weep alone,
  And see, to cheat their lips, thou driest thy
        tears.

Be it enough by night thy grief to pour,
  By night to commune with Cornelia's shade;   70
If to my likeness in thy secret bower
  Thou speakest, speak as though I answer made.

Should time bring on another wedding day,
  And set a stepdame in your mother's place,
My children, let your looks no gloom betray;   75
  Kind ways and loving words will win her grace.

Nor speak too much of me; the jealous ear
  Of the new wife perchance offence may take;
But ah! if my poor ashes are so dear
  That he will live unwedded for my sake,   80

---

[1] Its use was confined to the chief state officials.

Learn, children, to forestall your sire's decline,
  And let no lonesome thought come near his life;
Add to your years what Fate has reft from mine;
  Blest in my children let him bless his wife.

Though brief my day, I have not lived in vain;   85
  Mourning for child of mine I never wore;
When from my home went forth my funeral train,
  Not one was missing there of all I bore.

My cause is pleaded.   Now, ye mourners rise
  And witness bear till earth my meed decree;   90
If worth may claim its guerdon in the skies,
  My glorious ancestors may welcome me.
                                GOLDWIN SMITH.

OVID

BIOGRAPHICAL SKETCH

AT the end of the fourth book of the *Tristia*, Ovid, following a custom of Roman elegiac poets, has given a sketch of his life. He was born in 43 B. C., at Sulmo, a town of the Pelignians, about seventy miles east of Rome. His father, who belonged to the equestrian order, destined him for a legal and political career, and with this end in view sent him to Rome and afterwards to Athens to study under some of the distinguished rhetoricians of the day. His own inclinations, however, were towards literature rather than law, and when he was about twenty-four he abandoned his legal pursuits to devote himself entirely to poetry. The *Amores* made him famous as a writer of erotic elegies, and this success was followed up by the publication of the *Heroides*, a series of imaginary letters in elegiac verse from deserted women to their erring lovers, and the pseudo-didactic poem on the *Art of Love.* Later came the *Metamorphoses*, a collection of mythological stories in fifteen books, written in hexameters, and the *Fasti*, a poetical calendar of the first six months of the year. He was at the height of prosperity when in 8 A. D. he was struck down by a decree of Augustus which banished him to Tomi, a desolate place on the shores of the Black Sea. The cause of his banishment has never been accurately determined, but the conjecture that he had been in some way implicated in the intrigue of Julia, the notorious granddaughter of Augustus. with Decimus Silanus, has a fair degree of probability. The sentence was never remitted, and he died at Tomi in

18 A. D.   To the period of his exile belong the *Epistolae ex Ponto*, the *Tristia*, and other miscellaneous poems.

While Propertius puzzles us by his curious self-absorption, Ovid amazes us by his cleverness, his quickness, his versatility, and his astounding facility in metrical composition.   The *Metamorphoses* constitute one of the most remarkable *tours de force* in literary history.   They show, successfully combined in one whole, a bewildering array of myths that have as their only common theme some kind of change of form.   Fable is linked to fable, myth to myth, with a nicety of juncture that never fails, a variety of device that seems to be inexhaustible.   In the stories themselves we find all the qualities of the literary artist whose natural gifts have been supplemented by training and practice · verve in narration, picturesqueness in description, skill in the elaboration of simile or metaphor, and the faculty of writing in smoothly flowing verse that knows no pause. Swift, vivid, brilliant, never wearying us except by the infinity of his surprises, coercing our admiration of his storyteller's art, he carries us along through his strange world of ever changing forms that begin with Deucalion and end with Julius Caesar.   In the *Fasti*, with their explanations of the festivals of the different months, we see the same characteristics, but added to them something more serious, an aetiological spirit that makes them the most substantial of all the poet's works.   His erotic elegies and his *Art of Love*, written to amuse himself and others as flippant as himself, show him to have been, in some moods at least, frivolous to the last degree of frivolity, careless of himself and of the society in which he moved, such a man as could only have been produced by an age in which the old republican virtue and simplicity had given way to luxury and even immorality.

DIDO TO AENEAS [1]

(Heroides, VII)

So, on Maeander's [2] banks, when death is nigh,
The mournful swan sings her own elegy.
Not that I hope (for oh, that hope were vain!)
By words your lost affection to regain;
But, having lost whate'er was worth my care,   5
Why should I fear to lose a dying prayer?
'T is then resolved poor Dido must be left,
Of life, of honor, and of love bereft!
While you, with loosened sails, and vows, prepare
To seek a land that flies the searcher's care;   10
Nor can my rising towers your flight restrain,
Nor my new empire, offered you in vain.
Built walls you shun, unbuilt you seek; that land
Is yet to conquer, but you this command.
Suppose you landed where your wish designed,   15
Think what reception foreigners would find,
What people is so void of common sense,
To vote succession from a native prince?
Yet there new sceptres and new loves you seek,
New vows to plight, and plighted vows to break.   20
When will your towers the height of Carthage know?
Or when your eyes discern such crowds below?

[1] The visit to Carthage was one of the most important episodes in the long voyage of Aeneas and his Trojans from Troy to Italy. Driven by a storm on the coast of Africa, they had been hospitably entertained by Queen Dido. When, after some time, Aeneas announced his intention to depart, the queen, loving him, urged him to remain and share her kingdom with her. He, however, refused, and was making his final preparations to leave the country, when she sent him this letter as a last appeal.

[2] A river in Asia Minor.

If such a town and subjects you could see,
Still would you want a wife who loved like me.
For oh! I burn, like fires with incense bright;   25
Not holy tapers flame with purer light.
Aeneas is my thoughts' perpetual theme,
Their daily longing, and their nightly dream.
Yet he 's ungrateful and obdurate still;
Fool that I am to place my heart so ill!   30
Myself I cannot to myself restore;
Still I complain, and still I love him more.
Have pity, Cupid, on my bleeding heart,
And pierce thy brother's[1] with an equal dart.
I rave, nor canst thou Venus' offspring be,   35
Love's mother could not bear a son like thee.
From hardened oak, or from a rock's cold womb,
At least thou art from some fierce tigress come;
Or on rough seas, from their foundation torn,
Got by the winds, and in a tempest born: 40
Like that, which now thy trembling sailors fear;
Like that, whose rage should still detain thee here.
Behold how high the foamy billows ride!
The winds and waves are on the juster side.
To winter weather, and a stormy sea,   45
I 'll owe what rather I would owe to thee.
Death thou deserv'st from heaven's avenging laws;
But I 'm unwilling to become the cause.
To shun my love, if thou wilt seek thy fate,
'T is a dear purchase, and a costly hate.   50
Stay but a little, till the tempest cease,
And the loud winds are lulled into a peace.
May all thy rage, like theirs, inconstant prove!
And so it will if there be power in love.
Know'st thou not yet what dangers ships sustain?   55

[1] Aeneas was a son of Venus and so is called a brother of Cupid

So often wrecked, how darest thou tempt the main?
Which were it smooth, were every wave asleep,
Ten thousand forms of death are in the deep.
In that abyss the gods their vengeance store,
For broken vows of those who falsely swore;   60
There winged storms on sea-born Venus wait,
To vindicate the justice of her state.
Thus I to thee the means of safety show;
And, lost myself, would still preserve my foe.
False as thou art, I not thy death design;   65
O rather live, to be the cause of mine!
Should some avenging storm thy vessel tear,
(But heaven forbid my words should omen bear!)
Then in thy face thy perjured vows would fly,
And my wronged ghost be present to thy eye;   70
With threatening looks think thou behold'st me stare,
Gasping my mouth, and clotted all my hair.
Then, should forked lightning and red thunder fall,
What couldst thou say, but, " I deserved them all "?
Lest this should happen, make not haste away;   75
To shun the danger will be worth thy stay.
Have pity on thy son,[1] if not on me;
My death alone is guilt enough for thee.
What has his youth, what have thy gods deserved,
To sink in seas, who were from fires preserved?   80
But neither gods nor parent didst thou bear;
Smooth stories all, to please a woman's ear,
False as the tale of thy romantic life.
Nor yet am I thy first-deluded wife;
Left to pursuing foes Creüsa [2] stayed,   85
By thee, base man, forsaken and betrayed.

---

[1] Ascanius, who accompanied his father from Troy.
[2] Aeneas's Trojan wife Dido accuses him of having left her behind intentionally when he fled from Troy.

This, when thou told'st me, struck my tender heart,
That such requital followed such desert.
Nor doubt I but the Gods, for crimes like these,
Seven winters [1] kept thee wandering on the seas,   90
Thy starved companions, cast ashore, I fed,
Thyself admitted to my crown and bed.
To harbor strangers, succor the distressed
Was kind enough; but, oh, too kind the rest!
Curst be the cave which first my ruin brought,   95
Where, from the storm, we common shelter sought!
A dreadful howling echoed round the place;
The mountain nymphs, thought I, my nuptial grace.
I thought so then, but now too late I know
The furies yelled my funerals from below.   100
O chastity and violated fame,
Exact your dues to my dead husband's [2] name!
By death redeem my reputation lost,
And to his arms restore my guilty ghost!
Close by my palace, in a gloomy grove,   105
Is raised a chapel to my murdered love;
There, wreathed with boughs and wool, his statue stands,
The pious monument of artful hands.
Last night, methought, he called me from the dome,
And thrice, with hollow voice, cried, " Dido, come ! "
She comes; thy wife thy lawful summons hears,   111
But comes more slowly, clogged with conscious fears.
Forgive the wrong I offered to thy bed;
Strong were his charms, who my weak faith misled.
His goddess mother, and his aged sire [3]   115
Borne on his back, did to my fall conspire.

[1] Seven years had passed since the fall of Troy.

[2] Sychaeus, after whose murder by her brother Pygmalion, king of Tyre, Dido had fled to Africa and founded Carthage.

[3] Aeneas had told her how he saved his father Anchises on the night of the sack of Troy

Oh! such he was, and is, that, were he true,
Without a blush I might his love pursue;
But cruel stars my birthday did attend,
And, as my fortune opened, it must end.　　120
My plighted lord was at the altar slain,
Whose wealth was made my bloody brother's gain;
Friendless, and followed by the murderer's hate,
To foreign countries I removed my fate;
And here, a suppliant, from the natives' hands　　125
I bought the ground on which my city stands,
With all the coast that stretches to the sea,
E'en to the friendly port that sheltered thee;
Then raised these walls, which mount into the air,
At once my neighbors' wonder, and their fear.　　130
For now they arm; and round me leagues are made,
My scarce established empire to invade.
To man my new-built walls I must prepare,
A helpless woman, and unskilled in war.
Yet thousand rivals to my love pretend,　　135
And for my person would my crown defend;
Whose jarring notes in one complaint agree,
That each unjustly is disdained for thee.
To proud Iarbas[1] give me up a prey,
For that must follow, if thou goest away;　　140
Or to my husband's murderer leave my life,
That to the husband he may add the wife.
Go then, since no complaints can move thy mind;
Go, perjured man, but leave thy gods[2] behind.
Touch not those gods, by whom thou art forsworn,　　145
Who will in impious hands no more be borne;
Thy sacrilegious worship they disdain,
And rather would the Grecian fires sustain.

[1] A local prince, one of Dido's suitors.
[2] Aeneas had borne the images of his gods from Troy

.   .   .   .

Some god, thou sayest, thy voyage does command ;
Would the same god had barred thee from my land !
The same, I doubt not, thy departure steers,   155
Who kept thee out at sea so many years ;
While thy long labors were a price so great,
As thou, to purchase Troy, wouldst not repeat.
But Tiber [1] now thou seek'st, to be at best,
When there arrived, a poor precarious guest.   160
Yet it deludes thy search ; perhaps it will
To thy old age lie undiscovered still.
A ready crown and wealth in dower I bring,
And, without conquering, here thou art a king.
Here thou to Carthage may'st transfer thy Troy ;   165
Here young Ascanius may his arms employ ;
And, while we live secure in soft repose,
Bring many laurels home from conquered foes.
    By Cupid's arrows, I adjure thee stay !
By all the gods, companions of thy way !   170
So may the Trojans, who are yet alive,
Live still, and with no future fortune strive ;
So may thy youthful son old age attain,
And thy dead father's bones in peace remain ;
As thou hast pity on unhappy me,   175
Who knew no crime, but too much love of thee.
I am not born from fierce Achilles' line,
Nor did my parents against Troy combine.
To be thy wife if I unworthy prove,
By some inferior name admit my love.   180
To be secured of still possessing thee,
What would I do, and what would I not be !
    Our Libyan coasts their certain seasons know,
When, free from tempests, passengers may go ;

[1] Latium was the Trojans' promised land.

But now with northern blasts the billows roar,   185
And drive the floating sea-weed to the shore.
Leave to my care the time to sail away ;
When safe, I will not suffer thee to stay.
Thy weary men would be with ease content ;
Their sails are tattered, and their masts are spent. 190
If by no merit I thy mind can move,
What thou deniest my merit, give my love.
Stay, till I learn my loss to undergo,
And give me time to struggle with my woe :
If not, know this, I will not suffer long ;   195
My life 's too loathsome, and my love too strong.
Death holds my pen, and dictates what I say,
While cross my lap the Trojan sword I lay.
My tears flow down ; the sharp edge cuts their flood,
And drinks my sorrows, that must drink my blood. 200
How well thy gift [1] does with my fate agree !
My funeral pomp is cheaply made by thee.
To no new wounds my bosom I display ;
The sword but enters where love made the way.
But thou, dear sister,[2] and yet dearer friend, 205
Shalt my cold ashes to their urn attend.
Sychaeus' wife let not the marble boast ;
I lost that title, when my fame I lost.
This short inscription only let it bear ;
" Unhappy Dido lies in quiet here.   210
The cause of death, and sword by which she died,
Aeneas gave ; the rest her arm supplied."

ALEXANDER POPE.

[1] The sword   According to Virgil's story (Aeneid, IV.), Dido had given it as a present to Aeneas, and he had accidentally left it behind.

[2] Anna, who had been her confidante throughout the affair with Aeneas.

PHAETHON

(Metamorphoses II , 1–366.)

SUBLIME on lofty columns, bright with gold
And fiery carbuncle, its roof inlaid
With ivory, rose the Palace of the Sun,
Approached by folding gates with silver sheen
Radiant; material priceless, — yet less prized   5
For its own worth than what the cunning hand
Of Mulciber [1] thereon had wrought, — the globe
Of Earth, — the Seas that wash it round, — the Skies
That overhang it. 'Mid the waters played
Their Gods caerulean.   Triton [2] with his horn   10
Was there, and Proteus [3] of the shifting shape,
And old Aegeon, [4] curbing with firm hand
The monsters of the deep.   Her Nereids there
Round Doris [5] sported, seeming, some to swim,
Some on the rocks their tresses green to dry,   15
Some dolphin-borne to ride ; nor all in face
The same, nor different ; — so should sisters be.
Earth showed her men, and towns, and woods, and beasts,
And streams, and Nymphs, and rural Deities :
And over all the mimic Heaven was bright   20
With the twelve Zodiac signs, on either valve
Of the great portal figured, — six on each.

---

[1] Vulcan in his function as a smith.

[2] A son of Neptune, generally represented as blowing on a twisted sea-shell to raise or calm the waves.

[3] The keeper of Neptune's flocks (the seals)   He had the power of changing his shape at will

[4] Here represented as a god of the sea.

[5] A daughter of ocean, wife of Nereus, and mother of the Nereides, nymphs of the sea

And now the child[1] of Clymene the steep
Ascending, passed the threshold of his Sire
Yet unassured, and toward the Godhead bent   25
His steps, yet far off stood, nor nearer bore
The dazzling radiance.   Clad in flowing robe
Of purple, on a throne of state, that shone
Crusted with beryl, Phoebus sate.   To right
And left were ranged the Days, and Months, and
      Years,   30
And Ages, and the Hours, with each its space
Allotted equal.   Spring, with flowery crown
Round his young brows, — and Summer, lightly clad,
With wreath of odorous spices, — Autumn, stained
With juice of trodden wine-press, — and the head   35
Of Winter, white with frost and age, — were there.
Himself sits midmost: — nor escapes his eye
All-seeing long the youth, with wondering awe
Such marvels viewing: — and "What brings thee
      here,
My offspring, — for I recognize thee such, —   40
What wouldst thou of me?" asks the God.   To
      whom
The youth — "O common light of all the world,
Phoebus, my Sire, if by such name I dare
Address thee, nor hath Clymene her shame
With falsehood sought to veil, — give me, I pray,   45
Some pledge whereby henceforth I may be known
Thy son indeed, and all this doubt be cleared!"
He said — and straight the Godhead laid aside
The dazzling glories of his brow, and bade
Approach, and folded in his arms his child,   50
And — "O well worthy to be owned my Son,"

[1] Phaethon, whom Clymene, daughter of Tethys and wife of Merops, had borne to Phoebus Apollo

He said, " thy mother's tale was truth.   To still
All question, ask what boon thou wilt : — ere asked
I grant it thee.   By Styx, dread oath of Gods,
Which never yet these rays illumed, I swear ! "   55
Scarce uttered was the promise, when the youth
Demands his father's car, and, for one day,
The rein and guidance of its winged steeds.
Then rued the God his oath, and thrice and once
Shaking his radiant head, " Alas ! thy speech   60
Proves mine too rash ! " he cried, — " would yet my
      boon
I could deny, for thou the one sole thing
Hast asked I would not grant thee.   O my son,
Let me dissuade, if not refuse.   Thy wish
Is fraught with peril !   'T is no little thing   65
Thou seek'st, my Phaëthon ! a trust for heads
And years like thine unfitting.   Mortal, thou
Immortal function dar'st affect, and more
Than all Heaven's Gods may venture.   Whatsoe'er
His confidence, none save myself can guide   70
That fiery chariot, task for Jove himself,
Whose terrible right hand the thunder wields,
Too hard, — and where is greater strength than
      Jove's ?
Steep is the track at starting, even for steeds
Fresh with the morn no easy climb : — then lies   75
High across central Heaven, whence I, — even I, —
On Earth and Sea not without fear look down :
Then sheer again descends, — sure hand and strong
Demanding, where old Tethys' [1] self, whose waves
Beneath receive me, dreads some day to see   80
My headlong fall.   Add, that the heavens, around
In ceaseless revolution borne, attract

[1] The wife of Ocean.

And with them drag in dizzy whirl the stars.
Adverse to these my course.   All else they sweep
With them, — save me.   Against the rapid rush 85
Of the World I hold my way.   But *thou* — suppose
The chariot thine — couldst *thou* unswerving keep
The path 'twixt either Pole, or stem undazed
The whirl of Heaven?   Dost dream that journey
     winds
By groves, and towns, and fanes of Gods with gifts 90
Resplendent?   Through what perils, 'mid what forms
Of monsters lies it!   Shouldst thou keep the track
Perchance, nor deviate aught, still must thou tempt
The horns of hostile Taurus, and the shafts
Of that Thessalian archer, Leo's jaws 95
Terrific, Scorpio's cruel arms around
Groping for prey, and Cancer's claw which grasps
With backward clutch its spoil!   Nor light the task
That team to curb, impetuous, breathing flame
From mouth and nostril!   Scarce, when warmed, they
     bear 100
My hand, and toss with scornful neck the rein!
Bethink thee, O my son, nor let thy sire
With fatal gift undo thee!   While thou mayst,
Amend thy suit.   Thou wouldst by certain proof
Assure thy parentage.   My grief supplies 105
The pledge ; — my father's fears the father prove.
Look on me!   Would thy glance my inmost heart
Could penetrate, and read the sire within!
Oh! ransack all the treasures of the world,
Earth, sea, and sky, — choose what thou wilt of all 110
Their gifts, nor dread denial!   This alone
Forbear to seek, — false honor, — certain bane!
The boon thou seekest is thy doom, my son!
Nay, clasp not thus my neck — ah! rash and blind!

Whate'er thy wish, doubt not, 't is thine, for Styx   115
Hath heard my oath, — but oh, more wisely ask!"
      He ended, but the youth his warning scorned,
And urged his boon, and burned to guide the car,
Whereto at length the sire, with what delay
He could, unwilling led him.   Vulcan wrought   120
The chariot ; — gold its axle was, its pole
Golden, its wheels gold-tired, with silver spokes :
And from its seat unnumbered chrysolites
Flashed back reflected light.   The daring boy
Admiring scans the marvel.   And now wide   125
Aurora, blushing-born, her purple gate,
Wakeful, had flung, and all her roseate halls
Disclosed ; and Lucifer the gathered stars
Drove homeward, last himself to leave the skies.
And Phoebus, as he saw the rosy flush   130
Suffuse the world, and Luna's horns in light
Superior vanish, bade the rapid Hours
Yoke to the car the steeds.   The Hours obey
Instant, and from their stalls the coursers lead,
With juice ambrosial nourished, and attach   135
The harness resonant.   With drugs of power
The Sire anoints his offspring's brow, to bear
Unharmed the flames, and round his tresses binds
The radiant crown, and, with deep sighs, too well
Prescient of coming sorrow, speaks : " O son ! —   140
If thus much of thy father's warning thou
Canst follow, — spare the lash, and tightly hold
The rein.   My steeds spontaneous fly : thy task
Will be to check them.   Nor directly urge
Through the five zones thy way.   A path oblique   145
Winds curving through the central three.   Content
With these, and shunning either Pole, the track
Observe, where erst my wheels have marked the road,

Dispensing equal warmth to Earth and Heaven.
Nor be thy course too low depressed, nor urged   150
Too high aloft, lest Heaven or Earth in flames
Be wrapped, but safe the midway course pursue.
Nor toward the Serpent on thy right, nor near
The Altar on thy left, thy wheel incline:
At equal distance pass them. What remains   155
I trust to Fortune: — may she aid, and more
Consult thy weal than thou dost! While I speak
The night hath touched the borders of the west,
And darkness flies Aurora's face; nor more
May I delay; — the World demands me! Grasp   160
The reins, or — if thy breast may still be moved —
My counsel take, and not my car, while yet
Thou mayst, and from this steadfast seat — more safe
Than that thy ignorance covets — see thy Sire
Fulfil his proper task, and light the World!"   165
But the hot boy already in the car
Sate mounted, joyous in his grasp to feel
The trusted reins, and to his Sire profuse
Poured his unwelcome thanks. The steeds, mean-
    while —
Eous, Pyroëis, Aethon, and the fourth   170
Phlegon — with fiery neighings fill the air,
And plunge, impatient of restraint. And now
Tethys, unprescient of her grandson's doom,
Unbars her gates, and gives them way: the World
Immense is theirs to traverse! Forth they dash   175
And cleave th' opposing clouds, and with fleet wings
Outstrip the blast of Eurus,[1] like themselves
Eastern of birth. Nor failed their sense at once
The lighter load to feel, and car which lacked
Its wonted weight. And, as some bark which starts   180

---

[1] The east wind.

Too sparely ballasted, across the deep
Unsteady drives, the chariot now, unpressed
By its due burden, reels and rocks, and seems
As empty to those coursers, quick to snatch
Their liberty.   Wild dashing on, they quit   185
The beaten track, and all control disown.
Cold tremors seize the youth : — no more he knows
Which rein to try, or where his road, though vain
'T were now, when all command is lost, to know.
Now first those heavenly Oxen burned with heat   190
Unfelt before, and vainly longed to plunge
Beneath the wave denied them ; — and the Snake
Nighest the icy Pole, till now with cold
Inert, and terrible to none, conceived
Strange fury from the rays.   Even thou, they say,   195
Alarmed didst fly, Boötes, slow albeit
Of movement by thy tardy wain delayed.
But when the hapless Phaëthon looked down
From Heaven to Earth, so wide, so far below,
Together knocked his knees, and blanched his cheeks,
And darkness, born of too much light, his eyes   201
Confounded.   Would his hand had ne'er essayed
Those steeds to rule ! Ah, would he ne'er had won
With fatal prayer this proof of heavenly birth,
Content with Merops for a sire !   As drives   205
Some bark, when Boreas rages, and the helm
The o'ermastered pilot quits, nor hope has more,
Save in his prayers and Gods — so headlong now
The youth is borne. Behind him spreads the track
Of Heaven already passed — before him lies   210
A wider yet !   Both measuring, now with look
Strained to that west he ne'er is doomed to reach —
Now eastward — paralyzed in blank despair
He stands — the loose reins idle in his hands

Which neither drop nor manage them — nor knows
By name to call and pacify his steeds. 216
    A place there is in Heaven where Scorpio curves
In double bow his arms, and, with spread tail
And claws on either side outstretched, usurps
Space ample for two signs. When him the Boy 220
Beheld, black venom sweltering, and with sting
Exasperate threatening wounds and death, — all heart
Failed him, and icy terror numbed his hands,
And from them shook the reins ; no sooner felt
Loose floating on those coursers' backs, than wild 225
They swerve, and masterless through unknown realms
Of air, as impulse urges, bound, and dash
Against fixed orbs of stars, and whirl the car
Through space by track unmarked, and now aloft
They soar, now downward headlong plunge, too close
To Earth. Her brother's steeds beneath her own 231
Much marvelling Luna sees. The scorching clouds
Begin to smoke. Each loftier prominence
Of Earth takes fire, and flames, and splits, and gapes
In fissures, parched and moistureless. The meads 235
Turn ashy white, nor leaf nor trunk of tree
Escapes, and drying harvests court the blaze.
Light mischief this, when cities whole with all
Their walls in ruin tumble, and some heap
Of ashes only tells that underneath 240
A nation lies consumed ! Each mount with all
Its forests flames ! Flames Athos' height and thine,
Cilician Taurus : Tmolus, Oeta, burn,
And Ida, erst for many fountains famed,
Dry now, — and virgin-haunted Helicon, — 245
And Haemus, by that name of after time,
Aeagrius, yet unknown. With doubled blaze
Flames Aetna, — and Parnassus' cloven crest, —

Eryx, and Cynthus, Othrys, Rhodope
Now first of snow dismantled, Dindyma,   250
Mimas, and Mycale, and thou, for rite
Of Bacchus famed, Cithaeron.   Little now
May Scythia's snows avail her!   Caucasus
Flares with the rest: — Ossa and Pindus burn,
And, huger yet, Olympus, and the Alps   255
Heaven-towering, and the cloud-capped Apennine!
And now, where'er he turns his glance, the Youth
Sees but a world on fire; nor heat so great
Sustains, and, panting, draws each breath of air
Scorching as furnace-blast, and feels the car   260
Beneath him glow, — with ashes and thick shower
Of fiery fragments choked, and blind with cloud
Of stifling smoke: — nor where he was, or is,
Or goes, can longer tell, but at the will   264
Of those mad steeds whirls giddy through the skies!
   'T was then, they say, the Aethiop [1] — all his blood
Drawn outward to the surface — first assumed
That darker hue he wears: — then Libya first,
Of all her moisture drained, an arid waste
Became.   Then with dishevelled locks the Nymphs   270
For their lost founts went wailing.   Sudden ceased
Boeotian Dirce: — Amymone failed
Her Argives: — and in Ephyra thy wave,
Pirene, gushed no more.   Nor rivers, proud
Of widest bank and broadest flood, escaped   275
The ruin.   Tanais in mid-channel smoked,
And aged Peneus, and thy Mysian stream,
Caïcus, and Ismenus swift, and thine,
Arcadian Erymanthus, — Xanthus, doomed
Later again to burn, — thy yellow wave,   280
Lycormas, and Maeander, pleased to stray

———————
[1] Used generally of the inhabitants of Africa

In sportive windings numberless. Burned too
Mygdonian Melas, and Eurotas born
Of Spartan Taenarus, — Euphrates far
By Babylon, Orontes, and the flood   285
Thermodon downward hurries : — Ganges warmed,
And Phasis, and Danubius. All thy waves,
Alpheus, boiled and bubbled, and thy banks,
Spercheius, glowed. Tagus his golden freight
Rolled melted to the sea. The swans which haunt   290
Cayster's banks, and all Maeonian founts
Make famous with their music, in mid-stream
Sickened with heat. To the world's utmost end
Fled Nilus, burying deep in earth his head,
Ne'er since to light restored : — his mouth remains, —
Rivers, no more, — mere valleys, dry with dust.   296
Nor other lot befell that Thracian pair,
Hebrus and Strymon : — nor the western floods
Of Padus, Rhenus, Rhodanus ; nor thine,
Old Tiber, by the Fates in after years   300
Ordained to bear the Masters of the world.
Earth's surface yawns throughout, and piercing light
Illumes all Tartarus, and shakes with fear
Hell's Monarch and his Consort. Ocean shrinks,
And leaves a waste of sand what late was sea ;   305
And rocks jut out, late covered by the waves,
Like islands to the scattered Cyclades
New added. Fishes to the bottom dive,
Nor dare the dolphins more through air to try
Brief flight, and seals uncouth expiring float   310
Supine upon the deep. In lowest cave
Old Nereus, and his Doris, and their train
Of daughters, trembling hide. Thrice Neptune rears
His angry brow above the wave, and thrice
Withdraws, by heat o'ermastered. At the last   315

Old Tellus,[1] ocean-girdled, — all her founts
Or dried or in her bosom shrunk, — upraised
Her parching brow, and, shading from her eyes
With outspread hand the glare, and by her fears
Shaken to lesser bulk and lower place   320
Than erst she held, with gasping accents spake.
"O thou, of Gods the Sovereign![2] if thy will
Be thus, and I this fate have merited,
Why linger yet thy lightnings?   If by fire
I perish, let it be by thine!   My doom   325
Will come the easier from thy hand.   The prayer
Thou seest how scarce my parching lips have strength
To urge.   My brows are scorched! my eyes are
       seared
And blind with ashes!   Oh! is this the meed
Of all my faithful duty?   But for this   330
Have I endured, the long year through, the tooth
Of plough and gnawing harrow?   But for this
Borne for the herd its pasture, for the race
Of men my harvests, for the Gods themselves   334
Their incense?   Say my doom is just; — but what,
What hath my Brother[3] done?   Why thus from
       Heaven
More distant shrink the Waters to his rule
Assigned? — But, if nor he nor I have power
To move thee, let thy proper Heaven awake
Thy pity!   Look around thee!   Either pole   340
Already smokes — let these but burst in flame,
And all thy palace topples!   Atlas' self,
Half stifled, scarce the glowing globe sustains!
If Sea, and Land, and Sky must perish thus,
Chaos again confounds us!   Rescue yet   345
What rests, and in thy mercy help the World!"

[1] The goddess of the earth.   [2] Jupiter.   [3] Neptune.

She ceased, nor longer bore the heat, nor more
Could utter, and within herself withdrew
Low in her deepest cavern, neighboring close
On Hades.   Then the Sire Omnipotent   350
Calling all Gods to witness, — and, most, him
Who lent that fatal car, — how ruin threats
The world unless he aid it, to the top
And citadel of Heaven betakes him, whence
He darkens earth with storm-cloud, and bids roar   355
The thunder, and the brandished lightning flings:
Though now — so Fate would have it — was at hand
Nor cloud, nor shower, to darken or to drown.
But loud he thunders, and, with right hand high
Uplifted, on the hapless charioteer   360
Lets fly the bolts of fire, and hurls him down
Headlong at once from car and life, and quells
The fires with fire more potent.   Terror strikes
The steeds, and backward bounding from their necks
The yoke they dash, and spurn the broken reins; —
And here the curb, and here the axle lies,   366
And separate here the pole, and here the spokes
Of shattered wheels, and here what fragments else
Strewed piecemeal of the car.   Down, headlong down
Falls Phaëthon, his streaming locks ablaze   370
With flame, and shoots through air, as seems athwart
The cloudless sky some midnight star to fall,
Yet leaves no vacant space.   Eridanus,
Far from the land that gave him birth, receives
His corse, and from his face the death-sweat laves. 375

The Hesperian Naiads gave his blackened form
A tomb, and on the stone these lines engraved:
"This is the grave of Phaëthon, who strove
To guide his Father's car; and, if he strove

In vain, at least in no mean venture failed."   380
O'erwhelmed with grief that Father veiled, they say,
His head, and left the World — believe who will —
For one whole day without a Sun. The flames
Awful supplied his place : — so came of ill
Some good at least. But Clymene, when grief   385
With all wild words to such a sorrow due
Had spent its earliest force, forlorn and crazed
Of soul, with careless vest and torn, all Earth
Exploring traversed, in the hope to find
His limbs, or, when the hope grew vain, his bones.   390
To these, in that far land entombed, at last
She comes, and o'er them broods, and with her tears
Wets, as she reads, the name beloved, and warms
The marble to her bosom pressed. Nor less   394
His Heliad sisters [1] mourned; with sobs and tears, —
Vain gifts which Death not heeds, — and hands that beat
Their breasts, and linked around the tomb, by day,
By night, they call the Brother, whose dull ear
No plaints of theirs may reach. Four times the Moon
Her horns fresh filling, heard them, — for the wail 400
From use was custom now : — when, as she bent
To kneel, Phaëthusa, eldest born, her feet
Felt stiffen, and Lampetie, at her cry
Starting, took sudden root, and strove in vain
For motion to her aid. The third, her hair   405
In anguish tearing, tore off leaves! And now
Their legs grow fixed as trunks, their arms as boughs
Extend, and upward round them creeps a bark
That gradual folds the form entire, save yet
The head and mouth that to their mother shrieks 410
For help. What help is there to give? Now here,

[1] The three daughters of Phoebus Apollo and Clymene

Now there she rushes, frantic, kissing this
Or that while yet she can, and strives to rend
Their bodies from the clasping bark, and tears
The fresh leaves from their sprouting heads, and sees,
Aghast, red drops as from some wound distil.   416
And "Ah, forbear!" the sufferer shrieks — "Forbear,
O mother dear!   Our bodies in these trees
Alone are rent!   Farewell!"   And o'er the words
Scarce uttered closed the bark, — and all was still. 420

But yet they weep: — and, in the sun, their tears
To amber harden, by the clear stream caught
And borne, the gaud and grace of Latian maids.

HENRY KING.

LIVY

BIOGRAPHICAL SKETCH

THE greatest prose work of the Augustan age is the History of Rome from its earliest beginnings to 9 B. C. by Titus Livius. It was in all probability the author's intention to bring the narrative down to his own times, but he died before he had accomplished his task. There were one hundred and forty-two books in all, of which only thirty-five have survived, namely the first, third, fourth, and part of the fifth decade. The work was originally published in parts of varying length, as the presence of prefaces at various points in the narrative indicates. The division into decades was made by publishers of the fourth or fifth century.

According to St. Jerome's version of Eusebius, Livy was born at Padua in 59 B. C. He came of a good family and was carefully educated. Rhetoric was the most prominent element in the school curricula of the time, and in his case even special emphasis seems to have been laid upon it. He acquired, moreover, an adequate knowledge of literature, both Greek and Latin, and his interest in philosophy is attested by the fact that he wrote some dialogues on themes which fall within that field. He was probably about thirty years of age when he came to Rome, where he continued to reside till almost the close of his life. In the Civil War his sympathies had been with the party of Pompey, but Augustus harbored no resentment against him on this account, and the friendliest relations existed between the two men.

For the most part he kept aloof from public life and devoted himself exclusively to his historical work. The story that he was the tutor of Claudius, afterwards emperor, does not rest on very substantial foundations. It is, however, quite possible that it was on his suggestion that the prince turned his attention to historiography. It was after the accession of Tiberius that he retired to Padua, where he died in 17 A. D.

Judged from the point of view of modern historical research, Livy's work is open to criticism on many counts: there is a very limited use of original sources even where original sources were easily accessible; he shows but a scant knowledge of legal and constitutional history; he is not always wise in his choice of authorities; and very frequently we find a leaning in the direction of the picturesque and the dramatic that does not make for accuracy of statement. Yet whatever defects his work may have, its merits far outweigh them. And most conspicuous of these is his success in making his subject vital. He has revivified the dry bones of history found in the jejune accounts of the annalists. His own scepticism in all matters of early history has not prevented his giving us glowing pictures of the various alleged occurrences that had become a part of Rome's tradition. The personalities of the kings, of the first consuls, and of all the heroes who had added their quota to the sum of their country's greatness, stand out clearly defined, and this long gallery of national portraits is a notable feature of his history. Equally effective is his treatment of situations and events within historic times. He has the artist's gift of singling out important and interesting elements, and reproducing them in rich phrases and rolling periods that remind us of the best period of Roman oratory. Now it is a scene in the Roman senate, now some phase of the struggle between the patricians and the plebeians, now a foreign war; but everywhere, no matter what the subject is, we find the same charm, the same distinction of style, the same vivid imagination and descriptive power. His accounts of battles almost invariably occasion more or less difficulty to the topographical experts, but even they will not dispute the claim that they are good battles. His description of Hannibal's march across the Alps leaves us in doubt as to what route was taken, but no reader will easily forget the impression made by those graphic pages. If we are to believe the statement of a later critic, one at any rate of his contemporaries saw traces of provincialism in his style, but the charge has never been made good, and the so-called *Patavinitas* of Livy (from Patavium, his native town) remains a mystery, a stylistic will o' the wisp, which has eluded many generations of scholars. The story of the citizen of Cadiz who travelled to Rome for the express purpose of seeing the great historian may be fairly adduced as an indication of the reputation he had in his own time, and the number of references to his work by later writers shows the esteem in which he was held by posterity.

THE HISTORIAN'S PREFACE

WHETHER in tracing the history of Rome from the foundation of the city I shall employ my time to good purpose, is a question which I cannot positively determine; nor, were it possible, would I venture to announce such determination; for I am aware that the matter is of high antiquity, and has been already treated by many others; the latest writers always supposing themselves capable either of throwing some new light on the subject or, by the superiority of their talents for composition, of excelling the more inelegant writers who preceded them. However that may be, I shall, at all events, derive no small satisfaction from the reflection that my best endeavors have been exerted in transmitting to posterity the achievements of the greatest people in the world ; and if, amid such a multitude of writers, my name should not emerge from obscurity, I shall console myself by attributing it to the eminent merit of those who stand in my way in the pursuit of fame. It may be further observed that such a subject must require a work of immense extent, as our researches must be carried back through a space of more than seven hundred years ; that the state has, from very small beginnings, gradually increased to such a magnitude, that it is now distressed by its own bulk ; and that there is every reason to apprehend that the generality of readers will receive but very little pleasure from the accounts of its first origin or of the times immediately succeeding, but will be impatient to arrive at the period in which the powers of this overgrown state have been long employed in working their own destruction. On the other hand, this much will be derived from my labor, that, so long at least as I shall have my thoughts totally occupied in investigating the transactions of such distant ages, without being embarrassed by any of those unpleasant considerations in respect of later days, which, though they might not have power to warp a writer's mind from the truth, would yet be sufficient to create uneasiness, I shall withdraw myself from the sight of the many evils to which our eyes have been so long accustomed. As to the relations which have been handed down of events prior to the founding of the city, or to the circumstances that gave occasion to its being founded, and which bear the semblance rather of poetic fictions, than of authentic records of history, — these, I have no intention either to maintain or refute. Antiquity

is always indulged with the privilege of rendering the
origin of cities more venerable by intermixing divine
with human agency; and if any nation may claim the
privilege of being allowed to consider its origin as
sacred, and to attribute it to the operations of the
gods, surely the Roman people, who rank so high in
military fame, may well expect that, while they choose
to represent Mars as their own parent and that of
their founder, the other nations of the world may ac-
quiesce in this, with the same deference with which
they acknowledge their sovereignty. But what degree of attention or credit may be given to these and
similar matters I shall not consider as very material. To the following considerations I wish every one
seriously and earnestly to attend, — by what kind of
men, and by what sort of conduct, in peace and war,
the empire has been both acquired and extended:
then, as discipline gradually declined, let him follow
in his thoughts the structure of ancient morals, at
first, as it were, leaning aside, then sinking farther
and farther, then beginning to fall precipitate, until
he arrives at the present times, when our vices have
attained to such a height of enormity, that we can no
longer endure either the burden of them or the sharpness of the necessary remedies. This is the great advantage to be derived from the study of history; indeed the only one which can make it answer any profitable and salutary purpose; for being abundantly
furnished with clear and distinct examples of every
kind of conduct, we may select for ourselves and for
the state to which we belong such as are worthy of
imitation; and carefully noting such as, being dis-
honorable in their principles, are equally so in their
effects, learn to avoid them. Now, either partiality to

the subject of my intended work misleads me, or there never was any state either greater or of purer morals, or richer in good examples, than this of Rome; nor was there ever any city into which avarice and luxury made their entrance so late, or where poverty and frugality were so highly and so long held in honor; men contracting their desires in proportion to the narrowness of their circumstances. Of late years, indeed, opulence has introduced a greediness of gain, and the boundless variety of dissolute pleasures has created in many a passion for ruining themselves, and all around them. But let us, in the first stage at least of this undertaking, avoid gloomy reflections, which, when perhaps unavoidable, will not even then be agreeable. If it were customary with us, as it is with poets, we would more willingly begin with good omens and vows and prayers to the gods and goddesses that they would propitiously grant success to our endeavors in the prosecution of so arduous a task.[1]

THE RAPE OF THE SABINE WOMEN

(I, 4.)

THE Roman state had now attained such a degree of power that it was a match in arms for any of the neighboring nations; but from the small number of its women, its greatness was not likely to last longer than one age of man, as they had neither hopes of offspring among themselves nor had yet contracted any inter-marriages with their neighbors. Romulus, therefore, by advice of the senate, sent ambassadors round to all adjoining states, soliciting their alliance, and permis-

[1] Baker's translation has been used for all the selections from Livy.

sion for his new subjects to marry among them: he intimated to them that "cities, like everything else, rise from low beginnings; that in time those which are supported by their own merit and the favor of the gods procure to themselves great power and a great name; and that he had full assurance both that the gods favored the founding of Rome, and that the people would not be deficient in merit. Wherefore, as men, they ought to show no reluctance to mix their blood and race with men." In no one place were his ambassadors favorably heard; such contempt of them did people entertain, and at the same time such apprehensions of danger to themselves and their posterity from so great a power growing up in the midst of them. By the greater part they were dismissed with the question, "whether they had opened an asylum for women also, for that would be the only way to procure suitable matches for them?" This was highly resented by the Roman youth, to such an extent, indeed, that the business appeared evidently to point towards violence. Romulus, in order to afford them a convenient time and place for a design of that sort, dissembling his displeasure, prepared with that intent to celebrate solemn games in honor of the equestrian Neptune, to which he gave the name of Consualia. He then ordered the intended celebration to be proclaimed among the neighboring nations, while his people exerted themselves in making the most magnificent preparations that their knowledge and abilities allowed, in order to gain attention and raise expectation. Great numbers of people assembled; induced, in some measure, by a desire of seeing the new city: especially those whose countries lay nearest, the Caeninensians, Crustiminians and Antemnatians, in particular the whole multitude of the Sabines came with their wives and children. They were hospitably invited to the different houses, and when they viewed the situation and the fortifications and the city crowded with houses, they were astonished at the rapid increase of the Roman power. When the show began and every person's thoughts and eyes were attentively engaged on it, then, according to a preconcerted plan, on a signal being given, the Roman youth ran different ways to carry off the young women. Some they bore away as they happened to meet with them, without waiting to make a choice; but others of extraordinary beauty, being designed for the principal senators, were conveyed to their houses by plebeians employed for that purpose. It is said that one highly distinguished above the rest for her beauty was carried off by the party of one Talassius; and that in answer to many who eagerly inquired to whom they were hurrying her, they, every now and then, to prevent any interruption in their course, cried out that they were carrying her to Talassius:[1] this circumstance gave rise to the use of that word at weddings. The terror occasioned by this outrage put an end to the sports; and the parents of the young women retired, full of grief, inveighing against such a violation of the laws of hospitality, and appealing to the god to whose solemn festival and games they had come, relying on the respect due to religion and on the faith of nations. Nor did the women who were seized entertain better hopes with regard to themselves, or a less degree of indignation. However, Romulus went about in person

---

[1] " Talassio " was a cry raised at bridal processions. It was probably of Sabine origin, and the explanation given by Livy here is incorrect.

and told them that " this proceeding had been occasioned by the haughtiness of their parents, who refused to allow their neighbors to marry among them ;
that, notwithstanding this, they should be united to
his people in wedlock in the common enjoyment of
all property, and of their common children ; a bond
of union than which the human heart feels none
more endearing. He begged of them to soften their
resentment, and to bestow their affections on those
men on whom chance had bestowed their persons. It
often happened, he said, that to harsh treatment mutual regard had succeeded, and they would find their
husbands behave the better on this very account ; that
every one would exert himself, not merely in performing his duty as a husband, but to make up to
them for the loss of their parents and of their country." To these persuasions was added the soothing
behavior of their husbands themselves, who urged
in extenuation of their violence that they had been
tempted to commit the excess from passion and the
force of love : arguments, than which there can be
none more powerful to assuage the irritation of the
female mind.

HORATIUS [1]

(I, 10)

As the enemy drew nigh, every one moved hastily
from the country into the city, on every side of
which strong guards were posted. Some parts seemed

---

[1] Horatius' defence of the bridge took place on the occasion of an
attempt by Tarquinius Superbus, aided by Lars Porsena, king of the
Etruscan city of Clusium, to recover his sovereignty in Rome

well secured by the walls, others by the Tiber running close to them. The Sublician [1] bridge was very
near affording the enemy an entrance, had it not
been for one man, Horatius Cocles : no other bulwark
had the fortune of Rome on that day. He happened
to be posted on guard at the bridge, and when he
saw the Janiculum [2] taken by a sudden assault, and
the enemy pouring down thence in full speed, his
countrymen in disorder and confusion, no longer
attempting opposition but quitting their ranks, he
caught hold of every one that he could, and, appealing to gods and men, assured them that "it was in
vain that they fled, after deserting the post which
could protect them ; that if they passed the bridge
and left it behind them, they would soon see greater
numbers of the enemy in the Palatium and the Capitol than in the Janiculum ; wherefore he advised and
warned them to break down the bridge by their
swords, fire, or any other effectual means, while he
should sustain the attack of the enemy, as long as it
was possible for one person to withstand them. He
then advanced to the first entrance of the bridge, and
being easily distinguished from those who showed
their backs in retreating from the fight, facing to
the front, with his arms prepared for action, he
astonished the enemy by his wonderful intrepidity.
Shame, however, prevailed on two to remain with
him, Spurius Lartius and Titus Herminius, both of
them men of distinguished families and characters :
with their assistance he for a time supported the first
storm and the most furious part of the fight. Even
these he sent back, when the bridge was nearly de-

---

[1] Literally, the pile-bridge
[2] The hill on the Etruscan side of the Tiber

stroyed, and those who were employed in breaking it
down called on them to retire, then darting fierce,
menacing looks at each of the leaders of the Etrurians,
he sometimes challenged them singly, sometimes upbraided them all together, as slaves of haughty kings,
who, incapable of relishing liberty themselves, had
come to wrest it from others. For a considerable time
they hesitated, looking about for some other to begin
the combat. Then shame at length put their troops
in motion, and setting up a shout, they poured their
javelins from all sides against their single opponent.
But when all these stuck in the shield with which he
guarded himself, and he still persisted in keeping possession of his post, they had now resolved, by making
a violent push, to force him from it, when the crash of
the falling bridge, and at the same time a shout raised
by the Romans, filled them with sudden dismay, and
stopped them from proceeding in the attempt. Then
Cocles said, " Holy father Tiberinus, I beseech thee to
receive these arms, and this thy soldier, into thy propitious stream." With these words, armed as he was,
he leaped down into the Tiber, and through showers of
darts which fell around him, swam safe across to his
friends, having exhibited a degree of intrepidity which
in after times was more generally celebrated than believed. The state showed a grateful sense of such high
desert: a statue was erected to him in the Comitium,
and he was given a grant of land as large as he could
plough completely in one day. The zeal of private
persons too was conspicuous amidst the honors con-
ferred on him by the public; for, great as the scarcity
then was, every one contributed something to him,
in proportion to the stock of their family, abridging
themselves of their own proper support.

BEFORE THE WAR.[1]

(XXI., 1.)

To this division of my work I may be allowed to prefix a remark which most writers of history make in the beginning of their undertaking: that I am going to write of a war, the most memorable that was ever waged; that which the Carthaginians, under the conduct of Hannibal, maintained with the Roman people; for never did any other states and nations of more potent strength and resources engage in any contest of arms; nor did these same nations at any other period possess so great a degree of power and strength. The arts of war also, practised by each party, were not unknown to each other, for they had already gained some experience of them in the First Punic War; and so various was the fortune of this war, so great its vicissitudes, that the party which proved in the end victorious was at times brought the nearest the brink of ruin. Besides, they exerted in the contest almost a greater degree of rancor than of strength, the Romans being fired with indignation at a vanquished people presuming to take up arms against their conquerors; the Carthaginians, at the haughtiness and avarice which they thought the others showed in their imperious exercise of the superiority which they had acquired. We are told that when Hamilcar [2] was about to march at the head of an army into Spain, after the conclusion of the war in Africa, and was offering sacrifices on the occasion,

---

[1] The next seven selections give some of the more important events of the Second Punic War (219–202 B.C).

[2] The leader of the Carthaginians in the first war with Rome.

his son Hannibal, then about nine years of age, so-
licited him with boyish fondness to take him with
him. Whereupon he brought him up to the altars,
and compelled him to lay his hand on the consecrated
victims and swear that as soon as he should be in
power, he would show himself an enemy to the Roman
people. Being a man of high spirit, he was deeply
chagrined at the loss of Sicily and Sardinia; for he
considered Sicily as given up by his countrymen by
too hasty despair of their affairs, and Sardinia as
fraudulently snatched out of their hands by the Romans during the commotions in Africa, with the additional insult of a tribute imposed upon them.

HANNIBAL

(XXI, 4)

A FEW, particularly those of the best understanding, concurred in opinion with Hanno;[1] but, as it
generally happens, the more numerous party prevailed
over the more judicious. Hannibal was sent into
Spain, and upon his first arrival attracted the notice of
the whole army. The veteran soldiers imagined that
Hamilcar was restored to them from the dead, observing in him the same animated look and penetrating
eye, the same expression of countenance, and the
same features. Then, such was his behavior, that in
a short time the memory of his father was the least
among their inducements to esteem him. Never before had a man possessed a genius so admirably fitted
to the discharge of offices so opposite in their very

---

[1] A distinguished Carthaginian, who bitterly opposed the plans of
Hamilcar, and afterwards of Hannibal.

nature as obeying and commanding, so that it was not easy to discern whether he were more beloved by the general or by the soldiers. There was none to whom Hasdrubal[1] preferred to intrust the command in any case where courage and activity were required, nor did the soldiers ever feel a greater degree of confidence and boldness under any other commander. With perfect intrepidity in facing danger, he possessed, in the midst of the greatest, perfect presence of mind. No degree of labor could either fatigue his body or break his spirit: heat and cold he endured with equal firmness; the quantity of his food and drink was limited by natural appetite, not by the pleasure of the palate. His seasons for sleeping and waking were not distinguished by the day or by the night; whatever time he had to spare, after business was finished, he gave to repose, which however he never courted either by a soft bed or quiet retirement: he was often seen, covered with a cloak, lying on the ground in the midst of the soldiers on guard, and on the advanced posts. His dress had nothing in particular in it beyond that of others of the same rank; his horses and his armor he was always remarkably attentive to; and whether he acted among the horsemen or the infantry, he was eminently the first of either, the foremost in advancing to the fight, the last who quitted the field of battle. These great virtues were counterbalanced in him by vices of equal magnitude, — inhuman cruelty, perfidy beyond that of a Carthaginian, a total disregard of truth, and of every obligation deemed sacred; utterly devoid of

[1] Son-in-law of Hamilcar, in command of the Carthaginian forces in Spain He was assassinated in 220 B. C., and Hannibal was chosen to take his place.

all reverence for the gods, he paid no regard to an
oath, no respect to religion. Endowed with such disposition, a compound of virtues and vices, he served
under the command of Hasdrubal for three years,
during which he omitted no opportunity of improving
himself in every particular, both of theory and practice, that could contribute to the forming of an accomplished general.

THE MARCH ACROSS THE ALPS [1]

(XXI., 32-38.)

IN about three days after Hannibal's moving from
the bank of the Rhone, the consul Publius Cornelius had come with his forces in order of battle to
the camp of the enemy, intending to fight them without delay. But finding the fortifications abandoned,
and concluding that, as they had got the start of him
so far, it would be difficult to overtake them, he
marched back to the sea where his ships lay ; for he
judged that he might thus with greater ease and
safety meet Hannibal on his descent from the Alps.
However, not to leave Spain, the province which the
lots had assigned to his care, destitute of the aid of
the Roman troops, he sent his brother Cneius Scipio
with the greater part of his forces against Hasdrubal,[2]
with the expectation of not merely protecting old

---

[1] Hannibal had started from New Carthage, on the east coast of
Spain, in the spring of 218 B. C. In a few months he had reduced the
tribes north of the Ebro, crossed the Pyrenees, and advanced as far as
the Rhone. The consul Publius Cornelius Scipio had sailed with his
forces to Gaul, in hopes of intercepting him before he reached the
Alps.

[2] The brother of Hannibal See note on page 361.

allies, and acquiring new, but of driving him out of
Spain.   He himself, with a very small force, repaired
to Genoa, proposing, with the army which was
stationed on the Po, to provide for the security of
Italy.   From the Druentia, Hannibal, passing through
a tract in general level, without any molestation from
the Gauls inhabiting those regions, arrived at the
Alps.   And now, notwithstanding that the men had
already conceived notions from the reports, which in
cases capable of misrepresentation generally go beyond the truth, yet the present view exhibited such
objects as renewed all their terrors : the height of the
mountains, the snow almost touching the sky, the
wretched huts standing on cliffs, the cattle and beasts
shivering with the cold, the natives squalid and in uncouth dress, all things, in short, animate and inani-
mate, stiffened with frost, besides other circumstances
more shocking to the sight than can be represented
in words.   As they marched up the first acclivities,
they beheld the eminences which hung over them covered with parties of the mountaineers, who, if they
had posted themselves in the valleys out of view,
and, rushing out suddenly, had made an unexpected
attack, must have occasioned the most terrible havoc
and dismay.   Hannibal commanded the troops to
halt, and having discovered from some Gauls whom
he sent forward to examine the ground that there
was no passage on that side, encamped in the widest
valley which he could find, where the whole circuit
around consisted of rocks and precipices.   Then having gained intelligence by means of the same Gauls
(who differed not much from the others in language
and manners, and who had entered into conversation
with them) that the pass was blocked up only by day,

and that at night they separated to their several dwellings, he advanced at the first dawn to the eminences, as if with the design of forcing his way through the pass. This feint he carried on through the whole day, his men at the same time fortifying a camp in the spot where they were drawn up. As soon as he understood that the mountaineers had retired from the heights and withdrawn their guards, he made, for a show, a greater number of fires than was proportioned to the troops who remained in the camp, and leaving behind the baggage with the cavalry and the greater part of the infantry, he himself, with a light-armed band composed of the most daring men in the army, pushed rapidly through the pass, and took post on those very eminences of which the enemy had been in possession.

At the first dawn of the next day the rest of the army began to march forward. By this time the mountaineers, on a given signal, were coming together out of their fortresses to their usual station; when on a sudden they perceived a part of the enemy over their heads in possession of their own strong post, and the rest passing along the road. Both these circumstances striking them at once, they were for some time incapable of thought, or of turning their eyes to any other object. Afterwards, when they observed the confusion in the pass, and that the body of the enemy was disordered on their march by the hurry among themselves, and particularly by the unruliness of the affrighted horses, they thought that if they could augment in any degree the terror under which the army already labored, they could destroy it. They therefore ran down the rocks in an oblique direction through pathless and circuitous ways which habitual practice rendered easy to them. And now the

Carthaginians had to contend at once with the Gauls and the disadvantage of the ground, and there was a greater struggle among themselves than with the enemy, for every one strove to get first out of danger. But the greatest disorder was occasioned by the horses, which, affrighted at the dissonant clamors, multiplied by the echoes from the woods and valleys, became nearly unmanageable ; and when they happened to receive a stroke or a wound, grew so unruly as to overthrow numbers of men and heaps of baggage of all sorts ; and as there were abrupt passages on each side of the pass, their violence cast down many to an immense depth, so that the fall of such great masses caused a dreadful effect. Although these were shocking sights to Hannibal, yet he kept his place for a while, and restrained the troops that were with him, lest he should increase the tumult and confusion. Afterwards, seeing the line of the army broken, and that there was danger of their being wholly deprived of their baggage, in which case the effecting of their passage would answer no purpose, he hastened down from the higher ground ; and while by the mere rapidity of his motion he dispersed the forces of the enemy, he at the same time increased the confusion among his own. But this, when the roads were cleared by the flight of the mountaineers, was instantly remedied, and the whole army was soon brought through the pass not only without disturbance, but almost without any noise. He then seized a fort, which was the capital of that district, and several villages that lay around it, and fed his army for three days with cattle taken from the fugitives. During these three days, as he was not incommoded by the mountaineers, nor much by the nature of the ground, he made a considerable progress in his march.

He then reached the territory of another state, which was thickly inhabited for a mountainous country : there he was very near suffering a defeat, not only by open force, but by his own arts, treachery, and ambush. Some men of advanced age, governors of their forts, came to the Carthaginian as ambassadors, with humble representations that "as the calamities of others had afforded them a profitable lesson, they wished to make trial of the friendship rather than of the strength of the Carthaginians. That they were therefore resolved to yield obedience to all his commands, and requested him to accept provisions and guides on his march, and hostages to insure the performance of their engagements." Hannibal neither hastily crediting, nor yet slighting their offers, lest, if rejected, they might declare openly against him, after returning a favorable answer, accepted the hostages, and made use of the provisions which they had, of their own accord, brought to the road ; but followed the guides, not as through a friendly country, but with the strictest order in his march. The elephants and cavalry composed the van, and he himself followed with the main body of the infantry, carefully inspecting every particular. On their coming into a road narrower than the rest, confined on one side by an impending hill, the barbarians rising up on all sides from places where they had lain concealed, assailed them in front and rear, in close and in distant fight, rolling down also huge rocks on the troops. The most numerous body pressed on the rear. There the main force of infantry was ready to oppose them : but had not that been very

strong, it must have undoubtedly, in such a difficult
pass, have suffered very great loss : even as the case
stood, it was brought to the extremity of danger, and
almost to destruction : for whilst Hannibal hesitated
to lead his horsemen into the narrower road, though
he had left no kind of support at the back of the infantry, the mountaineers, rushing across and breaking
through between the two divisions of the army, took
possession of the pass, and Hannibal spent one night
separated from his cavalry and his baggage.

Next day, the barbarians having relaxed the violence of their attacks in the centre, the troops were
reunited, and carried through the defile, but not without loss; the destruction was greater however among
the beasts of burden than among the men. Thence-
forward the mountaineers made their attacks in
smaller parties, more like robbers than an army, at
one time on the van, at another on the rear, just as
the ground happened to afford them an advantage, or
as stragglers advancing before the rest, or staying behind, gave them an opportunity. Although the driving of the elephants through the narrow roads, even
with all the haste that could be made, occasioned much
loss of time, yet wherever they went they effectually
secured the troops from the enemy; who, being unaccustomed to such creatures, dared not to come near
them. On the ninth day the army completed the ascent to the summit of the Alps, mostly through pathless tracts and wrong roads; into which they had
been led either by the treachery of their guides, or
when these were not trusted, rashly, on the strength
of their own conjectures, following the courses of the
valleys. On the summit they remained encamped two
days, in order to refresh the soldiers, who were spent

with toil and fighting; and in this time several of
the beasts which had fallen among the rocks, following
the tracks of the army, came into camp. Tired as
the troops were of struggling so long with hardships,
they found their terrors very much increased by a
fall of snow, this being the season of the setting of
the constellation Pleiades.[1] The troops were put in
motion with the first light; and as they marched slowly
over ground which was entirely covered with snow,
dejection and despair being strongly marked in every
face, Hannibal went forward before the standards, and
ordering the soldiers to halt on a projecting eminence,
from which there was a wide extended prospect, made
them take a view of Italy, and of the plains about the
Po, stretching along the foot of the mountains; then
told them that "they were now scaling the walls,
not only of Italy, but of the city of Rome: that all
the rest would be plain and smooth; and after one
or at most a second battle, they would have the bulwark and capital of Italy in their power and disposal."
The army then began to advance, the enemy now de-
sisting from any farther attempts on them except by
trifling parties for pillaging, as opportunity offered.
But the way was much more difficult than it had been
in the ascent, the declivity on the Italian side of the
Alps being in most places shorter, and consequently
more perpendicular; while the whole way was narrow and slippery, so that the soldiers could not prevent their feet from sliding, nor, if they made the least
false step, could they, on falling, stop themselves:
and thus men and beasts tumbled promiscuously over
one another.

Then they came to a ridge much narrower than

---

[1] The beginning of November.

the others, and composed of rock so upright that a light-armed soldier, making the trial, could with difficulty by laying hold of bushes and roots, which appeared here and there, accomplish the descent. In this place the precipice, originally great, had by a late falling away of the earth been increased to the depth of at least one thousand feet. Here the cavalry stopped, as if at the end of their journey, and Hannibal, wondering what could be the cause of the troops' halting, was told that the cliff was impassable. Then going up himself to view the place, it seemed clear to him that he must lead his army in a circuit, though ever so great, and through tracks never trodden before. That way, however, was found to be impracticable. The old snow indeed had become hard, and being covered with the new of a moderate depth, the men found good footing as they walked through it; but when that was dissolved by the treading of so many men and beasts, they then trod on the naked ice below. Here they were much impeded, because the foot could take no hold on the smooth ice, and was besides more apt to slip on account of the declivity of the ground; and whenever they attempted to rise, either by aid of the hands or knees, they fell again. Add to this that there were neither stumps nor roots within reach, on which they could lean for support; so that they wallowed in the melted snow on one entire surface of slippery ice. This the cattle sometimes penetrated as soon as their feet reached the lower bed; and sometimes, when they lost their footing, by striking more strongly with their hoofs in striving to keep themselves up, they broke it entirely through; so that the greatest part of them, as if caught in traps, stuck fast in the hard, deep ice.

At length, after men and beasts were heartily fatigued to no purpose, they fixed a camp on the summit, having with very great difficulty cleared even the ground which that required, so great was the quantity of snow to be dug and carried off. The soldiers were then employed to make a way down the steep, through which alone it was possible to effect a passage ; and as it was necessary to break the mass, they felled and lopped a number of huge trees which stood near, which they raised into a vast pile, and as soon as a smart wind arose, to forward the kindling of it, set it on fire ; and then, when the stone was violently heated, made it crumble to pieces by pouring on vinegar. When the rock was thus disjointed by the power of the heat, they opened a way through it with iron instruments, and inclined the descents with it in such a manner, that not only the beasts of burden, but even the elephants could be brought down. Four days were spent about this rock, during which the cattle were nearly destroyed by hunger ; for the summits are for the most part bare, and whatever little pasture there might have been was covered with snow. In the lower parts are valleys and some hills, which, enjoying the benefit of the sun, with rivulets at the side of the woods, are better suited to become the residence of human beings. There the horses were sent out to pasture, and the men, fatigued with the labor on the road, allowed to rest for three days. They then descended into the plains, where the climate, like the character of the inhabitants, was of a milder cast.

In this manner, as nearly as can be ascertained, they accomplished their passage into Italy, in the fifth month, according to some authors, after leaving New Carthage, having spent fifteen days in crossing the

Alps. As to what number of forces Hannibal had
when he arrived in Italy, writers by no means agree.
Those who state them at the highest make them
amount to one hundred thousand foot and twenty
thousand horse; while those who state them at the
lowest say twenty thousand foot and six of horse.
The authority of Lucius Cincius Alimentus,[1] who
writes that he was taken prisoner by Hannibal, would
have the greatest weight with me, did he not confound the number by adding the Gauls and Ligurians. He says that, including these (who, it is more
probable, however, flocked to him afterwards, and so
some writers assert), there were brought into Italy
eighty thousand foot and ten thousand horse; and
that he heard from Hannibal himself, that from the
time of his passing the Rhone he had lost thirty-
six thousand men, together with a vast number of
horses and other beasts of burden, before he left the
country of the Taurinians,[2] the next nation to the
Gauls as he went down into Italy. That he came to
this state is agreed by all. I am therefore the more
surprised at its remaining doubtful by what road
he crossed the Alps, and that the opinion should commonly prevail that he passed over the Pennine Hill, and
that from thence that summit of these mountains got
its name.[3] Coelius says that he passed over the hill of
Cremo. Either of these passes would have led him
not in the territory of the Taurinians, but through
that of the mountaineers, called Salluvians, to the
Libyan Gauls. Nor is it probable that those roads

---

[1] A Roman annalist who wrote in Greek an account of the Second
Punic War

[2] Their chief town was Taurasia, the modern Turin

[3] A common designation of the Carthaginians was *Poeni*, with reference to their Phoenician origin.

into Hither Gaul should at that time have been open:
those, especially, which led to the Pennine Hill would
have been blocked up by nations half German. And
besides, if the assertions of the inhabitants be admitted
as an argument of any weight, it must be allowed that
the Veragrians, the inhabitants of that very hill, deny
that the name was given to these mountains from any
passage of the Carthaginians, and allege that it was
so named from a person, called by the mountaineers
Penninus, worshipped as a divinity on the highest peak.

THE BATTLE OF CANNAE [1]

(XXII, 44-49)

THE consuls pursued the Carthaginians, taking proper care to examine the roads: when they arrived
near Cannae, and had the foe in sight, they divided
their forces as before, and fortified two camps at nearly
the same distance from each other as they had been
at Geronium. As the river Aufidus ran by the camps
of both, the watering parties of both had access to it,
as opportunity served, but not without encountering
opposition. The Romans, however, in the smaller
camp, which was pitched on the other side of the
Aufidus, had greater liberty of supplying themselves
with water, because there were none of the enemy
posted on the farther bank. Hannibal now, conceiving
hopes that the consuls might be brought to an engagement in this tract, where the nature of the ground was
advantageous to cavalry, in which kind of force he had

[1] Hannibal had already defeated the Romans at the river Ticinus
(218 B.C.), at the river Trebia (218), and at Lake Trasimenus (217),
when he met them at Cannae, a village in Apulia, in 216

a manifest superiority, drew out his army in order of battle, and endeavored to provoke them by skirmishes of the Numidians. On this the Roman camp was again thrown into disturbance by mutinous behavior on the part of the soldiers, and dissension between the consuls; Paulus represented to Varro the fatal rashness of Sempronius and Flaminius; and Varro to him the example of Fabius as a specious precedent for timid and inactive commanders: the one [1] calling gods and men to witness that none of the blame was to be imputed to him of Hannibal's now holding Italy as if by prescriptive right of possession; for he was chained down by his colleague, while the soldiers, full of rage and ardor for the fight, were kept unarmed. To which the other replied that, if any misfortune should happen to the legions from their being hurried into an inconsiderate and rash engagement, he himself, although entirely free from all reproach, must yet bear a share of the consequences, be they what they might. Let him take care that those whose tongues were now so ready and impetuous showed the same alertness during the fight.

While, instead of deliberating on proper measures, they thus wasted time in altercation, Hannibal, who had kept his forces drawn up in order of battle during a great part of the day, led back the rest towards the camp, and despatched the Numidian horse to the other side of the river to attack a watering party, which had come from the smaller camp of the Romans. They had scarcely reached the opposite bank when, merely by their shout and the rapidity of their motions, they dispersed this disorderly crowd; and then pushed forward against an advanced guard stationed before the

---

[1] Varro.

rampart, and almost up to the very gates. The
Romans, in having their camp threatened by a band
of irregular auxiliaries, felt an intolerable affront, so
that nothing could have restrained them from drawing out their forces and passing the river, but from
the chief command being in the hands of Paulus. On
the next day, therefore, Varro, whose turn it was to
command, without conferring with his colleague, displayed the signal for battle, and, marshalling his forces,
led them over the river, while Paulus followed; because, though he did not approve of his design, yet
he could not avoid giving him his support. Having
crossed the river, they were joined by the troops from
the smaller camp, and formed their line in this manner: on the right wing, next the river, they placed the
Roman cavalry, and adjoining them the Roman infantry; the extreme of the left wing was composed of
the confederate cavalry; and, inclosed by these, the
confederate infantry stretched to the centre, so as to
unite with the Roman legions. The archers and other
light-armed auxiliaries formed the van. The consuls
commanded the wings, Terentius the left, Aemilius the
right; the charge of the centre was committed to
Geminus Servilius.

Hannibal, at the first light, sending before him the
Balearians and the other light-armed troops, crossed
the river, and posted each company in his line of
battle, in the same order in which he had led them
over. The Gallic and Spanish cavalry occupied the
left wing near the bank, opposite the Roman cavalry,
and the Numidian horse the right; the infantry forming the centre in such a manner that both ends of
their line were composed of Africans, and between
these were placed the Gauls and Spaniards. The
Africans, for the most part, resembled a body of Ro-

man troops, being furnished in great abundance with
the arms taken partly at Trebia, but the greater part
at Trasimenus. The shields of the Gauls and Spaniards were nearly of the same make; their swords
were different, both in length and form, those of the
Gauls being very long, and without points; those of
the Spaniards, whose practice was rather to thrust at
the enemy than to strike, light, handy, and sharp
at the point. The troops of these nations made a
more terrible appearance than any of the rest, on
account of the size of their bodies. The Gauls were
naked from their middle upward; the Spaniards clad
in linen tunics, of a surpassing and dazzling white-
ness, and bordered with purple. The whole number
of infantry drawn up in the field on this occasion
was forty thousand, of cavalry ten thousand. The
generals who commanded the wings were Hasdrubal[1]
on the left and Maharbal[2] on the right. Hannibal
himself, with his brother Mago, took the command of
the centre. The sun, very conveniently for both
parties, shone on their flanks, whether this position
was chosen designedly or that it fell out by acci-
dent; for the Romans faced the south, the Carthaginians the north. The wind, which the natives of
the country call Vulturnus, blew briskly against the
Romans; and, by driving great quantities of sand
into their faces, prevented them from seeing clearly.

The shout being raised, the auxiliaries advanced,
and the fight commenced, first between the light-armed
troops; then the left wing, consisting of Gallic and
Spanish cavalry, engaged with the right wing of the
Romans; but not in the usual method of fighting between horsemen, for they were obliged to engage front

[1] A brother of Hannibal
[2] One of the most efficient of Hannibal's officers.

to front, no room having been left for any evolutions, the river on the one side and the line of infantry on the other confining them, so that they could only push directly forward; at last, the horses being pressed together in a crowd and stopped from advancing, the riders, grappling man to man, dragged each other to the ground The contest was now maintained chiefly on foot, but was more furious than lasting; for the Roman horsemen, unable to keep their stand, turned their backs. When the fight between the cavalry was almost decided, the infantry began to engage. At first the Gauls and Spaniards maintained their ranks without betraying any inferiority in strength or courage. At length the Romans, by frequent and persevering efforts, with their front regular and in compact order, drove back a body which projected before the rest of the line in form of a wedge, and which, being too thin, consequently wanted strength, as these gave ground, and retreated hastily and in disorder, they pursued, and without slacking their charge, broke the dismayed and shattered battalions; at first, to their centre line, and at length, meeting with no resistance, they arrived at the reserved troops of the Africans, which latter had been posted on both flanks of the others, inclining backwards towards the rear, while the centre, composed of Gauls and Spaniards, jutted considerably forward. By the retreat of this prominent part the front was first rendered even; then by their proceeding still in the same direction, a bending inward was at length formed in the middle, on each side of which the Africans now formed wings; and the Romans incautiously rushing into the centre, these flanked them on each side, and, by extending themselves from the extremities, surrounded them in the rear also. In consequence of this, the Romans, who had already finished one battle, leaving the Gauls and Spaniards, whom they had pursued with much slaughter, began a new engagement with the Africans, in which they had not only the disadvantage of being hemmed in, and in that position obliged to fight, but also that of being fatigued, while their antagonists were fresh and vigorous.

By this time the battle had begun also on the left wing of the Romans, where the confederate cavalry had been posted against the Numidians: it was languid at first, and commenced with a piece of Carthaginian treachery. About five hundred Numidians, carrying, besides their usual armor and weapons, swords concealed under their coats of mail, rode up under the appearance of deserters, with their bucklers behind their backs; and having hastily alighted from their horses, and thrown their bucklers and javelins at the feet of their enemies, were received into the centre line, and conducted thence to the hindmost ranks, where they were ordered to sit down in the rear. There they remained quiet until the fight was begun in every quarter: when, however, the thoughts and eyes of all were deeply intent on the battle, snatching up the shields which lay in great numbers among the heaps of the slain, they fell on the rear of the Romans, and stabbing the men in the backs, and cutting their hams, made great slaughter, and caused still greater terror and confusion. While in one part dismay and flight prevailed, in another there was obstinate fighting in spite of despair. Hasdrubal, who commanded on the left wing, after entirely routing the

Roman cavalry, went off to the right, and, joining the Numidians, put to flight the cavalry of the allies. Then, leaving the Numidians to pursue them, with his Gallic and Spanish horse he made a charge on the rear of the Roman infantry, while they were busily engaged with the Africans.

On the other side of the field Paulus had, in the very beginning of the action, received a grievous wound from a sling; nevertheless, at the head of a compact band, he frequently opposed Hannibal; and in several places he restored the fight, being protected by the Roman horsemen, who in the end dismounted, because the consul's strength declined so far that he was not able even to manage his horse. Hereupon, some one telling Hannibal that the consul had ordered the cavalry to dismount, he answered, as we are told, "I should have been much better pleased if he had delivered them to me in chains." The fight maintained by the dismounted cavalry was such as might be expected, when the enemy had gained undoubted possession of the victory; and, as the vanquished chose to die on the spot rather than fly, the victors, enraged at them for retarding their success, put to death those whom they could not drive from their ground. They did, however, at length oblige them to quit the field, their numbers being reduced to a few, and those quite spent with toil and wounds. They were all dispersed, and such as were able repaired to their horses, in order to make their escape. Cneius Lentulus, a military tribune, seeing, as he rode by, the consul sitting on a stone and covered with blood, said to him, "Lucius Aemilius,[1] whom the gods ought to favor as the only person free

[1] Lucius Aemilius Paulus

from the blame of this day's disaster, take this horse while you have any remains of strength; I will raise you up and protect you. Add not to the fatality of the fight the death of a consul; without that there will be abundant cause of tears and mourning." The consul replied, "Your spirit, Cneius Cornelius,[1] I commend; but do not waste in unavailing commiseration the short time allowed you for escaping out of the hands of the enemy. Go, carry a public message from me to the Senate, that they fortify the city of Rome, and before the victorious Carthaginian arrives secure it with a powerful garrison. Carry also a private message to Quintus Fabius: tell him that Lucius Aemilius has lived, and now dies, in careful observance of his directions. As to myself, let me expire here, in the midst of my slaughtered soldiers, that I may neither be brought a second time to trial on the expiration of my consulship, nor stand forth an accuser of my colleague, as if my own innocence were to be proved by the impeachment of another." While they were thus discoursing, first a crowd of their flying countrymen, and afterwards the enemy, came on them; and these, not knowing the consul, overwhelmed him with their weapons. Lentulus, during the confusion, escaped through the swiftness of his horse. A general rout now took place; seven thousand men fled into the smaller camp, ten thousand into the greater, and about two thousand into the village of Cannae: but the town not being defended by any fortifications, these were instantly surrounded by Carthalo and the cavalry. The other consul, without joining any party of his routed troops, gained Venusia, with about seventy horsemen. The

---

[1] Cneius Cornelius Lentulus

number of the slain is computed at forty thousand foot and two thousand seven hundred horse, the loss of natives and of confederates being nearly equal. Among these were the quaestors belonging to both consuls, Lucius Atilius and Lucius Furius Bibaculus; twenty-one military tribunes; several who had passed through the offices of consul, praetor, or aedile, among whom were reckoned Cneius Servilius Geminus, and Marcus Minucius, who had been master of the horse in the preceding year, and consul some years before; likewise eighty who were members of the Senate, or had borne those offices which qualified them for membership in that body, and who had voluntarily enlisted as soldiers in the legions. The prisoners taken in this battle are reckoned at three thousand foot and three hundred horse.

THE CARTHAGINIANS IN CAPUA

(XXIII, 17.)

HERE,[1] during the greater part of the winter, Hannibal kept his forces lodged in houses, — men who had frequently and long endured with firmness every hardship to which human nature is liable, and had never been accustomed to, nor ever had experienced the comforts of prosperity. And it came about that they, whom no power of adversity had been able to subdue, were ruined by an excess of good fortune and by immoderate pleasures. These produced effects the more pernicious because, being hitherto unaccustomed, as I have said, to such indulgences, they plunged into them with greater avidity. Sleep and wine, feasting

[1] Capua, a rich city in Campania, which had opened its gates to Hannibal.

and harlots, with which through habit they became
daily more and more delighted, enervated both their
minds and bodies to such a degree that they owed
their preservation rather to the name they had acquired by their past victories than to their present
strength. In the opinion of persons skilled in the
art of war the general was guilty of a greater fault
in this instance than in not leading his army directly
to the city of Rome after the battle of Cannae; for
that dilatory conduct might be supposed only to have
deferred the conquest for a time, whereas this latter
error left him destitute of the strength to effect it.
Accordingly he marched out of Capua as if with a
different army, for it did not retain in any particular
the slightest remnant of the former discipline. Most
of the men returned to the field encumbered with
harlots; and, as soon as they began to live in tents,
and were obliged to undergo the fatigue of marches
and other military labors, like raw recruits, their
strength both of body and mind failed them; and
from that time, during the whole course of the summer campaign, great numbers used to steal away
from their standards without leave; and the only
lurking-place of all these deserters was Capua.

THE END OF THE WAR[1]

(XXX, 44, 45.)

THE last peace[2] with the Carthaginians had been
made forty years before this, in the consulate of Quin-

---

[1] On Hannibal's leaving Italy in 203 B. c, the Romans carried the
war into Africa, and, under the leadership of Publius Scipio Africanus, defeated the Carthaginians at Zama in 202. Peace was concluded in the following year

[2] In 241 B c., after the First Punic War

tus Lutatius and Aulus Manlius. The late war began twenty-three years after, in the consulate of Publius Cornelius and Tiberius Sempronius, and ended in the seventeenth year, when Cneius Cornelius and Publius Aelius Paetus were consuls. We are told that Scipio often said afterwards, that the ambition, first of Tiberius Claudius, and then of Cneius Cornelius, was what prevented that war from ending in the utter destruction of Carthage. The Carthaginians, having been exhausted by the long continuance of the late struggles, found it difficult to raise the first contribution money, so that the senate house was filled with grief and lamentations, on which occasion, it is said, Hannibal was observed to laugh; and that being reproved by Hasdrubal Haedus [1] for laughing in a moment of public sorrowing, and when he himself was the cause of their tears, he said, " If the inward thoughts could be perceived in the same manner as the look of the countenance is perceived by the eye, you would be immediately convinced that the laughter which you blame proceeds not from a heart elated by joy, but from one driven almost to madness by misfortunes; and yet it is not by any means so unseasonable as those absurd and inconsistent tears of yours. Then ought you to have wept when our arms were taken from us, our ships burned, and we ourselves forbidden to engage in foreign wars; that was the wound by which we fell. And do not imagine that the measures taken against you by the Romans were dictated merely by animosity. No great state can remain long at rest. If it has no enemies abroad, it finds them at home; as overgrown bodies seem safe from external injuries, but suffer grievous incon-

[1] Hasdrubal, " the Kid," an opponent of Hannibal's party.

venience from their own strength. We feel, it seems, for the public misfortunes, only in proportion as our private affairs are affected by them; and none of them stings more deeply than the loss of money. Thus, when the spoils were stripped off from vanquished Carthage, and you saw her left naked among so many armed states of Africa, not one of you uttered a groan; now, because a contribution must be made to the tribute out of your private properties, you lament as if the existence of the state were terminated. Much I dread lest you quickly feel that the subject of your tears this day is the lightest of your misfortunes." Such were Hannibal's sentiments which he delivered to the Carthaginians. Scipio, having called an assembly, bestowed on Masinissa,[1] in addition to his paternal kingdom, the city of Cirta, and other cities and lands belonging to the territories of Syphax,[2] which had fallen into the hands of the Roman people. He ordered Cneius Octavius to conduct the fleet to Sicily, and deliver it to the consul, Cneius Cornelius; and the ambassadors of the Carthaginians to go to Rome, in order that the terms stipulated for him might be ratified by the authority of the Senate and the order of the people.

Peace being established by sea and land, he embarked his army, and carried it over to Lilybaeum in Sicily; and from thence, sending a great part of his troops around by sea, he himself landed in Italy. As he proceeded through the country, he found it no less delighted at finding there was an end to the war than at the success in it, not only the inhabitants of the

[1] A king of Numidia who had aided Scipio against Hannibal

[2] A prince of western Numidia, who had fought on the side of tho Carthaginians.

cities pouring out to show their respect to him, but
crowds of the country-people also filling up the roads.
Thus he arrived at Rome, where he entered the city
in the most splendid triumph which had ever been
beheld. He carried into the treasury a hundred and
twenty-three thousand pounds weight of silver, and
out of the spoil distributed to each of his soldiers
four hundred asses.[1] The death of Syphax caused
some diminution in the splendor of the show, but none
in the glory of the general who triumphed. He died
a short time before at Tibur, to which place he had
been removed from Alba. His death, however, made
some noise, for he was honored with a public funeral.
Polybius, a writer of no contemptible authority, as-
serts that this king was led in triumph. I have not
been able to discover whether it was the affection of
the soldiers, or the attachment of the people, which
honored Scipio with the surname of Africanus; nor
whether it was brought into use by the flattery of
his friends, as that of Felix given to Sulla, and of
Magnus to Pompey, in the memory of our fathers.
He was certainly the first general distinguished by
the title of a nation which he had subdued. Others,
afterwards following his example, though far inferior
in the greatness of their achievements, assumed pompous inscriptions for their statues, and splendid sur-
names for their families.

---

[1] The coin known as the "as" was at this time worth about 14
cents

THE DEATH OF HANNIBAL[1]

(XXXIX., 51.)

TITUS QUINTIUS FLAMININUS came as ambassador to King Prusias, who had incurred the jealousy of the Romans by entertaining Hannibal after the flight of Antiochus, and by making war on Eumenes. Soon after his arrival, among other discourse, he remonstrated with Prusias on his giving protection to a person who, of all men living, was the most inveterate enemy to the Roman nation; who had incited, first his own country, and afterwards, when its power was reduced, King Antiochus, to make war on Rome. In consequence of this, or of Prusias having himself a desire of gratifying Flamininus, a party of soldiers was sent to guard Hannibal's house. The Carthaginian had always foreseen such end of his life, for he knew the implacable hatred which the Romans bore him, and placed little confidence in the faith of kings. Besides, he had experienced the fickle temper of Prusias, and had for some time dreaded the arrival of Flamininus, as an event fatal to him. Surrounded as he was by dangers on all sides, in order to have always some passage of flight open, he had made seven doors in his house, of which some were concealed lest they might be invested by a guard. But the imperious government of kings suffers nothing to remain secret, which they choose to discover. The troops formed a circle of

[1] Hannibal remained at the head of the government for six years after the conclusion of peace with the Romans. Then, accused by his political enemies of planning to join forces with Antiochus, king of Syria, in another attack upon Rome, he was compelled, on pressure from the Romans, to flee from Carthage. He went first to Tyre, then to Ephesus, and finally to the court of Prusias, king of Bithynia

guards around the house in such a manner that it was impossible to slip out. Hannibal, on being told that some of the king's soldiers were in the porch, endeavored to escape through a back door, which was the most private, and whence the passage was least likely to be observed, but, perceiving that to be guarded, and every avenue round to be shut by a body of soldiers, he called for poison, which he had long kept in readiness for such an event, and said, " Let us release the Romans from their long anxiety, since they have not patience to wait for the death of an old man. Flamininus will gain no very great or memorable victory over one unarmed and betrayed. What an alteration has taken place in the behavior of the Roman people, this day affords abundant proof. Their fathers gave warning to Pyrrhus, their armed foe, then heading an army against them in Italy, to beware of poison. The present generation have sent an ambassador, of consular rank, to persuade Prusias villanously to murder his guest." Then imprecating curses on the head of Prusias, and on his kingdom, and calling on the gods, the avengers of violated hospitality, to witness his breach of faith, he drank off the contents of the cup. In this manner did Hannibal end his life.

PETRONIUS

BIOGRAPHICAL SKETCH

" With regard to Caius Petronius, I ought to dwell a
little on his antecedents. His days he passed in sleep, his
nights in the business and pleasures of life. Indolence had
raised him to fame, as energy raises others, and he was
reckoned not a debauchee and spendthrift, like most of
those who squander their substance, but a man of refined
luxury. And indeed his talk and his doings, the freer they
were and the more show of carelessness they exhibited, were
the better liked, for their look of a natural simplicity. Yet
as proconsul of Bithynia and soon afterwards as consul,
he showed himself a man of vigor, and equal to business.
Then falling back into vice or affecting vice, he was chosen
by Nero to be one of his few intimate associates, as a critic
in matters of taste, while the emperor thought nothing
charming or elegant in luxury unless Petronius had expressed to him his approval of it. Hence jealousy on the
part of Tigellinus, who looked on him as a rival, and even
his superior in the science of pleasure. And so he worked
on the prince's cruelty, which dominated every other passion, charging Petronius with having been the friend of
Scaevinus, bribing a slave to become informer, robbing him
of the means of defence, and hurrying into prison the
greater part of his domestics.

" It happened at the time that the emperor was on his
way to Campania, and that Petronius, after going as far as
Cumae, was detained there. He bore no longer the sus-

pense of fear or of hope. Yet he did not fling away life with precipitate haste, but having made an incision in his veins and then, according to his humor, bound them up, he again opened them, while he conversed with his friends, not in a serious strain or on topics that might win for him the glory of courage. And he listened to them as they repeated, not thoughts on the immortality of the soul or on the theories of philosophers, but light poetry and playful verses. To some of his slaves he gave liberal presents, a flogging to others. He dined, indulged himself in sleep, that death, though forced on him, might have a natural appearance. Even in his will he did not, as did many others in their last moments, flatter Nero or Tigellinus or any other of the men in power. On the contrary, he described fully the prince's shameful excesses, with the names of his male and female companions, and their novelties in debauchery, and sent the account under seal to Nero. Then he broke his signet ring, that it might not be subsequently available for imperilling others." [1]

Such is the sketch which Tacitus [2] gives of the man who was in all probability the author of the *Satirae*, of which unfortunately only fragments of the fifteenth and sixteenth books remain. The work, which was for the most part in prose, contained an account of the adventures of one Encolpius and his companions on a journey in southern Italy. The interest which it has for us on the literary side as an example of the Roman novel, and on the linguistic side by reason of its contribution to our knowledge of colloquial Latin, is still further enhanced by its drastic representations of current abuses and strikingly realistic pictures of various aspects of the social life of the times.

[1] The translation is that of Church and Brodribb.
[2] *Annals*, xvi, 18, 19.

AT TRIMALCHIO'S DINNER[1]

(Satirae, 41–46.)

As his departure delivered us from his usurpation
of the talk, we tried to draw our neighbors into conversation. "What is a day?" cried Dama, after
calling for a larger glass. "Nothing! Before you
have time to turn round it is night. One should
therefore go straight from the bedroom to the dining-
room. And what a regular freezing we have been
having of late! I could scarcely get hot in my bath.
However, a hot drink is as good as a greatcoat. I've
had some stiff ones, and I am about full; it has got
into my head." Here Seleucus broke in with, "I
don't take a bath every day. Constant washing wears
out the body as well as the clothes; but when I've
put down my good posset of mead, I can tell the cold
go hang. However, I could not have bathed to-day
in any case, as I had to attend a funeral. Poor Chrysanthus, you know, a nice fellow, has just slipped his
wind. It was only the other day he said how d'ye
do to me. I can fancy I am talking to him now.
Ah, we are only air balloons, summer flies; this life's
a bubble. And it's not as if he hadn't tried the
fasting cure. For five days neither bit nor sup
passed his lips, and yet he's gone. Too many doc-
tors did for him, or else it was to be. A doctor's
really no use except to feel you did the right thing.

---

[1] The longest extant section of the *Satirae* is that which contains a
description of a dinner party given by Trimalchio, a rich parvenu of
the freedman class. This selection reproduces the conversation which
took place among some of the guests, freedmen like Trimalchio, during a temporary absence of the host.

An excellent funeral it was, — superior bier and trappings, and the mourners first class." He was becoming a bore, and Phileros interrupted him with, " Oh, let us leave the dead alone. He's all right. He had a decent life and a decent death. What has he to complain of ? He rose from the gutter, and was once so poor that he would have picked a farthing out of a midden with his teeth. But he grew like a honeycomb. I suppose he has left behind him a cool 100,- 000, and all in hard cash. To speak the truth — for, as you know, I wear my heart upon my sleeve — he was a rough-spoken fellow, quarrelsomeness personified. Now his brother was a fine, friendly, open-handed gentleman, and kept a good table. At first everything went ugly with him, but his first vine-crop pulled him together ; he sold his wine for whatever he chose to ask. But what really kept his head above water was that legacy, when he walked into a good deal more than was left him. That was why that blockhead Chrysanthus quarrelled with his own brother, and left away his money to some Tom, Dick, or Harry. It's an ill turn when a man turns his back on his own. He took all his slaves told him for gospel, and they played the deuce with him. Credulity is fatal, especially for a business man. However, he got far more than he deserved ; Fortune's favorite, lead turned to gold under his hands. And how many years do you think he had on his back ? Seventy and more, I should say. But he was as hard as nails, and carried his age splendidly, — as black as a crow. Ah, I knew him long, long ago, when he did something smack, something grow to. He had a general kind of taste. Well, he enjoyed himself, and I for one don't blame him. It's all he takes to the grave with him."

"How you go on talking," said Ganymedes, "about what has nothing to do with the heavens above or the earth beneath, and no one troubles his head about the supply of food. I declare I could not buy a mouthful of bread this day. It's the drought, and now we have had a year's fast. But luck to the aediles,[1] they have an understanding with the bakers : 'Scratch me and I'll scratch you.' So it's the folk in a small way bear the brunt, while the top-sawyers have high jinks all the time. Ah, if we had the giants now that we had when I came back from Asia ! How well I remember Safinius ! He lived near the Old Arch when I was a boy : a regular pepper-box, he'd knock sparks out of the ground under his feet. And so in his time food was cheap as dirt. You'd get for an as a loaf that two men could not eat; now you get a thing the size of a bull's eye. Ah, things are going from bad to worse every day. This place is growing downwards like a cow's tail But I'm hanged if I don't think it is all the irreligion of the age ; no one fasts or cares a jot for Jupiter. Time was when our ladies used to go in their robes with tossed hair, bare feet, and pure hearts, and pray for rain, and it used to rain bucketfuls at once, and they all came back like drowned rats. But now we have lost our religion, and the fields are feeling the effect of it." "Easy, easy," said Echion, a shoddy merchant; "there are ups and downs, as the peasant said when he lost his speckled pig : to-morrow may bring what we have n't to-day, — that's the way the world jogs along. There would not be a better country than this in the world, only for the men that are in it. It is in a poor way now, but

---

[1] It was one of their duties to superintend the food supply.

so are others. We must n't be too particular. The sky 's above us all. If you lived somewhere else, you would say that here the pigs were going about ready to roast, crying, ' Who 'll eat me? ' "

R. Y. TYRRELL.

MARTIAL

BIOGRAPHICAL SKETCH

BORN at Bilbilis, a town in the province of Tarraconensis in Spain, Martial came to Rome in 64 A. D., when he was about twenty years of age. Throughout the whole period of his residence in the capital he was a client, one of that numerous class of needy dependents who relied for their support solely upon the generosity of their patrons. It was not at any time a position of dignity, but in the case of Martial, who had no difficulty in securing the patronage of rich and influential citizens, it carried with it a fair competence, and afforded him boundless opportunities for coming in contact with those sides of Roman life which furnished the best material for the pen of the epigrammatist.

The *Liber Spectaculorum*, a collection of pieces on shows given mostly in the Flavian Amphitheatre, twelve books of *Epigrams*, and two books of *Xenia* and *Apophoreta*, distichs intended to accompany presents such as were exchanged on the Saturnalia, make up the list of Martial's extant works. In the *Epigrams*, which are the poet's most important contribution to Latin literature, we find a great variety of subjects. It was the field that he made peculiarly his own, and he worked in it with such success that from his time down to the present day his name has been identified with the *Epigram* as a literary type. When we attempt to select individual pictures from the long gallery which he has left us, we find ourselves confronted by an embarrassment of riches. He had a quick eye for the weaknesses of his fellows, and was merciless in attacking the hypocrisies and foibles of the age His was not, indeed, the standpoint of outraged morality, for many of his poems are marked by gross adulation and still grosser obscenity; but without making any pretences himself, he regarded the different types of character he saw around him as fair marks for his satire: Selius, who patrols the whole town in the hope of meeting some one who will invite him to dinner (II., 14); Tongilius, who pretends to be ill in order to obtain presents of wine and food (II., 40); Diaulus, who hit upon the lucrative combination of being at once physician and undertaker (I, 47), Symmachus, who, going out with a retinue of medical students to visit a patient, found him without a fever but left him with one (V, 9). These are a few examples chosen at random from a long list.

The greater part of Martial's work was done during the reign of Domitian, who showed him some signs of favor. After the death of the tyrant he seems to have found the atmosphere at Rome less congenial, and a few years later, early in Trajan's reign, he retired to Bilbilis, where he died about 104 A. D.

A FRIEND

(Epigrams, I, 39)

Is there a man whose friendship rare
With antique friendship may compare,
In learning steeped, both old and new,
Yet unpedantic, simple, true;
Whose soul, ingenuous and upright,
Ne'er formed a wish that shunned the light,
Whose sense is sound? If such there be,
My Decianus, thou art he.

GOLDWIN SMITH.

THE DINER-OUT

(Epigrams, II , 11.)

BEHOLD, on Selius' brow, how dark the shade;
How late he roams beneath the colonnade;
How his grim face betrays some secret wound;
How with his nose he almost scrapes the ground;
He beats his breast, he rends his hair.   What now?
Has Selius lost a friend, or brother?   No!
His brace of sons still live, long be their life!
Safe are his slaves, his chattels, and his wife;
His steward's, his bailiff's books are right—what doom
So dire has fallen on him?   He dines at home!

GOLDWIN SMITH.

A LITERARY HOST [1]

(Epigrams, III , 50)

THE single cause why you invite
Is that your works you may recite.
I hardly had my slippers [2] dropped,
Nor dream'd the entertainment stopp'd,
When, 'mid the lettuces and salad,
Is usher'd in a bloody ballad,
Then, lo! another bunch of lays,
While yet the primal service stays.
Another, ere the second course;
A third, and fourth, and fifth you force.
The boar, beroasted now to rags,
Appears in vain : the stomach flags.

[1] The epigram is addressed to one Ligurinus, who gave a dinner party for the sole purpose of reading his poems to the guests.
[2] The Romans used to have their sandals taken off on reclining at table.

The labors,[1] that destroy each dish,
Were useful coats for frying fish.
Affirm, my Bard, this dire decree :
Else you shall sup alone for me.

JAMES ELPHINSTON

A ROMAN DAY

(Epigrams, IV., 8)

VISITS [2] consume the first, the second hour ;
When comes the third, hoarse pleaders [3] show their
          power.
At four to business Rome herself betakes ;
At six she goes to sleep ; [4] by seven she wakes.
By nine, well breathed from exercise, we rest,
And in the banquet hall the couch is pressed.
Now, when thy skill, greatest of cooks, has spread
The ambrosial feast, let Martial's rhymes be read,
With mighty hand while Cæsar [5] holds the bowl,
When draughts of nectar have relaxed his soul.
Now trifles pass.   My giddy Muse would fear
Jove to approach in morning mood severe.

GOLDWIN SMITH.

THE TRUE BUSINESS OF LIFE

(Epigrams, V., 20.)

O COULD both thou and I, my friend,
    From care and trouble freed,

---

[1] The manuscripts of the poems would have been more useful as
wrappers for fish.

[2] It was customary for clients to assemble at their patron's house
for the *salutatio* early in the morning.

[3] In the law-courts

[4] The siesta was universal

[5] The Emperor Domitian

Our quiet days at pleasure spend
  And taste of life indeed,

We 'd bid farewell to marble halls,
  The sad abodes of state,
The law, with all its dismal brawls,
  The trappings of the great;

We 'd seek the book, the cheerful talk,
  At noonday in the shade,
The bath, the ride, the pleasant walk
  In the cool colonnade.

Dead to our better selves we see
  The golden hours take flight,
Still scored against us as they flee,
  Then haste to live aright.

GOLDWIN SMITH

A JUGGLER

(Epigrams, IX., 38.)

LITTLE, nimble Agathine,
What consummate art is thine!
Play thy postures, one and all;
Never will the target [1] fall.
Thee it follows everywhere:
Swooping through the easy air,
To thy hand or foot it flies,
On thy back or shoulder lies.
Slipp'ry footing proves no dread,
Though the shower Corycian [2] shed;

---

[1] Shield
[2] The stage was sprinkled with saffron from Corycus in Cilicia

Though the rapid southern gales
Strive to rend theatric veils.[1]
Still secure, the careless boy
Flings from limb to limb the toy;
And the artist well may brave
All the force of wind and wave.
Little, dextrous Agathine
To eschew should'st thou incline,
Poor thy chance, alone of this:
Who still hits can never miss.
Thou must change thy postures all;
Else the target ne'er will fall.

JAMES ELPHINSTON.

DEATH OF A CHARIOTEER

(Epigrams, X., 50)

LET Victory, sorrowing, cast her palm away,
Let Favor beat her breast and wail the day,
Let Honor don the mourner's dark attire,
And Glory fling her wreath upon the pyre.
Snatched in his prime, Scorpus, sad thought! must go
To yoke night's horses in the realm below.
Swift flew the chariot, soon the goal was won,
Another race thou hast too quickly run.

GOLDWIN SMITH.

---

[1] The awning which protected the spectators from the sun.

TACITUS

BIOGRAPHICAL SKETCH

LITTLE or nothing is known about the early life of Tacitus. The year of his birth can only be approximately given as 54 A. D., and the assertion sometimes made that Interamna in Umbria was his birthplace rests on extremely unsubstantial evidence. It is quite possible that he was born at Rome, and we know for certain that he studied rhetoric there. It has been suggested that possibly the Cornelius Tacitus mentioned by the elder Pliny as procurator of Belgic Gaul was the historian's father, but there is no proof of this, and the details of his family relations are unknown to us, except the fact that in 78 he married the daughter of Julius Agricola, the famous governor of Britain.

Tacitus' career was at first pursued along political lines. He held some minor office under Vespasian, was quaestor under Titus, and praetor under Domitian. After his praetorship (88 A. D.), he was absent from Rome for some years, possibly serving as propraetor of Belgic Gaul. He returned in 93, the year of Agricola's death, but does not seem to have taken any part in public life during the remainder of Domitian's reign. In 97, under Nerva, he was made consul. A few years later we hear of him as associated with his friend the younger Pliny in the indictment of Marius Priscus for extortion in the province of Africa. After this he retired, and devoted himself exclusively to his literary and historical pursuits. His death probably took place about 116 A. D.

His first literary work was the *Dialogus de Oratoribus*, a

charming little dialogue on the decline of oratory under the empire. The style, which differs in a striking manner from that of his other works, shows many signs of Ciceronian influence. In the *Agricola* and *Germania*, also of small compass, we see Tacitus tending in the direction of historiography, the field to which he afterwards confined himself. Yet neither of these monographs is, strictly speaking, an historical work. The *Agricola* is an example of encomiastic biography, in which the historical form is adopted only to give the encomiastic element greater effectiveness; while the *Germania*, formally and primarily an ethnographical treatise, seems from its idealization of the simplicity and virtue of the northern people to indicate some desire on the part of the author to reflect upon the deterioration of morals among the Romans.

Of much wider scope are the two great historical works, the *Historiae* and the *Annales*. The former, which in all probability originally consisted of fourteen books, was a history of the empire from 69 A. D. to the death of Domitian. Of this only the first four books and a part of the fifth have survived, containing an account of 69 and 70, the crowded years that saw the reigns of Galba, Otho, and Vitellius, and the triumph of the Flavians. The *Annales* (there were sixteen books in all, but the central portion of the work is lost) dealt with the period from the death of Augustus in 14 A. D. to the fall of Nero. It is the author's masterpiece: of prime importance, historically, for its masterly descriptions of political situations, and its subtle analysis of the characters of the great personages of the early empire; of rare stylistic effectiveness from its wonderful compression, the infinite variety shown in the structure of clause and period, and the skillful use of poetic word and phrase.

CUSTOMS OF THE GERMANS [1]

(Germania, XVI. - XXVII.)

THE Germans, it is well known, have no regular cities; nor do they allow a continuity of houses. They dwell in separate habitations, dispersed up and down as a grove, a meadow, or a fountain happens to invite. They have villages, but not with a series of connected buildings. Every tenement stands detached, with a vacant piece of ground round it, either to prevent accidents by fire, or for want of skill in the art of building. They do not know the use of mortar or of tiles. They build with rude materials, regardless of beauty, order, and proportion. Particular parts are covered over with a kind of earth so smooth and shining that the natural veins have some resemblance to the lights and shades of painting. Besides these habitations they have a number of subterranean caves, dug by their own labor and carefully covered over with dung: in winter their retreat from cold and the repository of their corn. In those recesses they not only find a shelter from the rigor of the season, but in times of foreign invasion their effects are safely concealed. The enemy lays waste the open country, but the hidden treasure escapes the general ravage; safe in its obscurity, or because the search would be attended with too much trouble.

The clothing in use is a loose mantle, made fast with a clasp, or, when that cannot be had, with a thorn. With only this on they loiter away whole days by the fire-side. The rich wear a more pretentious

[1] This and the following selections are from the translation of Arthur Murphy.

garment, not however displayed and flowing like the
Parthians or the people of Sarmatia, but drawn so
tight that the form of the limbs is palpably expressed.
The skins of wild animals are also much in use.
Near the frontier, on the borders of the Rhine, the
inhabitants wear them, but are wholly indifferent as
to the choice.   The people who live in the more remote regions near the northern seas, and who have
not acquired by commerce a taste for new-fashioned
apparel, are more careful in their selection.   They
choose particular beasts, and having stripped off the
furs clothe themselves with the spoil, decorated with
parti-colored spots, or fragments taken from the skins
of fish that swim the ocean as yet unexplored by
the Romans.   In point of dress there is no distinction
between the sexes, except that the garment of the
women is frequently made of linen, adorned with
purple spots, but without sleeves, leaving the arms
and part of the bosom uncovered.

Marriage is considered as a strict and sacred insti-
tution.   In the national character there is nothing so
truly commendable.   To be contented with one wife is
peculiar to the Germans.   They differ in this respect
from all other savage nations.   There are indeed a
few instances of polygamy; not however the effect of
loose desire, but occasioned by the ambition of various
families, who court the alliance of a chief distinguished
by the nobility of his rank and character.   The bride
brings no portion, but receives a dowry from her husband.   In the presence of her parents and relations
he makes a tender of part of his wealth; if accepted,
the match is approved.   In the choice of the presents
female vanity is not consulted.   There are no frivolous trinkets to adorn the future bride.   The whole

fortune consists of oxen, a caparisoned horse, a shield, a spear, and a sword. She in return delivers a present of arms, and by this exchange of gifts the marriage is concluded. This is the nuptial ceremony; this the bond of union; these their hymeneal gods. Lest the wife should think that her sex exempts her from the rigor of the severest virtue and the toils of war, she is informed of her duty by the marriage ceremony; and thence she learns that she is received by her husband to be his partner in toil and danger, to dare with him in war, and suffer with him in peace. The oxen yoked, the horse accoutred, and the arms given on the occasion inculcate this lesson; and thus she is prepared to live, and thus to die. These are the terms of their union: she receives her armor as a sacred treasure, to be preserved inviolate, and transmitted with honor to her sons, a portion for their wives, and from them going down to her grandchildren.

In consequence of these manners the married state is a life of affection and female constancy. The virtue of the woman is guarded from seduction: no public spectacles to seduce her, no banquets to inflame her passions, no baits of pleasure to disarm her virtue. The art of intriguing by clandestine letters is unknown to both sexes. Populous as the country is, adultery is rarely heard of; when detected, the punishment is instant, and inflicted by the husband. He cuts off the hair of his guilty wife, and having assembled her relations expels her naked from his house, pursuing her with stripes through the village. To public loss of honor no favor is shown. She may possess beauty, youth, and riches; but a husband she can never obtain. Vice is not treated by the Germans

as a subject of raillery, nor is the profligacy of cor-
rupting and being corrupted called the fashion of the
age.   By the practice of some states,[1] female virtue is
advanced to still higher perfection : with them none
but virgins marry.   When the bride has fixed her
choice, her hopes of matrimony are closed for life.
With one husband, as with one life, one mind, one
body, every woman is satisfied.   In him her happiness
is centred, her desires find their limit, and the result
is not only affection for the husband's person, but
reverence for the married state.   To set limits to
population by rearing up only a certain number of
children, and destroying the rest, is accounted a flagi-
tious crime.   Among the savages of Germany virtu-
ous manners operate more than good laws in other
countries.

In every family the children are reared in filth.
They run about naked, and in time grow up to that
strength and size of limb which we behold with wonder.   The infant is nourished at the mother's breast,
not turned over to nurses and to servants.   No distinction is made between the future chieftain and the infant son of a common slave.   On the same ground and
mixed with the same cattle they pass their days, till
the age of manhood draws the line of separation, and
early valor shows the person of free birth.   It is generally late before their young men come to manhood,
nor are the virgins married too soon.   Both parties
wait to attain their full growth.   In due time the
match is made, and the children of the marriage have
the constitution of their parents.   The uncle by the
mother's side regards his nephews with an affection
not at all inferior to that of their father.   With some

---

[1] *I e.* German states.

the relation of the sister's children to their maternal
uncle is held to be the strongest tie of consanguinity,
so that in demanding hostages that line of kindred is
preferred as the most endearing objects of the family
and, consequently, the most tender pledges. The son
is always heir to his father. Last wills and testa-
ments are not in use. In case of failure of issue, the
brothers of the deceased are next in succession, or else
the paternal or maternal uncles. A numerous train
of relations is the comfort and honor of old age. To
live without raising heirs to yourself is no advantage
in Germany.

To adopt the quarrels as well as the friendships of
your parents and relations is held to be an indispensable duty. In their resentments, however, they are not
implacable. Injuries are adjusted by a settled measure
of compensation. Atonement is made for homicide
by a certain number of cattle, and by that satisfaction
the whole family is appeased; a happy regulation
and conducive to the public interest, since it serves
to curb that spirit of revenge which is the natural
result of liberty in the excess. Hospitality and convivial pleasure are nowhere else so liberally enjoyed.
To refuse admittance to a guest were an outrage
against humanity. The master of the house wel-
comes every stranger, and regales him to the best of
his ability. If his stock falls short, he becomes a
visitor to his neighbor, and conducts his new acquaintance to a more plentiful table. They do not wait to
be invited, nor is this of any consequence, since a
cordial reception is always certain. Between an intimate and an entire stranger no distinction is made.
The law of hospitality is the same. The departing
guest receives as a present whatever he desires, and

the host retaliates by asking with the same freedom. A German delights in the gifts which he receives, yet by bestowing he imputes nothing to you as a favor, and for what he receives he acknowledges no obligation.

In this manner the Germans pride themselves on their frankness and generosity. Their hours of rest are protracted to broad daylight. As soon as they rise, they bathe, generally, on account of the intense severity of the climate, in warm water. They then betake themselves to their meal, each on a separate seat and at his own table. Having finished their repast they proceed completely armed to the despatch of business, and frequently to a convivial meeting. To devote both day and night to deep drinking is a disgrace to no man. Disputes, as will be the case with people in liquor, frequently arise, and are seldom confined to opprobrious language. The quarrel generally ends in a scene of blood. Important subjects, such as the reconciliation of enemies, the forming of family alliances, the election of chiefs, and even peace and war, are generally canvassed in their carousing festivals. The convivial moment, according to their notion, is the true season for business, when the mind opens itself in plain simplicity, or grows warm with bold and noble ideas. Strangers to artifice and knowing no refinement, they tell their sentiments without disguise. The pleasure of the table expands their hearts and calls forth every secret. On the following day the subject of debate is again taken into consideration, and thus two different periods of time have their distinct uses: when warm, they debate; when cool, they decide.

Their beverage is a liquor drawn from barley or

from wheat, and, like the juice of the grape, fermented to a spirit. The settlers on the banks of the Rhine provide themselves with wine. Their food is of the simplest kind : wild apples, the flesh of an animal recently killed, or coagulated milk. Without skill in cookery, or without seasoning to stimulate the palate, they eat to satisfy nature. But they do not drink merely to quench their thirst. Indulge their love of liquor to the excess which they require, and you need not employ the terror of your arms ; their own vices will subdue them.

Their public spectacles boast of no variety. They have but one sort, and that they repeat at all their meetings. A band of young men make it their pastime to dance entirely naked amidst pointed swords and javelins. By constant exercise this kind of exhibition has become an art, and art has taught them to perform with grace and elegance. Their talents, however, are not let out for hire. Though some danger attends the practice, the pleasure of the spectator is their only recompense. In the character of a German there is nothing so remarkable as his passion for play. Without the excuse of liquor, strange as it may seem, in their cool and sober moments they have recourse to dice, as to a serious and regular business, with the most desperate spirit committing their whole substance to chance, and when they have lost their all, putting their liberty and even their persons on the last hazard of the die! The loser yields himself to slavery. Young, robust, and valiant, he submits to be chained, and even exposed to sale. Such is the effect of a ruinous and inveterate habit. They are victims to folly, and they call themselves men of honor. The winner is always in a hurry to barter away the slaves acquired by success at play ; he is ashamed of his victory, and therefore puts away the remembrance of it as soon as possible.

The slaves in general are not arranged at their several employments in the household affairs, as is the practice at Rome. Each has his separate habitation, and his own establishment to manage. The master considers him as an agrarian dependent, who is obliged to furnish a certain quantity of grain, cattle, or wearing apparel. The slave obeys, and the state of servitude extends no further. All domestic affairs are managed by the master's wife and children. To punish a slave with stripes, to load him with chains or condemn him to hard labor is unusual. It is true that slaves are sometimes put to death, not under color of justice, or of any authority vested in the master, but in transport of passion, in a fit of rage, as is often the case in a sudden affray ; but it is also true that this species of homicide passes with impunity. The freedmen are not of much higher consideration than the actual slaves; they obtain no rank in the master's family, and, if we except the parts of Germany where monarchy is established, they never figure on the stage of public business In despotic governments they rise above the men of ingenuous birth, and even eclipse the whole body of the nobles. In other states the subordination of the freedmen is a proof of public liberty.

The practice of placing money at interest and reaping the profits of usury is unknown in Germany ; and that happy ignorance is a better preventive of the evil than a code of prohibitory laws. In cultivating the soil they do not settle on one spot, but shift from place to place. The state or community takes possession of a certain tract proportioned to its number of hands ; allotments are afterwards made to individuals according to their rank and dignity. In so extensive a country, where there is no want of land, the partition is easily made. The ground tilled in one year lies fallow the next, and a sufficient quantity always remains, the labor of the people being by no means adequate to the extent or fertility of the soil. Nor have they the skill to make orchard plantations, to enclose the meadow grounds, or to lay out and water gardens. From the earth they demand nothing but grain. Hence their year is not, as with the Romans, divided into four seasons. They have distinct ideas of winter, spring, and summer, and their language has terms for each ; but they neither know the blessings nor the name of autumn.

Their funerals have neither pomp nor vain ambition. When the bodies of illustrious men are to be burned, they choose a particular kind of wood for the purpose, and have no other attention. The funeral pile is neither strewed with garments nor enriched with fragrant spices. The arms of the deceased are committed to the flames, and sometimes his horse. A mound of turf is raised to his memory ; and this, in their opinion, is a better sepulchre than those structures of labored grandeur which display the weakness of human vanity, and are at best a burden to the dead. Tears and lamentations are soon at an end, but their regret does not so easily wear away. To grieve for the departed is comely in the softer sex. The women weep for their friends ; the men remember them.

THE MUTINY OF THE PANNONIAN LEGIONS[1]

(Annales, I., 16–30.)

SUCH was the situation of affairs at Rome when a fierce and violent mutiny broke out among the legions in Pannonia. For this insurrection there was no other motive than the licentious spirit which is apt to show itself in the beginning of a new reign, and the hope of private advantage in the distractions of a civil war. A summer camp had been formed for three legions[2] under the command of Junius Blaesus. The death of Augustus and the accession of Tiberius being known to the army, the general granted a suspension of military duty as an interval of grief or joy. The soldiers grew wanton in idleness; dissensions spread amongst them; the vile and profligate had their circles of auditors; sloth and pleasure prevailed; and all were willing to exchange a life of toil and discipline for repose and luxury. There happened to be in a camp a busy incendiary, by name Percennius, formerly a leader of theatrical factions,[3] and now a common soldier; a man fluent in words, and by his early habits versed in the arts of exciting tumults and sedition. Over the weak and ignorant, and such as felt their minds alarmed with doubts and fears about the future condition of the service, this meddlesome fellow began to exert his

---

[1] Pannonia, which lay between the Danube and the Alps, had been organized as a province in the reign of Augustus. There were three Roman legions posted there. The mutiny took place just after Tiberius' accession, 14 A D.

[2] The strength of a legion was from 5000 to 6000 men. It was commanded by a *legatus*, under whom were the tribunes, six in number, and under them the centurions.

[3] A leader of *claqueurs* in the theatre.

influence. In the dead of the night he mixed in cabals, and never failed at the close of day, when the sober and well disposed retired to their tents, to draw together the idle and most abandoned. Having gained a number of proselytes, he stood forth the orator of sedition, and harangued his confederates in the following manner: —

"How long, my fellow-soldiers, must we obey a small and despicable set of centurions? How long continue slaves to a wretched band of military tribunes? If we mean to redress our grievances, what time so fit as the present, when the new emperor is not yet settled on the throne? Relief may now be obtained, either by remonstrances, or sword in hand. By our passive spirit we have suffered enough; we have been slaves in thirty or forty campaigns; we are grown gray in the service, worn out with infirmities and covered with wounds. In that condition we are still condemned to the toils of war. Even the men who have obtained their discharge still follow the standard under the name of veterans: another word for protracted misery. A few, indeed, by their bodily vigor have surmounted all their labors; but what is their reward? They are sent to distant regions, and, under color of an allotment of lands, are settled on a barren mountain or a swampy fen. War of itself is a state of the vilest drudgery without an adequate compensation. The life and limb of a soldier are valued at ten *asses*[1] a day: out of that wretched pittance he must find his clothing, his tent equipage, and his arms; with that fund he must bribe the centurion; with that must purchase occasional exemptions from service; and with that must pay for a remission

---

[1] The *as* at this time was worth about a cent.

of punishment. But blows and stripes from our officers, wounds from the enemy, intense cold in winter and the fatigue of summer campaigns, destructive war, in which everything is hazarded, and peace, by which nothing is gained, are all the soldier's portion.

"For these evils there is but one remedy left. Let us fix the conditions of our service; let every soldier receive a *denarius*[1] a day, and at the end of sixteen years let him be entitled to his discharge; beyond that term no further service. Without detaining any man whatever, and without forcing him to follow the colors as a veteran, let every soldier receive the arrears that may be due to him; let him be paid in ready money on the spot, and in the very camp where he signalized his valor. The praetorian cohorts[2] receive two *denarii* for their daily pay; at the end of sixteen years they return to their families. Is superior merit the ground of this distinction? Do they encounter greater dangers? It is theirs to mount guard within the city, and the service may be honorable; but it is our lot to serve amidst savage nations in a state of perpetual warfare. If we look out of our tents the barbarians are in view."

This speech was received with acclamations. Various passions heaved in every breast. Some presented their bodies seamed with stripes; others pointed to their heads grown gray in the service; numbers showed their tattered clothing, and their persons almost naked. At length the frenzy of the malcontents knew no bounds. Their first design was to incorporate the three legions into one; but which should give

[1] About twenty cents

[2] The Praetorian Guard, numbering about 10,000 men, and kept in the neighborhood of Rome.

its name to the united body was the question. Mutual jealousy put an end to the project. Another plan was carried out: the eagles of the three legions, with the colors of the cohorts, were crowded together without preference or distinction. They threw up sods of earth, and began to raise a tribunal. Amidst the tumult Blaesus arrived. He called aloud to all, laid hold of individuals, offered himself to their swords. "Here," he said, "behold your victim; imbrue your hands in the blood of your general. Murder is a crime less horrible than treason to your prince. I will either live to command the legions intrusted to me; or, if you are determined to revolt, despatch me first, that, when the frenzy is over, you may wake to shame, horror, and remorse."

The work of raising a tribunal, in spite of all his efforts, still went on. Heaps of turf were thrown up, and rose breast high. Conquered at length by the perseverance of their general, the mutineers desisted. Blaesus exerted all his eloquence: "Sedition and revolt," he said, "could not serve the cause; the remonstrances of the army ought to be conveyed to the ear of the prince with respect and deference. The demands which they now made were new, unknown to former armies, and with the deified Augustus never attempted. In the present juncture, when the prince had just undertaken the cares of government, was that a time to add to his solicitude by tumult and insurrection? If they would still persist, in the season of profound peace, to urge a claim never demanded even by the conquerors in a civil war, why incur the guilt of rebellion? Why, in violation of all military discipline, urge their pretensions sword in hand? They might depute their agent to treat with the prince, and, in the presence of their general, give their instructions on the spot." This proposal was accepted : with one voice they called for the son of Blaesus, then a military tribune. The young officer undertook the charge. His directions were to insist that at the expiration of sixteen years the soldier should be discharged from the service. That point settled, it then would be time to enumerate other grievances. With this commission the general's son went forward on his journey. A calm succeeded, and lasted for some days. But the minds of the soldiers were still in agitation : their pride was roused ; the general's son was now the orator of the army ; and force, it was manifest, had at length extorted what by gentle measures could never have been obtained.

Meanwhile the detached companies, which before the disturbance had been sent to Nauportum, having heard of the commotion in the camp, seized the colors, and, after ravaging the adjacent villages, plundered Nauportum, a place little inferior to a municipal town. They treated the centurions with derision, from derision proceeded to opprobrious language, and in the end to blows and open violence. Aufidienus Rufus, the prefect of the camp,[1] was the chief object of their fury : they dragged him out of his carriage ; and, laying a heavy load on his back, obliged him to march in the foremost ranks, asking him with contemptuous insolence how he liked his burden and the length of his journey. Rufus had risen from a common soldier to the rank of centurion, and was afterwards made prefect of the camp. In that station he endeavored to recall the rigor of ancient discipline. A veteran in the service and long inured to fatigue,

---

His duties resembled those of a quartermaster.

he was strict and rigorous in his duty, expecting from others what he had practised himself.

The return of this tumultuous body renewed the troubles of the camp. The soldiers, without control, left the lines, and pillaged the country round. Some, more heavily loaded with booty than their comrades, were apprehended by the orders of Blaesus, and, after receiving due correction, thrown into prison, as an example to the rest. The authority of the general was still in force with the centurions and such of the common soldiers as retained a sense of their duty. The delinquents, however, refused to submit: they were dragged along, resisting with all their strength; they clasped the knees of the multitude round them; they called on their fellow-soldiers by name; they implored the protection of the company to which they belonged; they invoked the cohorts and the legions, crying out to all that the same lot would shortly be their portion. Against their general they omitted nothing that calumny could suggest; they appealed to heaven; they implored their gods; they tried by every topic to excite compassion, to inflame resentment, to awaken terror, and rouse the men to acts of violence. A general insurrection followed: the soldiers in a body rushed to the prison, burst the gates, unchained the prisoners, and associated with themselves the vilest of the army, a band of deserters, and a desperate crew of malefactors, then under condemnation for the enormity of their crimes.

The flame of discord raged with redoubled fury. New leaders joined the mutiny. Amidst the crowd, one of the common soldiers, a fellow known by the name of Vibulenus, mounted on the shoulders of his comrades before the tribunal of Blaesus, and addressed the multitude, all wild with fury, and eager to hear the language of sedition. "My friends," he said, "you have bravely interposed to save the lives of these innocent, these much-injured men; you have restored them to new life; but who will restore my brother? Who will give him to my arms? Sent hither from the German army, in concert with you to settle measures for our common safety, he was last night basely murdered by the hand of gladiators[1] whom Blaesus arms for your destruction. Answer me, Blaesus, where have you bestowed the body? The very enemy allows the rites of sepulture. When I have washed my brother with my tears, and printed kisses on his mangled body, then plunge your poniard in this wretched bosom. I shall die content, if these my fellow-soldiers perform the last funeral office, and bury in one grave two wretched victims, who knew no crime but that of serving the common interest of the legions."

This speech Vibulenus rendered still more inflammatory by the vehemence of his manner, by beating his breast, by striking his forehead, and pouring a flood of tears. A way being opened through the crowd, he leaped from the men's shoulders, and groveling at the feet of individuals, excited the passions of the multitude to the highest pitch of frenzy. In their fury some fell on the gladiators retained by Blaesus, and loaded them with irons; others seized the general's domestic train, while numbers dispersed themselves on every side in quest of the body; and if it had not been speedily known that no corpse could be found, that the slaves of Blaesus averred under the torture that no murder had been committed,

---

[1] Slaves trained as gladiators

and, in fact, that the incendiary never had a brother, Blaesus must have fallen a sacrifice. The tribunes and the prefect of the army were obliged to save themselves by flight. Their baggage was seized and plundered. Lucilius the centurion was put to death. This man, by the sarcastic pleasantry of the soldiers, had been nicknamed, "Give me another;" because, in chastising the soldiers, when one rod was broken, he used to call for "Another," and then "Another." The rest of the centurions lay concealed. Out of the whole number, Julius Clemens, a man of promptness and energy, was the favorite of the insurgents. He was spared as a fit person to negotiate the claims of the army. Two of the legions, the eighth and the fifteenth, were on the point of coming to the decision of the sword: the former bent on the destruction of Sirpicus, a centurion, and the latter determined to protect him The quarrel would have resulted in a scene of blood, if the soldiers of the ninth legion had not, by entreaties or menaces, appeased the fury of both parties.

When the account of these transactions reached Tiberius, that abstruse and gloomy prince, who loved to brood in secret over all untoward events, was so deeply affected, that he resolved to despatch his son Drusus and other nobles, together with two practorian cohorts, to quell the insurrection. In their instructions no decisive orders were given: they were left to act as emergencies might require. To the cohorts was added a select detachment, with a party of the practorian horse, and the flower of the Germans, at that time the body-guard of the emperor. In the train which accompanied Drusus, Aelius Sejanus was appointed to guide the inexperience of the

young prince. Sejanus,[1] at that time in a joint commission with his father Strabo, had the command of
the praetorian bands, and stood high in favor with
Tiberius. The army would of course consider him
as the fountain of rewards and punishments. As soon
as they approached the camp, the discontented legions,
by way of doing honor to Drusus, advanced to meet
him ; not, indeed, with colors displayed, as is usual
on such occasions, but in deep and solemn silence,
their dress neglected, and their whole appearance uncouth and sordid. In their looks was seen an air of
dejection, and at the same time a sullen gloom, that
plainly showed a spirit of mutiny still working in their
hearts.

Drusus was no sooner within the entrenchments than
the malcontents secured the gates. Sentinels were
posted at different stations, while the rest gathered
in a body round the tribunal. Drusus stood in act to
speak, with his hand commanding silence. The soldiers felt a variety of contending passions : they looked
around, and viewing their numbers grew fierce at the
sight, rending the air with shouts and acclamations ;
they turned to Drusus, and were covered with confusion. An indistinct and hollow murmur was heard,
a general uproar followed, and soon afterwards a deep
and awful silence. The behavior of the men varied
with their passions, by turns inflamed with rage or
depressed with fear. Drusus seized his moment, and
read his father's letter, in substance stating that
Tiberius had nothing so much at heart as the interest
of the gallant legions with whom he had served in
so many wars. As soon as his grief for the loss of
Augustus allowed him leisure, it was his intention to

[1] Afterwards the emperor's confidential minister

refer the case of the army to the wisdom of the senate. In the mean time he sent his son to grant all the relief that could then be applied. Ulterior demands he reserved for the deliberation of the fathers. To enforce authority, or to relax it, was the lawful right of that assembly, and the senate, beyond all doubt, would distribute rewards and punishments with equal justice.

The soldiers made answer that they had appointed Julius Clemens to speak in their behalf. That officer claimed a right of discharge from the service at the end of sixteen years, all arrears to be settled then; in the mean time a *denarius* to be the soldier's daily pay, and the practice of detaining the men beyond the period of their service, under the name of veterans, to be abolished forever. In a business of so much moment, Drusus observed, the senate and the emperor must be consulted. A general clamor followed. " Why did he come so far, since he had no authority to augment their pay, or to mitigate their sufferings? The power of doing good was not confided to him, while every petty officer inflicted blows and stripes, and even death. It had been formerly the policy of Tiberius to elude the claims of the army, by taking shelter under the name of Augustus; and now Drusus comes to play the same farce. How long were they to be amused by the visits of the emperor's son? Could that be deemed an equitable government that kept nothing in suspense but the good of the army? When the soldier is to be punished, or a battle to be fought, why not consult the senate? According to the present system reward is to be always a subject of reference, while punishment is instant and without appeal."

The soldiers, in a tumultuous body, rushed from

the tribunal, breathing vengeance, and wherever they met either men belonging to the praetorian bands, or friends of Drusus, they threatened violence, in hopes of ending the dispute by a sudden conflict. Gnaeus Lentulus, whose age and military character gave him considerable weight, was particularly obnoxious, he being regarded as the chief adviser of Drusus, and an enemy to the proceedings of the army. For the security of his person he went aside with Drusus, intending to repair to the winter camp. The mutineers gathered round him, demanding, with insolence, " Which way was he going? to the senate? perhaps to the emperor? Was he there to show himself an enemy to the demands of the legion?" Nothing could restrain their fury. They discharged a volley of stones, and Lentulus, wounded and covered with blood, had nothing to expect but instant death, when the guards that attended Drusus came up in time, and rescued him from destruction.

The night that followed seemed big with some fatal disaster, when an unexpected phenomenon put an end to the commotion. In a clear and serene sky the moon was suddenly eclipsed. This appearance, its natural cause not being understood by the soldiers, was deemed a prognostic announcing the fate of the army. The planet in its languishing state represented the condition of the legions; if it recovered its former lustre, the efforts of the men would be crowned with success. To assist the moon in her labors, the air resounded with the clangor of brazen instruments, with the sound of trumpets, and other warlike music. The crowd in the mean time stood at gaze. Every gleam of light inspired the men with joy, and the sudden gloom depressed their hearts with grief. The clouds condensed, and the moon was supposed to be lost in utter darkness. A melancholy horror seized the multitude, and melancholy is sure to engender superstition. A religious panic spread through the army. The appearance in the heavens foretold eternal labor to the legions, and all lamented that by their crimes they had called down on themselves the indignation of the gods. Drusus took advantage of the moment. The opportunity was the effect of chance, but, rightly managed, might conduce to the wisest purpose.

He gave orders that the men who by honest means were most in credit with the malcontents should go round from tent to tent. Among these was Clemens the centurion. They visited every part of the camp, applied to the guards on duty, conversed with the patrol, and mixed with the sentinels at the gates. They allured some by promises, and by terror subdued the spirit of others. "How long shall we besiege the son of the emperor? Where will this confusion end? Must we follow Percennius and Vibulenus? And shall we swear fidelity to those new commanders? Will their funds supply the pay of the legions? Have they lands to assign to the veteran soldier? For them shall the Neros and the Drusi be deposed? Are they to mount the vacant throne, the future sovereigns of Rome? Let us, since we were the last to enter into rebellion, be the first to expiate our guilt by well-timed repentance. Demands in favor of all proceed but slowly; to individuals indulgence is more easily granted; deserve it separately, and the reward will follow." This reasoning had its effect. Suspicion and mutual distrust began to arise; the soldiers recently recruited went apart from the veterans;

the legions separated, a sense of duty revived in the breasts of all; the gates were no longer guarded; and the colors, at first promiscuously crowded together, were restored to their proper stations.

At the return of day Drusus called an assembly of the soldiers. Though unused to public speaking, he delivered himself with the eloquence of a man who felt his own importance and the dignity of his rank. He condemned the past, and applauded the present. It was not, he said, a part of his character to yield to menaces, or to shrink from danger. If he saw them penitent, if he heard the language of remorse, he would make a report in their favor, and dispose his father to listen to their petition. The soldiers answered in humble terms. At their request the younger Blaesus, mentioned above, with Lucius Apronius, a Roman knight in the train of Drusus, and Justus Catonius, a centurion of the first rank, were despatched as the delegates of the army. In the councils afterwards held by Drusus various opinions were entertained, and different measures proposed. To wait the return of the deputies, and meanwhile to win the affections of the men by moderation, was the advice of many: others were for immediate coercion. "Lenity," they said, "makes no impression on the vulgar herd. Common soldiers, when not kept in subjection, are fierce and turbulent, yet ever ready to bend and crouch under proper authority. It was now the time, while they were overwhelmed with superstition, to infuse another fear, and teach them to respect their general The authors of the late sedition ought to be made a public example." Drusus, by the bent of his nature prone to vindictive measures, desired that Percennius and Vibulenus should be brought before him. By his

orders they were put to death; according to some
writers, in his own tent, and there buried; according
to others, their bodies were thrown over the entrenchments, a spectacle for public view.

Diligent search was made for the most active incendiaries. Some were found roving on the outside of
the lines, and were instantly cut off by the centurions
or the praetorian soldiers. Others were delivered up to
justice by their respective companies, as an earnest of
their own conversion. The rigor of the winter, which
set in earlier than usual, added to the afflictions of the
army. Heavy rains ensued, and fell with such violence
that the men could not venture from their tents. To
meet in parties, and converse with their comrades, was
impossible. The colors, borne down by torrents that
rushed through the camp, were with difficulty secured.
Superstition still continued to fill the mind with terror. In everything that happened imagination saw
the anger of the gods: it was not without reason that
the planets suffered an eclipse, and storms and tempests burst from the angry elements; the guilt of the
army was the cause of all. To avert impending vengeance, the only expedient was to depart at once from
an inauspicious camp, and by due atonement expiate
their past offenses in their winter quarters. In this
persuasion the eighth legion departed; the fifteenth
followed. The ninth remained behind, declaring aloud
that they would wait for orders from Tiberius, but
they soon saw themselves deserted, and therefore
struck their tents, willing to do by choice what in a
little time would be an act of necessity. Peace and
good order being thus restored, Drusus, deeming it
unnecessary to wait for the return of the deputies,
immediately set out for Rome.

THE GREAT FIRE AT ROME [1]

(Annales, XV, 38–41)

A DREADFUL calamity followed a short time afterwards, by some ascribed to chance, by others to the
execrable wickedness of Nero. There is authority
of historians on both sides, and which preponderates
it is not easy to determine. It is, however, certain,
that of all the disasters that ever befell the city of
Rome from fire, this was the worst, the most violent
and the most destructive. The flames broke out in
that part of the circus which adjoins on one side
the Palatine hill, and on the other the Caelian. It
caught a number of shops stored with combustible
goods, and gathering force from the winds spread with
rapidity from one end of the circus to the other.
Neither the thick walls of houses, nor the inclosure
of temples, nor any other building could check the
rapid progress of the flames. A dreadful conflagration followed. The level parts of the city were destroyed. The fire reached the higher buildings, and
again laying hold of lower places spread with a degree of velocity that nothing could resist. The form
of the streets, long and narrow, with frequent windings and no regular opening, contributed to increase
the mischief. The shrieks and lamentations of women, the infirmities of age, and the weakness of the
young and tender added misery to the dreadful scene.
Some endeavored to provide for themselves, others
to save their friends, in one part dragging along the
lame and impotent, in another waiting to receive the
tardy, or expecting relief themselves. They hurried,

[1] 64 A. D.

they lingered, they obstructed one another. They
looked behind, and the fire broke out in front;
they escaped from the flames, and in their place of
refuge found no safety. The fire raged in every
quarter; all were involved in one general conflagration.

The unhappy wretches fled to places remote and
thought themselves secure, but soon perceived the
flames raging round them. Which way to turn, what
to avoid or what to seek, no one could tell. Some
fell prostrate on the ground; others lay stretched in
the fields, in consternation and dismay resigned to
their fate. Numbers lost their whole substance, even
the tools and implements by which they gained their
livelihood, and, in that distress, did not wish to survive. Many, wild with affliction for their friends
and relations whom they could not save, embraced a
voluntary death and perished in the flames. During the whole of this dismal scene no man dared to
attempt anything that might check the violence of
the dreadful calamity. A crew of incendiaries stood
near at hand denouncing vengeance on all who offered to interfere. Some were so abandoned as to
heap fuel on the flames. They threw in firebrands
and flaming torches, proclaiming aloud that they had
authority for what they did. Whether in fact they
had received such horrible orders, or under that device meant to plunder with greater licentiousness,
cannot now be known.

During the whole of this terrible conflagration
Nero remained at Antium, without a thought of returning to the city, till the fire approached the building by which he had joined the gardens of Maecenas
with the imperial palace. All help, however, was too

late. The palace, the contiguous edifices, and every house adjoining were laid in ruins. To relieve the unhappy people, wandering in distress without a place of shelter, he opened the field of Mars, as well as the magnificent buildings raised by Agrippa, and even his own imperial gardens. He ordered a number of sheds to be thrown up with all possible despatch, for the use of the populace. Household utensils and all kinds of necessary implements were brought from Ostia and other cities in the neighborhood. The price of grain was reduced to three sesterces [1] a peck. For acts like these, munificent and well-timed, Nero might hope for a return of popular favor, but his expectations were in vain : no man was touched with gratitude. A report prevailed that, while the city was in a blaze, Nero went to his own theatre, and there, mounting the stage, sang the destruction of Troy, as a happy allusion to the present misfortune.

On the sixth day the fire was subdued at the foot of the Esquiline hill. This was effected by demolishing a number of buildings, and thereby leaving a wide space, where for want of materials the flame expired. The minds of men had scarce begun to recover from their consternation when the fire broke out a second time with no less fury than before. This happened, however, in a more open quarter, where fewer lives were lost : but the temples of the gods, the porticos and buildings raised for the decoration of the city, were levelled to the ground. The popular odium was now more inflamed than ever, as this second alarm began in the house of Tigellinus,[2] formerly the mansion of Aemilius. A suspicion prevailed that to build a new city and give it his own name was the ambi-

---

[1] Twelve cents.   [2] A favorite of Nero.

tion of Nero. Of the fourteen quarters into which
Rome was divided, four only were left entire, three
were reduced to ashes, and the remaining seven presented nothing better than a heap of shattered houses
half in ruins.

The number of houses, temples, and tenements destroyed by the fire cannot be ascertained. But the
most venerable monuments of antiquity, which the
worship of ages had rendered sacred, were laid in
ruins. Amongst these were the temple dedicated to
the moon by Servius Tullius, the fane and the great
altar consecrated by Evander to Hercules, the chapel
of Jupiter Stator, built by Romulus, the palace of
Numa, and the temple of Vesta, with the tutelary
gods of Rome. With these were consumed the tro-
phies of innumerable victories, and many precious
monuments of literature and ancient genius, all at
present remembered by men advanced in years, but
irrevocably lost. Not even the splendor with which
the new city rose out of the ruins of the old could
compensate for that lamented disaster. It did not
escape observation that the fire broke out on the nineteenth of July, a day remarkable for the conflagration kindled by the Senones, when those barbarians
took the city of Rome by storm, and burned it to
the ground. Men of reflection, who refined on everything with minute curiosity, calculated the number of
years, months, and days from the foundation of Rome
to its burning by the Gauls, and from that calamity
to the present they found the interval of time precisely
the same.

Nero did not blush to convert to his own use the
public ruins of his country. He built a magnificent
palace, in which the objects that excited admiration

were neither gold nor precious stones.   Those decora-
tions, long since introduced by luxury, were grown
stale and hackneyed to the eye.   A different species
of magnificence was now consulted : expansive lakes
and fields of vast extent were intermixed with pleasing variety ; woods and forests stretched to an immeasurable length, presenting gloom and solitude
amidst scenes of open space, where the eye wandered
with surprise over an unbounded prospect.   This prodigious plan was carried out under the direction of two
surveyors, whose names were Severus and Celer.
Bold and original in their projects, these men undertook to conquer nature, and to perform wonders even
beyond the imagination and the riches of the prince.
They promised to form a navigable canal from Lake
Avernus to the mouth of the Tiber.   The experiment,
like the genius of the men, was bold and grand.
The canal was to be made through a long tract of
barren land, and in some places through opposing
mountains.   The country round was parched and dry,
without one humid spot, except the Pomptinian marsh,
from which water could be expected.   A scheme so
vast could not be accomplished without immoderate
labor, and, if practicable, the end was in no proportion to the expense and labor.   But the prodigious
and almost impossible had charms for the enterprising
spirit of Nero.   He began to hew a passage through
the hills that surround Lake Avernus, and some traces
of his deluded hopes are visible at this day.

The ground which, after marking out his own domain, Nero left to the public, was not laid out for the
new city in a hurry and without judgment, as was the
case after the irruption of the Gauls.   A regular plan
was formed : the streets were made wide and long ;

the elevation of the houses was defined, with an open area before the doors, and porticos to secure and adorn the front. The expense of the porticos Nero undertook to defray out of his own revenue. He promised, besides, as soon as the work was finished, to clear the ground, and leave a clear space to every house, without any charge to the occupant. In order to excite a spirit of industry and emulation, he offered rewards proportioned to the rank of each individual, provided the buildings were finished in a limited time. The rubbish was removed by his order to the marshes of Ostia, and the ships that brought corn up the river were to return loaded with the refuse of the workmen. Besides all this the houses, built on a new principle, were to be raised to a certain elevation, without beams or woodwork, on arches of stone from the quarries of Alba or Gabii, those materials being impervious, and of a nature to resist the force of fire. The springs of water, which had been before that time intercepted by individuals for their separate use, were no longer suffered to be diverted from their channel, but left to the care of commissioners, that the public might be properly supplied, and in case of fire have a reservoir at hand to stop the progress of the mischief.

It was also settled that the houses should no longer be contiguous, with slight party-walls to divide them, but that every house should stand detached, surrounded and insulated by its own inclosure. These regulations, it must be admitted, were of public utility, and added much to the embellishment of the new city. But still the old plan of Rome was not without its advocates. It was thought more conducive to the health of the inhabitants. The narrowness of the streets

and the elevation of the buildings served to exclude
the rays of the sun, whereas the more open space,
having neither shade nor shelter, left men exposed to
the intense heat of the day.

These several regulations were, no doubt, the best
that human wisdom could suggest. The next care
was to propitiate the gods. The Sibylline Books[1] were
consulted, and the consequence was that supplications
were decreed to Vulcan, to Ceres, and to Proserpine.
A band of matrons offered their prayers and sacrifices
to Juno, first in the Capitol, and next on the nearest
margin of the sea, where they supplied themselves
with water to sprinkle the temple and the statue of
the goddess. A select number of women, who had
husbands actually living, laid the deities on their sacred beds,[2] and kept midnight vigils with the usual
solemnity. But neither these religious ceremonies
nor the liberal donations of the prince could efface
from the minds of men the prevailing opinion that
Rome was set on fire by his own orders. The infamy
of that horrible transaction still adhered to him. In
order if possible to remove the imputation, he determined to transfer the guilt to others. For this purpose he punished with exquisite cruelty a race of men
detested for their evil practices, by vulgar appellation
commonly called Christians.

The name was derived from Christ, who in the reign
of Tiberius suffered under Pontius Pilate, the procurator of Judea. By that event the sect of which he
was the founder received a blow which for a time

---

[1] A collection of oracles in Greek hexameters that had been
brought to Rome in the reign of Tarquinius Superbus.

[2] This was the ceremony of the *lectisternium*, in which images of gods
were laid upon couches, a table with food being placed beside them

checked the growth of a dangerous superstition; but it revived soon after, and spread with recruited vigor, not only in Judea, the soil that gave it birth, but even in the city of Rome, the common sink into which everything infamous and abominable flows like a torrent from all quarters of the world. Nero proceeded with his usual artifice. He found a set of profligate and abandoned wretches, who were induced to confess themselves guilty, and on the evidence of such men a number of Christians were convicted, not indeed on clear evidence of their having set the city on fire, but rather on account of their sullen hatred of the whole human race. They were put to death, and to their sufferings Nero added mockery and derision. Some were covered with the skins of wild beasts, and left to be devoured by dogs; others were nailed to the cross; numbers were burnt alive; and many, covered over with inflammable matter, were lighted, when the day declined, to serve as torches during the night.

For the convenience of seeing this tragic spectacle the emperor lent his own gardens. He added the sports of the circus, and assisted in person, sometimes driving a chariot, and occasionally mixing with the rabble in his charioteer's dress. At length the cruelty of these proceedings filled every breast with compassion. Humanity relented in favor of the Christians The manners of that people were, no doubt, of a pernicious tendency, and their crimes called for the hand of justice, but it was evident that they fell a sacrifice, not for the public good, but to glut the rage and cruelty of one man only.

JUVENAL

BIOGRAPHICAL SKETCH

THE paucity and meagreness of the traditions that have come down to us about the life of Juvenal preclude the possibility of anything but an extremely flimsy reconstruction of it. He lived during the last half of the first century of our era and the first part of the second, various activities, if we are to believe the ancient accounts, filling up his long life. He is said to have seen some military service, to have held certain municipal offices in Aquinum in Latium, presumably his native town, to have turned to the writing of satire only after spending many years in the practice of declamation, and finally in his eightieth year to have been banished to Egypt, under the pretext of a military command, as a penalty for having in one of his satires reflected upon an actor who was a favorite at court.

He has left us sixteen satires, some of them on general moral themes, but the majority satirizing conditions or tendencies in society at Rome. In some cases he handles the same topics as Martial, but instead of Martial's flippant light-heartedness we find bitterness and indignation, expressed with a rush of rhetoric and a mordancy of phrase that make them unique even in this kind of writing. His sincerity has often been impeached, but, while conceding that many passages are marred by exaggeration, and that in the heat of declamation the feeling is not infrequently forced, it seems probable that his work was for the most part based on genuine convictions. However this may be, there can be no question as to the brilliancy of his rhetoric, the effectiveness of his *sententiae*, and his powers of vivid portrayal and word painting. His canvas is crowded with realistic pictures of Roman life: as, for example, the swarm of toga-clad clients besieging the door of a rich patron at dawn, some of them not having even the excuse of poverty, others looking to the dole as their only means of subsistence, and to procure it resorting freely to lying and impersonation, and all the devices of shifty poverty; the scenes in the streets at Rome on the downfall of Sejanus; the crowded tenements whose shoddy construction offered to their occupants at best an option between collapse and conflagration, the legacy hunters, forgers, rioters, highwaymen, debauchees, adulterers, — all characters old to satire, it is true, but never placed before in so fierce a light.

ROME [1]

(III.)

GRIEVED though I am to see the man depart,
Who long has shared, and still must share, my heart,
Yet (when I call my better judgment home)
I praise his purpose to retire from Rome,
And give, on Cumae's [2] solitary coast,
The Sibyl — one inhabitant to boast!
  Full on the road to Baiae, Cumae lies,
And many a sweet retreat her shore supplies —
Though I prefer ev'n Prochyta's [3] bare strand

5

[1] This satire contains an account of the evils and discomforts of life in Rome. The speaker (vv 37 to end) is one Umbricius, who is leaving the capital in disgust. Juvenal represents himself (vv. 1–36) as having accompanied him to the valley of Egeria, just beyond one of the city gates, to say good-by

[2] On the coast of Campania, the dwelling-place of the famous Sibyl, priestess of Apollo

[3] A small island off the coast of Campania

To the Subura [1] — for, what desert land,   10
What wild, uncultured spot, can more affright
Than fires wide blazing through the gloom of night,
Houses with ceaseless ruin thundering down,
And all the horrors of this hateful town ?
Where poets, while the dog-star glows, rehearse   15
To gasping multitudes their barbarous verse !
  Now had my friend, impatient to depart,
Consigned his little all to one poor cart :
For this without the town he chose to wait;
But stopped a moment at the Conduit-gate. [2]   20
Here Numa [3] erst his nightly visits paid,
And held high converse with the Egerian maid :
Now the once-hallowed fountain, grove, and fane
Are let to Jews, a wretched, wandering train,
Whose furniture 's a basket filled with hay —   25
For every tree is forced a tax to pay ;
And while the heaven-born Nine in exile rove,
The beggar rents their consecrated grove !
  Thence slowly winding down the vale, we view
The Egerian grots — ah, how unlike the true !   30
Nymph of the Spring, more honored hadst thou been,
If, free from art, an edge of living green
Thy bubbling fount had circumscribed alone,
And marble ne'er profaned the native stone.
  Umbricius here his sullen silence broke,   35
And turned on Rome, indignant, as he spoke.
Since virtue droops, he cried, without regard,
And honest toil scarce hopes a poor reward ;
Since every morrow sees my means decay,

  [1] A densely populated district of Rome.
  [2] The Porta Capena, in the southeast part of the city. The Marcian aqueduct passed over it.
  [3] The second king of Rome, who was said to have received instruction from the nymph Egeria

And still makes less the little of to-day;   40
I go, where Daedalus, as poets sing,
First checked his flight, and closed his weary wing:
While something yet of health and strength remains,
And yet no staff my faltering step sustains,
While few gray hairs upon my head are seen,   45
And my old age is vigorous still, and green.
Here, then, I bid my much-beloved home farewell —
Ah, mine no more! — there let Arturius [1] dwell,
And Catulus,[1] knaves, who in truth's despite
Can white to black transform, and black to white,   50
Build temples, furnish funerals, auctions hold,
Farm rivers, ports, and scour the drains for gold!
    Once they were trumpeters, and always found
With strolling fencers in their annual round,
While their puffed cheeks, which every village knew,   55
Called to "high feats of arms" the rustic crew:
Now they give shows [2] themselves; and, at the will
Of the base rabble, raise the sign [3] — to kill,
Ambitious of their voice: then turn once more
To their vile gains, and farm the common shore!   60
And why not everything? — since Fortune throws
Her more peculiar smiles on such as those,
Whene'er, to wanton merriment inclined,
She lifts to thrones the dregs of human kind!
    But why, my friend, should I at Rome remain?   65
I cannot teach my stubborn lips to feign;
Nor, when I hear a great man's verses, smile,
And beg a copy, if I think them vile.
A sublunary wight, I have no skill

---

[1] Any swindlers   [2] Gladiatorial shows.
[3] To turn up the thumb was the signal that a fallen gladiator should be despatched It was properly done by the spectators, not by the giver of the games.

To read the stars; I neither can, nor will,   70
Presage a father's death; I never pried
In toads for poison, nor — in aught beside.
Others may aid the adulterer's vile design,
And bear the insidious gift and melting line,
Seduction's agents!   I such deeds detest;   75
And, honest, let no thief partake my breast.
For this without a friend, the world I quit,
A palsied limb, for every use unfit.
    Who now is loved, but he whose conscious breast
Swells with dark deeds, still, still to be supprest?   80
He pays, he owes, thee nothing (strictly just),
Who gives an honest secret to thy trust;
But, a dishonest! — there, he feels thy power,
And buys thy friendship high from hour to hour.
But let not all the wealth which Tagus pours   85
In Ocean's lap, not all his glittering stores,
Be deemed a bribe sufficient to requite
The loss of peace by day, of sleep by night: —
Oh take not, take not what thy soul rejects,
Nor sell the faith which he who buys suspects!   90
The nation, by the great admired, carest,
And hated, shunned by me above the rest,
No longer now restrained by wounded pride,
I haste to show (nor thou my warmth deride)
I cannot rule my spleen, and calmly see   95
A Grecian capital in Italy!
Grecian?   O no! with this vast sewer compared,
The dregs of Greece are scarcely worth regard:
Long since, the stream that wanton Syria laves
Has disembogued its filth in Tiber's waves,   100
Its language, arts, o'erwhelmed us with the scum
Of Antioch's streets, its minstrel, harp, and drum.
Hie to the Circus! ye who pant to prove

A barbarous mistress, an outlandish love ;
Hie to the Circus ! there in crowds they stand,   105
Tires on their head and timbrels in their hand.
    Thy rustic, Mars, the trechedipna[1] wears,
And on his breast, smeared with ceroma,[2] bears
A paltry prize, well pleased ; while every land,
Sicyon, and Amydon, and Alaband,   110
Tralles, and Samos, and a thousand more,
Thrive on his indolence, and daily pour
Their starving myriads forth : hither they come,
And batten on the genial soil of Rome ;
Minions, then lords, of every princely dome !   115
A flattering, cringing, treacherous, artful race,
Of torrent tongue, and never-blushing face ;
A Protean[3] tribe, one knows not what to call,
Which shifts to every form, and shines in all :
Grammarian, painter, augur, rhetorician,   120
Rope-dancer, conjurer, fiddler, and physician,
All trades his own your hungry Greekling counts ;
And bid him mount the sky — the sky he mounts !
You smile — was 't a barbarian, then, that flew ?
No, 't was a Greek ; 't was an Athenian,[4] too !   125
Bear with their state who will : for I disdain
To feed their upstart pride, or swell their train :
Slaves, that in Syrian lighters stowed so late
With figs and prunes (an inauspicious freight),
Already see their faith preferred to mine,   130
And sit above me ! and before me sign ![5]
That on the Aventine[6] I first drew air,

[1] Greek shoes.   [2] A mixture of wax, oil, and clay.
[3] Like Proteus, able to assume different forms
[4] Daedalus
[5] Take a higher place at dinner, and have precedence in signing a document.
[6] One of the hills of Rome.

And from the womb was nursed on Sabine fare,
Avails me not! our birthright now is lost,
And all our privilege an empty boast!   135
   For lo! where versed in every soothing art
The wily Greek assails his patron's heart,
Finds in each dull harangue an air, a grace,
And all Adonis in a Gorgon face;
Admires the voice that grates upon the ear,   140
Like the shrill scream of amorous chanticleer;
And equals the crane neck and narrow chest
To Hercules, when, straining to his breast
The giant son [1] of Earth, his every vein
Swells with the toil and more than mortal pain.   145
   We too can cringe as low, and praise as warm,
But flattery from the Greeks alone can charm.
No longer now the favorites of the stage
Boast their exclusive power to charm the age:
The happy art with them a nation shares,   150
Greece is a theatre, where all are players.
For lo! their patron smiles, — they burst with mirth;
He weeps, — they droop, the saddest souls on earth;
He calls for fire, — they court the mantle's heat;
'T is warm, he cries, — and they dissolve in sweat.   155
Ill-matched! — secure of victory they start,
Who, taught from youth to play a borrowed part,
Can with a glance the rising passion trace,
And mould their own, to suit their patron's face;
At deeds of shame their hands admiring raise,   160
And mad debauchery's worst excesses praise.
   Turn to their schools: yon gray professor see,
Smeared with the sanguine stains of perfidy!
That tutor most accursed his pupil sold!
That Stoic sacrificed his friend to gold!   165

---

[1] Antaeus, who lost his strength when lifted from the earth

A true-born Grecian ! littered on the coast [1]
Where the Gorgonian hack [2] a pinion lost.

    Hence, Romans, hence ! no place for you remains
Where Diphilus, where Erimanthus reigns ;
Miscreants, who, faithful to their native art,   170
Admit no rival in a patron's heart :
For, let them fasten on his easy ear,
And drop one hint, one secret slander there,
Sucked from their country's venom, or their own,
That instant they possess the man alone,   175
While we are spurned, contemptuous, from the door,
Our long, long slavery thought upon no more.
'T is but a client lost ! — and that, we find,
Sits wondrous lightly on a patron's mind :
And (not to flatter our poor pride, my friend)   180
What merit with the great can we pretend,
Though in our duty we forestall the day,
And, darkling,[3] run our humble court to pay ;
When the brisk praetor long before is gone,
And hastening with stern voice his lictors on,   185
Lest his colleagues o'erpass him in the street,
And first the rich and childless matrons [4] greet,
Alba and Modia, who impatient wait,
And think the morning homage comes too late !

    Produce at Rome your witness ; let him boast   190
The sanctity of Berecynthia's host,[5]

[1] At Tarsus, properly on the banks of the river Cydnus in Cilicia

[2] Pegasus, the winged horse, which sprang from the blood of the Gorgon Medusa.

[3] Before sunrise. It was the duty of a client to present himself at his patron's house early in the morning.

[4] The efforts of legacy hunters to get a place in the wills of the childless rich is a favorite theme with Roman satirists.

[5] P. Cornelius Scipio Nasica, chosen on account of his piety to receive the stone which represented the goddess Cybele (Berecynthia).

Of Numa, or of him [1] whose zeal divine
Snatched pale Minerva from her blazing shrine:
To search his rent-roll first the bench prepares,
His honesty employs their latest cares: 195
What table does he keep, what slaves maintain,
And what, they ask, and where, is his domain?
These weighty matters known, his fate they rate,
And square his probity to his estate.
The poor may swear by all the immortal Powers,   200
By the Great Gods of Samothrace,[2] and ours.
His oaths are false, they cry, he scoffs at heaven
And all its thunders, scoffs — and is forgiven!
Add that the wretch is still the theme of scorn,
If the soiled cloak be patched, the gown o'erworn; 205
If through the bursting shoe the foot be seen,
Or the coarse seam tell where the rent has been.
O Poverty, thy thousand ills combined
Sink not so deep into the generous mind,
As the contempt and laughter of mankind!   210
    "Up! up! these cushioned benches," Lectius [3] cries,
" Befit not your estates: for shame! arise."
For " shame!" — but you say well: the pander's heir,
The spawn of bulks and stews, is seated there;
The crier's spruce son, fresh from the fencer's school, 215
And prompt the taste to settle and to rule.
So Otho [4] fixed it, whose preposterous pride
First dared to chase us from their Honors' side.

---

[1] L Caecilius Metellus, who rescued the statue of Minerva when the temple of Vesta was burned

[2] A small island in the northern Aegean, the seat of the mystic worship of the Cabiri.

[3] Some official of the games, who ejects poor citizens from the seats reserved for members of the equestrian order.

[4] The law which reserved the first fourteen rows in the theatre for the equestrian order had been proposed by Roscius Otho in 67 B C

In these cursed walls, devote alone to gain,
When do the poor a wealthy wife obtain? 220
When are they named in wills? When called to share
The aedile's[1] council, and assist the chair?
Long since should they have risen, thus slighted,
    spurned,
And left their home, but — not to have returned!

    Depressed by indigence, the good and wise 225
In every clime by painful efforts rise;
Here by more painful still, where scanty cheer,
Poor lodging, mean attendance — all is dear.
In earthenware he scorns at Rome to eat,
Who, called abruptly to the Marsian's[2] seat, 230
From such well pleased would take his simple food,
Nor blush to wear the cheap Venetian hood.
    There 's many a part of Italy, 't is said,
Where none assume the toga but the dead:
There, when the toil foregone and annual play 235
Mark from the rest some high and solemn day,
To theatres of turf the rustics throng,
Charmed with the farce that charmed their sires so
    long;
While the pale infant, of the mask[3] in dread,
Hides in his mother's breast his little head. 240
No modes of dress high birth distinguish there;
All ranks, all orders, the same habit wear,
And the dread aedile's dignity is known,
O sacred badge! by his white garb alone.
But here, beyond our power arrayed we go, 245
In all the gay varieties of show;

[1] In his function as a police magistrate.
[2] The Marsi, whose country lay among the Apennines, east of
Rome, were proverbial for the simplicity of their lives.
[3] Masks were worn by the actors

And when our purse supplies the charge no more,
Borrow, unblushing, from our neighbor's store:
Such is the reigning vice; and so we flaunt,
Proud in distress, and prodigal in want!   250
Briefly, my friend, here all are slaves to gold,
And words and smiles and everything is sold.
What will you give for Cossus'[1] nod?   How high
The silent notice of Veiento[1] buy?

   One favorite youth is shaved, another shorn;   255
And while to Jove the precious spoil is borne,
Clients are taxed for offerings, and (yet more
To gall their patience) from their little store
Constrained to swell the minion's ample hoard,
And bribe the page for leave to bribe his lord.   260

   Who fears the crash[2] of houses in retreat
At simple Gabii, bleak Praeneste's seat,
Volsinium's craggy heights, embowered in wood,
Or Tibur, beetling o'er prone Anio's flood?
While half the city here by shores[3] is stayed,   265
And feeble cramps, that lend a treacherous aid;
For thus the stewards patch the riven wall,
Thus prop the mansion, tottering to its fall;
Then bid the tenant court secure repose,
While the pile nods to every blast that blows.   270

   O! may I live where no such fears molest,
No midnight fires burst on my hour of rest!
For here 't is terror all; mid the loud cry
Of " water! water! " the scared neighbors fly,
With all their haste can seize — the flames aspire,   275
And the third floor is wrapt in smoke and fire,
While you, unconscious, doze. Up, ho! and know,

[1] Put for any rich patron
[2] The large tenement houses, in which the majority of the people in Rome lived, not infrequently collapsed
[3] Props

The impetuous blaze which spreads dismay below
By swift degrees will reach the aërial cell,
Where crouching underneath the tiles you dwell, 280
Where your tame doves their golden couplets rear,
And you could no mischance but drowning fear!
  Codrus [1] had but one bed, and that too short
For his short wife; his goods, of every sort,
Were else but few : — six little pipkins graced , 285
His cupboard head, a little can was placed
On a snug shelf beneath, and near it lay
A Chiron,[2] of the same cheap marble — clay.
And was this all? O no: he yet possesst
A few Greek books, shrined in an ancient chest, 290
Where barbarous mice through many an inlet crept,
And fed on heavenly numbers while he slept. —
" Codrus, in short, had nothing." You say true;
And yet poor Codrus lost that nothing too!
One curse alone was wanting to complete 295
His woes : that cold and hungry through the street
The wretch should beg, and in the hour of need
Find none to lodge, to clothe him, or to feed!
  But should the raging flames on grandeur prey,
And low in dust Asturius' [3] palace lay, 300
The squalid [4] matron sighs, the senate mourns,
The pleaders cease, the judge the court adjourns;
All join to wail the city's hapless fate,
And rail at fire with more than common hate.
Lo! while it burns, the obsequious courtiers haste 305
With rich materials to repair the waste:
This brings him marble, that, a finished piece,

---

[1] Named as a representative of the poorer class of Romans.
[2] A statuette of the centaur Chiron.
[3] A rich man.
[4] In mourning

The far-famed boast of Polyclete[1] and Greece;
This, ornaments which graced of old the fane
Of Asia's gods; that, figured plate and plain;   310
This, cases, books, and busts the shelves to grace,
And piles of coin his specie to replace.
So much the childless Persian[2] swells his store,
(Though deemed the richest of the rich before)
That all ascribe the flames to thirst of pelf,   315
And swear Asturius fired his house himself.
    O, had you from the Circus[3] power to fly,
In many a halcyon village might you buy
Some elegant retreat, for what will here
Scarce hire a gloomy dungeon through the year!   320
There wells by nature formed, which need no rope,
No laboring arm to crane their waters up,
Around your lawn their facile streams shall shower,
And cheer the springing plant and opening flower.
There live delighted with the rustic's lot,   325
And till with your own hands the little spot;
The little spot shall yield you large amends,
And glad with many a feast your Samian friends.[4]
And sure, in any corner we can get,
To call one lizard ours is something yet!   330
    Flushed with a mass of undigested food,
Which clods the stomach and inflames the blood,
What crowds, with watching wearied and o'erprest,
Curse the slow hours, and die for want of rest!
For who can hope his languid lids to close,   335

---

    [1] The famous Greek sculptor of the latter half of the fifth century B C
    [2] Asturius
    [3] Juvenal in more than one passage deplores the abnormal interest of the majority of Romans in the games of the circus.
    [4] Pythagoreans, who were vegetarians. Pythagoras was a native of Samos

Where brawling taverns banish all repose?
Sleep to the rich alone his visits pays,
And hence the seeds of many a dire disease.
The carts' loud rumbling through the narrow way,
The drivers' clamors at each casual stay,   340
From drowsy Drusus[1] would his slumber take,
And keep the calves of Proteus[2] broad awake!
    If business call, obsequious crowds divide,
While o'er their heads the rich securely ride,
By tall Illyrians[3] borne, and read, or write,   345
Or (should the early hour to rest invite)
Close the soft litter, and enjoy the night.
Yet reach they first the goal; while, by the throng
Elbowed and jostled, scarce we creep along
Sharp strokes from poles, tubs, rafters, doomed to
     feel;   350
And plastered o'er with mud from head to heel;
While the rude soldier gores us as he goes,
Or marks in blood his progress on our toes!
    See, from the dole,[4] a vast tumultuous throng,
Each followed by his kitchen, pours along!   355
Huge pans, which Corbulo[5] could scarce uprear,
With steady neck a puny slave must bear,
And, lest amid the way the flames[6] expire,
Glide nimbly on, and gliding fan the fire;
Through the close press with sinuous efforts wind,   360
And, piece by piece, leave his botched rags behind.
    Hark! groaning on, the unwieldy wagon spreads

[1] The emperor Claudius, who was notoriously somnolent.
[2] A minor sea deity who tended the seals for Neptune.
[3] Commonly used as litter-bearers
[4] The portion given by the patron to his client. It consisted either
of food or of a small sum of money.
[5] Some Roman strong man.
[6] In the brazier which he carried to keep the food warm

Its cumbrous load, tremendous! o'er our heads,
Projecting elm or pine, that nods on high,
And threatens death to every passer-by.   365
Heavens! should the axle crack, which bears a weight
Of huge Ligurian stone,[1] and pour the freight
On the pale crowd beneath, what would remain,
What joint, what bone, what atom of the slain?
The body, with the soul, would vanish quite,   370
Invisible as air, to mortal sight!
Meanwhile, unconscious of their fellow's fate,
At home they heat the water, scour the plate,
Arrange the strigils, fill the cruse with oil,
And ply their several tasks with fruitless toil;   375
For he who bore the dole, poor mangled ghost,
Sits pale and trembling on the Stygian coast,
Scared at the horrors of the novel scene,
At Charon's threatening voice and scowling mien;
Nor hopes a passage, thus abruptly hurled,   380
Without his farthing,[2] to the nether world.

 Pass we these fearful dangers, and survey
What other evils threat our nightly way.
And first behold the mansion's towering size,
Where floors on floors to the tenth [3] story rise;   385
Whence heedless garreteers their potsherds throw,
And crush the unwary wretch that walks below!
Clattering, the storm descends from heights unknown,
Ploughs up the street, and wounds the flinty stone!
'Tis madness, dire improvidence of ill,   390
To sup abroad, before you sign your will;
Since fate in ambush lies, and marks his prey,
From every wakeful window in the way:

---

[1] Carrara marble   [2] Charon's fee
[3] The translator exaggerates   Augustus limited the height of
buildings in Rome to seventy feet.

Pray, then, and count your humble prayer well sped,
If pots be only emptied on your head. 395
    The drunken bully, ere his man be slain,
Frets through the night, and courts repose in vain;
And while the thirst of blood his bosom burns,
From side to side in restless anguish turns,
Like Peleus' son,[1] when, quelled by Hector's hand, 400
His loved Patroclus pressed the Phrygian strand.
    There are who murder as an opiate take,
And only when no brawls await them wake;
Yet even these heroes, flushed with youth and wine,
All contest with the purple robe decline; 405
Securely give the lengthened train to pass,
The sun-bright flambeaux and the lamps of brass.
Me, whom the moon, or candle's paler gleam,
Whose wick I husband to the last extreme,
Guides through the gloom,[2] he braves, devoid of fear:
The prelude to our doughty quarrel hear, 411
If that be deemed a quarrel, where, heaven knows,
He only gives, and I receive, the blows!
Across my path he strides, and bids me stand!
I bow, obsequious to the dread command; 415
What else remains, where madness, rage, combine
With youth and strength superior far to mine?
    " Whence come you, rogue?" he cries. " Whose
        beans to-night
Have stuffed you thus? What cobbler clubbed his mite
For leeks and sheep's-head porridge? Dumb! quite
        dumb! 420
Speak, or be kicked. Yet, once again! your home?
Where shall I find you? At what beggar's stand
(Temple or bridge) whimp'ring with outstretched
        hand?"

[1] Achilles.   [2] The streets of Rome were not lighted.

Whether I strive some humble plea to frame,
Or steal in silence by, 't is just the same;   425
I'm beaten first, then dragged in rage away;
Bound to the peace, or punished for the fray!

Mark here the boasted freedom of the poor!
Beaten and bruised, that goodness to adore,
Which at their humble prayer suspends its ire,   430
And sends them home with yet a bone entire!

Nor this the worst; for when deep midnight reigns,
And bolts secure our doors, and massy chains,
When noisy inns a transient silence keep,
And harassed nature wooes the balm of sleep,   435
Then thieves and murderers ply their dreadful trade.
With stealthy steps our secret couch invade:
Roused from the treacherous calm, aghast we start,
And the flashed sword is buried in our heart!

Hither from bogs, from rocks, and caves pursued
(The Pontine marsh and Gallinarian wood [1]),   441
The dark assassins flock as to their home,
And fill with dire alarms the streets of Rome.
Such countless multitudes our peace annoy,
That bolts and shackles every forge employ,   445
And cause so wide a waste, the country fears
A want of ore for mattocks, rakes, and shares.

O! happy were our sires, estranged from crimes:
And happy, happy, were the good old times
Which saw, beneath their kings', their tribunes' reign,
One cell the nation's criminals contain!   451

Much could I add, more reasons could I cite,
If time were ours, to justify my flight,
But see! the impatient team is moving on,
The sun declining, and I must be gone   455

---

[1] The Pontine marshes in Latium and the Gallinarian wood in Campania were infested by brigands

Long since the driver murmured at my stay,
And jerked his whip to beckon me away.
Farewell, my friend! with this embrace we part!
Cherish my memory ever in your heart;
And when from crowds and business you repair,   460
To breathe at your Aquinum freer air,
Fail not to draw me from my loved retreat
To Elvine Ceres, and Diana's seat:[1]
For your bleak hills my Cumae I'll resign,
And (if you blush not at such aid as mine)   465
Come well equipped to wage in angry rhymes
Fierce war with you on follies and on crimes.

WILLIAM GIFFORD.

[1] There were temples of Ceres and of Diana at Aquinum It has been suggested that the former was erected by a member of the Helvian gens, — hence the epithet.

PLINY THE YOUNGER

BIOGRAPHICAL SKETCH

PLINY's statement that he was in his eighteenth year at the time of the eruption of Vesuvius enables us to place his birth with certainty in 62 A. D. He was the nephew and adopted son of C. Plinius Secundus, the author of the *Natural History*, whose example undoubtedly did much to stimulate his literary ambitions. He studied rhetoric under Quintilian, and beginning the practice of law at an early age, soon became one of the leading advocates in Rome. He passed through the usual course of official honors, attaining the consulship in 100 under Trajan, and finally in 111 or 112 being appointed governor of Bithynia. He died about 114.

He published a number of speeches, some poems, and several books of letters. Of these one speech, the *Panegyric on Trajan*, and the *Letters* have survived. The *Panegyric* was delivered in the senate on the occasion of his election to the consulship, but was only published after careful revision. It is a conspicuous example of the florid type of oratory, shows many signs of studied elaboration, and is full of flattery of the emperor. Of much greater value and interest are the ten books of *Letters*, the first nine containing epistles on a great variety of subjects addressed to various friends, while the last is confined to correspondence with Trajan during Pliny's governorship of Bithynia. In the first group we have to deal with productions which were only ostensibly letters and which were written to be published, — each one dealing with a single theme, and the address to this or that individual apparently being a matter of form. In the precision and crispness of their style they differ greatly from the florid expansiveness of the *Panegyric*, the divergence indeed being so great as to point to a conscious and deliberate adaptation of manner to conventional standards of oratory on the one hand, and of epistolography on the other. In the tenth book, however, we find real letters, for in these Pliny writes to Trajan for advice on various problems of provincial administration, and the emperor replies in notes, the eminently practical spirit of which forms one of the most noticeable features of the correspondence.

From his works we are able to form a fairly adequate idea of our author's character: a man of little more than mediocre ability, upon whose imagination his own activities invariably loomed large; pedantic in matters of literature, irresolute and vacillating in matters of administration, vain to the extreme of vanity, of impenetrable complacency, yet withal amiable, kindly, conscientious, standing for what was good, and genuinely interested in literature.

The following letters are from Firth's translation.

TO CORNELIUS TACITUS [1]

(I, 6.)

You will laugh, and I give you leave to. You know what sort of sportsman I am, but I, even I, have bagged three boars, each one of them a perfect beauty. "What!" you will say, "you!" Yes, I, and that too without any violent departure from my usual lazy ways. I was sitting by the nets; I had by my side not a hunting spear and a dart, but my pen and writing tablets. I was engaged in some composi-

[1] The historian, one of Pliny's intimate friends.

tion and jotting down notes, so that I might have full
tablets to take home with me, even though my hands
were empty. You need not shrug your shoulders at
study under such conditions. It is really surprising
how the mind is stimulated by bodily movement and
exercise. I find the most powerful incentive to
thought in having the woods all about me, in the solitude and the silence which is observed in hunting. So
when next you go hunting, take my advice and carry
your writing tablets with you as well as your luncheon
basket and your flask. You will find that Minerva
loves to wander on the mountains quite as much as
Diana. Farewell.

TO SOSIUS SENECIO

(I , 13)

THIS year has brought us a fine crop of poets : right
through April hardly a day passed without some recital[1] or other. I am delighted that literature is so
flourishing and that men are giving such open proofs
of brains, even though audiences are found so slow in
coming together. People as a rule lounge in the
squares and waste the time in gossip when they should
be listening to the recital. They get some one to come
and tell them whether the reciter has entered the hall
yet, whether he has got through his introduction, or
whether he has nearly reached the end of his reading.
Not until then do they enter the room, and even then
they come in slowly and languidly. Nor do they sit
it out ; no, before the close of the recital they slip
away, some sidling out so as not to attract attention,

---

[1] The public recitations were one of the features of literary life in
Rome under the empire.

others rising openly and walking out bodily. And yet, by Hercules, our fathers tell a story of how Claudius Caesar one day while walking up and down in the palace, happened to hear some clapping of hands, and on inquiring the cause and being told that Nonianus was giving a reading, he suddenly joined the company to every one's surprise. But nowadays even those who have most time on their hands, after receiving early notices and frequent reminders, either fail to put in an appearance, or if they do come they complain that they have wasted a day just because they have not wasted it. All the more praise and credit, therefore, is due to those who do not allow their love of writing and reciting to be damped either by the laziness or the fastidiousness of their audiences. For my own part, I have hardly ever failed to attend. True, the authors are mostly my friends, for almost all the literary people are also friends of mine, and for this reason I have spent more time in Rome than I had intended. But now I can betake myself to my country retreat and compose something, though not for a public recital, lest those whose readings I attended should think I went not so much to hear their works as to get a claim on them to come and hear mine. As in everything else, if you lend a man your ears, all the grace of the act vanishes if you ask for his in return. Farewell.

TO SEPTICIUS CLARUS

(I, 15)

WHAT a fellow you are! You promise to come to dinner and then fail to turn up! Well, here is my

magisterial sentence upon you. You must pay the
money I am out of pocket to the last farthing, and
you will find the sum no small one. I had provided
for each guest one lettuce, three snails, two eggs, spelt
mixed with honey and snow (you will please reckon up
the cost of the latter as among the most costly of all,
since it melts away in the dish), olives from Baetica,
cucumbers, onions, and a thousand other equally ex-
pensive dainties. You would have listened to a come-
dian, or a reciter, or a harp-player, or perhaps to all,
as I am such a lavish host. But you preferred to dine
elsewhere — where I know not — off oysters, sows'
matrices, sea-urchins, and to watch Spanish dancing
girls! You will be paid out for it, though how I decline to say. You have done violence to yourself.
You have grudged, possibly yourself, but certainly
me, a fine treat. Yes, yourself! For how we should
have enjoyed ourselves, how we should have laughed
together, how we should have applied ourselves! You
can dine at many houses in better style than at mine,
but nowhere will you have a better time, or such a
simple free and easy entertainment. In short, give
me a trial, and if afterwards you do not prefer to excuse yourself to others rather than to me, why then
I give you leave to decline my invitations always.
Farewell.

TO CALPURNIA [1]

(VI , 4)

NEVER before have I chafed so much at being so
busy that I could not accompany you when you set
out for Campania to recruit your health, nor yet fol-

[1] His wife.

low and overtake you after you had started. For now
especially I should like to be with you to see with my
own eyes how much strength you are gaining, what
weight that delicate frame of yours is putting on, and
whether you are enjoying yourself without let or hindrance in the retirement and among the rich, generous
pleasures of Campania. I am quite anxiously longing to hear that you are strong again, for it makes
one nervous and troubled to get no news of those
whom we love very dearly, when they are away from
us, and your absence, coupled with your weak state of
health, keeps me constantly upon the rack. I am
afraid of all sorts of things; I fancy anything may
have happened, and, like all anxious people, I am
especially given to conjuring up the thoughts that I
most dread. I intreat you, therefore, to remember
how nervous I am about you, and to write me once,
or even twice a day. For while I am reading your
letters, I shall feel easier in my mind, though, when
I have read through to the end, my fears will immediately recur. Farewell.

TO TACITUS

(VI., 16.)

You ask me to send you an account of my uncle's
death, so that you may be able to give posterity an
accurate description of it. I am much obliged to you,
for I can see that the immortality of his fame is well
assured, if you take in hand to write of it. For although he perished in a disaster [1] which devastated
some of the fairest regions of the land, and though he

---

[1] The eruption of Vesuvius in 79 A. D.

is sure of eternal remembrance like the peoples and
cities that fell with him in that memorable calamity,
though, too, he had written a large number of works
of lasting value, yet the undying fame of which your
writings are assured will secure for his a still further
lease of life. For my part, I think that those people
are highly favored by Providence who are capable
either of performing deeds worthy of the historian's
pen or of writing histories worthy of being read, but
that they are peculiarly favored who can do both.
Among the latter I may class my uncle, thanks to his
own writings and to yours. So I am all the more
ready to fulfill your injunctions, nay, I am even prepared to beg to be allowed to undertake them.

My uncle was stationed at Misenum, where he was
in active command of the fleet, with full powers.
On the 23d of August, about the seventh hour, my
mother drew his attention to the fact that a cloud of
unusual size and shape had made its appearance. He
had taken his sun bath, followed by a cold one, and
after a light meal he was lying down and reading.
Yet he called for his sandals, and climbed up to a
spot from which he could command a good view of
the curious phenomenon. Those who were looking
at the cloud from some distance could not make out
from which mountain it was rising, — it was afterward discovered to have been Mount Vesuvius, — but
in likeness and form it more resembled a pine-tree
than anything else, for what corresponded to the trunk
was of great length and height, and then spread out
into a number of branches, the reason being, I imagine, that while the vapor was fresh, the cloud was
borne upwards, but when the vapor became wasted,
it lost its motion, or even became dissipated by its

own weight and spread out laterally. At times it looked white, and at other times dirty and spotted, according to the quantity of earth and cinders that were shot up.

To a man of my uncle's learning, the phenomenon appeared one of great importance, which deserved a close study. He ordered a Liburnian galley to be got ready, and offered to take me with him, if I desired to accompany him, but I replied that I preferred to go on with my studies, and it so happened that he assigned me some writing to do. He was just leaving the house when he received a written message from Rectina, the wife of Tascus, who was terrified at the peril threatening her, — for her villa lay just beneath the mountain, and there were no means of escape save by shipboard, — begging him to save her from her perilous position. So he changed his plan and carried out with the greatest fortitude the ideas which had occurred to him as a student.

He had the galleys launched and went on board himself, in the hope of succoring, not only Rectina, but many others, for there were a number of people living along the shore, owing to its delightful situation. He hastened, therefore, towards the place whence others were flying, and steering a direct course, kept the helm straight for the point of danger, so utterly devoid of fear that every movement of the looming portent and every change in its appearance he described and had noted down by his secretary, as soon as his eyes detected it. Already ashes were beginning to fall upon the ships, hotter and in thicker showers as they approached more nearly, with pumice-stones and black flints, charred and cracked by the heat of the flames, while their way was barred by the

sudden shoaling of the sea bottom and the litter of
the mountain on the shore. He hesitated for a moment whether to turn back, and then, when the helms-
man warned him to do so, he exclaimed, "Fortune
favors the bold; try to reach Pomponianus." The
latter was at Stabiae, separated by the whole width
of the bay, for the sea there pours in upon a gently
rounded and curving shore. Although the danger
was not yet close upon him, it was none the less
clearly seen, and it traveled quickly as it came nearer,
so Pomponianus had got his baggage together on shipboard, and had determined upon flight, and was waiting for the wind which was blowing on shore to fall.
My uncle sailed in with the wind fair behind him,
and embraced Pomponianus, who was in a state of
flight, comforting and cheering him at the same time.
Then in order to calm his friend's fears by showing
how composed he was himself, he ordered the servants
to carry him to his bath, and, after his ablutions, he
sat down and had dinner in the best of spirits, or
with that assumption of good spirits which is quite as
remarkable as the reality.

In the meantime broad sheets of flame, which rose
high in the air, were breaking out in a number of
places on Mount Vesuvius and lighting up the sky,
and the glare and brightness seemed all the more
striking owing to the darkness of the night. My
uncle, in order to allay the fear of his companions,
kept declaring that the country people in their terror
had left their fires burning, and that the conflagration
they saw arose from the blazing and empty villas.
Then he betook himself to rest and enjoyed a very
deep sleep, for his breathing, which, owing to his bulk,
was rather heavy and loud, was heard by those who

were waiting at the door of his chamber. But by this time the courtyard leading to the room he occupied was so full of ashes and pumice-stones mingled together, and covered to such a depth, that if he had delayed any longer in the bed-chamber there would have been no means of escape. So my uncle was aroused, and came out and joined Pomponianus and the rest who had been keeping watch. They held a consultation whether they should remain indoors or wander forth in the open; for the buildings were beginning to shake with the repeated and intensely severe shocks of earthquake, and seemed to be rocking to and fro, as though they had been torn from their foundations. Outside again there was danger to be apprehended from the pumice-stones, though these were light and nearly burnt through, and thus, after weighing the two perils, the latter course was determined upon. With my uncle it was a choice of reasons which prevailed, with the rest a choice of fears.

They placed pillows on their heads and secured them with napkins, as a precaution against the falling bodies. Elsewhere the day had dawned by this time, but there it was still night, and the darkness was blacker and thicker than any ordinary night. This, however, they relieved as best they could by a number of torches and other kinds of lights. They decided to make their way to the shore, and to see from the nearest point whether the sea would enable them to put out, but it was still running high and contrary. A sheet was spread on the ground, and on this my uncle lay, and twice he called for a draught of cold water, which he drank. Then the flames, and the smell of sulphur which gave warning of them, scattered the others in flight and roused him. Leaning on two slaves, he rose to his feet and immediately fell down again, owing, as I think, to his breathing being obstructed by the thickness of the fumes and congestion of the stomach, that organ being naturally weak and narrow, and subject to inflammation. When daylight returned — which was three days after his death — his body was found untouched, uninjured, and covered, dressed just as he had been in life. The corpse suggested a person asleep rather than a dead man.

Meanwhile my mother and I were at Misenum. But that is of no consequence for the purposes of history, nor indeed did you express a wish to be told anything except of my uncle's death. So I will say no more, except to add that I have given you a full account both of the incidents which I myself witnessed and of those narrated to me immediately afterwards, when, as a rule, one gets the truest account of what has happened. You will pick out what you think will answer your purpose best, for to write a letter is a different thing from writing a history, and to write to a friend is not like writing to all and sundry. Farewell.

TO SURA

(VII, 27.)

THE leisure we are both of us enjoying gives you an opportunity of imparting, and me an opportunity of receiving, information. So I should very much like to know whether in your opinion there are such things as ghosts, whether you think they have a shape of their own and a touch of the supernatural in them, or whether you consider they are vain, empty shadows and mere creatures of the imaginations. For my own part, I feel led to believe that they have a real existence, and this mainly from what befell Curtius Rufus.

In the days when he was still poor and obscure, he had attached himself to the person of the governor of Africa. One evening at sundown he was walking in the portico, when the figure of a woman — but taller and more beautiful than mortal woman — presented itself before him and told Rufus, who was terrified with fright, that she was Africa and could foretell the future. She declared that he would go to Rome and hold high offices of state, and that he would also return with plenary powers as governor to that same province, and there meet his death. All these details were fulfilled. Moreover, when he was entering Carthage and just stepping out of his ship, the same figure is said to have met him on the beach. Certain it is that when he was attacked by illness, he interpreted the future by the past, and his coming adversity by his present prosperity, and, though none of his people were despairing of his recovery, he cast aside all hope of getting better.

Now I want you to consider whether the following story, which I shall tell you just as I heard it, is not even more terrifying and no less wonderful than the other. There stood at Athens a spacious and roomy house, but it had an evil reputation of being fatal to those who lived in it. In the silence of the night the clank of iron and, if you listened with closer attention, the rattle of chains were heard, the sound coming first from a distance and afterwards quite close at hand. Then appeared the ghostly form of an old man, emaciated, filthy, decrepit, with a flowing beard and hair on end, with fetters round his legs and chains

on his hands, which he kept shaking. The terrified
inmates passed sleepless nights of fearful terror, and
following upon their sleeplessness came disease and
then death, as their fears increased. For every now
and again, though the ghost had vanished, memory
conjured up the vision before their eyes, and their
fright remained longer than the apparition which had
caused it. Then the house was deserted and condemned to stand empty, and was wholly abandoned
to the spectre, while the authorities forbade that it
should be sold or let to any one wishing to take it,
not knowing under what a curse it lay.

The philosopher Athenodorus came to Athens, read
the notice board, and on hearing the price, hesitated,
because the low rent made him suspicious. Then he
was told the whole story, and, so far from being de-
terred, he became the more eager to rent it. When
evening began to fall, he ordered his people to make
him up a bed in the front part of the house, and
asked for his tablets, a pen, and a lamp. Dismissing
all his servants to the inner rooms, he applied mind,
eyes, and hand to the task of writing, lest by having
nothing to think about he might begin to conjure up
the apparition of which he had been told and other
idle fears. At first the night was just as still there
as elsewhere, then the iron was rattled and the chains
clanked. Athenodorus did not raise his eyes, nor cease
to write, but fortified his resolution and closed his
ears. The noise became louder and drew nearer, and
was heard now on the threshold and then within the
room itself. He turned his head, and saw and recognized the ghost which had been described to him. It
stood and beckoned with its finger, as if calling him;
but Athenodorus merely motioned with his hand, as

if to bid it wait a little, and once more bent over his
tablets and plied his pen. As he wrote the spectre
rattled its chains over his head, and looking round he
saw that it was beckoning as before, so, without further delay, he took up the lamp and followed. The
spectre walked with slow steps, as though burdened
by the chains, then it turned off into the courtyard of
the house and suddenly vanished, leaving its companion alone, who thereupon plucked some grass and
foliage to mark the place. On the following day he
went to the magistrates and advised them to give orders that the place should be dug up. Bones were
found with chains wound round them. Time and the
action of the soil had made the flesh moulder, and left
the bones bare and eaten away by the chains, but the
remains were collected and given a public burial.
Ever afterwards the house was free of the ghost, which
had been thus laid with due ceremony.

I quite believe those who vouch for these details,
but the following story I can vouch for to others. I
have a freedman who is a man of some education.
A younger brother of his was sleeping with him in
the same bed, and he thought he saw some one sitting
upon the bed, and applying a pair of shears to his
head, and even cutting off some hair from his crown,
and the locks were found lying close by. A little
time elapsed, and a similar incident occurred to make
people believe the other story was true. A young
slave of mine was sleeping with a number of others
in the dormitory, when, according to his story, two
men clothed in white tunics entered by the window
and cut his hair as he slept, retiring by the way they
came. Daylight revealed that his hair had been cut,
and the locks lay scattered around. No incident of

any note followed, unless it was that I escaped prosecution, as I should not have done if Domitian, in whose reign these incidents had taken place, had lived any longer than he did. For in his writing-desk there was discovered a document sent in by Carus which denounced me. This gives rise to the conjecture that, as it is the custom for accused persons to let their hair go untrimmed, the fact that the hair of my slaves was cut was a sign that the peril overhanging me had passed away.

I beg of you to bring your erudition to bear on these stories. The matter is one which is worth long and careful consideration, nor am I altogether undeserving of your imparting to me your plentiful knowledge. I will let you follow your usual habit of arguing on both sides of the case, but be sure that you take up one side more strongly than the other, so that I may not go away in suspense and uncertainty, when the reason I asked your advice was just this —that you put an end to my doubts. Farewell.

TO GEMINUS

(IX., 11.)

I RECEIVED your letter, which afforded me great pleasure, especially as you say that you wish me to write you something to be inserted in your books. I shall find a subject, either the one you suggest or some other, for there are certain objections to yours, as you will see if you look around you. I did not think that there were any booksellers at Lugdunum,[1] and I am delighted to hear from you that my books are being

---

[1] Lyons.

sold there, for it is gratifying to find that they retain in foreign parts the popularity they have won at Rome. I begin to think that they must be fairly good when there is such unanimity about their merits in lands so far apart and in the judgment of persons so dissimilar. Farewell.

TO MAXIMUS

(IX, 23)

WHEN I have been pleading, it has often happened that the Centumviri,[1] after strictly preserving for a long time their judicial dignity and gravity, have suddenly leaped to their feet *en masse* and applauded me, as if they could not help themselves but were obliged to do so. I have often again left the Senate-house with just as much glory as I had hoped to obtain, but I never felt greater gratification than I did a little while ago at something which Cornelius Tacitus told me in conversation. He said that he was sitting by the side of a certain individual at the last Circensian games, and that, after they had had a long and learned talk on a variety of subjects, his acquaintance said to him: "Are you from Italy or the provinces?" Tacitus replied: "You know me quite well, and that from the books of mine you have read." "Then," said the man, "you are either Tacitus or Pliny." I cannot express to you how pleased I am that our names are, so to speak, the property of literature, that they are literary titles rather than the names of two men, and that both of us are familiar by our writings to persons who would otherwise know nothing of us.

[1] The court of one hundred judges.

A similar incident happened a day or two before. That excellent creature, Fadius Rufinus, was dining with me on the same couch, and next above him was a fellow-townsman of his who had just that day come to town for the first time. Rufinus, pointing me out to this man, said, "Do you see my friend here?" Then they spoke at length about my literary work, and the stranger remarked, "Surely, he is Pliny." I don't mind confessing that I think I am well repaid for my work, and if Demosthenes was justified in being pleased when an old woman of Attica recognized him with the words, "Why, here is Demosthenes," ought not I too to be glad that my name is so widely known? As a matter of fact, I am glad and I say so, for I am not afraid of being considered boastful, when it is not my opinion about myself but that of others which I put forward, and especially when you are my confidant, — you who grudge no one his fair praise, and are constantly doing what you can to increase my fame. Farewell.

TO FUSCUS

(IX, 36.)

You ask me how I spend the day at my Tuscan villa in summer time. Well, I wake at my own sweet will, usually about the first hour, though it is often before, and rarely later. I keep my windows shut, for it is remarkable how, when all is still and in darkness, and I am withdrawn from distracting influences and am left to myself, and free to do what I like, my thoughts are not led by my eyes, but my eyes by my thoughts; and so my eyes, when they have nothing else to look at, only see the objects which are present before my mind. If I have anything on hand, I think it over, and weigh every word as carefully as though I were actually writing or revising, and in this way I get through more or less work, according as the subject is easy or difficult to compose and bear in mind. I call for a shorthand writer, and, after letting in the daylight, I dictate the passages which I have composed; then he leaves me, and I send for him again, and once again dismiss him.

At the fourth or fifth hour, according as the weather tempts me, — for I have no fixed and settled plan for the day, — I betake myself to my terrace or covered portico, and there again I resume my thinking and dictating. I ride in my carriage, and still continue my mental occupation, just as when I am walking or lying down. My concentration of thought is unaffected, or rather is refreshed by the change. Then I snatch a brief sleep, and again walk, and afterwards read aloud a Greek or Latin speech, as clearly and distinctly as I can, not so much to exercise the vocal organs as to help my digestion, though it does at the same time strengthen my voice. I take another walk, then I am anointed, and take exercise and a bath. While I am at dinner, if I am dining with my wife or a few friends, a book is read to us, and afterwards we hear a comic actor or a musician; then I walk with my attendants, some of whom are men of learning. Thus the evening is passed away with talk on all sorts of subjects, and even the longest day is soon done.

Sometimes I vary this routine, for, if I have been lying down, or walking for any length of time, as soon as I have had my sleep and read aloud, I ride on horseback instead of in a carriage, as it takes less time, and one gets over the ground faster. My friends come in from the neighboring towns to see me, and monopolize part of the day, and occasionally, when I am tired, I welcome their call as a pleasant relief. Sometimes I go hunting, but never without my tablets, so that though I may take no game, I still have something to bring back with me.   Part of my time, too, is given to my tenants — though in their opinion not enough — and their clownish complaints give me a fresh zest for my literary work and my round of engagements in town.   Farewell.

TO TRAJAN

(96.[1])

IT is my custom, Sire, to refer to you in all cases where I do not feel sure, for who can better direct my doubts or inform my ignorance?   I have never been present at any legal examination of the Christians, and I do not know, therefore, what are the usual penalties passed upon them, or the limits of those penalties, or how searching an inquiry should be made.   I have hesitated a great deal in considering whether any distinctions should be drawn according to the ages of the accused; whether the weak should be punished as severely as the more robust; whether if they renounce their faith they should be pardoned, or whether the man who has once been a Christian should gain nothing by recanting; whether the name itself,

---

[1] This letter is not only typical of the whole correspondence between Pliny and Trajan, but is of special importance in that it indicates the policy of the Roman authorities towards the Christians at this period.   The next letter is the emperor's answer.

even though otherwise innocent of crime, should be
punished, or only the crimes that gather round it.

In the mean time, this is the plan which I have
adopted in the case of those Christians who have been
brought before me. I ask them whether they are
Christians; if they say yes, then I repeat the question a second and a third time, warning them of the
penalties it entails, and if they still persist, I order
them to be taken to prison. For I do not doubt that,
whatever the character of the crime may be which
they confess, their pertinacity and inflexible obstinacy
certainly ought to be punished. There were others
who showed similar mad folly whom I reserved to be
sent to Rome, as they were Roman citizens. Subsequently, as is usually the way, the very fact of my
taking up this question led to a great increase of ac-
cusations, and a variety of cases were brought before
me. A pamphlet was issued anonymously, containing
the names of a number of people. Those who denied
that they were or had been Christians and called
upon the gods in the usual formula, reciting the words
after me, those who offered incense and wine before
your image, which I had given orders to be brought
forward for this purpose, together with the statues
of the deities, — all such I considered should be discharged, especially as they cursed the name of Christ,
which, it is said, those who are really Christians
cannot be induced to do. Others, whose names were
given me by an informer, first said that they were
Christians and afterwards denied it, declaring that
they had been but were so no longer, some of them
having recanted many years before, and more than
one so long as twenty years back. They all worshiped
your image and the statues of the deities, and cursed

the name of Christ. But they declared that the sum
of their guilt or their error only amounted to this,
that on a stated day they had been accustomed to
meet before daybreak and to recite a hymn among
themselves to Christ, as though he were a god, and
that so far from binding themselves by oath to commit any crime, their oath was to abstain from theft,
robbery, adultery, and from breach of faith, and not
to deny trust money placed in their keeping when
called upon to deliver it. When this ceremony was
concluded, it had been their custom to depart and
meet again to take food, but it was of no special character and quite harmless, and they had ceased this
practice after the edict in which, in accordance with
your orders, I had forbidden all secret societies. I
thought it the more necessary, therefore, to find out
what truth there was in these statements by submit-
ing two women, who were called deaconesses, to the
torture, but I found nothing but a debased superstition carried to great lengths. So I postponed my
examination, and immediately consulted you. The
matter seems to me worthy of your consideration,
especially as there are so many people involved in the
danger. Many persons of all ages, and of both sexes
alike, are being brought into peril of their lives by their
accusers ; and the process will go on   For the contagion of this superstition has spread not only through
the free cities, but into the villages and the rural dis-
tricts, and yet it seems to me that it can be checked
and set right. It is beyond doubt that the temples,
which have been almost deserted, are beginning again
to be thronged with worshipers, that the sacred rites
which have for a long time been allowed to lapse are
now being renewed, and that the food for the sacrifi-

cial victims is once more finding a sale, whereas, up to recently, a buyer was hardly to be found. From this it is easy to infer what vast numbers of people might be reclaimed, if only they were given an opportunity of repentance.

TRAJAN TO PLINY

(97.)

You have adopted the proper course, my dear Pliny, in examining into the cases of those who have been denounced to you as Christians, for no hard and fast rule can be laid down to meet a question of such wide extent. The Christians are not to be hunted out; if they are brought before you and the offense is proved, they are to be punished, but with this reservation, — that if any one denies that he is a Christian and makes it clear that he is not, by offering prayers to our deities, then he is to be pardoned because of his recantation, however suspicious his past conduct may have been. But pamphlets published anonymously must not carry any weight whatever, no matter what the charge may be, for they are not only a precedent of the very worst type, but they are not in consonance with the spirit of our age.

APULEIUS

BIOGRAPHICAL SKETCH

APULEIUS, one of the most prominent of the African writers who contributed so largely to Latin literature in the second century A. D., was born at Madaura in Numidia about 130.   He was educated at Carthage and Athens, and afterwards lived for a few years in Rome.   The greater part of his life, however, was spent in Africa, where he lectured on rhetoric and philosophy in many different cities. We gain some knowledge of his private life from the *Apologia*, in which, shortly after his marriage with a rich widow, he successfully defended himself against his wife's relatives, who had accused him of resorting to magic in the furtherance of his suit.

Of his other works there are extant some philosophical treatises, a collection of excerpts from his lectures, and, most important of all, the *Metamorphoses*, in eleven books. In these he describes the adventures of one Lucius, who, transformed by a magic potion into the semblance of an ass but retaining still such wits as he had originally possessed, met with divers strange experiences.   Like the *Satirae* of Petronius, the work belongs to the novel class, so sparsely represented in Latin literature, but while Petronius deals with the everyday life of certain sections of Italian society, Apuleius handles mysteries and magic. His style is one of singular opulence of phraseology, interwoven with reminiscences of the poets and showing many highly colored passages in which image follows image with wonderful profusion of detail. It is artificial to be sure, yet, in spite of its manifestly studied elaborateness, has a certain glamour of its own.

CUPID AND PSYCHE [1]

(Metamorphoses, IV , 28–VI., 24)

IN a certain city lived a king and queen who had three daughters exceeding fair. But the beauty of the elder sisters, though pleasant to behold, yet passed not the measure of human praise, while such was the loveliness of the youngest that men's speech was too poor to commend it worthily and could express it not at all. Many of the citizens and of strangers, whom the fame of this excellent vision had gathered thither, confounded by that matchless beauty, could but kiss the finger-tips of their right hands at sight of her, as in adoration to the goddess Venus herself And soon a rumor passed through the country that she whom the blue deep had borne, forbearing her divine dignity, was even then moving among men, or that by some fresh germination from the stars, not the sea now, but the earth, had put forth a new Venus, endued with the flower of virginity.

This belief, with the fame of the maiden's loveliness, went daily further into distant lands, so that many people were drawn together to behold that glorious model of the age. Men sailed no longer to Paphos, to Cnidos or Cythera, to the presence of the goddess Venus : her sacred rites were neglected, her

---

[1] This fairy-tale is one of the numerous episodes introduced into the *Metamorphoses*. It is said to have been overheard in a robbers' cave by Lucius, as it was told by an old woman to a captive girl.

images stood uncrowned, the cold ashes were left to disfigure her forsaken altars. It was to a maiden that men's prayers were offered, to a human countenance they looked, in propitiating so great a godhead : when the girl went forth in the morning they strewed flowers on her way, and the victims proper to that unseen goddess were presented as she passed along. This conveyance of divine worship to a mortal kindled meantime the anger of the true Venus. "Lo! now, the ancient parent of nature," she cried, "the fountain of all elements! Behold me, Venus, benign mother of the world, sharing my honors with a mortal maiden, while my name, built up in heaven, is profaned by the mean things of earth! Shall a perishable woman bear my image about with her? In vain did the shepherd of Ida prefer me! Yet shall she have little joy, whosoever she be, of her usurped and unlawful loveliness!" Thereupon she called to her that winged, bold boy, of evil ways, who wanders armed by night through men's houses, spoiling their marriages, and stirring yet more by her speech his inborn wantonness, she led him to the city, and showed him Psyche as she walked.

"I pray thee," she said, "give thy mother a full revenge. Let this maid become the slave of an unworthy love." Then, embracing him closely, she departed to the shore and took her throne upon the crest of the wave. And lo! at her unuttered will, her ocean-servants are in waiting : the daughters of Nereus are there singing their song, and Portunus, and Salacia, and the tiny charioteer of the dolphin, with a host of Tritons leaping through the billows. And one blows softly through his sounding sea-shell, another spreads a silken web against the sun, a third presents the mirror to the eyes of his mistress, while the others swim side by side below, drawing her chariot. Such was the escort of Venus as she went upon the sea.

Psyche meantime, aware of her loveliness, had no fruit thereof. All people regarded and admired, but none sought her in marriage. It was but as on the finished work of the craftsman that they gazed upon that divine likeness. Her sisters, less fair than she, were happily wedded. She, even as a widow, sitting at home, wept over her desolation, hating in her heart the beauty in which all men were pleased.

And the king, supposing the gods were angry, inquired of the oracle of Apollo, and Apollo answered him thus: "Let the damsel be placed on the top of a certain mountain, adorned as for the bed of marriage, and of death. Look not for a son-in-law of mortal birth; but for that evil serpent-thing, by reason of whom even the gods tremble and the shadows of Styx are afraid."

So the king returned home and made known the oracle to his wife. For many days she lamented, but at last the fulfillment of the divine precept is urgent upon her, and the company make ready to conduct the maiden to her deadly bridal. And now the nuptial torch gathers dark smoke and ashes: the pleasant sound of the pipe is changed into a cry: the marriage hymn concludes in a sorrowful wailing: below her yellow wedding-veil the bride shook away her tears; insomuch that the whole city was afflicted together at the ill-luck of the stricken house.

But the mandate of the god impelled the hapless Psyche to her fate, and, these solemnities being ended, the funeral of the living soul goes forth, all the peo-

ple following.   Psyche, bitterly weeping, assists not
at her marriage but at her own obsequies, and while
the parents hesitate to accomplish a thing so unholy
the daughter cries to them: "Wherefore torment
your luckless age by long weeping?   This was the
prize of my extraordinary beauty!   When all people
celebrated us with divine honors, and in one voice
named the New Venus, it was then ye should have
wept for me as one dead.   Now at last I understand
that that one name of Venus has been my ruin.   Lead
me and set me upon the appointed place.   I am in
haste to submit to that well-omened marriage, to behold that goodly spouse.   Why delay the coming of
him who was born for the destruction of the whole
world?"

She was silent, and with firm step went on the way.
And they proceeded to the appointed place on a steep
mountain, and left there the maiden alone, and took
their way homewards dejectedly.   The wretched parents, in their close-shut house, yielded themselves to
perpetual night; while to Psyche, fearful and trembling and weeping sore upon the mountain-top, comes
the gentle Zephyrus.   He lifts her mildly, and, with
vesture afloat on either side, bears her by his own soft
breathing over the windings of the hills, and sets her
lightly among the flowers in the bosom of a valley
below.

Psyche, in those delicate grassy places, lying sweetly
on her dewy bed, rested from the agitation of her
soul and arose in peace.   And lo! a grove of mighty
trees, with a fount of water, clear as glass, in the
midst; and hard by the water, a dwelling-place, built
not by human hands but by some divine cunning.
One recognized, even at the entering, the delightful

hostelry of a god. Golden pillars sustained the roof, arched most curiously in cedar-wood and ivory. The walls were hidden under wrought silver, — all tame and woodland creatures leaping forward to the visitor's gaze. Wonderful indeed was the craftsman, divine or half-divine, who by the subtlety of his art had breathed so wild a soul into the silver! The very pavement was distinct with pictures in goodly stones. In the glow of its precious metal the house is its own daylight, having no need of the sun. Well might it seem a place fashioned for the conversation of gods with men!

Psyche, drawn forward by the delight of it, came near, and, her courage growing, stood within the doorway. One by one, she admired the beautiful things she saw; and, most wonderful of all! no lock, no chain, nor living guardian protected that great treasure-house. But as she gazed there came a voice, — a voice, as it were, unclothed of bodily vesture. "Mistress!" it said, "all these things are thine. Lie down, and relieve thy weariness, and rise again for the bath when thou wilt. We thy servants, whose voice thou hearest, will be beforehand with our service, and a royal feast shall be ready."

And Psyche understood that some divine care was providing, and, refreshed with sleep and the bath, sat down to the feast. Still she saw no one: only she heard words falling here and there, and had voices alone to serve her. And the feast being ended, one entered the chamber and sang to her unseen, while another struck the chords of a harp, invisible with him who played on it. Afterwards the sound of a company singing together came to her, but still so that none was present to sight, yet it appeared that a great multitude of singers was there.

.   .   .   .

One night the bridegroom spoke thus to his beloved, " O Psyche, most pleasant bride ! Fortune is grown stern with us, and threatens thee with mortal peril. Thy sisters, troubled at the report of thy death and seeking some trace of thee, will come to the mountain's top. But if by chance their cries reach thee, answer not, neither look forth at all, lest thou bring sorrow upon me and destruction upon thyself." Then Psyche promised that she would do according to his will. But the bridegroom was fled away again with the night. And all that day she spent in tears, repeating that she was now dead indeed, shut up in that golden prison, powerless to console her sisters sorrowing after her, or to see their faces; and so went to rest weeping.

And after a while came the bridegroom again, and embracing her as she wept, complained, " Was this thy promise, my Psyche ? What have I to hope from thee ? Even in the arms of thy husband thou ceasest not from pain. Do now as thou wilt. Indulge thine own desire, though it seeks what will ruin thee. Yet wilt thou remember my warning, repentant too late." Then, protesting that she is like to die, she obtains from him that he suffer her to see her sisters, and present to them moreover what gifts she would of golden ornaments; but therewith he ofttimes advised her never at any time yielding to pernicious counsel, to inquire concerning his bodily form, lest she fall, through unholy curiosity, from so great a height of fortune, nor feel ever his embrace again. "I would die a hundred times,' she said, cheerful at last, "rather than be deprived of thy most sweet usage." I love thee as my own soul, beyond comparison even with

Love himself. Only bid thy servant Zephyrus bring hither my sisters, as he brought me. My honeycomb! My Husband! Thy Psyche's breath of life!" So he promised; and ere the light appeared, vanished from the hands of his bride.

And the sisters, coming to the place where Psyche was abandoned, wept loudly among the rocks, and called upon her by name, so that the sound came down to her, and running out of the palace distraught, she cried, " Wherefore afflict your souls with lamentation? I whom you mourn am here." Then, summoning Zephyrus, she reminded him of her husband's bidding; and he bare them down with a gentle blast. " Enter now," she said, " into my house, and relieve your sorrow in the company of Psyche your sister."

And Psyche displayed to them all the treasures of the golden house, and its great family of ministering voices, nursing in them the malice which was already at their hearts. And at last one of them asks curiously who the lord of that celestial array may be, and what manner of man her husband? And Psyche answered dissemblingly, "A young man, handsome and mannerly, with a goodly beard. For the most part he hunts upon the mountains." And lest the secret should slip from her in the way of further speech, loading her sisters with gold and gems, she commanded Zephyrus to bear them away.

And they returned home, on fire with envy. " See now the injustice of fortune!" cried one. " We, the elder children, are given like servants to be the wives of strangers, while the youngest is possessed of so great riches, who scarcely knows how to use them. You saw, Sister! what a hoard of wealth lies in the house; what glittering gowns; what splendor of precious gems, besides all that gold trodden under foot. If she indeed hath, as she said, a bridegroom so goodly, then no one in all the world is happier. And it may be that this husband, being of divine nature, will make her too a goddess. Nay, so in truth it is. It was even thus she bore herself. Already she looks aloft and breathes divinity, who, though but a woman, has voices for her handmaidens, and can command the winds." "Think," answered the other, "how arrogantly she dealt with us, grudging us these trifling gifts out of all that store, and when our company became a burden, causing us to be hissed and driven away from her through the air! But I am no woman if she keep her hold on this great fortune; and if the insult done us has touched thee too, take we counsel together. Meanwhile let us hold our peace, and know nought of her, alive or dead. For they are not truly happy of whose happiness other folk are unaware."

And the bridegroom, whom still she knows not, warns her thus a second time, as he talks with her by night: "Seest thou what peril besets thee? Those cunning wolves have made ready for thee their snares, of which the sum is that they persuade thee to search into the fashion of my countenance, the seeing of which, as I have told thee often, will be the seeing of it no more forever. But do thou neither listen nor make answer to aught regarding thy husband. Besides, we have sown also the seed of our race. Even now this bosom grows with a child to be born to us, a child, if thou but keep our secret, of divine quality; if thou profane it, subject to death." And Psyche was glad at the tidings, rejoicing in that solace of a divine seed, and in the glory of that pledge of love to be, and the dignity of the name of mother. Anx-

iously she notes the increase of the days, the waning
months. And again, as he tarries briefly beside her,
the bridegroom repeats his warning : " Even now the
sword is drawn with which thy sisters seek thy life.
Have pity on thyself, sweet wife, and upon our child,
and see not those evil women again." But the sisters
make their way into the palace once more, crying to
her in wily tones, "O Psyche ! and thou too wilt be a
mother ! How great will be the joy at home ! Happy
indeed shall we be to have the nursing of the golden
child. Truly if he be answerable to the beauty of his
parents, it will a birth of Cupid himself."

So, little by little, they stole upon the heart of their
sister. She, meanwhile, bids the lyre to sound for
their delight, and the playing is heard : she bids the
pipes to move, the quire to sing, and the music and
the singing come invisibly, soothing the mind of the
listener with sweetest modulation. Yet not even
thereby was their malice put to sleep : once more they
seek to know what manner of husband she has, and
whence that seed. And Psyche, simple over-much,
forgetful of her first story, answers, " My husband
comes from a far country, trading for great sums. He
is already of middle age, with whitening locks."
And therewith she dismisses them again.

And returning home upon the soft breath of Zephyrus
one cried to the other, " What shall be said of so ugly
a lie ? He who was a young man with goodly beard
is now in middle life. It must be that she told a false
tale : else is she in very truth ignorant of what manner of man he is. Howsoever it be, let us destroy her
quickly. For if she indeed knows not, be sure that
her bridegroom is one of the gods : it is a god she
bears in her womb. And let that be far from us ! If

she be called the mother of a god, then will life be more than I can bear."

So, full of rage against her, they returned to Psyche, and said to her craftily, " Thou livest in an ignorant bliss, all incurious of thy real danger. It is a deadly serpent, as we certainly know, that comes to sleep at thy side. Remember the words of the oracle, which declared thee destined to a cruel beast. There are those who have seen it at nightfall, coming back from its feeding. In no long time, they say, it will end its blandishments. It but waits for the babe to be formed in thee, that it may devour thee by so much the richer. If indeed the solitude of this musical place, or it may be the loathsome commerce of a hidden love, delight thee, we at least in sisterly piety have done our part." And at last the unhappy Psyche, simple and frail of soul, carried away by the terror of their words, losing memory of her husband's precepts and her own promise, brought upon herself a great calamity. Trembling and turning pale, she answers them, " And they who tell those things, it may be, speak the truth. For in very deed never have I seen the face of my husband, nor know I at all what manner of man he is. Always he frights me diligently from the sight of him, threatening some great evil should I too curiously look upon his face. Do ye, if ye can help your sister in her great peril, stand by her now."

Her sisters answered her, " The way of safety we have well considered, and will teach thee. Take a sharp knife, and hide it in that part of the couch where thou art wont to lie : take also a lamp filled with oil, and set it privily behind the curtain. And when he shall have drawn up his coils into the accus-

tomed place, and thou hearest him breathe in sleep,
slip then from his side and discover the lamp, and,
knife in hand, put forth thy strength, and strike
off the serpent's head." And so they departed in
haste.

And Psyche left alone (alone but for the furies
which beset her) is tossed up and down in her distress, like a wave of the sea ; and though her will is
firm, yet, in the moment of putting hand to the deed,
she falters, and is torn asunder by various apprehensions of the great calamity upon her. She hastens and
anon delays, now full of distrust, and now of angry
courage : under one bodily form she loathes the monster and loves the bridegroom. But twilight ushers
in the night ; and at length in haste she makes ready
for the terrible deed. Darkness came, and the bridegroom ; and he first falls into a deep sleep.

And she, erewhile of no strength, the hard purpose
of destiny assisting her, is confirmed in force. With
lamp plucked forth, knife in hand, she put by her sex ;
and lo ! as the secrets of the bed became manifest,
the sweetest and most gentle of all creatures, Love
himself, reclined there, in his own proper loveliness !
At sight of him the very flame of the lamp kindled
more gladly ! But Psyche was afraid at the vision,
and, faint of soul, trembled back upon her knees, and
would have hidden the steel in her own bosom. But
the knife slipped from her hand ; and now, undone,
yet ofttimes looking upon the beauty of that divine
countenance, she lives again. She sees the locks of
that golden head, pleasant with the unction of the
gods, shed down in graceful entanglement behind and
before, about the ruddy cheeks and white throat.
The pinions of the winged god, yet fresh with the

dew, are spotless upon his shoulders, the delicate plumage wavering over them as they lie at rest. Smooth he was, and touched with light, worthy of Venus his mother. At the foot of the couch lay his bow and arrows, the instruments of his power, propitious to men

And Psyche gazing hungrily thereon, draws an arrow from the quiver, and trying the point upon the thumb, tremulous still, drave in the barb, so that a drop of blood came forth. Thus fell she, by her own act, and unaware, into the love of Love. Falling upon the bridegroom, with indrawn breath, in a hurry of kisses from eager and open lips, she shuddered as she thought how brief that sleep might be. And it chanced that a drop of burning oil fell from the lamp upon the god's shoulder. Ah! maladroit minister of love, thus to wound him from whom all fire comes; though 't was a lover, I trow, first devised thee, to have the fruit of his desire even in the darkness! At the touch of the fire the god started up, and beholding the overthrow of her faith, quietly took flight from her embraces.

And Psyche, as he rose upon the wing, laid hold on him with her two hands, hanging upon him in his passage through the air, till she sinks to the earth through weariness. And as she lay there, the divine lover, tarrying still, lighted upon a cypress tree which grew near, and, from the top of it, spake thus to her, in great emotion. "Foolish one! unmindful of the command of Venus, my mother, who had devoted thee to one of base degree, I fled to thee in his stead. Now know I that this was vainly done. Into mine own flesh pierced mine arrow, and I made thee my wife, only that I might seem a monster beside thee — that thou shouldst seek to wound the head wherein lay the eyes so full of love to thee! Again and again, I thought to put thee on thy guard concerning these things, and warned thee in lovingkindness. Now I would but punish thee by my flight hence." And therewith he winged his way into the deep sky.

Psyche, prostrate upon the earth, and following far as sight might reach the flight of the bridegroom, wept and lamented; and when the breadth of space had parted him wholly from her, cast herself down from the bank of a river which was nigh. But the stream, turning gentle in honor of the god, put her forth again unhurt upon its margin. And as it happened, Pan, the rustic god, was sitting just then by the waterside. Hard by, his flock of goats browsed at will. And the shaggy god called her, wounded and outworn, kindly to him and said, " I am but a rustic herdsman, pretty maiden, yet wise, by favor of my great age and long experience; and if I guess truly by those faltering steps, by thy sorrowful eyes and continual sighing, thou laborest with excess of love. Listen then to me, and seek not death again, in the stream or otherwise. Put aside thy woe, and turn thy prayers to Cupid He is in truth a delicate youth: win him by the delicacy of thy service."

So the shepherd-god spoke, and Psyche, answering nothing, but with a reverence to this serviceable deity, went on her way. And while she, in her search after Cupid, wandered through many lands, he was lying in the chamber of his mother, heart-sick. And the white bird which floats over the waves plunged in haste into the sea, and approaching Venus, as she bathed, made known to her that her son lies afflicted with some grievous hurt, doubtful of life. And Venus cried,

angrily, "My son, then, has a mistress! And it is
Psyche, who witched away my beauty and was the
rival of my godhead, whom he loves!"

Therewith she issued from the sea, and returning
to her golden chamber, found there the lad, sick, as
she had heard, and cried from the doorway, "Well
done, truly! to trample thy mother's precepts under
foot, to spare my enemy that cross of an unworthy
love; nay, unite her to thyself, child as thou art, that
I might have a daughter-in-law who hates me! I will
make thee repent of thy sport, and the savour of thy
marriage bitter. There is one who shall chasten this
body of thine, put out thy torch and unstring thy
bow. Not till she has plucked forth that hair, into
which so oft these hands have smoothed the golden
light, and sheared away thy wings, shall I feel the injury done me avenged." And with this she hastened
in anger from the doors.

And Ceres and Juno met her, and sought to know
the meaning of her troubled countenance. "Ye come
in season," she cried; "I pray you, find for me Psyche.
It must needs be that ye have heard the disgrace of
my house." And they, ignorant of what was done,
would have soothed her anger, saying, "What fault,
Mistress, hath thy son committed, that thou wouldst
destroy the girl he loves? Knowest thou not that he
is now of age? Because he wears his years so lightly
must he seem to thee ever but a child? Wilt thou
forever thus pry into the pastimes of thy son, always
accusing his wantonness, and blaming in him those
delicate wiles which are all thine own?" Thus, in
secret fear of the boy's bow, did they seek to please
him with their gracious patronage. But Venus, angry
at their light taking of her wrongs, turned her back

upon them, and with hasty steps made her way once more to the sea.

Meanwhile Psyche, tost in soul, wandering hither and thither, rested not night or day in the pursuit of her husband, desiring, if she might not soothe his anger by the endearments of a wife, at the least to propitiate him with the prayers of a handmaid. And seeing a certain temple on the top of a high mountain, she said, " Who knows whether yonder place be not the abode of my lord?" Thither, therefore, she turned her steps, hastening now the more because desire and hope pressed her on, weary as she was with the labors of the way, and so, painfully measuring out the highest ridges of the mountain, drew near to the sacred couches. She sees ears of wheat, in heaps or twisted into chaplets; ears of barley also, with sickles and all the instruments of harvest, lying there in disorder, thrown at random from the hands of the laborers in the great heat. These she curiously sets apart, one by one, duly ordering them; for she said within herself, "I may not neglect the shrines, nor the holy service, of any god there be, but must rather win by supplication the kindly mercy of them all."

And Ceres found her bending sadly upon her task, and cried aloud, "Alas, Psyche! Venus, in the furiousness of her anger, tracks thy footsteps through the world, seeking for thee to pay her the utmost penalty; and thou, thinking of anything rather than thine own safety, hast taken on thee the care of what belongs to me!" Then Psyche fell down at her feet, and sweeping the floor with her hair, washing the footsteps of the goddess in her tears, besought her mercy, with many prayers: " By the gladdening rites of harvest, by the lighted lamps and mystic marches of the marriage

and mysterious invention of thy daughter Proserpine,[1]
and by all beside that the holy place of Attica veils
in silence, minister, I pray thee, to the sorrowful heart
of Psyche! Suffer me to hide myself but for a few
days among the heaps of corn, till time have softened
the anger of the goddess, and my strength, outworn
in my long travail, be recovered by a little rest."

But Ceres answered her, "Truly thy tears move
me, and I would fain help thee; only I dare not incur
the ill-will of my kinswoman. Depart hence as quickly
as may be." And Psyche, repelled against hope, afflicted now with twofold sorrow, making her way back
again, beheld among the half-lighted woods of the valley below a sanctuary builded with cunning art. And
that she might lose no way of hope, howsoever doubtful, she drew near to the sacred doors. She sees there
gifts of price, and garments fixed upon the door-posts
and to the branches of the trees, wrought with letters
of gold which told the name of the goddess to whom
they were dedicated, with thanksgiving for that she
had done. So, with bent knee and hands laid about
the glowing altar, she prayed saying, "Sister and
spouse of Jupiter! be thou to these my desperate
fortunes Juno the Auspicious! I know that thou
dost willingly help those in travail with child; deliver
me from the peril that is upon me." And as she
prayed thus, Juno in the majesty of her godhead was
straightway present, and answered, "Would that I
might incline favorably to thee; but against the will
of Venus, whom I have ever loved as a daughter, I
may not, for very shame, grant thy prayer."

And Psyche, dismayed by this new shipwreck of

---

[1] The reference is to the festival celebrated in the autumn at Eleu-
sis in Attica, in honor of Demeter (Ceres) and Persephone (Proserpina).

her hope, communed thus with herself, "Whither, from the midst of the snares that beset me, shall I take my way once more? In what dark solitude shall I hide me from the all-seeing eye of Venus? What if I put on at length a man's courage, and yielding myself unto her as my mistress, soften by a humility not yet too late the fierceness of her purpose? Who knows but that I may find him also whom my soul seeketh after, in the abode of his mother?"

And Venus, renouncing all earthly aid in her search, prepared to return to heaven. She ordered the chariot to be made ready, wrought for her by Vulcan as a marriage-gift, with a cunning of hand which had left his work so much the richer by the weight of gold it lost under his tool. From the multitude which housed about the bed-chamber of their mistress, white doves came forth, and with joyful motions bent their painted necks beneath the yoke. Behind it, with playful riot, the sparrows sped onward, and other birds sweet of song, making known by their soft notes the approach of the goddess. Eagle and cruel hawk alarmed not the quireful family of Venus. And the clouds broke away, as the uttermost ether opened to receive her, daughter and goddess, with great joy.

And Venus passed straightway to the house of Jupiter to beg from him the service of Mercury, the god of speech. And Jupiter refused not her prayer. And Venus and Mercury descended from heaven together; and as they went, the former said to the latter, "Thou knowest, my brother of Arcady, that never at any time have I done anything without thy help; for how long time, moreover, I have sought a certain maiden in vain. And now nought remains but that, by thy heraldry, I proclaim a reward for whomsoever shall find her. Do thou my bidding quickly." And therewith she conveyed to him a little scrip, in the which was written the name of Psyche, with other things; and so returned home.

And Mercury failed not in his office; but departing into all lands, proclaimed that whosoever delivered up to Venus the fugitive girl, should receive from herself seven kisses — one thereof full of the inmost honey of her throat. With that the doubt of Psyche was ended. And now, as she came near to the doors of Venus, one of the household, whose name was Use-and-Wont, ran out to her crying, "Hast thou learned, Wicked Maid! now at last! that thou hast a mistress?" and seizing her roughly by the hair, drew her into the presence of Venus. And when Venus saw her, she cried out, saying, "Thou hast deigned, then, to make thy salutations to thy mother-in-law. Now will I in turn treat thee as becometh a dutiful daughter-in-law."

And she took barley and millet and poppy-seed, every kind of grain and seed, and mixed them together, and laughed, and said to her: "Methinks so plain a maiden can earn lovers only by industrious ministry: now will I also make trial of thy service. Sort me this heap of seed, the one kind from the others, grain by grain; and get thy task done before the evening." And Psyche, stunned by the cruelty of her bidding, was silent, and moved not her hand to the inextricable heap. And there came forth a little ant, which had understanding of the difficulty of her task, and took pity upon the consort of the god of Love, and he ran deftly hither and thither, and called together the whole army of his fellows. "Have pity," he cried, "nimble scholars of the Earth, Mother of all things!—have pity upon the wife of Love, and hasten to help her in her perilous effort." Then, one upon the other, the hosts of the insect people hurried together; and they sorted asunder the whole heap of seed, separating every grain after its kind, and so departed quickly out of sight.

And at nightfall Venus returned, and seeing that task finished with so wonderful diligence, she cried, "The work is not thine, thou naughty maid, but his in whose eyes thou hast found favor." And calling her again in the morning, "See now the grove," she said, "beyond yonder torrent. Certain sheep feed there, whose fleeces shine with gold. Fetch me straightway a lock of that precious stuff, having gotten it as thou mayst."

And Psyche went forth willingly, not to obey the command of Venus, but even to seek a rest from her labor in the depths of the river. But from the river, the green reed, lowly mother of music, spake to her: "O Psyche! pollute not these waters by self-destruction, nor approach that terrible flock; for, as the heat groweth, they wax fierce. Lie down under yon plane-tree, till the quiet of the river's breath have soothed them. Thereafter thou mayst shake down the fleecy gold from the trees of the grove, for it holdeth by the leaves."

And Psyche, instructed thus by the simple reed, in the humanity of its heart, filled her bosom with the soft golden stuff, and returned to Venus. But the goddess smiled bitterly, and said to her, "Well know I who was the author of this thing also. I will make further trial of thy discretion, and the boldness of thy heart. Seest thou the utmost peak of yonder steep mountain? The dark stream which flows down thence

waters the Stygian fields, and swells the flood of Cocytus Bring me now, in this little urn, a draught from
its innermost source." And therewith she put into
her hands a vessel of wrought crystal.

And Psyche set forth in haste on her way to the
mountain, looking there at last to find the end of her
hapless life. But when she came to the region which
borders on the cliff that was showed to her, she understood the deadly nature of her task. From a great
rock, steep and slippery, a horrible river of water
poured forth, falling straightway by a channel exceeding narrow into the unseen gulf below. And lo !
creeping from the rocks on either hand, angry serpents, with their long necks and sleepless eyes. The
very waters found a voice and bade her depart, in
smothered cries of, Depart hence ! and, What doest
thou here ? Look around thee ! and Destruction is
upon thee ! And then sense left her, in the immensity
of her peril, as one changed to stone.

Yet not even then did the distress of this innocent
soul escape the steady eye of a gentle providence.
For the bird of Jupiter spread his wings and took
flight to her, and asked her, " Didst thou think, simple
one, even thou ! that thou couldst steal one drop of
that relentless stream, the holy river of Styx, terrible
even to the gods ? But give me thine urn." And
the bird took the urn, and filled it at the source, and
returned to her quickly from among the teeth of the
serpents, bringing with him of the waters, all unwilling — nay ! warning him to depart away and not
molest them.

And she, receiving the urn with great joy, ran back
quickly that she might deliver it to Venus, and yet
again satisfied not the angry goddess. " My child ! "

she said, " in this one thing further must thou serve me. Take now this tiny casket, and get thee down even unto hell, and deliver it to Proserpine. Tell her that Venus would have of her beauty so much at least as may suffice for but one day's use, that beauty she possessed erewhile being forworn and spoiled, through her tendance upon the sick-bed of her son ; and be not slow in returning."

And Psyche perceived there the last ebbing of her fortune — that she was now thrust openly upon death, who must go down, of her own motion, to Hades and the Shades. And straightway she climbed to the top of an exceeding high tower, thinking within herself, " I will cast myself down thence: so shall I descend most quickly into the kingdom of the dead." And the tower again broke forth into speech . " Wretched Maid ! Wretched Maid ! Wilt thou destroy thyself ? If the breath quit thy body, then wilt thou indeed go down into Hades, but by no means return hither. Listen to me. Among the pathless wilds not far from this place lies a certain mountain, and therein one of hell's vent-holes. Through the breach a rough way lies open, following which thou wilt come, by straight course, to the castle of Orcus. And thou must not go empty-handed. Take in each hand a morsel of barley-bread, soaked in hydromel; and in thy mouth two pieces of money. And when thou shalt be now well onward in the way of death, then wilt thou overtake a lame ass laden with wood, and a lame driver, who will pray thee reach him certain cords to fasten the burden which is falling from the ass ; but be thou cautious to pass on in silence. And soon as thou comest to the river of the dead, Charon, in that crazy bark he hath, will put thee over upon the further side.

There is greed even among the dead ; and thou shalt
deliver to him, for the ferrying, one of those two
pieces of money, in such wise that he take it with his
hand from between thy lips.   And as thou passest
over the stream, a dead old man, rising on the water,
will put up to thee his mouldering hands, and pray
thee draw him into the ferry-boat.   But beware thou
yield not to unlawful pity.

" When thou shalt be come over, and art upon the
causeway, certain aged women, spinning, will cry to
thee to lend thy hand to their work ; and beware
again that thou take no part therein ; for this also is
the snare of Venus, whereby she would cause thee to
cast away one at least of those cakes thou bearest in
thy hands.   And think not that a slight matter, for
the loss of either one of them will be to thee the losing
of the light of day.   For a watch-dog exceeding fierce
lies ever before the threshold of that lonely house of
Proserpine.   Close his mouth with one of thy cakes ;
so shalt thou pass by him, and enter straightway into
the presence of Proserpine herself.   Then do thou
deliver thy message, and taking what she shall give
thee, return back again ; offering to the watch-dog the
other cake, and to the ferryman that other piece of
money thou hast in thy mouth.   After this manner
mayst thou return again beneath the stars.   But
withal, I charge thee, think not to look into, nor open,
the casket thou bearest, with that treasure of the
beauty of the divine countenance hidden therein."

So spake the stones of the tower ; and Psyche delayed not, but proceeding diligently after the manner
enjoined, entered into the house of Proserpine, at
whose feet she sat down humbly, and would neither
the delicate couch nor that divine food the goddess

offered her, but did straightway the business of Venus. And Proserpine filled the casket secretly, and shut the lid, and delivered it to Psyche, who fled therewith from Hades with new strength. But coming back into the light of day, even as she hasted now to the ending of her service, she was seized by a rash curiosity. "Lo! now," she said within herself, "my simpleness! who bearing in my hands the divine loveliness, heed not to touch myself with a particle at least therefrom, that I may please the more, by the favor of it, my fair one, by beloved." Even as she spoke, she lifted the lid; and behold! within, neither beauty, nor anything beside, save sleep only, the sleep of the dead, which took hold upon her, filling all her members with its drowsy vapor, so that she lay down in the way and moved not, as in the slumber of death.

And Cupid being healed of his wound, because he would endure no longer the absence of her he loved, gliding through the narrow window of the chamber wherein he was holden, his pinions being now repaired by a little rest, fled forth swiftly upon them, and coming to the place where Psyche was, shook that sleep away from her, and set him in his prison again, awaking her with the innocent point of his arrow. "Lo! thine old error again," he said, "which had like once more to have destroyed thee! But do thou now what is lacking of the command of my mother: the rest shall be my care." With these words, the lover rose upon the air; and being consumed inwardly with the greatness of his love, penetrated with vehement wing into the highest place of heaven, to lay his cause before the father of the gods. And the father of the gods took his hand in his, and kissed his face, and said to him, "At no time, my son, hast thou regarded me with due honor. Often hast thou vexed my bosom, wherein lies the disposition of the stars, with those busy darts of thine. Nevertheless, because thou hast grown up between these mine hands, I will accomplish thy desire." And straightway he bade Mercury call the gods together; and, the council-chamber being filled, sitting upon a high throne, "Ye gods," he said, "all ye whose names are in the white book of the Muses, ye know yonder lad. It seems good to me that his youthful heats should by some means be restrained. And that all occasion may be taken from him, I would even confine him in the bonds of marriage. He has chosen and embraced a mortal maiden. Let him have fruit of his love, and possess her forever."

Thereupon he bade Mercury produce Psyche in heaven, and holding out to her his ambrosial cup, "Take it," he said, "and live forever; nor shall Cupid ever depart from thee." And the gods sat down together to the marriage-feast. On the first couch lay the bridegroom, and Psyche in his bosom. His rustic serving-boy bare the wine to Jupiter: and Bacchus to the rest. The Seasons crimsoned all things with their roses. Apollo sang to the lyre, while a little Pan prattled on his reeds, and Venus danced very sweetly to the soft music Thus — with due rites — did Psyche pass into the power of Cupid; and from them was born the daughter whom men call Voluptas.

WALTER PATER, in *Marius the Epicurean*.

CPSIA information can be obtained at www.ICGtesting.com
Printed in the USA
BVOW081406050412

286973BV00006B/7/P